TIGHTEN

THE HISTORY OF REGGAE IN THE UK

UP!

D1452499

Printed and bound in the UK by MPG Books, Bodmin

Distributed in the US by Publishers Group West

Published in the UK by Sanctuary Publishing Limited, Sanctuary House, 45–53 Sinclair Road, London W14 0NS, United Kingdom

www.sanctuarypublishing.com

Copyright © Michael de Koningh and Marc Griffiths, 2003

Photographs: Courtesy of Micheal de Koningh unless otherwise stated

Cover design: Mystery

All rights reserved. No part of this book may be reproduced in any form or by any electronic or mechanical means, including information storage or retrieval systems, without permission in writing from the publisher, except by a reviewer, who may quote brief passages.

While the publishers have made every reasonable effort to trace the copyright owners for any or all of the photographs in this book, there may be some omissions of credits, for which we apologise.

ISBN: 1-86074-559-8

TIGHTEN
THE HISTORY OF REGGAE IN THE UK
UP!

Michael de Koningh & Marc Griffiths

Sanctuary

Contents

CD Notes

1   RICO'S COMBO: 'YOUTH BOOGIE'
    Original UK issue: Planetone RC5 (1962)
    Rico Rodriguez, recently arrived from Jamaica, flexes his trombone at the tail
    end of this sprightly UK-produced harmonica instrumental. Recorded at Sonny
    Roberts' Planetone studio, the uncredited band play a more R&B-based sound
    than ska. Rico went on to become one of the foundation players on the British
    reggae scene.

2   THE PLANETS: 'WATER FRONT'
    Original UK issue: Sway SW002 (1963)
    Recorded at the same studio as the above Rico record, the now-forgotten Planets
    cut the rug with an uptempo, very R&B-influenced early ska instrumental.

3   DANDY AND HIS GROUP: 'EAST OF SUEZ'
    Original UK issue: Giant GN3 (1967)
    A moody rocksteady instrumental track from a stalwart of the London scene,
    Robert 'Dandy' Thompson. The jazz influences give this particular track a more
    Jamaican feel, where at the time brass-masters such as Tommy McCook and
    Roland Alphonso were creating masterpieces of jazz-centred mellow rocksteady.

4   JOE MANSANO: 'LIFE ON REGGAE PLANET'
    Original UK issue: Blue Cat BS150 (1969)
    Influential producer Mansano talks his way through a highly popular track with
    Rico weaving his lazy trombone in the background. This style of UK reggae was
    highly regarded by the white skinheads of the time, and helped to cross-pollinate
    the sounds from West Indian quarters to the high street record retailers.

5   RICO RODRIGUEZ: 'THE BULLET'
Original UK issue: Blue Cat BS160 (1969)
Rico again, with the record that lead producer Joe Mansano to work for Trojan Records and ultimately have his own sub-label, 'Joe'. Selling in huge quantities (for a reggae record), 'The Bullet' was a staple in both West Indian and white skinhead's record boxes. Trojan saw the popularity of the record and snapped up Mansano to produce for them.

6   SELWYN BAPTESTE: 'MO'BAY'
Original issue: Black Swan BW1402 (1970)
The Trojan production team of Webster Shrowder, Desmond Bryan and Joe Sinclair were really finding their feet as they laid down this steel-pan version of Freddie Notes' classic 'Montego Bay'. An unusual move to utilise steel drums, but one that worked well. A good seller for Trojan Records.

7   PAMA DICE: 'THE WORM'
Original UK issue: Attack ATT8019 (1970)
Two more stalwarts of the UK scene combine on this popular DeeJay outing. Produced by Cuban-born singer-cum-producer Laurel Aitken, chirpy Pama Dice chats out just the sort of lyrics that kept the skinhead buyers happy. Aitken above all others knew just what his selected white audience wanted.

8   CHARLIE BOY: 'FUNKY STRIP'
Original UK issue: Trojan TR7823 (1971)
The original backing track was recorded in Kingston by producer Herman Chin-Loy with funky overdubs overseen at Chalk Farm Studios, London, by Dave Bloxham.

9   SYDNEY, GEORGE AND JACKIE: 'FEELING HIGH'
Original UK issue: Attack ATT8054 (1973)
By 1973, when this track was recorded, Jamaica was going roots, while London stayed with the lighter chart-friendly sound. The re-named Pioneers scored well with this happy song, and it remains one of their best later-period works.

10 PAT RHODEN: 'BOOGIE ON REGGAE WOMAN'
Original UK issue: Horse HOSS59 (1974)
Singer–songwriter Pat Rhoden goes for the soul-to-reggae cover on this spirited version of a Stevie Wonder song. Many saw the soul cover as an easy option, as it was sure to grab some fallout from the original in the way of sales. In this case there is obvious thought and plenty of talent behind the reinterpretation of the song.

11 LOUISA MARKS: 'KEEP IT LIKE IT IS'
Original UK issue: Trojan TR9005 (1977)
Teenage Louisa was one of the Lovers Rock queens with her sweet voice underpinned by deep, heavy rhythms. A very British substrate of reggae, Lovers Rock produced some massive-selling records which went unnoticed by the general public until Janet Kay's 'Silly Games' cracked the national charts.

12 ONE LOVE: 'THE SLAVE TRADE'
Original UK issue: Lightning TR9025 (1977)
An unknown British group produced by an equally unknown producer, Bill Spencer, create a very UK-sounding hard-roots outing. The sound is typical of what was coming out of every youth club and rehearsal studio across the inner cities, as the Red, Gold and Green blew in from Africa via Jamaica. Exemplary sounds, many of which never found their way onto vinyl and are now forgotten.

Foreword

With the exception of *Young, Gifted And Black: The Story Of Trojan Records* (Sanctuary Publishing, 2003) and *Boss Sounds: Classic Skinhead Reggae* (ST Publishing, 1996), few books about reggae music written to date have really talked in any depth about the people responsible for recording and issuing the music in the UK. We've heard a lot about Dodd, Perry, Reid, Buster, Kong, Bunny Lee *et al* – and rightly so – but who were the singers and players on British-recorded material? Who set up the labels for issuing the music? Who ran the shops that sold the records to the eager punters?

The 1976 *Aquarius* TV programme on UK reggae, written and narrated by Carl Gayle, was a major breakthrough in that it filmed the very people that this book discusses – all right, some of the old faces from the '60s had disappeared from the scene by then or were unable to be interviewed, but it was still the reggae we knew. The packed Saturday afternoon shops, the booming speaker boxes and the wildly desirable records were all shown, as were the now settled (in the sense that London was home) West Indian communities. Home-grown names like Delroy Washington, Aswad, Matumbi, The Cimarons and Lloyd Coxson all said or played their piece, pulling together a picture not of Jamaica away from Jamaica, but the brave new world of the London reggae vibe.

Without these people, there would have been no Jamaican music scene in the UK. Sales would have been limited to establishments like Dyke and Dryden who, in the 1960s, were importing records direct from Jamaica (complete with 'By Air Mail' stickers on them) and selling them to those in the know, or who lived close enough to get to the shop at Seven Sisters. This was to be a pretty limiting arrangement, and it took a while for entrepreneurs like Sonny Roberts and Rita and Benny Izons (not King or Issels as has so often been stated) to set about thinking, 'Why can't we do all this over here?' So this book is dedicated to all those people.

The three Palmer brothers were almost certainly playing second fiddle to Trojan during the 1967–73 period and their Pama label was just waiting to be given the coverage it deserved. While Pama may have justified a dedicated book, we could never ignore the likes of Count Shelly, Larry Lawrence, Dandy, Joe Mansano, Junior Lincoln, Pat Rhoden, Joe Sinclair and the like. Without these people, this music would not have reached the market in the way that it did.

In putting all this together, however, we have tried to avoid covering already well-trodden ground. For example, quite a comprehensive account of Island Records has already been presented in *Young, Gifted And Black*, and we didn't necessarily want to recount it all. Similarly, Trojan is covered here in the sense that the company's downfall and that of its distributor B&C in 1975 created the vacuum that gave rise to the proliferation of the independents and thus provided them with room for manoeuvre. Also, without B&C as linchpin reggae distributor, the smaller outfits generally had to build up their own distribution networks through much blood, sweat and tears. These were dedicated people who had to build from the ground up.

It remains for us to thank the many people who, in one way or another, helped us put this together – we could never have done it alone. It has to be said what helpful and kind people inhabit the UK reggae world, and what a joy it has been meeting and speaking to so many of our musical heroes in the course of writing this book.

So our major thanks go to Mike Atherton for being our 'third author' and also for his knowledge of the UK labels scene, which is second to none. In addition, his manipulation of our words into readable sentences was much needed and appreciated.

Our very grateful thanks also to the following people: Alan Wallace (Mood Reaction), Bob Andy, Brian Harris (Icicle), Bruce Ruffin, Bruce White (Creole), Chris Cracknell (Greensleeves), Count Suckle, Dave Barker, Dave Hendley, DD Dennis, Dub Vendor, Freddie Notes, Glenroy Oakley (Greyhound), Howard Palmer, Ian Smith, Jack Price, Jackie Robinson, Janis at I-Anka, John Kpiaye, John Reed, Kathy de Koningh, Keith Stone (Daddy Kool), Laurence Cane-Honeysett, Mike Cole, Monty Neysmith, Noel Hawks, Pat Rhoden, Pete Fontana, Rico Rodriguez, Rob Bell, Roy Shirley, Sid Bucknor, Siggy Jackson, Steve Jukes, Tom Wegg-Prosser (Virgin) and, last but not least, Winston Groovy.

Like the business we're writing about, there are a lot of people involved!

Michael de Koningh and Marc Griffiths
December 2003

1 Many Rivers To Cross

JAMAICANS INFLUENCE THE UK

On 23 June 1948, the SS *Empire Windrush* docked at Tilbury and deposited 492 hopeful young Jamaican men, and a few women, into a post-war Britain that was grey, cold, rationed and short of workers. Many of the arrivals were ex-servicemen who had fought for the mother country in the war, and were tempted by the perceived high standard of living to make the move to Great Britain. The British government had some concerns as to what would happen as these Empire citizens settled in to their new lives. How would the white working class and the trades unions view the new recruits to the collective workforce? In consequence, the government sat on the fence and said nothing as the West Indians scraped together the princely sum of £24 each for the long one-way journey. Questions were asked in Parliament in 1949 regarding who had actually invited the immigrants over to the motherland. The answer was that no one had. They had come under their own steam, spurred on by the hope of profitable employment and a better standard of living. Most of these pioneers were skilled people, many having gained their experience in the services.

Many of the existing generation of Britons had given their all for king and country, as in the First World War, which had left empty places at every family table, and with the Second World War only a memory away, more chairs stood idle. The British labour pool was struggling to fill nursing, milk delivery, sewage treatment and just about any other necessary, but unappreciated, jobs. Europe was the first port of call for the British government, which hoped to attract workers from the still war-ravaged main continent. As the UK economy boomed and pulled out of the recession created by the war, Europe and the British workforce could not fill the jobs created by the expanding economy.

London Transport was in particular need and was very active in the early 1950s recruiting West Indians for all manner of jobs within its bus and tube depots. LT even sent Charlie Gomm, its recruitment officer, out to the West Indies to drum up takers for the passage to a better life. By this time, the British government had realised two main points: first, that all West Indians were citizens of the British Empire and so had every right to relocate to the cooler climes of the UK; second, that the growing economy needed more workers, whether they be black or white.

So from the early 1950s onwards, with the cessation of European workers crossing the English Channel, the West Indians were enticed to Britain's cold shores by promises of plentiful work and a higher standard of living than imaginable back home. In particular, the fragile Jamaican economy had taken a heavy blow during the war, as it depended on the export of sugar to the motherland, and with the war interrupting trade the price of sugar had fallen dramatically. A violent hurricane in 1944 had caused widespread destruction and crop disasters, and the small island was still feeling the repercussions. This caused even more depression; many were tempted by the enticing offer made by the British government and they booked their one-way passage.

For many, when they arrived, the reality was somewhat different from that presented in the cheery posters they had seen back home: they found chilly summers and bitter winters, and were housed in inner-city streets full of bleak untended tenement lodgings or Victorian and Edwardian bay-fronted middle-class houses that had seen better days. One room per family was the norm, and the unlucky single man would find many a landlady displaying 'No coloured men' signs prominently below the cheery and welcoming 'Vacancy' notice in their window.

Home ownership was on the rise and, with the destruction of so much property due to the war, there was an acute housing shortage. The new overspill towns such as Harlow and Basildon were in the making, and many unskilled and middle-class white workers were vacating half-bombed-out streets in areas like London's Notting Hill for brand new homes on greenfield sites just beyond the city boundary.

Into these semi-derelict streets came the new immigrants, charged double the rent of a white worker just for the privilege of being black and having nowhere else to go. As the whites moved out, so the 'coloureds' moved in, with their new ways and looks, causing concern for the remaining indigenous inner-city dwellers.

Pete Fontana, a long-term Harlesden resident, recalls his childhood in the late 1950s as the West Indian population increased around his district: 'As far as I can remember the first West Indian family moved into my part of

Harlesden in 1957. I was eight years old. My memory says that the grown-ups weren't very happy about it, but I could be wrong.

'The indigenous white population were mostly confused and I guess the black people were as well. All of a sudden large numbers of immigrants were moving in to what was a very close-knit community, with no explanation from the councils or officialdom in general. There was a lot of resentment as people saw their lifestyles and the community changing forever with no consultation or explanation. To give an idea of the scale of the change, when I started at Wesley Road Secondary Modern school in 1960 there were three black boys at the school (I didn't take much notice of girls at age 11): Frank Windsor in the fourth year, a lad in the second year (can't remember his name) and John Shaw in the same year as me. When I left in 1965, about a third of the boys were black.'

Even skilled immigrants were normally only able to find manual jobs as the industry bosses feared strikes should a coloured person be elevated above the intrinsic white workers. The stigma of colour struck hard, with toilet and canteen areas in some larger premises segregated for black and white.

There was no doubt that jobs were available and, even though no Londoner desired to clean the sewers, many resented the opportunity being taken away and handed to the newcomers. Grumblings and mumblings soon appeared, sometimes in the form of 'KBW' (Keep Britain White) graffiti on inviting blank walls, as houses and whole streets filled with the new workers from the Caribbean. By 1954, 10,000 mainly Jamaican West Indians had relocated, principally to the inner cities of the isle's major conurbations – London, Birmingham, Nottingham, Bristol – with smaller communities converging on many other towns. By 1958 this number had risen to 125,000 West Indians resident in the UK, all of them passport-holding Commonwealth citizens.

In 1958 a bout of unemployment hit the UK, affecting 2 per cent of the workforce (half a million people). There was bitterness at the perceived removal of job opportunities by the newcomers, with the resentment jumped upon and boosted by Oswald Moseley's fascist movement as it attempted to whip up anti-black feeling. These agitators moved among the crowds, causing anger and spreading rumour, much like the 1990s Poll Tax riots when outside forces infiltrated the protesting crowds causing violence to ensue.

With their rhetoric about potential job losses and fears of 'womenfolk' being stolen by hot-blooded young West Indian males, the agitators touched on the worries of young working-class whites and manipulated their feelings into revolt.

Over the previous 18 months Nottingham had seen attacks on coloured people by roving groups of vigilante-style whites, conveniently lumped together by the frenzied press as teddy boys, and spurred on by Moseley and his followers.

Then over the August bank holiday weekend in Notting Hill, London, following clashes the previous week in Nottingham, the so-called Notting Hill race riots began, whipped up by the press into anti-black hysteria.

A young Swedish girl was knocked to the ground with an iron bar by a mob as she walked with her West Indian boyfriend, and this incident lighted the blue touchpaper. The mob then turned on a West Indian house – where a party was under way with Count Suckle (Wilbert Campbell) running his formative sound system – and began pelting the windows with bricks and bottles. That was the start of four days of the worst rioting Great Britain had ever seen.

The sorry affair was commented on by Mighty Sparrow with his 45 'Carnival Boycott'. The record, on Melodisc's Kalypso label, was one of the first UK-pressed discs aimed at the new audience of British West Indians and, like the calypsonian/talking newspaper man back home, made social comment on a situation for all to hear. The Prime Minister of Jamaica, Norman Manley, came to London in that year to try to find a solution to the unease, and while the general call for calm resulted in an uneasy truce between the warring factions, tension still existed.

Trombone master and committed Rastafarian Rico Rodriguez (aka Reco or El Reco), a long-term player on the UK reggae scene arrived in 1962 after playing with Count Ossie and all the stars of Jamaican R&B in Kingston. He has a familiar story to tell of his move to London: 'I loved the excitement of music but I just wasn't making a living – Jamaica is the land of my birth and I love it, but it just wasn't happening. The police were very oppressive at this time [of the Rasta] and Ossie encourage me to go to England. So I stow away a few times but never make it, then Randy [Vincent Chin] pay for me to come over.

'There were signs in the boarding house windows "No blacks, no Irish"; it was very hard. I stayed with friends in Tottenham and I worked at Ford Motor Factory and did other dirty jobs. One time I worked in a rubber factory and I had to take my clothes off outside as I was so dirty. My friends were into different things so then I moved to south London.'

So the next decade found many cold, disillusioned Jamaicans congregated in areas like southeast London's Brixton, Liverpool's Toxteth or Nottingham's St Ann's, where they established communities and made new homes.

With these new homes came a longing for the old familiar things such as the taste of their own food and the sound of their own music: a recreation of the Jamaican culture in Britain. House parties, known as 'blues dances', became common on a Friday and Saturday nights, illegal shebeens (from the Irish word for weak beer) quickly established themselves by word of mouth and, later, clubs sprung up, all catering for the Jamaican population.

These venues were run by enterprising men from overseas like the aforementioned Count Suckle and the legendary Duke Vin, who is reputed to have inspired Clement Dodd to move into the sound system stakes in Jamaica. Vin relocated to London in 1954 and little more than a year later became the very first UK-based sound system owner and operator. Suckle recalls that he 'stowed away on a banana boat with Duke Vin and came here in 1954. And then open the Cue Club for them people.'

These men were pioneers in a new country, playing for their fellow new arrivals, and bringing with them the dancehall culture along with their precious boxes of records. Vin's sound system and Suckle's Cue Club – originally a snooker hall, hence the name – played the staple US R&B and latterly the Jamaican offshoot sound to visiting GIs and the growing West Indian population, while more mainstream venues like the Wag (Whisky A Go-Go) in London's West End tried out Jamaican DJs and their music to pleasing effect on their collective pockets. Amusingly, the Cue Club is listed in 1963 as sharing premises with HM Customs & Excise, presumably with the club downstairs and the Customs offices in the upper storeys of the building.

Pete Fontana recalls the early blues dance days around his native Harlesden: 'My first memories of the music were from the blues parties that the black people held in their houses; these caused lots of problems with the white adults due to their loudness and how late they went on 'til. I know on many occasions the police would be called out, and on one occasion there was an epic battle in my road when a single constable arrived and told them to stop the party. There was an altercation and a vanload of police arrived and literally broke the party up. The music was universally known as "blue beat". I became aware of ska later on and thought it was a different type of music.'

Pete picked up the beat, developing an interest he has kept to this day. 'The main shop I remember was in Library Parade, part of Craven Park Road, the main street in Harlesden. I can't remember its name [number 3 Library Parade was the Harlesden Music Salon in 1968] but I can remember the Island Records chart that used to be in the front window; I always used to read it while waiting for the bus to go to school, popping in to listen on the way home. I bought my first Blue Beat record from there in 1963: BB130 –

"Time Longer Than Rope"/"Fake King" by Prince Buster. The only other proper West Indian record shop that I knew at that time was at the Kilburn end of Willesden Lane; again I can't remember the name. There were of course many other shops, like hairdressers, that had a rack of records for sale.'

As the West Indian population increased, the wise shopkeepers and businessmen in the area would move to make money out of these newly arrived prospective customers. One such person was Pete's uncle. 'This was my biggest involvement with the local black community. My uncle, Fred Stephens, had been made redundant as a docker and was looking to invest his redundancy money in a business. He had made friends with a Trinidadian couple, George and Rose, and they remarked that there was nobody catering for West Indian greengrocery and grocery needs. So in 1961 he opened his shop on the corner of Burns Road and Ashdon Road selling both. In 1962 I started to work for him at weekends delivering the boxes of groceries etc to the houses. I was always getting into trouble for stopping to listen to the latest tune instead of getting back to the job!

'Within a year I was also serving in the shop, selling all the favourite West Indian foods, this was where I developed my taste for patties, mangoes etc. I really enjoyed this work as it gave me the opportunity to chat up the girls that came to get their mum's shopping (it's amazing how grateful people can be when you give them an extra pound of spuds). One of the downsides was when somebody asked for a mackerel – I hated putting my entire arm in that brine barrel that they came in, as the first fish I pulled out was inevitably too big or too small and your arm would smell all day.'

Rico was working regularly by this time and recalls, 'I was playing R&B sessions for Blue Beat as well as Planetone – [Emil] Shallit and [Siggy] Jackson treat me good. I also worked regularly with Georgie Fame's band The Blue Flames at the Roaring Twenties – I didn't see Georgie much though. I'd walk in with my trombone and they'd say, "Hey man, come and have a blow." I also used to see Count Suckle, who's done a lot for the people, you know. But I never did any work for Island at this time.'

Former Island and then Trojan employee Rob Bell recalls a particularly magical night at Suckle's well-known club in the mid-1960s. 'I was taken to Count Suckle's Cue Club a few times, in Paddington. Suckle was a large man, whom I later got to know when I worked at Trojan in the later '60s. He had a very briefly active label, Q, which released four records, including a few sides by Suckle himself. As I recall, he was possibly the world's worst singer. His club was very popular for many years, and catered to a crowd that included both old and young folks.

'I well remember one night there when, after two or three hours of non-stop ska, the DJ put on a jump side, from the late 1940s or early 1950s. I don't remember the title – it's really immaterial anyway – but the floor cleared to make way for an immaculately dressed man who was probably in his 50s or 60s. He had a vaguely Asian look – in the same way that Muddy Waters had – and he was dancing with a very blowsy blonde of similar age. His body remained fairly still and upright, one hand leading his woman, the other holding a large white handkerchief, with which he frequently mopped his brow. It was his feet that fascinated me – they moved with the beat, almost twinkling in rhythmic flashes.

'They lindy-hopped from one end of the floor to another, and the entire crowd watched with a glee that was equally rhythmic. He spun her, moved past her, holding out his hand behind his back as they passed, caught her outstretched hand and then pulled her close, feet pumping, mopping at his forehead, upper body showing minimal movement – released her and they both spun, he doing a slow split and then coming up right on the beat just at the moment you thought he'd never make it, make hand contact again. They shuffled in unison to the far end of the floor, and then strolled back the length of it again, apart from each other yet united in feel, and the crowd shouted, downed rum and Red Stripe, and clapped.

'The jock spun tune after tune, upping the tempo by degrees until the couple, by now drenched in sweat, was a blur of motion. The sound was everything, was everywhere, in every corner of the club, conversation was not only impossible, it was unnecessary, at that point obsolete. And all the while the man's expression had hardly altered – it was as if he was entranced, in another world that counted its vitality by tone, and its heart by feeling and its time by measure – all absorbed by the ears, soul and feet.

'I left that night knowing I had experienced something ultimately unknowable, something really undefinable, and yet something that was interestingly commonplace, and that was to prove to be the stock in trade of my future career. It was witnessing the power of music to transform people, witnessing how the very vibrations of sound induced this happiness, this otherworldliness, this bliss.'

The inner-city supper club culture was transforming into something more dynamic, as Rob was discovering as the 1960s rolled in, with the power and quality of recorded music used to greater effect and supplanting a live ever-so-smooth combo with exciting dance records. The development from skiffle milk bars and rock 'n' roll dance halls to swish clubs took less than a decade, but the effect it had on the younger generation of both black and white youth was immense. Rob Bell's story epitomises that of many of the new breed of young white men who embraced the black working-class sounds of US R&B and then moved on to the Jamaican beat.

'The first record I ever bought was Bill Haley's "Rock Around The Clock" in 1955. I was nine. Dug the sound and the excitement, plus Danny Cedrone's round-toned hollow-body guitar sound on the b-side, "Thirteen Women". From there I tuned in to Chuck Berry, Little Richard, Fats Domino and Joe Turner. It was all rock 'n' roll to me – guess it still is. I was hooked. I hung around the record store after school. This was when they had little booths and you could take a stack of 78s into a booth, close the door, and crank up "Reet Petite", "Jenny, Jenny" or whatever.

'My friends and I were on first-name terms with the record counter clerks at the four or five record stores in our home town of Winchester. It was a great time to grow up listening to music. Because of these stores' policies of letting us hear what we wanted, we played dozens of artists before buying something – we got to find out who was hip and who wasn't by listening. Not from ads, or even hearing a tune on the radio. Radio pretty much sucked in England then, anyway.

'We'd check out junk stores, picking up Elvis 78s on HMV, Louis Jordan on Brunswick, beat-up Fats Domino 45s on London. On bicycles, we'd ride the 12 miles to Southampton, and scour junk stores in an area that I think was around St Mary's. Because Southampton was a port city, with ships docking there after transatlantic trips, there were many American 45s to be found in the junk stores. We'd pick up things like "Zing Zing" by Art Neville, or "Lights Out" by Jerry Byrne, both on Specialty, or perhaps Tiny Bradshaw, Little Willie John or Wynonie Harris on King. Then ride back late in the day, saddle bags bulging with trophies, eager to get the record player fired up and the music heard. So I went from rock 'n' roll to R&B and blues and, through friends, also to jazz.

'I think I first heard Jamaican music around 1963 or so. Scored a copy of "Going Crazy" by The Continentals on a little label I had never heard of before: Island (Island WI 010). I found it in a junk store, took it home hoping for an R&B sound. It wasn't R&B as I knew it. It was sort of different. I started subscribing to *Blues Unlimited* and *R&B Monthly* in late '63 or '64, and heard about Sue Records, who were doing what London American, Stateside and Top Rank had been doing earlier – issuing cool R&B. I noticed that Island Records were somehow involved in the label.'

Youths like Rob wanted not only to listen to their preferred music in a smoky club (if they were old enough), but to carry it home to their bedrooms as the new consumer generation moved into full swing. It was in the inner-city clubs that the young black met with the young white, and each took something from the other. The West Indian style of sharp clothes and a unquenchable thirst for good driving music was soon to be adopted by trendy white males as the mod era dawned and British youth began a long love affair with Jamaican music.

THE EARLY LABELS LINE UP

Sonny Roberts And Planetone Records

Sonny Roberts has the distinction of founding probably the first black-owned record shop and the first black-owned record label in Britain. He came to London from Jamaica in 1953 and worked as a carpenter for some years before founding, in the early '60s, Planetone Records and the similarly named shop Orbitone Records, which was just across the road from Willesden Junction railway station. Rico recalls Sonny having a partner named only 'Reg', who now sells insurance back in Jamaica.

Planetone started life in 1962. Its studio was situated in the basement of 108 Cambridge Road, London NW6, later to become the famous address of Island Records. Sonny lined the studio walls with egg boxes to provide sound insulation, and either the recording equipment was very crude or Sonny was still learning to use it, for many Planetone records sound under-produced. Apparently he had a one-track machine, with little remixing capability. He even cut his own masters in the room next to the studio – a real cottage industry.

The label introduced some artists who would become mainstays of the London black music scene, such as Dimples (Hinds) And Eddie, alias The Marvels or Marvelles, and Robert Thompson aka Dandy. The studio band consisting of Rico Rodriguez, Lovett Brown (sax), Mike Elliott (sax) and Jackie Edwards (piano) seems to have been called The Planets when Rico was not present, and Rico's Combo when he was. That scarlet pimpernel of the London scene, Sugar Simone, also cropped up in one of his guises, as Jackie Foster, having singles issued both on Planetone and its short-lived sister label Sway in 1963.

It is possible that Marty Robinson, also on Sway, was the reasonably well-known Martell Robinson, in which case his single predates his *Port-o-Jam* outing, usually considered to be his first disc, by a year. Other protagonists, such as Perry Moon, Ernie Faulkner and Mike Elliott, were rarely heard from

19

again, although Elliott did surface with a single on Ackee in 1972, assuming he's the same fellow of course.

Planetone's labels were initially halved red over yellow; towards the end of the company's existence they changed to plain white with black writing, perhaps as an economy measure. That much is simple, but Planetone's numbering, or sometimes lettering, system has defied all attempts at understanding it for 40 years.

For instance, the first issue, 'Midnight In Ethiopia' [*sic*] by Rico's Combo bears '45/PT/A' in large letters, with 'RC1' in small letters beneath it, presumably denoting Rico's Combo. But its matrices are PLA-12 and PLA-13, suggesting that these were not the first in the series. But 'Fleet Street' by Dimples And Eddie is labelled '45/PT/B', suggesting that it was the second release unless Sonny hadn't learned his alphabet as a boy. Now the fun starts: the smaller legend beneath states 'RC3', destroying two theories at a stroke: that RC meant Rico's Combo, who aren't named on the label, and that the release letters followed a logical alphabetical progression. The matrices PLA-15 and PLA-16 substantiate this, showing that there was a release in between these two.

Confused? You will be, for '45/PT/C', 'Hitch And Scramble' by Rico's Combo, is numbered 'RC6' and its matrices are PLA-21 and PLA-22, showing that there were two releases in between 'B' and 'C'. Just to defy any further attempt at logical progression, '45/PT/D', perhaps the best-known single on the label, Rico's 'Youths Boogie', is RC5 and its matrices are PLA-18 and PLA-20. By the time The Marvelles released 'Tell All Those Girls', still in 1962, the letter sequence had disappeared and the number was '45/PT/35' (and so was the matrix), posing yet another query: it is most unlikely that a tiny label like Planetone could have released 35 singles in a year, so why the jump in numbers?

One possible explanation for some of this numerical eccentricity was that Sonny would make one-off 'specials' for sound systems. He started doing this before he released any records commercially, so it's possible that the early matrix numbers were taken up by sides that only circulated on acetates and were never on public sale. Those that did go on sale, along with Island's product, were distributed by a new company called Beat & Commercial Records, headed by a man who would be vital to the story of black music in Britain: Lee Gopthal.

By the end of 1963, Planetone had ceased trading and the Cambridge Road premises had been taken over by Island. Sonny Roberts would appear to have leased some masters to Melodisc, judging by Blue Beat BB206, which is by C

Sylvester And The Planets (Sylvester had previously had a Planetone release). This disc's b-side asks another question as it is credited to Little Joyce; was this future UK ska mainstay Joyce Bond's first appearance on disc?

Melodisc/Blue Beat

The exact origins of Melodisc Records are not clear. The label was founded by Emil E Shallit in 1946. There had already been a Melodisc label in the United States, operational in 1945 and, as Mr Shallit was apparently an American citizen, he could have been involved in it.

Emil Shallit was by all accounts an extraordinary man. Of European-Jewish extraction, he was a fluent multilinguist, a talent that led to him being parachuted behind Nazi lines in occupied Europe during the Second World War. Why he chose to enter the music business is unclear, as he did not seem to be a particularly avid music fan. Indeed, he once likened selling records to selling potatoes: you buy some potatoes, you sell them at a profit, you buy some more potatoes.

By the beginning of the 1950s, Melodisc Records, at 48 Woburn Place, London WC1 (the label would move to its long-time base at 12 Earlham Street, London WC2, just off Charing Cross Road, later in the decade), was off and running. Any independent outfit, denied radio or TV exposure, could not hope to compete with the major companies on a level playing field: so Emil Shallit sought niche markets that would be too specialised for the big boys to bother with.

A glance at Melodisc's 1952 catalogue, price 3d, shows how successfully he had done so. Over 200 78s were available at the time. Not surprisingly, a Jewish series was offered, with waxings of songs like 'Mein Yiddische Mamma', 'Gefilte Fish' and the intriguing 'Ich Bin A Fartiker'. Jazz was taking off in a big way in the London of the early 1950s, and Melodisc catered for the bearded beatniks with records by popular British artists like the Crane River Band and Tommy Whittle's Group, as well as US recordings by such top names as Stan Getz, Charlie Parker, JJ Johnson (the trombonist whose name would later be assumed by a Jamaican record producer) and Nat King Cole

In those days, blues was seen as a division of, or spin-off from, jazz, and appealed to a similar audience. Melodisc served up a series of 78s leased from Moe Asch's Disc and Asch labels in New York, where ironically the blues was seen as a department of folk music, not jazz (Asch would found the successful and long-lived Folkways label soon afterwards). Artists included Josh White, Brownie McGhee and Leadbelly, and two 78s by Big Bill Broonzy, recorded in London in 1951, augmented the blues roster.

Significantly, also on catalogue were a whole slew of calypso 78s – some, such as Bertie King's Royal Jamaicans, recorded in London, but most, including half a dozen each by Lord Kitchener and Lord Beginner, emanating from the Caribbean. So Mr Shallit was keeping the Jewish people of Golders Green, the bearded weirdoes of Soho and the small but burgeoning black enclaves of Notting Hill and Brixton supplied with their favourite sounds.

During the 1950s, following the keen young Sigismund 'Siggy' Jackson's appointment to the company, Melodisc expanded in leaps and bounds. By 1959, its catalogue, now running to 15 pages, embraced a quantity of African music by artists like The Nigerian Union Rhythm Group and Ginger Johnson, lashings of jazz both home grown (Acker Bilk) and American (Wild Bill Davison), Latin sounds from Hernandos Deniz, gypsy music possibly recorded in a knackered Ford van in a lay-by, and a smattering of pop recordings in a 'P' series – though how far these penetrated the popular market is questionable. A plethora of EPs and a smattering of 10- and 12-inch albums were also in print.

Caribbean music occupied a large proportion of the release schedule, however. Melodisc actively sought out and recorded UK-based artists, such as Russell Henderson, whose band had a residency at the Coleherne pub in West London for many years. The bulk of these releases, though, consisted of calypsos from the islands, with regular singles by Lord Melody, Mighty Sparrow and Lord Kitchener. The label had prepared a ready-made niche market for a music that was about to burst out of Kingston and capture the imagination of Britain's ever-increasing black immigrant population. That music was based on American R&B and was variously known as Jamaican blues or blues beat.

In 1959 Melodisc launched the Kalypso label, issuing singles in an XX series. Early Duke Reid and Federal productions, as well as some calypsos from what was then British Guyana, came out, but it was XX16, released in late 1959 or early 1960 depending on which reference book you believe, that pointed the way forward. Entitled 'Aitken's Boogie' by popular singer/pianist Laurel Aitken, the crudely recorded disc sounded like a Jamaican band that wanted to play R&B but hadn't learned the rules yet, which is exactly what it was. The flip, 'Cherrie', was less remarkable and hinted at Laurel's Cuban origins. Crude and erratic or not, this was the first Jamaican R&B music to see issue in Britain.

Aitken and his boys got it right next time round. 'Boogie In My Bones' was fully formed R&B, with walking bass, a snarling sax solo, a nimble guitar solo (which sounds like the work of the technically brilliant Ernest Ranglin) and pounding piano, it appeared more or less simultaneously in mid-1960 on Kalypso and on Carlo Krahmer's Starlite label. This was the one that broke the music in Britain, as evidenced by the copies that frequently turn up second-hand, all of which have clearly been played and enjoyed to a great degree! The Kalypso issue (XX18) is an oddity, for it shares its issue number with another 45 by Count Sticky, and it's much rarer than the Starlite disc. It also credits the Jamaican copyright holders as Caribou Records, a company run by one Dada Tewari, whereas in fact the disc first appeared in Jamaica on a label run by a young Chris Blackwell.

Whatever the legal ins and outs, this exciting new music was off the launchpad. Melodisc put out another R&B single by The Mellowlarks (though credited to Lord Tanamo) on Kalypso, and recorded Aitken, newly arrived in Britain, for their main label.

Encouraged by the record's sales to the West Indian communities, Shallit decided to start a label devoted to this new style of music. Siggy Jackson suggested the name of the label, a slight adaptation of the term 'blues beat', which was being used to describe Jamaican-style R&B, and soon the first two Blue Beat singles reached the shops: Laurel Aitken's 'Boogie Rock', leased from Clement Dodd's Downbeat label, and established show band Byron Lee And The Dragonaires' version of Doc Bagby's R&B tune 'Dumplins', from future Jamaican Prime Minister Edward Seaga's WIRL label.

Seaga also furnished Blue Beat's third release, Higgs & Wilson's 'Manny Oh', which saw the debut of the famous navy-blue label with its blocked silver logo; the initial releases had featured a lighter-blue script on a white background. Word spread through Jamaica's fast-expanding music business that Melodisc in London was seeking releases for its new label, and numerous producers sent over recordings.

Siggy Jackson recalls that Emil Shallit 'was an American, who spent most of his time in America and only occasionally came to England. Then when I got Blue Beat established, he went to the West Indies quite a few times to sign other [Jamaican] labels which we didn't previously have.'

So Shallit struck many leasing deals, and in its first year of operation, Blue Beat issued material from Dodd, Seaga, Duke Reid, Simeon L Smith, Trenton Spence and Fay Abrahams, as well as a couple of in-house recordings by Bobby Muir, and Lynn Hope's instrumental 'Shocking' from the US King label, as this record had the shuffling beat the dancers desired.

Siggy Jackson remembers the Blue Beat boom: 'When we released the Blue Beat records they became so popular that we had Blue Beat hats, Blue Beat skirts, all sorts of merchandise. And I had a weekly show going at the

Marquee Club, where I featured the Blue Beat scene and afterwards when that stuff waned a bit, we began releasing records that were known as ska.'

Blue Beat released a further 16 Aitken singles, along with tracks from Joe Higgs, Delroy Wilson, a young Owen Gray, the mods' mate Derrick Morgan and Clue J And The Blues Blasters. Surprisingly, the most consistent seller of those early records was a ballad, Keith Stewart And Enid Campbell's 'Worried Over You'. The duo soon split up, but their rather contrived recording remained available until the late 1970s, such was its enduring appeal within the West Indian community.

For the first couple of years of the 1960s, Blue Beat had little real competition. The Starlite label was releasing Chris Blackwell's Ja productions, alongside a few from other sources, but these were jumbled in with a mixture of pop and rock 'n' roll releases. Other labels, like Planetone and its subsidiary Sway, sold hardly enough copies to warrant the pressing of the record and remained firmly in the background of the burgeoning Jamaican music scene.

With at least one new release every week Blue Beat very quickly took the lead in issuing Jamaican sounds within the UK, and the music-hungry punters could be assured of a sizzling selection of either the hottest Kingston sounds or a UK-recorded piece in the same style. Blue Beat was lucky in that as it gained the upper hand in the retailing of Jamaican music to the relocated listeners in the UK, the actual blues beat was transforming into the rip-roaring sounds of ska.

By the end of 1962, however, the label faced competition from Chris Blackwell, who had moved to England at about the time of Jamaican independence in August of that year, and who had established his Island label. Undeterred by this threat, Blue Beat continued its rapid-release schedule to an audience now bolstered by young white mods. Sub-labels such as Chek and Duke were also launched, although only Dice survived beyond three issues.

In 1961, on the flip side of a Rico Rodriguez instrumental, there appeared Buster's Group's 'Little Honey', this being the first vocal record by the man who was increasingly to dominate Blue Beat: Cecil 'Prince Buster' Campbell. Along with running a sound system, Voice of the People, in Kingston, Buster also tried his hand at production. First off, he produced other artists, such as the Folks Brothers with 'Carolina', but once he got in front of the microphone there was no stopping him. By 1963 he was, along with Derrick Morgan, top of the pile. The two had wrung a lot of mileage out of a series of singles in which they took turns to slander each other to music, with records like Morgan's 'Blazing Fire' and Buster's 'Black Head Chineman'.

Aware of the threat posed by rival labels like Island competing in the ska market, Shallit brought Buster and Morgan to London for live appearances and to record a few tracks. Derrick cut his 'Telephone' single here, backed by Georgie Fame And The Blue Flames, and Prince Buster's massive seller, 'Wash Wash', was accompanied by the (non-comedian) Les Dawson Blues Unit led by white drummer Dawson. Shallit had them sign exclusive contracts to Melodisc, which were designed to prevent the two stars' recordings appearing on any label other than his imprints.

The Jamaican government later declared these contracts invalid and Derrick Morgan's work once more became available on Island as well as Blue Beat. Prince Buster, however, must have been satisfied with his contract as he stayed with Melodisc for virtually the whole of his long and prolific career.

Despite limited radio exposure and promotion, gems such as Prince Buster's 'Madness', The Maytals' 'Treating Me Bad' and the Prince Buster All Stars' instrumental 'Al Capone' all sold in their thousands at the time, though sales were largely confined to non-chart return shops in West Indian areas. With a fairer chart compilation system, these and several other Blue Beat issues could have been top 50 hits.

The year 1966 saw an exceptionally hot summer in Kingston. Coinciding with this was the appearance of the cool and deadly rude boys, dressed crisply and sporting dense dark shades, these young ghetto gangsters wanted to look hip, and flying round the dance floor to the ripping ska tempo wasn't for them. So with the oven-hot summer and the need of the many cooler members of the dancehall crowd to look mean (as indeed many were), the rapid tempo of ska was slowed down. By mid-1967 the new, slower style, called rocksteady, had winged its way over to the UK. Blue Beat, as ever up with the latest trends, issued the new sounds of rocksteady such as 'Take It Easy' by Hopeton Lewis and Prince Buster's own 'Judge Dread'.

Meanwhile, Melodisc had started a new pop-aimed label called Fab, but after a few releases by the likes of American star PJ Proby, the imprint became the one to launch the new image of Jamaican music for the Melodisc group. More soul-styled recordings by Jamaican artists like Errol Dixon were diverted to the Rainbow label, and by the end of 1967 – after almost 400 singles, two EPs and nine LPs – there was no longer a place for Blue Beat as an outlet for new Jamaican music. However, several classics, like 'Al Capone' and 'Ten Commandments', continued to be re-pressed on Blue Beat for the newer generation of aficionados of Jamaican sounds.

Oddly, there was also an isolated release in 1972 with John Holt's 'OK Fred' issued on BB 424. As the 1970s progressed, Prince Buster became a major shareholder in Melodisc, with his own production work emerging on the new Prince Buster label until the following year when he effectively retired to concentrate on his other business interests. The Fab label continued until 1977, although with a greatly reduced market share in the face of competition from the younger, more aggressively marketed, Trojan and Pama companies.

But the label still offered quality music. In the mid-1970s Emil Shallit revived his long-standing connection with Clement Dodd and issued a splendid series of Studio One recordings such as Burning Spear's fearsome 'Foggy Road' and Freddie McGregor's take on the Cat Stevens chestnut 'Wild World' as 'Wise Words', as well as some compilation LPs, one of which claimed to include tracks by one 'Bob Morley'.

Shallit was now past his 70th year and had slowed down; he had also lost the services of the dynamic Siggy Jackson and his mercurial successor Jack Price. He decided to lease out the rights to three of his best-selling singles – Buster's 'Al Capone', 'Ten Commandments' and 'Big Five' – as well as the renowned Prince Buster *Fabulous Greatest Hits* LP, to his Midlands distributors HR Taylor & Co of Birmingham. These reissues came with mid-green, blue or purple labels, with the Blue Beat logo cheaply laid out with letraset, and bearing the legend 'Under licence from Melodisc Music'.

The Prince Buster label was also reissued at this time using a drab single-colour label or sporting a 'brick wall' design that made the title and artist almost indecipherable. Finally, a couple of years before Shallit's death, a clutch of 12-inch disco 45s emerged. The first was simply 'Al Capone' and its flip 'One Step Beyond' in a larger format with a cartoon-style picture sleeve. Later issues in the series had three or four tracks each, featuring Buster, The All Stars and/or The Tennors. These have the letraset-style Blue Beat logo on an almost illegible spotty label of various colours.

Little of the catalogue has been reissued to date, and the label is avidly collected mainly for the fine ska sides it issued back in the 1960s.

Though they never issued a Jamaican record, the importance of Vogue Records of Fulham cannot be overemphasised. While Melodisc was leasing calypsos to please immigrants from Trinidad and elsewhere, Vogue was the first label to give expatriate Jamaicans what they wanted; the myriad Shirley And Lee, Amos Milburn and Wynonie Harris discs were aimed at them alone, as these records were hopelessly out of step with what white British blues enthusiasts were buying. Early white blues fans wanted either cotton-pickin' country blues strummers or gritty, electric Chicago stuff with harmonica and guitar to the fore, and would consider Vogue's big-city artists, with their booting sax-led combos, to be over-commercialised and therefore to have sold out.

Significantly, Melodisc picked up the rights to a few such discs. Some, including singles by Louis Jordan, were issued on the main label or on Downbeat, but sides by Hank Marr, Titus Turner and Wynonie Harris were placed on Blue Beat – a sure indication of the market to which they appealed.

Starlite Records

Carlo Krahmer, a prominent drummer on the London jazz scene since the 1940s, who had played with Ronnie Scott, Johnny Dankworth, George Chisholm and just about everyone else on the circuit, founded Esquire Records in the early 1950s. He ran it, helped by his wife Greta, from his mansion flat at 76 Bedford Court, London WC1, and built up a strong catalogue of mainly jazz releases on 78 rpm (prefix 10), 10-inch LP (prefix 20) and later on 12-inch LP (oddly, prefix 32).

A particular coup for the optically myopic but musically far-sighted Carlo was when he gained the rights to issue the Prestige catalogue in the UK. This brought major jazz names like Gene Ammons and the Modern Jazz Quartet to his label, no doubt leading to healthy sales among the beard-and-duffle-coat brigade. By 1957, he was seeking to expand his releases beyond the boundaries of jazz, and decided that these would best be issued on a new imprint. Starlite was born.

Kicking off in January 1958, the initial batch of singles on the beautiful plum-and-gold label were in a pop vein, including artists such as US hitmaker Jodie Sands and home-grown thrush Shelley Moore, allegedly 'The girl with the mink voice'. The label lay fallow through 1959, but returned in the new decade with a much more eclectic bunch of 45s, perhaps reflecting the fact that Carlo Krahmer, like any good Jewish record man, was willing to take a chance on anything that might sell.

The release sheet for 1960 included jazz from Kenny Graham, R&B from Sonny Thompson, gospel from the Rev AA Childs helped by his Congregation, strict-tempo dance tunes by Norman Grant, a rendering, or perhaps rending, of 'Happy Wanderer' by the Ballarat YWCA Choir and, tellingly, releases by a number of artists who were unfamiliar to most Britons, but whose names would undoubtedly strike an instant chord with newly arrived immigrants from the West Indies: Laurel Aitken, Owen Gray and Wilfred Edwards.

These were probably licensed from Chris Blackwell's R&B and Island labels in Jamaica; some sources have suggested that they were pressed in Britain without Blackwell's knowledge or permission, but it is unlikely that the businesslike Krahmer would do this. Why he picked up the rights is a mystery: possibly his 'Screaming Boogie' by Sonny Thompson (ST 008), issued in March 1960, had sold well in areas of high immigrant population, leading him to seek similar music to aim at this new and growing market.

Whatever the reason, the flow of Jamaican R&B and occasional calypso releases on Starlite started in June 1960 with Laurel Aitken's 'Boogie In My Bones' and continued unabated until October 1962, when singles by Owen Gray and Kes Chin were issued. Other West Indian-oriented music on Starlite included items by Azie Lawrence and the Palmetto Kings, which were UK recordings originally produced by Sam Manning for the short-lived Mezzotone imprint in 1959, and material from Eddie Seaga's WIRL label (Higgs & Wilson, Chuck And Dobby), plus one each from Byron Lee and Prince Buster.

These were, in Starlite's typical fashion, interspersed with rock 'n' roll, country, pop and strict-tempo releases. The label's last singles appeared in November 1963, and its EP series ended in early 1964 with a gospel set by the Faithful Wanderers. Starlite put out a limited number of LPs, just 15 in four years, of which STLP5, *Owen Gray Sings*, vies with Blue Beat's *Jamaican Blues* LP as the first long-player of Jamaican R&B ever released in Britain. The notorious rarity of both albums suggests that the market wasn't yet ready for microgroove.

Carlo Krahmer's death in the mid-1960s did not spell the end of the Esquire group, by now trading as Esquire Records Talent Ltd. His widow Greta, a formidable lady, reissued some of the old EPs and LPs with a GRK prefix, put out innumerable strict-tempo EPs by her pet studio band Norman Grant And His Orchestra and had a fruitful ten-year contract with Bob Koester's Chicago-based Delmark label, which resulted in a flow of fine blues LPs and EPs. The last of these, Otis Rush's *Cold Day In Hell* album, appeared in 1976, after which Esquire ticked over on its back catalogue until Mrs Krahmer's death a few years later.

Control of the label then passed to the Krahmers' long-time associate Peter Newbrook, who reissued many of the albums – but alas no Jamaican music – from his base in Norwich. He was still trading in the mid-1990s, by which time he owned the rights only to Esquire's original British jazz recordings. Nowadays Starlite, a label once overlooked by collectors (*Let It Rock* magazine unkindly described its Jamaican issues as 'pre-bluebeat records of no interest'), is recognised as the pioneering and important label it was, and some singles, such as those by Derrick Harriott's group The Jiving Juniors, command inflated prices among enthusiasts.

R&B Discs

Founded in 1959 by husband and wife Rita and Benny Izons, Jewish immigrants who had anglicised their surname to King, their record shop at 282a Stamford Hill, London N16 operated for over 25 years, during which time they also ran a chaotic extended family of record labels. Their imprints included the following.

- **King** (1964) – The flagship label that carried all types of music – pop, soul, Jamaican, rock 'n' roll and surf music. King scored the group's only national chart success, with Irish country & western artist Larry Cunningham!
- **R&B** (1963–65) – Ska all the way, with plenty of major producers' work from the likes of Clement Dodd and Duke Reid.

  Then, with the same number series, R&B became:
- **Ska Beat** (1965–67) – Correctly named at its outset but much of its later output was rocksteady. Again, plenty of issues from major producers along with some home-grown ones including material from the up-and-coming Robert 'Dandy' Thompson.
- **Port-o-Jam** (1964) – Short for 'Port of Jamaica' (ie Kingston), this seems to have been an overspill label for Dodd productions, but changed halfway through its run to become an outlet for Ossie Irving's UK productions.
- **Prima Magnagroove** (1964) – An inexplicable label devoted to the product of the US Prima label owned by Italian-American singer Louis Prima, whose chart heyday had been from 1958 to 1960 and who never meant much in the UK. Most issues featured Prima, plus a couple by his backing band Sam Butera And The Witnesses. R&B went all the way on this label with special company sleeves and even *NME* advertising.
- **R&B Discs** (1965) – Unlike its namesake, this silver-on-blue series, with dedicated company sleeves, actually did issue American blues and R&B, though branching out into pop later in its run. It is notable for issuing the first UK record on which Barry White's voice can be heard: the walroid soulman sings back-up on The Bel Cantos' rather splendidly titled 'Feel Aw Right'.
- **Giant** (1967–68) – The successor to Ska Beat, and mainly a rocksteady label. The majority of releases were UK productions by Dandy, who also featured as an artist. A handful of Jamaican releases included a couple of Studio One recordings, notably Albert Tomlinson's 'Don't Wait For Me' and The Wrigglers with 'The Cooler'.
- **Caltone** (1967–68) – Issued mainly Ken Lack productions, with a handful by the likes of Phil Pratt, newly emerging producer Bunny Lee and one by the ubiquitous Dandy. Caltone was the home of some particularly good rocksteady releases.

- **Jolly** (1968–69) – A hotchpotch of rocksteady and reggae, sometimes with UK artists singing over Jamaican rhythm tracks.
- **Domain** (1968) – Cheerful-looking orange-and-white label owned by the Kings and studio whiz Vic Keary. Scored a big hit on the UK soul charts with 'Mellow Moonlight' by Roy Docker.
- **Sound System** (1969) – An eclectic run of just five singles from various Jamaican sources, including an early Keith Hudson production on The Chuckles. Presumably the name was meant to suggest to punters that the label offered tunes that were currently hot on sound systems.
- **Moodisc** (1971–72) – Reggae from Harry Mudie most of the way (save one Ewan McDermott production) on this black-on-red imprint, which was less colourful than its Trojan-owned precursor.
- **Hillcrest** (1971–72) – This elusive label marked the end of Rita and Benny's direct involvement in releasing Jamaican music, though their Stamford Hill shop would continue for a further decade. At least two of its seven issues, King Cannon's 'Reggae Got Soul' and Glen Adams' 'The Lion Sleeps', were issued concurrently on Junior Bradley's Birmingham-based Junior label.

That's about it, except that all sorts of oddities turn up that are R&B-related. Keith Stone of Daddy Kool recalls finding a white-label Jimi Hendrix LP while clearing out the stockroom after Rita and Benny's deaths in the 1980s. One of the authors has a white-label copy of a single by Donnie Elbert, an American singer but singing to a reggae beat, on R&B 2000, and doubtless there are many more such oddities from this group of labels' prolific ten-year span.

Island

White upper-class Jamaican Chris Blackwell's Island empire is founded partially on his country's music from the formative R&B and ska days, with a good boost from Marley's electric international dread in the 1970s.

The Island story is well known and, not wishing to cover well-worn ground, we offer only a brief summary here.

Blackwell relocated to London just as Jamaica gained independence in 1962 and began his Island label as a cottage industry, working from his mews flat in Rutland Gate in west London.

The idea was for Jamaican producer Leslie Kong (who was a close friend of Blackwell's) to supply all the releases in the UK, but Kong could not fill the orders, forcing Blackwell to look elsewhere in Kingston for product. He consequently leased some outstanding sides from all the top-name producers of the day, as well as issuing a few London-recorded sides.

Island Records rapidly outgrew his small flat, and he began to lease rooms at the spacious shop-cum-house located at 108 Cambridge Road that was owned by Lee Gopthal. Sonny Roberts' Planetone set-up inhabited the basement and Island gradually took over the rest – bar Gopthal's bedroom. Gopthal would become a partner in the newly formed Island sub-label Trojan, as well as forming the B&C (Beat & Commercial) distribution company

Even with all the growing musical input via Jamaica, from the mid-1960s, Blackwell took an increasing interest in white rock, which was where he perceived a considerably more lucrative income could be made than from small-run West Indian-aimed records. Consequently, in 1968 he sold off his Trojan label and its satellite subsidiaries to Gopthal so he could concentrate on the white rock market, and did not re-enter the Jamaican music fray until his signing of Marley in 1972. Jimmy Cliff and Wilfred 'Jackie' Edwards did stay with Island but the idea was to groom them for a pop/international market.

Columbia/Columbia Blue Beat
The major label Columbia, part of EMI, licensed and released a few Jamaican recordings by the likes of Winston Samuels as well as issuing home-grown recordings by Laurel Aitken in 1964.

The Columbia Blue Beat label, launched in 1967, was set up by ex-Melodisc/Blue Beat manager Siggy Jackson and he is credited as producer on most of its issues, which feature UK bands like The Bees and The Mopeds.

Siggy recalls the birth of Columbia Blue Beat: 'Around 1967 [while still employed by Melodisc], we had a bit of a disagreement [he and Shallit], because I had many ideas, such as opening our own record shops so we have complete control over what we were selling. Because we always had to compete against the big companies, such as EMI, Decca, Philips, and so forth. But Emil wasn't for that, so I left and had my own label with EMI [Columbia Blue Beat]. I was quite successful with that, then I began to branch out into African music, which was very good indeed.'

Presumably Columbia had an eye as to where Melodisc's Blue Beat was heading and wanted to gain market share in the new audience, much like Atlantic Records, which issued product from Byron Lee. But the success of these major-label forays was hampered by their lack of understanding of the distribution and promotion patterns needed to sell this still largely 'underground' music. The little guys won hands down, although, as we shall see, a couple of them would grow into major players in the black music business.

2 Putting Down Roots

UK REGGAE ON THE RISE

It was not just new labels that were springing up, but also Jamaican artists picking up on the boomtime and moving to London. In addition, many new UK-based groups were taking the initiative to start making music. Most of the new bands started out backing visiting Jamaican or UK stars before moving into the studio to make their own music.

Jackie Robinson/The Pioneers

The Pioneers were indeed pioneers in being one of the first groups to cross the Atlantic and settle in the UK as reggae took a hold of the charts. 'Longshot Kick The Bucket' climbed to Number 21 in the pop-pickers' favourite chart show in October 1969, and soon afterwards Sidney Crooks, George Dekker (aka George Agard) and Jackie Robinson touched down in London. Of their biggest hit Jackie recalls, 'It was my father who pointed out in a newspaper about Longshot [a horse that died in racing service] and said why not write a song about it.' Jackie and Sidney had already written the song 'Longshot', which The Pioneers had recorded for Joel Gibson to great Jamaican acclaim, and then recorded a follow-up, detailing the nag's sad death, for producer Leslie Kong a year later. 'Leslie wasn't even in the country when we recorded it – I produced it myself,' says Jackie proudly of their best-seller.

The Pioneers found life in the UK very rewarding, as Jackie recalls: 'We arrived at Gatwick on the 22nd of November 1969 after a stopover at New York. We came with The Upsetters and didn't intend to stay long. It was a six week-promotional tour, which ended up as six months!' He credits Trojan boss Lee Gopthal as the single person that enticed the group over to the UK with 'an attractive advance and contract'.

With the tour, 'We hoped for more money [than available back home], new fans, a better lifestyle – adventure.' And once they were here it was 'happiness – bliss. [The UK was] a more advanced society with more venues to perform and more avenues for record sales. You see, we were versatile – we could sing pop, soul, reggae – so we got loads of work.'

The group flew back to Kingston in the spring of 1970 to lay down some more tracks for Leslie Kong. Some of these recordings surfaced on the Trojan LP *Longshot*. They were soon back in London 'doing plenty of shows. We had TV shows in Europe and Ireland, and then early 1971 we did a tour of the Middle East. We were in Cairo and discovered that our backing band there couldn't read music and didn't know some of the words [to our songs]. Luckily as the audience was Arabic most of them couldn't understand English so we were OK. Our first own backing band was called Sweet Blindness, by the way.'

Lee Gopthal had a song he particularly liked called 'Let Your Yeah Be Yeah' and was determined to see it a hit, as Jackie remembers: 'Well he'd played it to various other singers and they found the key too high for them, so he played it to me and, like him, I believed it to be a hit.' History shows that this was a super-smash for the group, taking them beyond the reggae market, and well and truly into the mainstream.

'Trojan treated us like stars…we were perhaps their biggest-selling group…we were pretty consistent with our chart entries and sales', Jackie says proudly. 'We did backing and session work for Jimmy Cliff, Dandy Livingstone, Winston Groovy, Eddy Grant, Desmond Dekker and many more. As we were so versatile we moved into cabaret work through 1971, 1972, 1973, doing soul and reggae [as the reggae boom faded in the UK], and by this time we'd already decided to stay for good in the UK as we had easy access to the continent and plenty of work. We capitalised on foreign markets by touring places like Canada, Japan and the Middle East…life was still good – better than it was in Jamaica. Actually I think, along with The Cimarons, we were the first reggae band to tour Japan – that was 1975.'

Jackie comments on the UK studios compared with their Jamaican equivalents: 'Chalk Farm was a good studio although there was no comparison to Jamaica – in Ja the musicians nurtured you – they were long-term players – while in London the bands were still learning. "Let Your Yeah Be Yeah" was voiced at Chalk Farm on a rhythm track cut at Dynamics. We always went back to Jamaica to lay tracks so we could keep in touch with our roots – get a feel for what was current down there and add our flavour to it. [In the UK] we used The Cimarons and The Rudies interchangeably [presumably for overdubs] and most of those recordings were done at Chalk Farm Studios. We had the licence to decide on what product to go with, including producing, arranging and harmonies, except a few Jimmy Cliff songs. We laid down most of the tracks then overdubbed the voices.'

Credited as Sidney, George And Jackie, because 'We wanted to slow the pace down with The Pioneers name a bit', some chart-bound releases such as 'Feeling High' backed with a moody retake of The Temptations' 'Papa Was A Rolling Stone' were issued on Trojan's Attack subsidiary label. The basis of both tracks was recorded in Jamaica with additional work done at Chalk Farm Studios. '"Papa" went down really well in our stage shows so we decided to record it, and the a-side did very well for us,' remembers Jackie.

Another track that has lived on from the Sidney, George And Jackie period is 'Reggae Fever', to be found on the flip of the jolly retread of Chubby Checker's 'At The Discotheque'. 'We wrote that around 1969–70, although we didn't record it until 1973, I think,' recalls Jackie. This would explain the reference to skinheads, who by this time had all but disappeared from the scene.

A move to solo work resulted in Jackie's popular 1974 single 'Homely Girl'. 'I suggested this cover of The Chi-Lites song to the group but they weren't interested so I did it alone. 'Homely Girl' was also covered by UB40 later on, who gave credence to my version on their album cover as their inspiration for doing the song, and not The Chi-Lites' original version.

'Then,' recalls Jackie, 'in 1975–76, as The Pioneers once again, we cut some funky-soul work for Eddy Grant at his Coach House studio. I also filled in by doing some acting starting in the late 1970s.' In fact, he appeared in both the first *Batman* movie and *Highlander*, while putting his luck at getting parts down to his 'being a rare commodity – I can speak with a good US accent'.

Since then, the three Pioneers have been active in solo projects as well as coming together to tour all over the world, perennial favourites with fans of vintage reggae music.

Dave Barker

Dave Barker was another artist, along with Ansel Collins, who came to the UK on the reggae boom, although Dave's tale is something of a contrast to Jackie's.

The pair were lured by the massive reaction to 'Double Barrel', which took both the reggae and pop charts by storm, hitting the coveted Number One spot in March 1971. The track was originally funded and produced by organist Ansel Collins as an instrumental, which he then passed on to producer Winston Riley and his brother Buster. Riley wanted to spice up the track with the patent Barker 'Yankee style' DJing that had made him a star in Jamaica, and called him to the studio.

Dave's story tells of the joys and hardships of the horizon of reggae in London: 'I didn't like the rhythm tape [that became "Double Barrel"]; it was too light – it didn't have the power that other reggae tracks had at the time. Anyway, I couldn't find inspiration when Winston Riley played me the tape, so Buster Riley who was standing in the studio next to me said "think about James Bond, imagine you're a giant standing on top of a mountain", and it happened – just one take, that's all. It was voiced at Joe Gibbs' studio and I got paid $20 for it.'

Presumably the producer dreamed up the song title as Dave was unaware of the track having any name at all. The follow-up, 'Monkey Spanner', was also untitled after Dave had done his thing. 'I never could work out why they called it that,' says Dave, 'as my lyrics didn't fit the title at all – it was Sid Bucknor who was the engineer on that one, by the way'.

'Double Barrel' was subsequently licensed to Trojan in the UK and issued on its Techniques subsidiary, which was dedicated to Riley's production work. In 99 per cent of cases, that would have been that: a quick session, limited UK sales within the underground reggae market, another day, another dollar. But this one was different, as Dave recalls: 'A few months went by and we were out by West Street [Kingston] where Winston Riley and his family lived, and the phone rang. He came out all excited saying it was Trojan calling him from London and saying "it seems like we may have to go on tour" as "Double Barrel" had taken off over there.

'Then a few days later the phone rang again and Riley said, "We have to leave for England like now." He took us to buy a stage suit each and get me a passport as I didn't have one. Then we were on the BOAC flight – I didn't even have a chance to tell my family I was leaving for England!'

The Dave & Ansel Collins band comprised Dave Barker, Ansel Collins on keyboards, Rad Bryan on guitar, Bobby Davis on harmonies, and Winston Riley.

Dave recalls the landing in the UK as being 'very chilly – we'd left Jamaica, which was hot, and I didn't have any socks or vest. We were told by Trojan that we had to go straight to *Top Of The Pops* [the BBC Studios], and Winston Riley had found these guys from Trinidad or Dominica – one of those places – to mime on *Top Of The Pops* with us – they wore grass skirts. Tony Blackburn was the host and I got the chance to meet Rod Stewart and Lulu.

'We were staying at first in a small place in North End Road, Kensington, and the payment for the lodgings didn't seem to be happening. We'd signed an agreement with Trojan for £40 a week each – work or not – and we were doing three shows a night, rushing to the car, changing as we ran. Anyway, Winston Riley paid us each the £40 a week, which he would come round with and he would deduct so much towards our air fares each time.

'After a while we moved to a shabby place in Ladbroke Grove, which I believe Winston Riley found for us. Our tour car was an old Rover, which you couldn't tell the colour of as its bodywork was so bad – this was while The Pioneers had a real flash car. We would park way down the street so no one saw us get out of this thing we were using!

'At this time Winston Riley brought Jackie Paris from Jamaica to play drums, and Trevor Star as our bass player. The tour lasted about five months, and at times we were flat broke with little to eat.

'I had only the one stage suit, and one night this fan that followed us around shouted as I was doing my thing "Mind the suit, Dave" and it made me realise. I had strong words with Winston Riley and I got £1,000 from him and Lee Gopthal and…bought myself some decent clothes.'

Riley and Dave flew back to Kingston some three to four months into the tour to record tracks for the forthcoming *Double Barrel* LP, which Trojan had scheduled for issue. 'We spent three weeks in Jamaica, where I recorded a number of tracks for the album,' says Dave. 'Yet these weren't the tracks that appeared on the LP – they were old tracks – not the new ones I'd recorded at Dynamic Studio.'

Soon after the tour was completed Winston Riley and Ansel Collins flew back to the sunnier climes of Jamaica, leaving the rest of the group in London. This was the beginning of the 'hard times' as Dave dropped out, 'depressed and disillusioned': 'I wrote the track "Money Is The Poor People's Cry" just then – and boy was it true for me.' The track later appeared on a Trojan album called *In The Ghetto*.

'It was Larry Lawrence that really got me out of my room – I'd just stay there all day except to go out for food or something…he said we should check Creole. I was working as Dave Collins then and it [the surname change] didn't bother me at all. Larry encouraged me to record again and we started an album for Creole with songs like "Keep on Trying", "Shakatak" and "Ton Up Kids", to name a few. Although there was some sort of disagreement between Larry, myself and Creole, and Larry took control of the master tape.

'Larry and I went our separate ways and then the album appeared on Trojan – it was me and Bobby Davis, no Ansel [the *In The Ghetto* Album issued by Trojan was credited to Dave & Ansel Collins] – I was unaware of it being put out at all.'

Dave's sporadic career continued as, in the mid-1970s, he joined Chain Reaction – a group tipped for the top, which achieved a Radio 1 record of the week. With Chain Reaction, Dave was able to demonstrate that, as well as being an explosive DJ artist, he was also one of Jamaica's most soulful singers. Signed to the Gull label, things looked good for Dave until group member Bruce Ruffin and producer Stanley Pemberton fell out with Gull, and the group members went their separate ways.

The Cats

Legends about this mystery group abound: they were black, they were white, they were Dutch... According to their main man, John Kpiaye, the real story is that The Cats were formed in Mile End, east London, in September 1967, with a personnel of Tyrone Patterson (b. 1940, Jamaica) on keyboards; bass, Richard Archer (b. 1946, Guyana); guitar, John Kpiaye (b. 1948, London); and drums, Michael Okoro (b. 1951, London). Initially, says John, they were called The Hustlin Kind: 'We were a four-piece ska/soul instrumental band. We played Booker T, Skatalites, Willie Mitchell-style numbers, at local clubs, pubs, office parties, etc. We changed our name to The Cats in summer 1968.

'We recorded "Swan Lake" and nine other tracks in a three-hour session at Maximum Sound studios in the Old Kent Road in September 1968. The tracks were recorded straight on to a two-track master, no overdubs or mixing. The flute was played by Nigerian saxophonist/flautist Peter King.

'"Swan Lake" was released on our own label, Baf Records. It was a big hit with the ska/rocksteady fans and the original skinheads. It reached Number 48 in the national charts, without any promotion or airplay. It was the first chart entry by any UK reggae band. Baf Records was set up by the band, because we could not get a record deal for "Swan Lake". The label was administered by an accountant named Mr Craig, and we released four more singles [and one Baf various artists album] before disbanding in 1970.'

Interestingly, another participant in that session remembers it slightly differently. Mike Cole, then a teenage roadie with top UK country act Tex Withers And The Sidetrackers, confirms some of the personnel John mentions, but reckons that 'Swan Lake' was cut, along with its b-side 'Swing Low', in spare time at the end of a Withers session.

'Session pianist Tyrone Patterson and a couple of other black musicians were drafted in to give the recording a more professional sound,' recalls Mike, who now runs a computer company in Buckinghamshire. 'At the end of Tex's session, the pianist started playing around with "Swan Lake"; his mates joined in with a reggae beat, a couple of Tex's band joined in too, and I played percussion. The engineer Vic Keary rolled the tape, and cut those two tracks.'

Those of you with sharp eyes will have noticed that 'Baf' spells 'Fab' backwards, which was the general idea when the guys cooked up their label name. So at last you have the lowdown on the mysterious Cats. Well, almost. Mike Cole still has an acetate of the two tracks, on which the group is named as 'The Snoog' – which is, of course, 'Goons' backwards.

Jubilee Stompers

Another band that has always been very much in the background, and that has puzzled many reggae fans, is The Jubilee Stompers. The name sounds more like that of a Dixieland outfit, but the band's music sounds like reggae. Behind the enigma lies a band that changed its style but not its name.

In 1962 saxophonist Ken Patton arrived in Britain from his native Jamaica. He soon found able and willing friends to make music with in London, and The Jubilee Stompers were born. They started playing mainly jazz, hence the 'Stompers', but swiftly changed style to Latin American, progressed to soul and, when reggae became the craze in the clubs and discotheques, again changed style to suit. In a very short time the eight-piece band, still known as The Jubilee Stompers, was in great demand for live work, both at home and abroad.

The band's reggae work, mainly covers of current reggae raves, appeared on a number of budget-priced albums in 1970 such as the Siggy Jackson-produced *Reggae Tight*, which was issued on the Hallmark label. The band initially recorded one single for Doctor Bird Records in 1968 – DB1151 'Give Your Love To Me'/'I Cry My Heart', which was also released on the obscure Amusicon label – and then, for Trojan Records, TR7725 'Lucianna'/'I Really Like It', which was issued in February 1970. One wonders how many bearded jazz fiends have picked up copies from junk shops, thinking that they've found an unknown gem of hot jazz, only to be perplexed by the Caribbean rhythms when they played the record.

Bees/Pyramids/Symarip

One of the earliest UK bands to form was The Bees, whose work appeared on the Blue Beat and Columbia Blue Beat labels. The group had further incarnations as The Pyramids and finally Symarip, under which name they struck skinhead gold with the anthemic 'Skinhead Moonstomp'. The core members were Montgomery 'Monty' Neysmith, Josh Roberts, Ray Knight, Roy Ellis, Roy Barrington, Frank Pitter and Mick Thomas.

'I came over to England when I was a teenager in the early 1960s,' recalls founder member Monty, 'and went to stay with my cousin Barry Biggs in Tooting. Barry's best friend was Roy Ellis. I was sent over by my father to study law, so soon after I began my studies and around this time, Frank [Pitter] and Mick [Thomas] started this band with Roy and Johnny Orlando as the lead singer, and there was a guitarist as well.

'Roy knew Josh Roberts, so he brought him into the band. At this time Barry went back to Jamaica, but Roy and I had become good friends and I used to go to the rehearsals with them – their band was called The Bees.

'I used to just play on the piano and things, as I used to play piano back home in Jamaica, and I also had a singing group in Jamaica – I used to love music. They asked me to join the band, but I didn't want to give up my studies, as my father would be really angry. So they started gigging at weekends and they said, "Gigging at the weekend won't really interrupt your studies", so I said OK. I went and bought myself an organ (I remember my first organ was a Vox) and I started playing and we started getting more and more work, and I found it more and more difficult to get up in the morning to go to class, so I started skipping class more and more.

'Then the opportunity came to tour with Prince Buster, being his backing band as well as opening up for him. It started as a six-week tour and it was so successful they had to extend it. For us, it was like a coming-out party, because we got exposed at all the clubs, and many of the agencies and everybody wanted us back. After Prince Buster left [to return to Jamaica], we had so much work, we all went full-time.

'Siggy Jackson was our manager, but he didn't produce any of our recordings – Laurel Aitken actually did the producing and, in fact, he was the one who got us signed to EMI, when we were The Bees. He didn't have a deal with them himself, but he got us on the label. It was really great of him.

'Then Eddy Grant came in – he was with The Equals at the time and they'd had big hits in England and Germany and all over, with "Baby Come Back" and things like that. He wanted us to play ska, because that was really the music he loved, not pop music.

'We went into the studio and we did a few songs and, right away, "Train Tour To Rainbow City" became a hit, with Eddy Grant naming the group The Pyramids and signing them with Edward Kassner, who owned President Records. 'We did an album and songs like "All Change For The Bakerloo Line", which although it wasn't a hit on the British chart, was very successful, because it was used for TV shows and radio plays. "Do Re Mi" got a lot of plays on the BBC, as well as "Wedding In Peyton Place" and "Rough Rider".

'Then a big controversy came up again, because a couple of the guys in the band didn't really want to play ska. They wanted to play pop. So I wrote a song called "Mexican Moonlight", which Edward Kassner wanted to release as a single, and Eddy Grant said, "No, you've built up an identity, stick to it."

'I remember Edward Kassner said, "Well, it's better to be king of something than just to be one of many." The big mistake we made was when we released "Mexican Moonlight", because we went from one extreme to the other – it was a ballad and although it was a hit in Germany and Austria, it kind of messed us up. That was the end of us. The deal with President Records did not work out after we found out that "Mexican Moonlight" was a hit on the continent – we did not find out until a year later.'

It's worth noting that The Pyramids also recorded in a reggae style for President's Jay Boy subsidiary under various guises, such as The EK Bunch, The Alterations, The Rough Riders and The Bed Bugs. Their best-known name change was, however, just around the corner, in 1969, as Monty explains: 'We were still under contract with Kassner, when we made "Skinhead Moonstomp", so we could not release it under The Pyramids. We said, "What can we call ourselves?" I came up with the idea of turning 'Pyramids' around and you leave out the 'd'. So [it was] originally Simaryp…if you look at the old records, you'll see. I don't know how it came to be Symarip… I don't know who changed it or how it changed. Anyway, Graeme Goodall, who was in charge of Doctor Bird Records, which was affiliated with Trojan…we started to work with him.

'At this time, while we were playing live, a lot of skinheads used to come to our shows, and Roy and myself said, "Boy, it would be good to write a song for skinheads." You remember the song where they said, "I want everybody to get up off your seat and give me some of that old soul music" ["I Thank You" by Sam And Dave]? I got the idea and said let's change the words and put, "I want all you skinheads to get up off your feet, put your braces together, your boots on your feet and give me some of that old moonstompin'." I said, "Moonstompin' – Skinhead Moonstomp!" Then I remember our old road manager started singing this song, "yeah, yeah, yeah, yeah, yeah…", something similar to that. At that time, we did not hear Derrick Morgan's "Moon Hop". So we said, "That sounds good!" We kind of twisted it and Roy and I wrote the words. Then we went down to Graeme and we said, "Graeme, we've got a real hot song" and Graeme said, "Let's record it". We recorded it on a Monday and by the Saturday it was in the stores, especially in London. The first day it was released it sold something like 5,000 copies in London alone. We thought, we've got a hit here, so we started recording for an album right away.'

The group also recorded during this time as The Seven Letters. This was a prolific time for them, says Monty: 'All those things were done at Graeme Goodall's studio in Fulham. In fact, we did so many things at this time. We did a couple of things with Desmond Dekker; we did a couple of things with Creole – Bruce White and Tony Cousins – that was really for Trojan Records. We did "To Sir With Love", we did over "Telstar", "All For You" and The Pioneers recorded an album with us as well. We used to record with people like Owen Gray, Laurel Aitken, The Ethiopians, Toots And The Maytals (we did shows with them), Desmond Dekker, and we did an album with Millie Small [*Time Will Tell*] that we did at EMI Studios or the Marquee.'

The group had a very active touring schedule as well. According to Monty, they played in 'every little town in England, Wales, Scotland. And we were a good stage band. I think the peak of the stage concerts was the one at Wembley [Sunday 26 April 1970, at the Empire Pool] that appeared in the movie *Reggae*. I remember about 14,000 people there and when we started playing and the skinheads started stompin' and it was really a sight to see – fantastic!'

After the *Skinhead Moonstomp* album the group reverted to being called The Pyramids and relocated to Germany. They gigged all over the country playing afro-rock in the vein of Osibisa. Still on the afro-trip, they moved back to London and recorded under the name of Zubaba. When 'Skinhead Moonstomp' became a hit for the second time in 1980 in the wake of the Two-Tone ska revival, the band were together in Switzerland. 'We took photos and everything, and agreed to do a tour if it went into the top 50, but it didn't [it peaked at 54], so we didn't bother with the tour. At this time, we were very successful as a club band in Germany, Austria and Switzerland, but more and more we were just taking it as a day-to-day job, and I didn't want that.'

When Monty left in the 1980s, the band found a replacement and continued, but soon they were to part for good. Monty now works as Monty Montgomery, has performed at Reggae Sunsplash a couple of times, toured Africa and recorded a new CD. Roy Ellis, meanwhile, is now resident in Switzerland, where he has forged a very successful career as a gospel vocalist.

Pat Rhoden

Among the first wave of Jamaicans to relocate to London was singer Winston 'Pat' Rhoden, who arrived in 1961 at the tender age of 19. 'My parents sent me over to be with my older brother who was already here,' says Pat, 'and my first recording was at TMC studio at Tooting: I did a couple of songs with a young girl called Marie for R&B Discs. They were issued as "Pat And Marie". I only got royalties, and we got on OK in terms of business. Then I did "Jezebel" and "Santa Claus" – Ranny Bop [Williams] played on that. I was working with musicians like Rico and Tan Tan [trumpeter Eddie Thornton – another early arrival to these shores], although I have to say I was disappointed as there wasn't a lot of musicians you could work with in the UK. Really, before The Rudies band there was only session musicians – Sonny Binns is a guy who played a big part in early UK reggae. I met Denzil Dennis at Rio and we've been friends ever since. I have to say that Denzil is one of the best singers to leave the shores of Jamaica – so underrated.'

The problem of culture clash also affected the aspiring artists, as Pat recalls: 'It was hard to find somewhere to rehearse as we didn't want to disturb the neighbours. They weren't used to hearing next door's music, and liked a quiet life. I never had any problems with this really, but plenty of artists did have the police round.'

After Pat recorded the Fontana album for Jack Price, he moved to Pama Records. 'My first song, "Happiness", was a big seller – it stood for a long time at the top of the chart. Pama always saw me in a commercial way – a crossover artist. 'Maybe The Next Time' sold 19,000 copies; that was produced by Derrick Morgan in 1970.

'I was recording an LP at Pama when they hit financial problems so it never got finished. It was a shame, as they had just started an agreement with Tony Pike's studio to make studio time available for all of us artists, which would've been good. So I went to Trojan. I took them "Nose For Trouble", which I recorded independently, and on the strength of that they signed me up. I did Stevie Wonder's "Living For The City" and "Boogie On Reggae Woman" for Trojan. "Boogie On" was looking good [for mainstream chart action]. Trojan paid me [royalties] for 12,000 records with that one. Then Trojan went down, just as I had seven or eight tracks finished for an album with them. Somewhere they still have those tapes.'

From that disappointment Pat went on to jointly found one of the top UK labels of the mid-1970s as we'll see a little later.

Roy Shirley

A Jamaican performer who has been resident in Britain for pretty much all of the last 30 years is Roy Shirley. 'I first came to the UK in 1972, although I'd met Dave Betteridge of Island around 1967 when he visited Jamaica with the intention of licensing music for Island to release over in Britain,' he says. 'It was then that I introduced Dave to Bunny Lee who, along with Joe Gibbs, I had brought into the record business.' Bunny Lee would later become a frequent visitor to Britain during his dealings with Island, R&B Discs, Pama and Trojan.

With his distinctive vocal style, Roy recorded several classics, which have ensured his continuing popularity in the world of West Indian music – most notably 'Hold Them' (Doctor Bird), 'The Winner' (Island), 'Get On The Ball' (Caltone) and 'Warming Up The Scene' (Giant). Roy would go on to open his own record shop in Jamaica and launch his Public record label.

'My first visit here came about as a result of Bunny Lee passing my contact details on to Rita King [Izons] of R&B Discs. Rita had apparently liked my records.' So much so in fact that, unbeknown to Roy, R&B Discs had clandestinely issued one of his self-productions from his Public label – 'Where In This World'/'Truly' – on a blank label during 1969. 'Rita wanted to contact me with a view to licensing my music and arranging a UK tour with U Roy, John Holt and Max Romeo. But John Holt never actually came. The tour, which started with a first date in Croydon, was not a financial success and, although Rita promised ten grand for each of us artists, I only ever saw £30. I stayed in Rita and Benny's house, and at the end of it Rita just gave me back my passport and made excuses about the tour.' Things couldn't have got worse. Or could they?

'I heard from some associates back home that my record shop had been smashed up and looted. There was little to go back to Jamaica for, so I settled in Stoke Newington's Brighton Road.'

Now forced to make his own way in the British reggae business, Roy gave a few sides to Count Shelly for his newly formed Count Shelly label ('This World' and 'Return To Me', the latter of which had actually come via Lord Koos). Meanwhile, Roy had been surprised to find some of his music on various Pama and Trojan subsidiaries (notably 'Jamaican Girl' and 'A Sugar', the latter appearing on both labels).

'I moved on from Shelly in 1973 and was introduced to Dennis Harris [and his new DIP label] by Barry Howard of The Aces, and 'I Fancy You' was one of the company's first releases. At the same time, Russell Coke [of Magnet] gave me about £600 to record eight or nine tracks with The Undivided Band, out of which I had to pay the band and other expenses. Some of these tunes, like "Endlessly" and "When You're Young", were sellers. Coke also gave me a promise of about 5p per copy in royalties, but no money ever passed.'

A trip to Brixton market saw Roy link up with Joe Mansano for a cover of current chart hit 'Welcome Home', although Roy says he never saw any money from this one-shot venture either. Yet he persevered.

'In 1974, I started a short-lived publishing company with an associate by the name of Earl and launched a label called Leroy. Only one single, "Don't Destroy The World", came about, but we could only afford to press up 500 copies. We had to close the company down.'

It was not long after this that Roy went into partnership with a Mrs Johnson. 'She would run a West Indian restaurant at the front of the shop in Sandringham Road, Dalston, and I would set up my own record shop called "Imperial Records" at the back. The shop became famous because it was painted in so many bright colours, and soon people were coming to paint on extra bits. It was here that I was filmed for the *Aquarius* TV programme on British reggae – you can see me walking outside the shop. Then I was taken, with Rico Rodriguez, to Phebes' club in Amhurst Road.' In the programme Roy gives a thoroughly spirited performance of his 1967 classic 'Get On The Ball'.

'Me and Mrs Johnson put out "Heart Breaking Gypsy", which I recorded at Gooseberry Studio in Wardour Street, and we released it on our own R&JJ label and Eddy Grant's Torpedo. We gave it to Eddy since Torpedo was owned by President and we wanted to get it into the national charts. The tune did well, but the shop started to attract a bad crowd, thieving the records. Some people upstairs used an extension to use the shop's telephone, so I get some high phone bills.

'I then went to this German guy, Robby Day, and his Trenchtown label and recorded the LP *The Winner* with Black Slate, who were very young guys then. There were some singles off that like "Rasta Love Is The Greatest Love" and "Crying Time". That album sell some, but I never heard from Robby Day again.' But at least the money Trenchtown gave him was sufficient to cover the cost of the phone bill and, closing down the record shop and generally cutting his losses, Roy moved away from the area altogether.

Later, in 1982, Roy caused a sensation with his performance at Jamaica's Reggae Sunsplash and has continued to record sporadically for a number of small labels during the last 20 years or so. Still touring as far afield as the USA and Canada, Roy is keen to further youth talent through the various shows he puts on, and is a strident voice for those artists that have not received their due reward from the jungle that is the reggae music business.

The Cimarons

One of the longest-serving London-based groups were The Cimarons, named after The Cimaroons, an African tribe shipped to Jamaica in the days of slavery, whose descendants, known as Maroons, still live within the small island's interior today.

The band formed around the Willesden area of north London in 1967 and comprised Locksley Gichie (guitar/vocals), Carl Levy (keyboards), Franklyn Dunn (bass), Maurice Ellis (drums), with 'Mingoes' taking lead vocal duties. He was to leave before the band departed on a tour of West

Africa in 1968 and a guy only remembered as Patrick took to the microphone. Carl Lewis was the next vocalist before Winston Reed took up residence in 1973 and remained with the group until he too embarked on a very profitable solo career in the early 1980s as Winston Reedy. Sonny Binns of The Rudies fame played keyboards with The Cimarons after the departure of Carl Levy in the later 1970s.

Initially, the fledgling Cimarons played only at local youth clubs with nothing but a self-taught feel for how to play their instruments. Their influences were wide, with Gichie digging the soul of Marvin Gaye, Levy into the heavy muthafunk of James Brown and Ellis checking out Buddy Rich and Ginger Baker, but it was their precision at playing the then new rocksteady beat that got them invited to tour West Africa. While still steeped in cover versions of soul records, The Cimarons slowly increased their rocksteady sound as the tour progressed. They also started to understand their instruments more fully and really see themselves as working musicians. Their confidence was boosted by the increasing amount of backing and session work they were given on the West African tour.

On their return, the now confident band were quickly hot property on the session scene, often recording under various aliases as 'The So-and-so All Stars'. They were soon doing work for Pama via Laurel Aitken, recording for Lambert Briscoe (as The Hot Rod All Stars), laying down some tracks for Bamboo and moving in on the expanding empire of Trojan. They still hit the funk spot on occasion, and under the guidance of London-based producer Mike Dorane they rocked out 'Penguin Funk', which found no favour at the time but has since become a rare groove classic.

At that time (the late 1960) Count Suckle's Cue Club on the corner of Edgware Road and Praed Street in west London was a top venue to play – and to catch the ear of talent scouts, as Carl Levy remembers: 'We were the first English band to play reggae at the Cue Club. It was our ambition to try and capture the Cue Club crowd because they didn't really dig reggae down there. When they heard us play it was so tight and purposeful they had to accept it. A tune called "Fire Corner" by Clancy Eccles And The Dynamites had just been released and we played it one night. Webster Shrowder from Trojan was there, and he said that it was the first time he had heard a band play reggae so tight. That's when we started to do sessions for Trojan and they asked us to do backing tracks for nearly all their artists whenever they recorded in England.'

While Carl is quite correct in saying that The Cimarons were responsible for a vast amount of the reggae recorded in the UK, The Rudies, too, were very prolific in their work, while other groups such as The Pyramids and The Pacesetters also took a small portion of the musical pie.

The Cimarons recorded a number of singles under different aliases as well as 'Mammy Blue', credited to themselves and produced by Dandy, which failed to create much of a ripple in the pond. Their 1974 *In Time* LP appeared on Trojan, with obligatory (for the time) bare-chested afro-wearers on the sleeve, and contained a fair smattering of covers plus the odd original recording such as 'Time Passage', which Ken Boothe also voiced on the same rhythm track for his *Everything I Own* album (also for Trojan). The group were unhappy with the album as they saw it as contrived to please roots fans and easy listeners in one go, with Trojan insisting on pop and standards covers. Hence it pleased neither and sold poorly.

It was at this time that The Cimarons decided to cut back on backing and session work to establish their own identity within the reggae marketplace: 1975 found them on Junior Lincoln's new Vulcan label slipping out a reggaefied single covering The Fatback Band's funk favourite 'Wicky Wacky'. The flip side of the Vulcan single was 'Tradition', a near note-perfect retread of the heavy roots sound of the major hit for Burning Spear. It would seem Vulcan was hedging its bets with a funky number on one side and the new sound of hard roots reggae on the other. Sadly neither side attracted much attention and the record failed to move many units.

The Cimarons' second LP, 1976's *On The Rock* (also on Vulcan), found the group both in Jamaica and London to lay down some serious roots music with a certain Mr Perry's involvement on a few tracks. Once again The Cimarons couldn't crack the market although they had scored well with a single, Marley's 'Talking Blues' in 1975, issued on Trojan's subsidiary label Horse, and credited to The Maroons. Producer-cum-engineer Sid Bucknor, who laid the track at Chalk Farm, cites 'Talking Blues' as a 'close shave with realism' in catching the 'Kingston sound', which is quite true as it also sold well in Jamaica, where it was issued on the Talent Corp label.

A move to a major label, Polydor, found the group recording perhaps their best album, *Maka*, in a very uncompromising roots vein with a distinct feel of London in the synthesiser overdubs. Initial copies came in groovy green vinyl, in keeping with the 1978 disco era, and the album was well received by the critics but, alas, once again it just didn't sell. Polydor then went for the live option album before it and the group parted company.

The band's swansong was an album of pop covers, recorded in 1982 and entitled *Reggaebility* for the budget label Pickwick, with the original concept coming from none other than Paul McCartney. By then the only members of the original band present were Dunn, Gichie and Reed, with Sonny Binns on keyboards and Lloyd 'Jah Bunny' McDonald from Matumbi drafted in on drums. Sid Bucknor, the original producer of the album alongside Vic Keary, recalls, 'It was recorded at Chalk Farm but not mixed there. Paul McCartney had a production company and wanted to do something…it was a strange album and we laid down some Buddy Holly covers including "Peggy Sue" along with the rest of the tracks, but they didn't make the album. ["Peggy Sue" surfaced as a single on the Imp label.] I didn't actually produce all the album, I left the project and I think Sonny Binns took over.' Sadly the album is only noteworthy for the full-colour sleeve photograph, which was taken by Linda McCartney.

By this time Winston Reed was moving out as the solo 'Reedy' and went on to score highly with a recut of his enduring lovers' tune 'Dim The Lights' in 1983 – a song originally recorded by the band and issued on Vulcan some years previously.

The Rudies

One of the best-known, and best, early reggae bands, both on record and live, were The Rudies whose work has appeared on just about every specialist UK label. The original group comprised Errol Dunn (lead guitar), Trevor Ardley White (bass), Sonny Binns (keyboards) and Danny Bowen Smith (drums). They got their first break through established singer Denzil Dennis, who recalls bringing the fledgling group to the attention of producer-cum-singer Dandy.

'In 1968 Dandy, myself and Laurel Aitken – whenever we heard a good group, our idea was to take them into the studio. At this time, I was living in south London – Brixton – and Dandy was living in Stamford Hill… So he asked me about this group I had heard called The Rudies, as at this time he used to pick and choose who he wanted to record. When he heard them, he said they were good enough, so we took them to record in a studio in Old Kent Road called Maximum Sound.

'We recorded "Hush" there and "Donkey Train" and "Down By The Riverside" and a few other ones – "Dream", "Sincerely". So we were the Brother Dan All Stars – me and Pat Rhoden – and anybody else who was in the studio. And when I wasn't singing lead, I did the background vocals.'

Freddie Notes

'I was born on the 4th of January 1943 in Kingston, Jamaica,' says the affable Alfred Peters, 'and as a youth used to sing jazz music from people like Oscar

Brown Junior on street corners. The passers-by used to toss me money and say, "Why there's Mr Notes again", and the name kinda stuck: Freddie Notes.'

After winning the infamous Vere Johns Talent hour like so many of his contemporaries, Freddie teamed up with Vic Brown, Donald Francis and Jah Ringles to form The Mellownotes. Their 'Album Of Memory' single for producer SL Smith sold well in Ja, and crossed the Atlantic in 1960 to appear on the newly formed Melodisc offshoot label Blue Beat in the UK, although it was credited to the 'Magic Notes'. Freddie would soon make the same trip in person.

'I had two kids in Jamaica, and the parents of their mother were already in England, and they sent for her,' explains Freddie. 'Then she sent for me, and I arrived in 1964. My first memory was of it being cold and very different from back home, but many of my friends were already here so it wasn't too bad.

'I formed a UK version of The Mellownotes with Jerome on drums, Kouie on organ, Webster playing bass and Dennis Smith on sax. We toured a little, until I joined The Coloured Raisins, after they were impressed by my dancing and singing, and worked all over the country performing at army and airforce bases playing mainly soul and ska numbers.'

The Coloured Raisins had a couple of well-received 45s out on the Major Minor and Trojan labels, including a version of Sam And Dave's 'I Thank You', together with a very worthwhile album. Their line-up included a young Gordon Greenidge, then combining music with playing cricket for Hampshire's second XI; he went on to become one of the West Indies' greatest test batsmen.

'Sonny Binns called me up,' continues Freddie, 'and asked if I'd like to join this group he'd started called The Rudies [Sonny formed the group around 1966], as they needed a vocalist and frontman. At the time Sonny was really the only professional in the band and they needed polish to get them out on the stage. So we debuted at the Ram Jam Club after just two hours' rehearsal in this sweatbox under a dry cleaners.'

By the time of the reggae boom fuelled by the white skinheads, Freddie Notes And The Rudies had become the number one UK band because, as Freddie says, 'We were so tight and professional. I loved the skinheads – I thought they were great – they liked my music and followed us everywhere. We make music for everyone – we're entertainers – I don't care who you are as long as you dig my sound. We backed just about everyone in them days: Owen Gray, Pat Kelly, Max Romeo, Jackie Edwards, Rico. It was me on drums on "Brixton Cat", you know. And that was me on the opening drum roll of "Moon Hop",' enthuses Freddie. 'I was a Burru drummer back in Jamaica – you know the Rasta drums, and I've always played drums since.'

Freddie and the guys took up residency at Count Suckle's Cue Club as well as providing studio duties on, as Freddie puts it, 'so many records that I can't remember them all. We were Dandy's Music Doctors, and did things for Joe Mansano along with backing Laurel Aitken and Derrick Morgan. We were popular in Jamaica too.' This is certainly true, as Ja-pressed copies of 'Moon Hop' do appear now and again.

'One day Vic [Keary, Chalk Farm Studios owner] and Graham [Walker of Trojan] suggested we cover this song by a white guy, Bobby Bloom, that had made the charts: "Montego Bay". I was sick with flu when they called round to get me to record it, but as a true professional entertainer I knew I had to do the job, and it came out OK.' In fact, 'Montego Bay' came out better than OK: it sold by the cartload to reggae buyers and became the pop-pickers' Number 45 in October 1970.

'I met Bobby Bloom when I was on tour soon after our hit and he said, "Man you sung my song much better than I could", and then later I met Joe South and he said the same of me.' (Freddie recorded South's 'Walk A Mile In My Shoes' soon after 'Montego Bay', although it failed to emulate the former record's success outside the reggae market.)

'We always arranged and produced our own music,' says Freddie of the production credits on his records, which often cite other people being involved with his work, 'and I never saw a penny from the sales of "Montego Bay" – I don't know where the money went.'

One bizarre record that was recorded by The Rudies is 'Devils Lead Soup'. Freddie chuckles an explanation, 'Well, you see, soup is normally nourishing and good for you, while this soup is the opposite – from the devil and full of bad things.

'The first time Bob Marley And The Wailers were to come over [on tour] they wanted The Rudies to work with them as they'd heard such good things about us in Jamaica,' says Freddie proudly, 'although for some reason we never got to do anything – I think the record companies didn't want it – I'm not sure why. We never did get to meet The Wailers. We did record with Clyde McPhatter [the ex-Drifters lead singer] and the folk singer Donovan wanted a reggae vibe on one track so we did that – although the cheque bounced on that one!'

Just as 'Montego Bay' was hitting the charts, divisions started to appear between him and the band, as Freddie explains: 'Pama said to the group they would do well continuing to back everyone, and I wanted to go out and perform. I'm an entertainer and do James Brown and funky stuff, not just reggae. I out-did Little Richard on one show and he refused to be on the same bill as me after that!

'We did one more song ["Black And White", released under the new group name of Greyhound] before I went off to tour Persia, Morocco, Hong Kong, New Zealand, Singapore and Australia. My band then was The Unity Band, who were The Coloured Raisins renamed – they played on 'Walk A Mile In My Shoes', not The Rudies. I've toured ever since all over the world for six or seven months of the year.'

With Freddie leaving, The Rudies were in need of a new singer. That replacement was to be a young man by the name of Glenroy Oakley.

Glenroy Oakley And Greyhound

'I was 11 when I arrived in London – that would be 1960,' says the quietly spoken and affable Glenroy. 'I lived in Stamford Hill and my first memories of music would have been the old Blue Beat records, which I heard while I was at school.

'At 16 I was an apprentice tailor and helped make jackets for Winston Churchill and Edward Heath among others. I used to go to this club run by Ken Boothe [not to be confused with the noted Jamaican singer of the same name], or Admiral Ken as he was known – Bluesville. He used to manage groups and run a sound system as well as having this club, and Mike Raven [later of pirate radio and Radio 1 fame] was one of the DJs there at the time. He would play all the latest records from the R&B right through to pop stuff – I loved pop records: Herman's Hermits, Georgie Fame… I'd sung in school competitions and they'd said I was a natural. Dandy lived quite near me in the early days and encouraged me to sing.

'One day I saw this ad in a newspaper for a Tom Jones-style singer and I thought I'd call it up. I went along and auditioned, and ended up in this six-piece called The Transactions. We rehearsed stuff like Wilson Pickett and The Animals – all the popular records of the day, and did a few gigs – no recording at all. The Skatalites were on tour over here in about 1967 and they were looking for a vocalist for the tour. I auditioned for that job and got accepted, so I did a few dates with them. They wanted me to carry on with them but I didn't really want to…

'I then formed a group called Glenroy Oakley And The Stax, which included Ruby James the session singer; and then I formed Glenroy Oakley And The Oracles. We gigged all over the UK – universities and such – and then we went to Italy for four weeks and on to Israel where we played in cinemas and other concert venues. We were the support for acts like Major Lance, Arthur Conley, Ben E King and Albert King before we split in 1969.'

Fortune would smile on Glenroy as, at this time, Freddie Notes was looking to leave The Rudies just as 'Montego Bay' was riding high in the national charts. 'The Rudies approached me to see if I'd like to join them. They didn't know me but they'd seen me on stage performing. Anyway we started doing some live stuff – still as The Rudies – playing "Montego Bay", some other reggae numbers – a bit of soul and, believe it or not, some rock, like Deep Purple's "Black Night". We liked to try all sorts of things, and I like rock so we'd do a few numbers.

'Our first record was called "Be Loving To Me", which was withdrawn because Dave Bloxham [the producer] had found the song "Black And White" (composed by two Americans, Dave Arkin and Earl Robinson, in 1955) and thought it was much better. He wanted me to record it solo as Glenroy Oakley, but I said no, we're a group, so that's how it came about.' ('Be Loving To Me'/'Judgement Rock' was actually issued on the Trojan subsidiary label Duke in early 1971, and credited to The Tillermen.)

'It was at this time we jointly decided to change our name to Greyhound, and "Black And White" became Tony Blackburn's record of the week.' (It subsequently hit the Number Six spot in June 1971.)

All the recordings were done at Chalk Farm Studios with Dave Bloxham in the producer's chair, assisted by the studio owner Vic Keary. The next chart attack came in the shape of the old Danny Williams standard 'Moon River', which took Glenroy and the band to Number 12 in January 1972.

The flip side to 'Moon River' carried two songs. The first, 'I've Been Trying', was a rhythmic Cat Stevens-style social-comment song, while the second, entitled 'The Pressure Is Coming On', is an outstanding piece of early roots-reality reggae. Glenroy admits that both songs are a long way from the smiley pop-reggae that Greyhound were making inroads into the national charts with: 'You have to sing what you feel, and the music can make a statement – that's what we were doing on those. Sometimes it's the only way to get a point across.'

'We did TV appearances with "Black And White", "Moon River" and our last pop hit "I Am What I Am",' recalls Glenroy, '"Moon River" went to Number One in Holland and we flew over to do their *Top Of The Pops*. One time we were in the [UK] *Top Of The Pops* studios we met Curtis Mayfield and then ended up as his support in Birmingham.' By this time the group owned two greyhounds, kennelled at the Essex seaside town of Southend, and were looking to be one of Trojan's best bets for pop chart dominance as 'I Am What I Am' charted at Number 20 in March 1972. 'We were playing commercial reggae,' explains Glenroy. 'You make things popular and people like it – that's what it's all about.'

The flip side to 'I Am What I Am' was a searing Hammond instrumental workout called 'Sky High', which not only harked back to The Rudies' skinhead sides but moved plenty of feet in the nightspots of 1972. Glenroy, in his usual unassuming way, comments, 'Well I'm the band's singer so I'm not on that one. You see, you can't take all the limelight and this [record] was to feature the band.'

Live work was also plentiful, 'We backed so many people on tour, like The Maytals, where I was the opener and Greyhound actually backed The Maytals, and we did the Alexandra Palace Reggae Festival in 1971. I personally preferred (and still prefer) live work to making records. We were on the Trojan live LP (*Trojan Reggae Party*), and although they kept asking me to be in the cover shot I wouldn't do it.' The problem with Trojan was that 'everything was always rushed,' observes Glenroy on the subject of the group's label.

At this time Greyhound relocated to the Island label and recorded for its Blue Mountain imprint. 'I wasn't on the Island single "Dream Lover",' says Glenroy, 'although we did do a few things for Virgin – I don't know if they came out – and as a side project I was in Erasmus Chorum, a black six-piece funk-rock band, produced by John Schroeder.'

Greyhound then moved across to the EMI offshoot label Retreat, and recorded an album, *Leave The Reggae To Us*, which was issued on the Transatlantic label in 1975. By this time Greyhound had run its course. The reggae boom had petered out and, as Glenroy puts it, 'We went our separate ways – we'd had enough and couldn't get any further.'

Glenroy went on to form the Atlantic Soul Band before working with big-name blues artists like Buddy Guy and Homesick James, while three original Rudies/Greyhound members (Binns, White and Dunn) moved on to form the nucleus of Dansak, a seven-piece band.

While The Rudies/Greyhound were riding high in the pop charts, Trojan was rapidly expanding as reggae moved into the big time with mainstream chart hits being clocked up. The resulting boom time for the company (and partially for its competitors like the Pama group) encouraged more visiting Jamaican artists to either relocate or tour extensively, including popular vocal trio The Pioneers.

Bob And Marcia

Bob Andy and Marcia Griffiths had toured countrywide in the wake of their smash 'Young, Gifted And Black' single and ensuing album of the same name. In a revolutionary step, Bob Andy decided to record the follow-up album to his and Marcia's hit at Chalk Farm Studios. This was 1971 and the stigma of only Kingstonians being able to play reggae was still running high. It would be almost the first time that a Jamaican artist had recorded a complete album in London with all UK-based musicians. The only other album to try this was Max Romeo's *Wet Dream*, although that did actually use some Jamaican rhythm tapes. Bob And Marcia's new album was to be called *Pied Piper*, released by Trojan (TRL26), and named after their second hit single, which climbed to Number 11 in June.

'It was Webster [Shrowder] who suggested that Marcia and I record "Pied Piper" when I was round his flat one evening,' says Bob Andy, 'He played Rita Marley's version [issued on the UK Rio label] to me and we both thought it would make a good record for us.'

The album was recorded with The Rudies band and used all new rhythm tracks bar two, with Bob as producer. Trojan gave Bob an unusually free hand with the album – beyond financing it, they let him do it his way.

'From the choice of songs to the final mix, it was all left to me,' reveals Bob. 'I even sat in with Tony King (who orchestrated some of the arrangements), and had input on the overdub side of things. I would decide on the songs and work out the rhythm patterns with the band and Vic [Keary, the studio owner].'

The major question had to be 'Why record in the UK when he had all of Kingston to work with?' 'Well, it was exciting being in England and I liked the rounder sound that Chalk Farm gave with its 24 tracks.'

Bob is sad to recount that Trojan was 'only interested in the record and had no interest in the artist at all. All they could see were hit records and it didn't matter who sang them.'

THE GROWING INDUSTRY

As the 1960s moved along, additional record labels sprang up to challenge the established masters like Blue Beat and Island, and to satisfy the demands of the ever-growing West Indian population relocating to the UK, along with the new white fans of the sound.

Rob Bell, who in his time worked for both Island and Trojan, gives his learned view of how and why the UK reggae recordings came about: 'I think the UK stuff was the result of Jamaican expatriates living in London who basically wanted to be connected to the scene. Cutting records was a way of being connected, if one was an aspiring producer, and part of the business of being a musician if one was such. I agree that some of the UK-recorded stuff sucked, just as (some) UK-recorded blues sucked to most blues fans. In both cases, the UK sessions attempted to get a sound, get a feeling.

'It ain't that easy! Look at how many labels tried to copy Sun Records or Stax or Motown; just the same with all those Jamaican guys. They had the cream of the crop down there [in Jamaica] in terms of both engineers/producers and musicians. Nevertheless, in the music business, there is always the possibility of lightning striking, and it is that possibility that keeps folks keeping on!

'For instance, we did hit with Joyce Bond's "Ob-La-Di Ob-La-Da" on Island. Also "Reggae Christmas" [issued late 1972 on Trojan] – a forgettable piece of fluff, I know, but business is business! It made Number 49 or 50.'

So how did this slightly bizarre Christmas hit for Trojan come about? 'It was Dave Bloxham's project. He started at Island as a van rep, in the London market,' continues Rob. 'He joined Trojan around 1970 to develop radio promotion. I imagine that as he became familiar with radio and TV, it became rapidly obvious that he could use this access to his advantage by getting into production. He had a few successes – Greyhound's "Black And White" and "Moon River", Scott English's "Brandy" and one or two others.

'Christmas tunes are kind of a given in the record business. Get a good 'un, and it sells each season for a long long time. I can't remember exactly how the Gable Hall Choir came into the picture. Perhaps an enterprising choir mistress contacted us. That's my daughter Mandy singing lead on that tune! She was about eight or nine, I think, and her two younger brothers were also invited to the session, but they got cold feet at the last minute.'

It must also be remembered that the UK was seen as a place where enterprising individuals could get on in business, and have a far better standard of living than in the somewhat run-down Kingston suburbs. The expanding West Indian and newly emerging white skinhead/pop markets of the late 1960s were well known in Jamaica, and many artists headed for the white cliffs of Dover with the hope of making their musical fortune in London. In addition, the popularity of UK-based touring artists like The Shadrocks and Joyce Bond would no doubt create a demand for their records to which their record label, in this case Island, would be only too happy to cater.

Graeme Goodall's Doctor Bird group of labels, distributed by Island, was one of the new breed taking an increasing market share as the 1960s moved past the halfway mark, alongside the mysterious Rio imprint, which ultimately was taken over by Doctor Bird. Long-term UK-based vocalist Denzil Dennis appeared on Rio and takes up the story.

'I arrived in London in June 1962. I came to England expecting to go to school, and I went to Earlham Street [the Melodisc offices] and they signed me up... So, my first recordings here were "Seven Nights In Rome" and

"Love Is For Fools", which came out on Blue Beat – they were produced between Siggy Jackson and Laurel Aitken and I recorded them in Advision Studio in Bond Street; Beres Ricketts also recorded at the session.

'William Rickard [aka Don Rickles] was at Blue Beat when I went there in '62 and then, in 1963, he started Rio Records and I began helping him run the label. The first thing I put out on it was "Blazing Fire" by Derrick Morgan, but we didn't know it was Chris Blackwell who owned it and he came on the phone to Rio and told us we had to withdraw it. He [Rickard] was an American and his wife was from Trinidad, and he was the one who paid for Owen Gray to come over [to England], but when Owen arrived, he was already signed to Blue Beat. Blue Beat was signing all these artists.'

Rio was a very small concern, as Denzil explains: 'It was just me, William Rickard and another fellow – an English man called Barry, who used to take the records around. He would pick up the records from the pressing plant, take them to a few shops, even a few white shops would take a lot of records from us at that time – there were a lot. Just like Lee Gopthal, he used to do with Island. I was the only one over here recording for Rio, unless I recommended someone, like with Milton Hamilton, but most of our other stuff came from Jamaica – from King Edwards. Edwards would send us things like Bobby Aitken or Shenley Duffus, because he was also from Trinidad. We had "Shame And Scandal In The Family" by Shawn Elliott and that was a seller – R-52 [the catalogue number]. Anyway, I recorded 15 songs for Rio as Alan Martin.'

Denzil explains why he chose such a different name to record under: 'I'd previously recorded with Frank Cosmo, as Cosmo And Dennis, and nobody knew me as a solo artist, so I chose Alan Martin. Dandy played harmonica on my first song for Rio – "The Party" – and Graham Hawk from The Mohawks, he was the keyboard player, because The Mohawks hadn't formed yet. Owen Gray, he was the piano player and producer, because William Rickard, he didn't produce anything. So Owen Gray played piano on most of my sessions. The bass player was Frank Burrell, he now represents some Jubilee Steel band. Tenor sax was Mike Elliott and Sonny Burke – the drummer, I can't recall his name – and Eddie "Tan Tan" [Thornton] played trumpet, because me and him go way back – and, of course, Dandy [Robert Thompson], the harmonica.

'Those things were recorded at Planetone, run by Sonny Roberts... Most of the [British] Rio recordings were made at Planetone and some at Advision in Denmark Street. Laurel Aitken used Advision a lot. You know, Laurel produced all the Melodisc recordings over here.

55

'I was at Rio up until 1966–7, when they sold out to Island. They bought it because where our shop was in Brixton tube station, on the Victoria line, London Transport bought the ground, so we had to sell up to Desmond [Bryan] from Desmond's Hip City. Graeme Goodall knew me from Jamaica, because he engineered my first record. Later, I went over with him to his studio in Fulham Road with Laurel Aitken and recorded the *Fire In My Wire* album. Graeme Goodall made some good sounds – "I Wanna Be Loved" by Pat Rhoden and Winston Groovy together, "The Same Thing For Breakfast" and that Laurel Aitken album.

Island's Rob Bell recalls a slightly different take on the change of ownership of Rio, however, with a financial problem resulting in the label gaining its new masters.

Charles Ross/Sugar

A particularly mysterious label was Sugar, run by Charles Ross – an interesting figure, if only for his uniqueness.

It seems that he was an Anglo-Indian who began producing pop music in the UK in the late 1950s or early 1960s. He then produced a few UK ska records in 1964, before returning to making pop records. Then, from 1967 to 1970, he spent extensive periods in Jamaica producing local talent, paying for sessions at Treasure Isle, WIRL and Studio One, with much of the material seeing release on Blue Cat, Duke and, finally, his two Sugar labels – the first version being distributed by Pye in 1969 and the second by Decca the following year. He then seems to have completely disappeared from the reggae scene.

Fab Records

Melodisc's Fab subsidiary, which operated from 1966 until the effective end of the Melodisc group's existence with founder Emil Shallit's death in 1982, is a collector's dream and a discographer's nightmare. Collectors will discover fascinating records by the score. Some of them, such as Prince Buster's 'Shaking Up Orange Street' or Burning Spear's 'Foggy Road', rank with the greatest classics of Jamaican music. Others, such as The Sugar Plums' reggae rendering, or perhaps rending, of 'Red River Rock', or future trouser-splitter PJ Proby's cheery early pop waxing 'I Need Love', are interesting oddities. A few, like 'Take You For A Ride' by Girl Satchmo (yes, indeed, a female Louis Armstrong impersonator) frankly defy belief. But a Fab record is always worth listening to, just in case it's one of those classics.

For that harmless drudge the discographer, it's a different story. Starting as a normal, well-behaved label with a sensible numbering system, and clear artist and production credits, it gradually went off the rails and ended up in a state of pure anarchy. First, numbers were missed out, unsurprisingly in the case of FAB-13, as there had been no Blue Beat BB13 either and we can assume that Mr Shallit was superstitious. However, when, for example, numbers 151 to 159 seem just not to exist, nor even to have been scheduled for release, it does not make the vinyl archaeologist's task any easier. Fab thoughtfully made up for this by duplicating, and even triplicating, some issue numbers, then starting again at Number 14, but not putting any labels on the records, so no one knew what they were anyway.

In order to throw the hapless researcher off the scent further, from about halfway through its life Fab changed its logo like other people change their socks, issued some singles with all the label copy (including the label name) typewritten, some of which credited the song title but not the artist, and a few that claimed to be on the Copyright Control label – only the FAB issue number revealed the records' true identity, or at least part of it, as once again the artists' names were omitted. The whole venture smacked of the lunatics running the asylum, yet among the confusion Fab issued many Prince Buster classics, some rare Wailers music and, at a time when it appeared to have become a home-made label, an awesome run of Studio One singles as Coxson Dodd entrusted his product to no other UK licensee.

It should not, then, surprise the reader to learn that Fab's first release was an EP that was in fact a perfectly normal two-track single. Melodisc launched Fab as a pop label, its name inspired by the *Thunderbirds* children's TV series of which Mr Shallit was an unlikely fan. The label's debut was either Errol Dixon's brash, brassy and beaty 'Need Someone To Love Me', assigned the number FAB EP1, or Phase Four's pop record 'What Do You Say About That', on FAB1. (In case anyone is wondering, there was an EP2, which was really a four-track extended-play disc, but don't hunt too hard for it as it's a set of square dances from a Butlin's holiday camp.) After a few more pop issues on the gold-coloured label, from PJ Proby and Jack Riding, the ubiquitous Laurel Aitken got in on the act on FAB5 and, from then on, the label assumed a more and more Jamaican aspect.

Although it was not conceived as a replacement for Blue Beat, that's effectively what it became. The two labels overlapped considerably – Blue Beat continued well into 1967 after which, in a true strike of marketing flair, Melodisc discontinued it just as Buster's 'Al Capone' hit the pop charts and raised the public's awareness of the label – but from FAB10 onwards, when Prince Buster first appeared on the label, it was rocksteady and reggae most of the way. As you would expect, there were a few aberrations, such as FAB129 by The Minstrels, which appears from its titles to be a Jewish record. One of the writers of this book saw this one on display alongside the latest reggae releases in Junior's Music Spot in Finsbury Park, and wondered what the shop's reggae-hungry clientele must have made of it.

The small number of pop records still issued by the company, by such great stars as Shovelville K Jackson and Gay Emma, reverted to the flagship Melodisc label, and 1967 and 1968 were great years for Fab. Classics like Prince Buster's 'Julie On My Mind' and 'Johnny Cool', Buster And Teddy King's 'Shepherd Beng' (twice), The Tennors' 'Ride Your Donkey' (possibly four times, and you could buy it on Island as well) and The Maximum Band's 'Hold Me Tight', probably Fab's biggest seller (it made the UK soul charts) crammed the release schedules. At this stage, the label was giving upstarts like Pama and Trojan a good fight for market share and musical quality – but there were ominous portents. FAB77, for example, purporting to be by Hank Williams on one side and Trevor Reel on the other, has the same track titles as the illustrious Shovelville K Jackson disc mentioned above. Was it the same record, and if so what the hell was it doing on Fab?

In 1969 and 1970 the wheels hadn't fallen off yet, but they were wobbling a bit on their axles. Most Jamaican-sourced Fab singles still emanated from producer Prince Buster who, if he didn't make a classic every time, never made a bad record: 'Tie The Donkey's Tail' and the amusing 'Ganja Plant' by himself, and two singles by The Clarendonians (labelled, in typical fashion, as The Caledonians, possibly the first north-of-the-border reggae group) were among the best. More UK Melodisc productions featured in the catalogue, many of them by seasoned singer Owen Gray whose 'Apollo' 12-inch was a good skinhead-style tune, but who leaned more and more towards depressing do-overs of 'Release Me', 'Three Coins In The Fountain' and other chestnuts. Home-grown reggae by The Rudies ('Brixton Rocket' on FAB104) and soul like 'Boom Biddy Boom' (FAB106) by the apparently multi-named Larry Foster alias Sugar Simone (but issued on white label as by Duke Lloyd) did some business, but records by The Max Group (probably the Maximum Band/Breed) and The Fruit Gums, among others, found few buyers.

From 1971 on, Fab's singles schedule careered about like a headless chicken. Yawning gaps appeared in the number series, the label design variations noted above kicked in with a vengeance and the label became increasingly eccentric and invisible, its market share declining steeply. Few Fab singles numbered above 176 ('Police Trim Rasta', Prince Buster's last issue on the label) turn up very often, suggesting that they had small pressing runs. During these years – and, because P-dates (issue dates) weren't printed on the labels after 1972, no one accurately knows how many years, but certainly they were still releasing in 1976 – several early productions by future top UK producer Larry Lawrence were issued, as was a series of five discs by 'The Great Aces' but patently not all by the same artist, which were possibly Joe Mansano productions. True to form, Fab also reissued The Folks Brothers' 'Oh Carolina' with a Fab label, a Blue Beat number and two different b-sides.

Few punters, however, heard most of these issues, just as, almost criminally, they didn't hear the splendid run of Studio One issues that filled most of Fab's declining years. Starting with The Ethiopians' trenchant 'Monkey Money' (FAB180, actually issued at the tail end of 1971 according to Roger Dalke's exhaustive listing), top Coxson artists like John Holt, Winston Francis and Bob Andy adorned the release sheets, and more top Coxson artists like Cornel Campbell, The Gladiators and Delroy Wilson saw anonymous issues on Fab's parallel white-label series.

In terms of LPs, Fab behaved itself in a comparatively demure way, releasing the solid compilation *15 Oldies But Goodies*, comprising mainly Buster ska (confusingly issued both on the Fab label and main Melodisc imprint – either issue appearing in the same sleeve), the Prince's strong-selling oldies compilation *FABulous Greatest Hits*, his new LPs *Wreck A Pum Pum* and *The Outlaw*, and Big Youth's debut LP *Chi Chi Run*. The rarest Fab LP is Buster's *The Message Dub Wise*, which came out, apparently in a pressing of 1,000 only, around 1973 and promptly sank without trace. It was as if the big grown-up LPs were above the confused catalogue shenanigans of their wee 7-inch counterparts. But wait: two of Buster's Fab LPs have Blue Beat catalogue numbers, and the Big Youth LP is actually a various artists compilation, which includes tracks by Buster's All Stars and Dennis Brown!

When Emil Shallit died in 1982, the stalwart *FABulous Greatest Hits* LP was still in print, sub-let to Melodisc's Birmingham distributors HR Taylor & Sons. According to Melodisc's long-time London distributor, John Jack of Cadillac Music, the album sold enough to have earned a gold disc, but Shallit wasn't interested in such trophies. As we saw earlier, he just wanted to get to the next sack of potatoes...

Prince Buster Label

'Prince Buster never liked being on Fab,' John Jack once observed. So the Prince must have been pleased when, in 1970, Melodisc gave him his own label, Prince Buster, in the same way that Trojan was then allocating labels to producers like Harry Johnson and producer/artists like Derrick Harriott.

Melodisc reproduced Buster's Jamaican label design, with its sun, moon and stars, and its red-over-white colour scheme. However, numerous colour variations cropped up over the years, such as red over yellow, black over yellow and the truly delicious chocolate over peppermint. The label kicked off with one of the Prince's slacker records, 'Big Five' (PB1), a rude adaptation of Brook Benton's US smash 'Rainy Night In Georgia', which proved to be one of Buster's biggest sellers, remaining in press until the early 1980s. A not atypical Melodisc cock-up gave the P-date as 1967, even though Benton's song didn't hit the American charts until January 1970. The following issue helps fill in some of those gaps in the Fab numbering series, pairing 'Rat Trap' by Buster and 'Black Organ' by Ansel Collins, whose matrix numbers show us that they were pencilled in for release as FAB142 and FAB141 respectively.

Prince Buster made good use of his dedicated label, releasing some 27 singles with himself as artist on one or both sides over the next three years. The prolific singer/producer covered soul songs like 'Sister Big Stuff' and 'I Stand Accused', together with country weepies such as 'Still', and offered a couple more of his own slack numbers in 'Kinky Griner' and 'Baldhead Pum Pum'. Other artists, almost all produced by the Prince, included John Holt smoothing his way through melodic songs like 'Rain From The Skies' and 'The First Time Ever I Saw Your Face', toasters Dennis Alcapone (usually uncredited as he is on 'It Mash Up') and Big Youth and The Ethiopians, whose lone Prince Buster single offers one of the idiosyncrasies so beloved of Melodisc collectors: it is numbered PB28 on one side and PB38 on the other. To compound the confusion, the matrix number of the latter assures us that it is 'PB37A'.

In 1973 the Prince largely withdrew from performance and production to concentrate on his jukebox business, so the stream of releases, about 36 in three years, dried to a trickle. One of these was an oddity, a coupling of Keith And Enid's ancient end-of-dance ballad 'Worried Over You' from 1960 with Derrick Morgan's 'Tears On My Pillow' from the rocksteady era circa 1966. Issued on PB60, this was the only non-Buster production on the label, and the label copy split the date difference by ascribing both sides to 1963! The final 45 release came as late as 1976: 'Uganda' credited to Prince Buster And The Revolutionaries.

Four LPs were issued on the label. *Big Five*, from 1972, offered a dozen of the Prince's slackest, most disgusting and often very funny waxings, such as the utterly sacrilegious rendition of the hymn tune 'At The Cross'. It was numbered in the main Melodisc series (MLP12-157). The following year, three valuable volumes of *Prince Buster Record Shack Presents The Original Golden Oldies* hit the racks: Volume 1 was Buster ska all the way, classics like 'Black Head Chineman' and 'They Got To Come', and it had 12 tracks even though only 10 were listed on the sleeve and label; Volume 2 offered more ska by various artists such as Derrick Morgan, Bobby Aitken and Eric Morris, as well as two Buster tracks already included on Volume 1; and Volume 3, a scorching set of Maytals oldies like 'Pain In My Belly' and 'Light of The World', is renowned for its cover photo of Toots Hibbert with a tree growing out of his shoulder.

What may appear to be a final idiosyncrasy is in fact a flash of true logic, by 1973 a rarity at Melodisc. These LPs are numbered PB9, PB10 and PB11; as there are no LPs numbered PB1 to PB8, readers may feel that this is yet another of those numerical gaps that pepper the catalogue. Not so. Issued at budget price, the trio simply followed on from the previous budget LP *Chi Chi Run*, which was MS8, and in fact the matrices state 'MS', not 'PB'. Despite this burst of rationality, there can be no group of labels that has issued so much wonderful Jamaican and black British music in so disorganised a fashion as Melodisc.

Torpedo

A label that has a much higher profile now than when it emerged in 1970 is Torpedo. It had two series, the first being an all-UK production outlet and the 1975 second incarnation issuing Ja-produced work, the majority of which was new roots material such as Johnny Osbourne's 'Put Away Your Gun' and a remixed version of 'Move Up Blackman' from future Lovers star Tyrone Taylor, plus the odd oddity like Ken Boothe's rocksteady oldie 'Lady With The Starlight', presumably issued in the wake of Ken's chart success with 'Everything I Own'.

Torpedo was founded by The Equals' Eddy Grant, who in an interview with Roger St Pierre in a 1976 issue of *Black Echoes* says that the parent company President 'didn't back me up with the right promotion… [although] I learned a lot from the way Eddie Kassner runs the company'. South London resident Lambert Briscoe was also involved, when he wasn't running his Hot Rod sound system.

The label had only one reggae hit (and saw no mainstream action at all), this being 'Please Don't Make Me Cry' from Birmingham-based singer Winston Groovy. The first cut of 'Please Don't Make Me Cry' was recorded in 1970 under Briscoe's direction (a second cut was produced by Sidney Crooks for Trojan a little later on). 'I did that for Rod at Chalk Farm Studio, and he then leased it to Eddy Grant and his Torpedo label. That was really the only seller Torpedo ever had – it was huge. I also had 'Gal You Think You Nice', which I did as Winston James,' said the affable Winston in a recent interview.

As we shall see in Chapter 5, 'Please Don't Make Me Cry' was particularly big in the Birmingham area. Talking about their 1983 cover of the song in a TV programme about their recording career, UB40 band members reminisce about seeing 'skinheads dancing to it in crowded dancehalls' and how the band had been so influenced by the tune. The song is probably the one with which Winston's name is most associated. Although 'Please Don't Make Me Cry' sold well to the reggae market, and the label was affiliated with President Records (The Equals' label), it remained firmly an underground hit.

Singer Denzil Dennis was an artist who worked for the small label and recalls that 'Torpedo was Eddy Grant's thing. I had a friend, Winston Groovy, and he was working with Laurel Aitken, and Eddy Grant wanted to start his own company, so I went there and did six songs for them. Me and Milton [Hamilton] recorded for them as The Imitations, because in those days when you're versatile you do these things. When I was DD Dennis I sang baritone and when I was Denzil Dennis, I sang tenor.'

The all-encompassing house band, The Hot Rod All Stars, named after Briscoe's Hot Rod sound system, specialised in brash instrumental sides with titles like 'Skinheads Don't Fear', confirming the new white market at which they were aimed. This band was originally the ubiquitous Cimarons under one of their many *noms des disques*, although some of the sides have a very much rounder sound, suggesting that The Rudies, and possibly The Pacesetters, had an outing or two with Mr Briscoe.

Torpedo may have had a target audience in mind, but those very punters it hoped to attract obviously had other labels to spend their hard-earned cash on, as few 'old timers' can even recall the label, let alone actually buying some of the sides. Further evidence of the lack of sales of the first-series Torpedo label *en masse* was the enormous quantity of unplayed boxes full of titles that surfaced in the 1980s. Every reggae stall and shop had copious quantities at 50p a throw, and absolutely no one wanted them – where the majority went can only be a matter for conjecture. It is quite likely that council waste tips all over London hold piles of the discs, which stall holders dumped as a dead-loss purchase.

Sioux

This small early 1970s label, with its stylish design, has always been of interest to collectors. Jack Price, the label owner, had a distinguished career in mainstream popular music, first in New Zealand and then in the UK, before entering the Jamaican field at Melodisc. 'At the beginning of 1968,' he remembers, 'I replaced Siggy Jackson as the label manager and PA for Emil Shallit, who was of course the managing director of Melodisc Records. Apart from his ability to speak a number of languages, Emil possessed the most fantastic photographic memory – he had instant recall and was able to remember almost every record matrix number he ever issued, and could put the song and title to these numbers. Whenever we had a quiet moment, I would test him and he was nearly always correct.

'Of course, before he began releasing records on Blue Beat, he'd released all sorts of music – folk, classical, country, blues – you name it, Emil had issued it. But Melodisc was essentially a very small operation – just Emil and myself. I used to drive him all over the place – we often went back and forth, to and from Paris, for business trips. He told me about working for the American government during the Second World War, and for the British during the German occupation [of Europe]. There was quite a bit he wouldn't talk about, but I rated him as one very clever, shrewd guy and I liked him a great deal. I think he was very underrated in the music business, which I thought was a bit shabby.'

After a year or so, Jack felt the need to break out on his own. 'I became a freelance producer and had meetings with most of the major companies, all of whom seemed to be very slow in picking up on this fantastic new form of music – well, new to them, that is. It was Paddy Fleming of Mercury Records, which was a part of the giant Philips Record Company, who gave me the break I had been looking for. So the first of the albums I produced was *Rocksteady Hits 1969*, featuring Pat Rhoden and DD Dennis as principal artists, which was issued on the Fontana label and went into the top ten of the mid-price range album charts almost straight away. That was produced for under £600, including session fees and studio time.'

Pat Rhoden recalls the memorable *Rocksteady Hits of 1969* album: 'I knew Lloyd Campbell who was working at Nat Cole's wig and record store, and one day out of the blue he introduces me and Denzil [Dennis] to Jack Price, who's looking to record this album. He thought we were OK so we started rehearsing in his place in Peckham. Jack picked the songs although he actually didn't have a lot of experience in producing reggae. We were just paid for the sessions, and as there was no hit single from the album we asked to be released from our contracts, which we were.'

'Actually,' continues Jack, 'I later took up a position as sort of manager-cum-consultant with Philips Records, at the start of their Mirto label. During this time, I did nearly 20 albums and a number of singles for companies like Fontana, Mercury, Philips, Pye, Decca, President, Rediffusion and Saga, and these records made reggae available nationwide for the first time – until then, it was only available at specialist shops.'

At that time, Jack also was involved in the single 'Pharaoh's Walk' by Exodus. 'I co-wrote "Pharaoh's Walk" with Terry Dwyer, who was also Eddy Grant's roadie. I can remember Eddy and his group [The Equals], along with Terry, visiting me at Melodisc one Saturday morning, prior to a tour of Germany, to borrow a microphone from me. Terry and I were both members of Exodus – the third member was Colin Dowl, a great West Indian flute player, and this multi-track project was recorded at my mother's house, and ended up being used as the theme to Emperor Rosko's *Radio 1 Club* show. Around this time, the record was actually issued on three different labels: Sioux, Saga and Trojan.

'By this time, 1971, I'd got to know Graeme Goodall, who had run Doctor Bird Records, having worked with him at his studio in Fulham Road – I'd played harmonica, keyboards and mellotron for Graeme on some of his records, and on some of my own productions that he's engineered. Anyway, Graeme had been very successful and he encouraged me to start my own label, so we ended up going to America and Jamaica together. He introduced me to a lot of the well-known producers out there, such as Byron Lee and Harry J. I remember on one occasion, when we were at Dynamic Studio, I played harmonica on a reggae version of a Chi-Lites song, by Barry Biggs, who of course later had some big hits over here ["Side Show", "Three Ring Circus", etc].

'When I used to visit Jamaica, I was always astounded at just how fast they changed tape into vinyl – it was just days, whereas in the UK it used to take weeks for the actual record to be released. Even with all the chart entries during the late '60s and early '70s, the major British record companies still didn't recognise what was happening. The word "muppets" springs to mind! I set up Sioux in 1971, once I had enough material to release. My daughter, who was pretty young at the time, actually designed the label and she's now a professional artist. We issued 25 singles on the label and we did four LPs in total. We put out a real mix of Jamaican and UK productions – many of the records I issued were by me using pseudonyms – I recorded as Jackie Rowland, Jumbo Sterling, Montego Melon, King Reggie and, of course, Exodus – it was all good fun.'

As was so often the case with such brave ventures, the label's demise was due to money, or lack of it. 'We lacked the finances to sustain the company, which was a great pity as Sioux could've been a good outlet for product, while the established labels were arguing over who had the rights to issue this or that. Still it was a great experience and a lesson for us.'

Creole Records

This label, which would take a market share of the reggae pie in the early 1970s and taste mainstream action with Bruce Ruffin and perhaps more notably Judge Dread, began in the mid-1960s as an entertainment agency.

Co-owner Bruce White confirms this, saying, 'Tony Cousins and I began as Commercial Entertainments (a management and agency company), who were responsible for introducing reggae acts into the UK in the mid-1960s. We handled such artists as Desmond Dekker And The Aces, Lee Perry And The Upsetters, Harry J All Stars, The Pioneers, Max Romeo, Millie Small, Pat Kelly, Symarip, The Maytals, The Melodians, The Ethiopians, The Clarendonians, Byron Lee And The Dragonaires on the reggae side, and Status Quo, Dave Dee, Dozy, Beaky, Mick And Tich, The Average White Band etc on the pop side. Initially it was hard to get bookings with unknown (to the majority of the UK) artists, although weekend bookings were OK. The Mecca and Baileys circuits up north were good for us. The artists were excited to be here and were normally very helpful, and we used self-contained London bands like The Rudies and The Cimarons for support and backing.

'It wasn't too long before Commercial Entertainments became the second largest entertainment organisation in Europe. We were instrumental in bringing Desmond Dekker to England and the subsequent enormous success of his Number One record released in 1969. It was this record, "Israelites", that really acquainted the ordinary British record buyer with the reggae sound. This led us to acquire a defunct music publishing company and a record company, Creole Music Ltd and Creole Records Ltd, to handle product from our Commercial Entertainments artists.

'A partnership was formed with Island Records and Trojan Records in 1971, and the first release was Bruce Ruffin's hit single "Rain", which Tony and I produced [in the UK] as Bruce Anthony [ie 'Bruce and Tony']. It went to Number 19 in the national charts.'

Bruce Ruffin recalls how he came to record 'Rain', which had the basic rhythm track and vocal laid in Kingston, with Bruce and Tony adding the overdubs in London. 'Herman [Chin-Loy] suggested I record "Rain". I thought "Why not?" I'd found the song on the b-side of a José Feliciano record and thought it was a great song, so began performing it live with the Inner Circle band. We went into the studio and recorded it. The man who actually produced the song [in Jamaica] was Geoffrey Chung, who became a great friend. Herman put up the money, but he didn't produce it as such.

'Herman sent the tape of "Rain" to Trojan and they had Tony King put all the strings and things on it. After that, the record went on to become a big hit all over Europe. I remember when I went to Spain and they asked me why I'd copied José Feliciano, who was of course a king in Spanish-speaking countries. So I told them I wasn't copying him: I loved the song. When "Rain" was a hit in Europe, I came over to England and did some things for Trojan, things like "Songs Of Peace", which came out on the first Trojan maxi-single.'

In the meantime Bruce and Tony's management company had added to its artists roster Dave & Ansel Collins, Bob And Marcia, The Pioneers and Greyhound, and had been instrumental in the promotion of their hit records – including Dave & Ansel's 'Double Barrel', a million seller and a hit on both sides of the Atlantic – and was directly responsible for five silver and three gold records in the UK, as well as other successful releases worldwide.

'In October 1971,' continues Bruce White, 'we broke off our partnership with Island/Trojan to concentrate on further record production on our own Creole label, and Bruce Ruffin was the first artist we signed exclusively to publishing and recording.'

'I signed with Bruce White and Tony Cousins,' says Ruffin. 'They were good friends with Graham Walker, who ran Trojan with Lee Gopthal, and when they set up Creole Records, I recorded for them. I didn't really have a follow-up, so I took a pile of songs I'd written when I was 13, 14, 15 and sang "Mad About You" to Bruce White, and he said, "That's a great song", so we decided to record it. I remember, it was during the three-day week; we went to Chalk Farm Studios and the great Vic Keary, who was the engineer, said we had two hours to record the track. So I did the track then boof! The lights went out and we had to go home [due to the state-enforced power cuts]!'

'I had to go back the next day and do the vocals. Then Tony Cousins took this cup and started doing this stupid voice and they decided to put that on. After that, they put vari-speed on it. EMI, who were doing the distribution for the record, had just moved at this time and could only press 18,000 copies, although it still went straight to Number Nine in the charts. But they couldn't press enough records, so it never went to Number One.

'After "Mad About You", I did "Coming On Strong", which again they changed. It was written as a slow song, but again they sped it up.'

In 1972, at MIDEM, the record industry's annual trade gathering in Nice, Bruce and Tony met Roy Featherstone, MD of EMI Records Ltd, London, and secured a deal for EMI to distribute Creole and the newly formed label Rhino Records. It was a coup for an independent to secure major distribution through a giant like EMI.

'We returned to the studios to produce Bruce Ruffin,' recalls Bruce White. 'The net result became the first Rhino release in May 1972. "Mad About

You" was an instant top ten hit in the UK, earning a silver disc and also becoming a best-seller worldwide. As a result of Rhino's early success, other artists from our stable signed directly to Creole/Rhino, including Desmond Dekker, Dave & Ansel Collins and newcomer Winston Francis.'

One very short-lived label that Creole started was Spur in 1972, which had just three very highly regarded releases to its name, all produced by premier Jamaican boardman Keith Hudson.

'Keith Hudson was visiting the UK,' explains Bruce White, 'and staying in west London, he contacted us, among others, to see if we were interested in releasing his singles. He brought three and a deal was agreed for his own label [Spur] and all three singles were released at the same time. I think they were actually recorded in 1971 or 1972 using the Soul Syndicate Band. They were aimed at the roots underground market and sold a few copies, but we never heard from him again!'

Thus the three highly desirable Hudson-produced singles – SP1 ('Darkest Night On A Wet Looking Road' with vocal by Keith Hudson), SP2 ('Adisababa' from Delroy Wilson) and SP3 ('All We Need Is Love' by veteran vocalist Alton Ellis) – arrived and promptly disappeared again.

In 1974 Creole formed a further, and much longer-lasting label, Cactus, largely to handle the more ethnic type of reggae. Artists included Honey Boy, Rupie Edwards, Judge Dread and others. Unlike Rhino, Cactus was still distributed by EMI, but Bruce and Tony had to do the promotion for the label themselves.

'Once a week there'd be a meeting,' says Bruce, 'with me, Tony, Richard Johnson, who was head of A&R, our press officer and our radio plugger. Over the course of a week records would be dropped off to us by various producers and we'd take a listen and decide which we'd like to release.

'"Ire Feelings" was played at the meeting and we all thought it was good, so we took it and started to promote it. The big breakthrough was when Emperor Rosko played it – then the demand took off. Two weeks later we sent an air ticket to Rupie Edwards for him to come over. It [the UK Cactus pressing] was actually mastered off a Jamaican 45.

'In November 1974, then, Cactus scored its first hit, "Ire Feelings" by Rupie Edwards, which reached Number Nine in the UK national charts and sold in excess of 250,000. Rupie's follow-up, released in February 1975, was "Leggo Skanga", which made the UK top 30.

'In July 1975 Judge Dread made his debut hit single for Cactus, "Je T'aime", which reached Number Nine and sold over 400,000 copies. We had to promote Judge Dread differently to the other reggae acts. For one thing he wouldn't get any airplay, but he had a big following in the clubs. So we did special promotions in the record shops and clubs.'

A string of releases followed between 1975 and 1978, which all made the UK national charts: 'Big 10', 'Christmas In Dreadland', 'Come Outside', 'The Winkle Man', 'Y Viva Suspenders', '5th Anniversary EP', 'Up With The Cock' and 'Big Punk'.

Bruce White continues, 'In 1975 we decided to release Desmond Dekker on the Cactus label, as Creole had now acquired the rights to his previously recorded material. It was at this stage that we re-released "Israelites", which became a top ten hit – for the second time – and sold a further 100,000 copies for Cactus. This we followed up with a Bruce And Tony production, "Sing A Little Song", which went top 30 in August 1975. This song was composed by Desmond and published by Creole Music Ltd.

In 1976 Bruce successfully negotiated a deal with Byron Lee to represent his Dynamic Sounds and Sheila Music catalogues from Jamaica. From 1976 to date, through Dynamic, Creole has released product by major Jamaican reggae artists including Byron Lee And The Dragonaires, Boris Gardiner, The Blues Busters, The Maytals, Hopeton Lewis, Barry Biggs and many more. Barry Biggs was the first artist from Dynamic to have a hit, with the rootsy 'Work All Day', which entered the top 30. This was followed by 'Side Show', which went to Number Two in December 1976 and sold in excess of 500,000 copies in the UK alone. Barry continued to have hits until 1981 with You're My Life', 'Three Ring Circus', 'What's Your Sign Girl' and 'Wide Awake In A Dream'. A surprise hit for Creole's Dynamic label was 'Only A Fool Breaks His Own Heart' by Mighty Sparrow, which hit the top ten in Holland.

In 1975 Creole was the first company to release a single by Boney M, entitled 'Baby Do You Wanna Bump'. Unfortunately this just failed to make the top 50 by two places, hitting Number 52.

Into the 1980s, Creole's reggae labels continued to prosper with the addition of new outlets Revue and Winner; the latter released Sophia George's 'Girlie Girlie', which made the top ten in the UK in December 1985, and charted in many other territories throughout Europe. 'It was different and the whole office loved it,' says Bruce.

Boris Gardiner's debut single for the Revue subsidiary, 'I Want To Wake Up With You', topped the UK national charts for three weeks in the summer of 1986, with sales in excess of 800,000 and also obtained high chart positions throughout Europe. 'We thought it sounded commercial and worth a crack,' says Bruce, 'and it was never pressed after recording – it just stayed on the master tape.'

Good old Boris, who had tasted chart success as early as 1970 with 'Elizabethan Reggae', won for Creole the Music Week Award for the best-selling single that year. His follow-up 'You're Everything To Me' reached Number Nine in the autumn, and his third release, 'The Meaning Of Christmas', achieved mild success in the festive season of 1986.

In late 2003, Creole became part of the Sanctuary Group, which also own Trojan, bringing to an end a long and successful, if often low-profile, existence as an independent reggae company.

Trojan was easily the leader in the chart stakes, due not only to its grasp of the need to sweeten the sound with string overdubs (which would ultimately cause its downfall), but also its chain of Musicland, and latterly Musik City, shops, which pushed its product right out on to the high street. This was aided by the distribution network of B&C, a sister company, which enabled its records to be stocked rapidly by high-street majors like HMV. Trojan's dominance in the marketplace is discussed in detail in *Young, Gifted And Black*. That said, within the reggae (as opposed to mainstream pop) market, Trojan did have competition, as Rob Bell notes:

'That Trojan aspired to world domination (outside of Ja) is pretty well known. Nevertheless, while the company had those aspirations, it understood and accepted the fact that there would always be competitors. It had no choice! Bamboo, Ackee, Fab, Pama, and earlier R&B Discs, with Ska Beat, were facts of life. I don't really recall any major flare-ups with Junior Lincoln [Bamboo and Ackee]. Pama was, during my Trojan years [1968–72], the main competitor by far.

'We probably clashed more because of the double-dealings of [some of] the producers of the world than because of any built-in rivalry. Producer X was in the habit of flying over to London on a Monday, visiting Trojan on Tuesday morning, selling us some masters, and then visiting Pama in the afternoon, and selling them duplicate tapes of the same tunes. Come Wednesday, he'd be on his way back to Ja. The next week, Trojan and Pama would release the same record. Thirty-odd years later it is very funny, but we were certainly a bit steamed at the time. Producer X wasn't the only one to do this – it was a popular practice for many for quite a while.

'Melodisc were pretty much a spent force by this time. They still had Buster, but I don't really remember them as a competitor in the way Pama was. Emil Shallit would come by Music House occasionally, to meet with DB [David Betteridge] or Lee Gopthal. A scruffy guy, in a dirty overcoat – unkempt hair. Always arrived in a taxi, and though I rarely saw him flash it, he always had a big roll of money in his pocket. I dealt with him in 1979–80 when Island licensed a few cuts for *The Blue Beat Years: The Birth Of A Music* album that I put together, attempting to trace the influence of R&B on Jamaican music. For some reason or other, he changed his mind after Island pressed the thing, and it got withdrawn. (The LP briefly surfaced in Germany only, and is now a considerable rarity.)

'I returned to Island in the winter of 1979–80 for a few months. I had left Somerset where I had been farming and planned on visiting the USA for an extended summer vacation in 1980. I went up to London and made some money organising Island's archives. During that time I did the *Birth* album, a Melodians album, and *Catch This Beat*, a rocksteady anthology. Steve Barrow gave me invaluable assistance on the first and the latter, as did Roger Dalke.'

Rob tried to act as Trojan's archivist, with only fleeting success. 'I kept three mint copies of all the Trojan stuff, and delivered them to the stores manager for safe keeping when I left the company in 1972, and they were promptly stolen! My brief in 1979 was to track down all the Island WI catalogue.

'My biggest break was Harry Tipple, who had been president of the GRRA [Gramophone Record Retailers Association]. His store had been selling records since his father opened it in the '20s or '30s. It was a tobacconists/newsagents-cum-record store. Funny sort of place. He had a few boxes of 45s on the counter, a rack or two of LPs, and that was about it. Hardly the kind of store you'd figure the president of the GRRA would have.

'It turned out it had been store policy since the '30s to buy six of *every* new release on *every* label! He had a warehouse out back full of...well, everything. He was, when I met him, putting together a list of all his London-American releases. I'm sure he made a fortune auctioning them off. I scored early Islands by the dozen. I think we were paying 50 pence each. All brand new, of course.'

Reggae was getting noticed in the 1970s, and even *The Sunday Times Magazine* ran a front page and colour feature entitled 'Reggae Reggae Reggae' on 4 February 1973. It was written by Colin McGlashan, and trombonist Rico Rodriguez featured prominently both in the text and in photos. 'Richard Williams [*Sunday Times* reporter] came to see me and he came to a Rasta party with us,' recalls Rico. 'He stayed all night – I think he was one of the first [to report on the scene].'

Rico's impressive pedigree meant that he had worked with all the UK-based producers and labels. 'I did plenty of work for Dandy [Livingstone], and Webster and Desmond and Joe [Shrowder, Bryan and Sinclair respectively – Trojan]. I also did work for Pama – they all used to call me – I never pestered for work, it came to me.

'I was a freelance – and Joe Mansano I did work for as well, and he only paid session fees. Me and Dice the Boss would play over backing tapes. He's also called Pama Dice and maybe BaBa Dice.' So while some of Mansano's finest recordings, such as the classic 'Skinhead Revolt', feature the DJ jiving of Dice and Rico's jazz-fuelled trombone, in some cases the actual session was dubbed over existing rhythm tracks.

There was no doubt that by the end of the 1960s just two labels controlled the majority of the reggae market. Trojan was hitting the mainstream charts with regularity, but the rawer-sounding sides were coming from another company literally just along the road. It didn't go in for the overdub and just issued what came to it from Jamaica or was cooked up on the London side. It would never hit the big time like Trojan, but for the fans then and the collectors now some of its records have become the most desirable bits of vinyl in the universe.

It was Pama Records.

3 Straighten Up: The History Of Pama Records

BEGINNINGS

The three Palmer brothers – Harry, Jeff and Carl – arrived in the UK from Jamaica at various times during the 1950s and early 1960s. Like many other arrivals from the West Indies, they looked to the motherland for greater opportunity, a more forward-looking society and a more financially rewarding future. For them, Jamaica offered only a life of drudgery involving farming a few crops and scraping a meagre existence.

Jeff, the eldest brother and first arrival, went into the engineering profession and settled in northwest London. Harry, second to make the journey, went into an unskilled factory position but, alongside this, studied for a qualification in business studies. Carl, the youngest, arrived in the early '60s. Always looking for ways to advance their entrepreneurial flair, the brothers went into the record business with a jack-of-all-trades record shop at the Willesden Junction end of the seedy Harrow Road. This worked out well for a few years until the shop was gutted by fire, following which the brothers opened an estate agency nearby. In those days, there was money to be made from the abundance of short-life accommodation in run-down areas like north Kensington and Paddington. The property business thrived, and a year or so later they moved to more prestigious premises a few miles further north at 16 Peterborough Road in leafier Harrow-on-the-Hill.

It was during this period that Jeff went into nightclub management, running Club 31 (which was also known as Club West Indies) at 31 Harrow Road (long since demolished) in the Stonebridge Park area. A year or so later he bought the lease of the Apollo Club, a couple of miles away at 375 Willesden High Road. They may also have had an interest in a club at High Wycombe, possibly the Newlands, at which a young Judy Boucher made her debut (her band was known as Judy Jack And The Beanstalks).

Monty Neysmith of The Pyramids clearly remembers Jeff Palmer and his clubs: 'I remember in the early days it was a real struggle. We asked Mr Palmer to play at his club and he said, "No, you guys play too much ska!" We pleaded and he finally gave in. We packed that place, every time we played there, which was pretty often. We had a real hard time when we first started. Not meaning to toot our horn but, looking back, I feel we deserve a lot of credit. We took a lot of abuse – people laughed at us. It was like playing ska was something bad.'

Of the three Palmer brothers Harry was probably most closely involved with the music business, particularly in the very early days, although Jeff and Carl were often credited on some early Pama labels as producers.

The brothers started the Pama label in 1967, initially as a sideline to their other business interests. The label's administrative offices were based at the estate agency in Harrow but later (probably mid- to late 1968) moved to premises at 78 Craven Park Road, Harlesden. At that time Harlesden was an area with a developing West Indian population, due largely to the massive Stonebridge Park Estate development and the general migration outwards following demolition of many of the north Kensington slum areas.

In addition to being the label's base, Number 78 was also a retail outlet for the brothers, and a number of people involved in reggae music worked there over the years, most notably Adrian Sherwood of On-U-Sound and roots reggae vocalist Delroy Washington. It is interesting to note that the official Post Office street directories for the address of 78 Craven Park Road list it as 'David Gregg – grocer' from 1967 to 1973. In the 1974 listing, Number 78 is missing altogether, which could be taken to mean that the premises were either empty or derelict. It reappears in 1975 as 'Sound Ville Records', and was still listed as such in 1978. In fact, none of the chain of Pama Record Shops is listed in the street guide at all for the whole period they were in operation. Official sources and the authors have no explanation for this bizarre error on the part of the Post Office.

Around the time of Pama's launch, there were to be some quite significant changes to some of the companies issuing Jamaican music in the UK. In particular, William Rickard's Rio label was to fold; Melodisc's Blue Beat imprint would be superseded by the more hip-sounding and ultimately less successful Fab and R&B Discs would scrap its Ska Beat label in favour of the less specific Giant and Jolly imprints. Ska had changed into rocksteady and some of the labels clearly wished to shed an outdated image. In the cases of Blue Beat and Ska Beat, this had somewhat adverse consequences and neither Melodisc nor R&B ever recaptured quite the success they had achieved earlier. There was certainly room for at least one newcomer to the market, and Pama would be one among several hopeful new labels launched during that era, including Collins Down Beat (put out by Clancy Collins), Double D (Len Dyke and Dudley Dryden) and Columbia Blue Beat (Siggy Jackson in association with EMI Records).

Harry Palmer had in fact already leased two fledgling Pama productions – 'Tell Me What It's All About' by Joyce Bond in 1966 and 'Go Go Special' by Kensal Rise band Little John And The Shadrocks around April 1967 – to Chris Blackwell's Island label for release. Around that time, Island stood predominant in the West Indian market, with its main Island label (the red and white series and the recently launched pop/soul pink one) and its Coxson, Studio One and Treasure Isle subsidiaries. It also had some involvement in the administration of Graeme Goodall's Doctor Bird and Pyramid labels, and had a fair degree of success in the national charts with pop/rock act Traffic and soul music (Robert Parker's 'Barefootin' and Roy C's 'Shotgun Wedding'). Chris Blackwell was becoming increasingly influential and, with this success in the mainstream market, was progressively moving his label away from West Indian music. The formation of Trojan/B&C was still a year or so off.

Harry Palmer had also spotted a niche market for soul music. Apart from one or two companies (including Island's Sue imprint), soul tended to be issued by labels associated with one or other of the major British mainstream concerns – Stax, Stateside and Tamla Motown, for example. The 'majors' were in fact responsible for putting out sounds licensed from some of the smaller US companies – and there were plenty of them. A lot of worthy material was clearly passing the large British concerns by, however, particularly since they were largely operating at the more commercial end of the soul market. To illustrate the demand for such small specialist soul outlets, it is worth noting that B&C's Action and Dave Godin's Soul City labels were set up around the same time as Pama started issuing soul records from the USA.

THE SOUL CONNECTION

A fair amount of Pama's soul output came from the Bell label in the USA and its many subsidiaries like Amy and Mala. One story has it that Bell was then (1967–68) being so successful with its more poppy product by the likes of Reparata And The Delrons, The Box Tops and Bruce Channel that it couldn't devote sufficient time to promoting the lesser-known soul material. That's why then label manager Trevor Churchill, now a director of leading indie label Ace Records, offered to license it free to whatever company wanted it. This was on the understanding that royalties would be paid on units sold. On the face of it, it looks as though Pama got hold of several batches of this US soul material and then issued it in a steady flow over an

18-month to two-year period. It dried up around the middle of 1970, presumably after Pama had put all of it out. By that stage, the soul boom of 1967–69 was largely over and the likes of Action and Soul City had been supplanted by newer 'into the '70s' companies such as Hot Wax, Invictus and Mojo.

At the UK end, it was clear that the nightclubs they ran gave the Palmer brothers a headstart so far as the A&R and management side of the business was concerned, and a number of London-based soul artists were recruited and signed to the label, almost certainly through initial exposure at Club 31 and the Apollo. These included Joyce Bond (dubbed 'the female Prince Buster'), Nola Campbell, The Mohawks (with a young Sidney Rogers in the line-up) and The Crowns, who were clearly strongly influenced by The Impressions. Another artist who debuted at the 31 was Junior English, who was to have a career in reggae music lasting into the 1980s. Later, the brothers would run an agency through which Pama artists could be booked.

For reasons unknown, Joyce Bond did not stay long with Pama and left the label at the close of 1968 after just one single – 'They Wash' – which was strongly based around Prince Buster's 'Wash All My Troubles Away'. The previous year, Harry Palmer had leased Bond's 'Do The Teasy' (an adaptation of Hopeton Lewis's 'Take It Easy') to Island for release on its new pink pop label, probably since it was better able to promote and distribute a potential chart winner than Pama. 'Teasy' actually did very well and in fact only narrowly missed the national chart. Island also saw fit to finance the issue of an entire Joyce Bond album (*Soul And Ska*) but seemed unsure of how to market her image (which seemed a tad aggressive) and her vocal style, which seemed to hark back to the faster sounds of ska rather than the current rocksteady. Beyond a cover of 'Ob-La-Di Ob-La-Da' for Island at the close of 1968, she pretty much disappeared from the scene, to return a couple of years later as lead singer of a band called The Colour Supplement, who had a small-label album issued entitled *Wind Of Change*.

In fact, of all the homegrown soul talent on Pama, only The Mohawks tasted any real success. Their first release, 'The Champ', more or less broke the company into the major league and was a massive underground success in the soul clubs. Demand was such that the Palmer brothers leased it to record companies in France (where it apparently went top ten), Germany and the USA. The disc itself was an instrumental version of Otis Redding and Carla Thomas's Stax hit 'Tramp', featuring prominent Hammond organ. While it was a decent enough effort, it was clearly heavily inspired by something else and could not therefore be considered particularly original.

The Mohawks' later records, such as 'Baby Hold On' and a cover of Lee Dorsey's 'Ride Your Pony' were similarly influenced and could not follow the success of the debut.

The Mohawks essentially suffered from an inability to come up with their own original material (the Geno Washington syndrome). An album named after the hit single was released later, with a sleevenote revealing 'Mo Hawk' – actually organist Alan Hawkshaw – as a reclusive, mean and moody character who spoke little, was educated to a degree and drove a fast car. The writer? One of the Palmer brothers no doubt. Alan Hawkshaw was in fact a veteran of various UK beat groups, beginning with Emile Ford And The Checkmates as far back as the late 1950s, and playing later, in the mid-1960s, with bands that had residences in Hamburg. He later played session organ on many UK pop and soul records.

From here on, things get a bit confusing. The Alan Hawkshaw Mohawks lasted only until about 1968–69 but the name continued for several years after that. Hawkshaw, in 2003, in a brief email to one of the authors of this book, said that he had little to do with The Mohawks beyond *The Champ* and a few other tracks on the album of the same name. So what is almost certain to have happened is that the Palmer brothers continued The Mohawks' 'brand' (it was already well known, so why drop it?) and simply used an ever-changing personnel for what were increasingly reggae-influenced sounds. Jamaican keyboardist Graham Hawk (or Hesketh Graham) was to be the mainstay of the band and, because of the similarities with the name, a lot of people have believed him to be Alan Hawkshaw. The change to the Mk II version of The Mohawks probably took place around the middle of 1970, about the time 'Skinhead Shuffle' and 'Let It Be' were issued, but they still made forays into soul territory with 'Cheer Me Up', 'Then You Can Tell Me Goodbye' and 'And I Love Her' (all on Pama Supreme). This version of the band would also back Pama sessions produced by the likes of Sidney Crooks and Derrick Morgan.

Former Mohawks' member Sidney Rogers, who had big reggae sellers in the mid-1970s with 'Miracle Worker' and 'Another Lonely Night' for Larry Lawrence's Ethnic label, told *Black Music* magazine in October 1974 that the band were always reluctant to record any of his own original compositions and just wanted to cover the tried and trusted. Sid's 'Looking Back', tucked away on the flip of the band's reggae cover of 'Let It Be' (Supreme SUP 204) is superb and well worth picking up. In fact, it is without doubt the best thing The Mohawks ever did. The band (or the band's name at any rate) were, however, important throughout Pama's history since they lasted almost as long as the label and played on many of the UK-recorded sides. Graham Hawk also worked with Pama and, later, Jetstar in various capacities, including sales and administration.

The other significant soul artist Pama had on its books was Beverley Simmons (aka 'Little Beverley'), who Harry Palmer had signed up during one of his early visits to Jamaica to license music. He arranged for her to come over to the UK to record an album of Otis Redding songs. The great man had died tragically in December 1967 and the idea was that a 'tribute' album would be better coming from a female singer than a male, who would have just been seen as a mere Otis copyist. Also, Pama would have been selling an already well-known brand rather than risking anything new by an unknown singer. The *Remember Otis* set was issued twice but, judging by the number of times it turns up, can't have been a particularly great seller. Another number, 'Please Don't Leave Me', was also licensed to Island by Harry Palmer and relegated to b-side status. It is not clear what happened to Simmons after this.

The company was keeping its irons in two fires: soul and rocksteady/reggae. While soul was to do good business for the label in the short-term (1968–69), the biggest area of sales was always going to be reggae music. Pama would therefore need to compete in a marketplace dominated by Island/B&C and, a little later, Trojan/B&C. Harry Palmer (often credited as Harry Dee, H Dee or, on one occasion, Harold Deeland) apparently produced the indigenous soul sounds, while Jeff Palmer produced just a few of the UK-recorded rocksteady sides for Pama's first subsidiary, Nu-Beat. It is now believed, however, that while Harry Palmer was actively involved in the production side early on, he did relatively little in this sphere after early 1969. This was something the Palmer brothers would engage other producers to do once the company had begun to make some money.

BOSS SOUNDS

Prior to the establishment of Pama as a company, Harry Palmer had visited Jamaica to investigate licensing material from up-and-coming Ja producers such as Clancy Eccles, Lynford Anderson and minor production players/record shop owners such as H Robinson (but see the information about him in the notes that precede the discography, on p288), Roy Bennett and Eric and Dorothy Barnett. Oddly, copies of Jamaican-pressed discs from those in the latter category (Carib-Disc-O for Robinson and Deltone for Barnett, for instance) are almost impossible to find, perhaps indicating that they weren't particularly successful in Ja. As already mentioned, Harry Palmer also happened upon Beverley Simmons.

The first release on Pama, around September 1967 – a production by small-time Ja artist Roy Bennett – was Carlton Alphonso's 'Where In This World'/'Peace Makers'. Despite a five-star rocksteady backing, it was a somewhat dreary song that ended up doing little business. The flip side in particular was heavily derived from Keith and Ken's 'Groove To The Beat', which had already been issued on Island/B&C's Coxson label. The 'Peace Makers' credit has nothing to do with the song and was perhaps an omen of what was to come in the company's later years.

Better things were round the corner, however. Pama's second release came out around a month later and was Clancy Eccles' 'What Will Your Mama Say', which enjoyed healthy sales and a few airplays on the fledgling BBC Radio 1. Big hits in the rocksteady style followed, with Lloyd Tyrell's suggestive 'Bang Bang Lulu' (a very big seller indeed over a couple of years), Eric 'Monty' Morris's 'Say What You're Saying', Alton Ellis's 'My Time Is The Right Time', Lyn Taitt's 'Soul Food' and The Termites' 'Push It Up'.

In terms of output, Eccles and Ellis had provided Pama with the bulk of its feedstock in the early stages, although Harry Palmer was later to rue the large advances he had given both men, particularly as this had set a precedent in a business where a company needed to sell a lot of vinyl to recoup an outlay of a couple of thousand pounds. And, of course, in Jamaica news about what a particular label owner or producer was paying went round very quickly, and the stakes were upped accordingly.

Oddly enough, though, despite the comparative success of these early Pama label rocksteady sides, hundreds of unplayed copies emanating from Exchange and Mart Fair at 319 Portobello Road, London, turned up in the mid-1980s, complete with the shop's rubber stamp. This being the case, few of them (ie those with issue dates of 1967 and 1968) are currently difficult to track down. The apparent reason for this surfeit of Pama vinyl is that when Island's HQ at 108 Cambridge Park Road was cleared out prior to demolition, hundreds of singles were offloaded for a few pence each at the aforementioned shop. Also included were singles on red and white Island (unsurprisingly perhaps), Studio One, Coxson and Treasure Isle (in fact, all of Island's subsidiaries from this time). From this, then, we may infer that Island actually distributed Pama product at its inception.

RHYTHM OF THE NEW BEAT

Following the success of the main Pama label during the first six months of its operation, the first subsidiary label – Nu-Beat – was launched in April 1968 to deal exclusively with both Ja and UK-produced rocksteady. Its first release was the highly commendable 'Train To South Vietnam' by recently formed local band The Rudies, who would also record for Island/B&C's Blue Cat label ('7.11') and Melodisc's Fab imprint ('Mighty Meaty' and 'Give Me The Rights') around this time. UK-based trombonist Rico Rodriguez, who debuted on Pama with a cover of Sam And Dave's 'Soul Man' (PM 706), went on to record some outstanding sides for the company. It also issued one LP of his work, entitled *Rico In Reggae Land*, which was devised as a tribute to The Skatalites trombone player and close friend of Rico's, Don Drummond, who had just passed away.

There was also a brief input from Dandy around this period. He approached Pama with a view to the company issuing what ultimately became his *Dandy Returns* album. Almost simultaneously, however, Lee Gopthal of the about-to-be-formed Trojan/B&C offered Dandy his own Down Town label and a producer's role in the new company. The Pama deal was, then, effectively off. One single on Nu-Beat featuring Dandy ('Engine 59') was issued, although it is not known whether this was part of the 'package' Dandy brought to Pama or the result of something entirely separate.

Further successes followed for Nu-Beat with Clancy Eccles' scorching 'This Festival '68' (NB 006), Derrick (Morgan) And Patsy (Todd)'s 'Hey Boy, Hey Girl' (NB 008) and Alton Ellis's classic cut of the Delfonics' 'La La Means I Love You' (NB 014). All three showed the development of the slower rocksteady into the faster reggae beat. In fact, Pama had been quick to catch on to the new reggae sound and most of these formative Nu-Beat releases really were exceptionally good, with only the odd UK side proving a flop (Junior Smith's ineffective 'Searching', for example).

By early 1969, Nu-Beat had also become something of a Laurel Aitken speciality outlet, and hits for him such as 'Woppi King', 'Pussy Price' and 'Haile Selassie' followed. Laurel in fact recorded and produced his records himself, licensed them to Pama (a standard arrangement he adopted with other UK issuing companies) and retains all the issuing rights to this day.

At the start of 1970, the label would change its name slightly to Newbeat and begin a policy of issuing only UK-produced discs (again, mostly from Laurel Aitken), although the Ja sounds did pick up again towards the end of the label's run. Denzil Dennis was a member of the London-based Classics, who recorded for the Newbeat label. 'That was me and Milton Hamilton and, later, Eugene Paul [as The Classics],' he recalls. 'We did a lot of tunes. At Pama, they asked me to do a lot of things. Me and Eugene Paul did "Cherry Oh Baby" with Lee Perry, and "Monkey Spanner" was me and Pete Campbell. I recorded all the Crab singles at Tony Pike's [studio] in Tooting. With The

Classics, it was Laurel Aitken who produced us…like with Crab, which Derrick Morgan produced – he produced everything I did that came out on Crab. "Nothing Has Changed" on Pama Supreme – that was my biggest hit with Pama – in 1971.'

THE LEE CONNECTION: THE UNITY LABEL

Ideally, however, Harry Palmer needed a solid business link with a Jamaican producer who could supply his label with a wealth of material that had already achieved consistent success in Jamaica. That man was to be Bunny Lee, who had recently produced solid gold tracks in the rocksteady style for Slim Smith and The Uniques ('My Conversation' and 'Gypsy Woman'), Val Bennett ('The Russians Are Coming'), Ken Parker ('A Change Is Gonna Come') and Pat Kelly ('Twelfth Of Never' and 'Somebody's Baby'). Since 1967, he had been licensing the bulk of this material to Island but, as that label handled a host of product from other producers, there was no single British label that specifically showcased his talents.

The Palmer brothers linked up with Lee during one of his first trips to London. The basis of the negotiations was that the company's previous arrangements with other Ja producers had not provided Pama with anything but short-term business, and that the brothers wished to have a more stable and direct link into the Jamaican music arena with a rising star of the Jamaican music world. They gave Lee an advance with which to produce some inaugural releases, which would see issue both in the UK and Ja. Unity was the chosen title for the new joint Palmer brothers/Bunny Lee imprint. The deal was essentially a mutually beneficial co-arrangement whereby the Palmers paid for the records to be recorded in Ja and both parties released them in their respective countries (although the actual releases would not necessarily correspond with each other, as we shall see).

The first official release on Unity came out towards the end of 1968 and was Stranger Cole And Tommy McCook's 'Last Flight To Reggae City', which did very well for a first disc. Cut at the same session as 'Last Flight' was Stranger Cole And Lester Sterling's 'Bangarang', which was the Christmas '68 reggae Number One and was *the* title all reggae fans were asking for. The tune was largely an instrumental with a jerking organ line (played either by Lloyd Charmers or Glen Adams, depending on whose account you accept) with Stranger intoning 'Mama no wan' Bangarang'. Furthermore, 'Bangarang' is often cited – along with Larry And Alvin's 'Nanny Goat', Clancy Eccles' 'Feel The Rhythm' and The Beltones 'No More Heartaches' – as the first bona fide reggae record.

Around the latter part of 1968 Bunny Lee began issuing discs on the Unity label in Ja, the label design of which would be faithfully reproduced for the UK counterpart. The only minor difference with the Ja imprint was that, in addition to the little circular 'Pama' logo on the lower-left of the label, there was an another identical logo with the word 'Lee' featured on the right-hand side. Similarly, Lee would later issue Ja discs on a Pama label almost identical in design to the UK one. There seems in fact to be relatively few discs on Ja Pama (Pat Kelly's 'Festival Time' and 'Troubling Mind' were two). Unity was instead to become synonymous with Lee's productions, both in this country and in Jamaica, until it was largely supplanted by Trojan's Jackpot subsidiary in the early 1970s.

Bunny Lee also established a short-lived Pama record shop in Ja above H Robinson's Carib-Disc-Co retail and record distribution operation. Robinson also had some tenuous links with certain records appearing on Pama labels in the formative years of the company's operation and clearly Lee would have been placed conveniently close to Mr R. The shop did not last anywhere near as long as the British Pama operation and later became subsumed into Lee's general retail set-up, presumably at about the time that his arrangement with the Palmer brothers concluded.

One of the first releases on Ja Unity was veteran US soul and R&B singer Donnie Elbert's 'Without You', which was backed with Derrick Morgan's 'River To The Bank'. 'Without You' also appeared in the UK on Decca's Deram imprint on an obscure and short-lived subsidiary of Melodisc entitled New Wave, and on an R&B Discs white-label issue. Apparently, Elbert arranged for the side to be recorded in the UK with Decca producer John Fiddy at the controls, and then proceeded to peddle it to record companies everywhere. The Palmer brothers may have been unwitting recipients, and they probably passed it on to Bunny Lee for Jamaican release after discovering its existence on these other UK labels. Another early Jamaican Unity release was Roland Alphonso's '1,000 Tons Of Megaton', which appeared later on Gas in the UK. Oddly, 'Bangarang' appeared not on Ja Unity but on Bunny Lee's 'Lees' label and another imprint called Carifta.

Derrick Morgan was also involved with Bunny Lee around this time – possibly as a co-producer – and may well have featured in the deal with Harry Palmer. He was also Lee's brother-in-law, so there were family as well as musical ties. Certainly, Derrick Morgan retains the rights to his own material on Unity and other Pama label releases in the UK, the earliest of which seem to be characterised by a more chugging sound than Lee's.

What complicates the picture further is that he and Bunny Lee used to swap their respective backing tracks around quite a bit – for example, Lee's 'Everybody Needs Love' (by Slim Smith) was used as the basis for Morgan's production of '1,000 Tons Of Megaton' by Roland Alphonso. So it isn't clear exactly what part each played in the productions. Derrick set up home in the UK around mid- to late 1969 when he was invited by Harry Palmer to become Pama's in-house producer, doing the honours for The Marvels, Pat Rhoden, Sketto Richards and Jennifer Jones, among others. He maintained that position for some two years and his role in the development of Pama should not be underestimated.

Turning back to the UK counterpart of Unity, the third release was Bunny Lee's production of Max Romeo's legendary 'Wet Dream'. Utilising Derrick Morgan's 'Hold You Jack' rhythm, the tune was picked up by West Indians and skinheads who, after a few months' momentum had built up, catapulted it into the UK charts during May 1969, where it eventually reached the highly respectable position of Number Ten. Not surprisingly, it attracted a complete BBC Radio ban. It remained on the chart for six months – no mean feat given that most top ten titles drop out of the national listings after a couple of months. It seems incredible even now that a record that received a total airplay ban could sell so many copies and do so well. It was simply bought by those who'd either heard it in the clubs or had picked up on it via the grapevine or plain word of mouth.

The fourth issue on UK Unity was Slim Smith's 'Everybody Needs Love', another seller during Christmas 1968 and the early months of 1969. This was cut at the same very productive session as 'Last Flight' and 'Bangarang', and was the last in a quartet of releases that completely stole the show from Pama's biggest competitor, Trojan/B&C. It was at this time that Pama was eclipsing Trojan, but more about that later. As for Slim Smith (who had broken away from The Uniques by that stage), his records were to do very well for Pama during the next couple of years. Other early successes for Unity included Lester Sterling's 'Reggae On Broadway' (the fifth release), Stranger Cole's 'When I Get My Freedom' (UN 514), the Reggae Boys' 'What You Gonna Do?' (UN 530) and Jackie Mittoo's 'Hook Up' (UN 533). There is a stray Laurel Aitken track on the flip side of UN 506 – 'Donkey Man' – which could be about Dandy ('you copy de donkey') and his relationship with Rita King of R&B Discs (it refers to 'the lady from Stamford Hill' taking him in). Clearly, there was some animosity between the two men, and lyrically this is a fascinating tune. Each to their own, of course, but the worst track on the label just has to be Doreen Shaeffer's 'How Much Is That Doggie In The Window?' The title pretty much speaks for itself.

The Palmer brothers' arrangement with Bunny Lee lasted throughout 1969 and into 1970, although it is impossible to say when it actually stopped. Basically, Lee had started his meteoric rise in the production world and had also began licensing material to Trojan, which had dedicated its Jackpot subsidiary to him. Jackpot was in fact the British counterpart of a label Bunny Lee had by then established in Ja. All things being equal, Lee's stock would have increased and the asking price for his wares surely followed suit. The quality of British Unity releases seemed to decline in 1970 and it may be that Pama was offered only what Trojan didn't want.

What has also become clear in recent years is that Bunny Lee often had little to do with a lot of the later UK Unity sides, with Niney (Winston Holness) often at the control board. Ultimately, however, Lee was probably responsible for around 70 per cent of Unity's total UK output during its three-year run until 1971, after which two one-off issues were put out in 1973. Aside from Trojan, in the early part of the '70s, Lee also began to develop a similar 'Ja to UK' link role with UK sound system operators and label owners Count Shelly and Lord Koos.

ALL SYSTEMS GO: THE LAUNCH OF CRAB AND GAS

All systems certainly were go in the closing months of 1968 when, in addition to Unity and Nu-Beat, Pama launched two further subsidiaries. The first, Crab, would handle product from various producers, notably H Robinson (in the early stages, but his involvement is tenuous), Derrick Harriott, Lee Perry, Albert George Murphy, Lloyd Daley, Rupie Edwards and Harry Mudie. Major successes included The Versatiles' 'Children Get Ready' (the first release), The Ethiopians' 'Reggae Hit The Town' (CR 4), Ernest Wilson's double-speed cover of William Bell And Judy Clay's 'Private Number' (CR 9) and The Viceroys' jerky 'Work It' (CR 12). Also featured were a great many Derrick Morgan outings recorded in Jamaica, most of which were to be included on the classic *Derrick Morgan In London* album (ECO 10).

The label ended up as something of a Derrick Morgan powerhouse with some 40 per cent of the label's total output performed and/or produced by him. His UK-recorded 'Moon Hop' (CR 32), backed by The Rudies, became the label's biggest seller. Most of Derrick's material from 'A Night At The Hop' (CR 44) onwards was, however, recorded in the UK with The Mohawks and seems to suffer as a result. It is likely that these tracks were cheaply and hurriedly recorded with the minimum of instrumentation and backing vocals. The Mohawks' backing is particularly limp, whereas The Rudies, who had completely moved over to Trojan by the early part of 1970, had really done the business on Derrick's 1969 Crab output. The same can be said of most of the material Derrick was producing for Crab roster artists like Denzil Dennis and Jennifer Jones, which is why Crab's 1970–71 output is generally not too collectable.

Gas, the second subsidiary, was to be something of a rag-bag and pretty much the only common threads seemed to be Eric Barnett productions and Pat Kelly numbers. The latter sides were mostly Bunny Lee productions, which for some curious reason never appeared on Unity. Despite the hotchpotch nature of the label, there was some superb music. The first single was Barnett's production of 'The Horse' by Theo Beckford's Group – a disc that did big business in the discos and had some crossover success in the mainstream market. Other productions came in the main from Winston Lowe, Ranny Williams, Derrick Morgan, Lloyd Daley and Winston Riley. There was even a lone one from Mr Studio One himself, Coxson Dodd (Marcia Griffiths' brilliant 'Tell Me Now').

Other strong sellers on Gas included Lester Sterling's 'Reggae In The Wind' (GAS 103), The Melodians' 'Ring Of Gold' (GAS 108), Roland Alphonso's aforementioned '1,000 Tons Of Megaton' (GAS 112), Martin Riley's wonderful 'Walking Proud' (GAS 114) and Pat Kelly's 'How Long Will It Take' (GAS 115) and 'If It Don't Work Out' (GAS 125), a reggae version of The Casinos' chart hit 'Then You Can Tell Me Goodbye'. There was also a smattering of releases credited to The Soul Rhythms and The Soul Cats, which seem to bear no aural relation to discs by the same artists on other Pama subsidiaries. This will be discussed in more depth later.

ANOTHER BIG FIVE

While Trojan/B&C seemed to operate a general policy of putting a particular producer's material on one subsidiary label – Bunny Lee for Jackpot (with some exceptions), Dandy for Down Town, Joe Gibbs for Amalgamated, and so on – the Palmer brothers' concern had a much more flexible approach to the allocation of records to particular labels, with the exception of Unity and, later, Success. In fact, if there was any real consistency at all it tended to go via artist rather than producer, with Pat Kelly's singles appearing on Gas, generally speaking, Derrick Morgan's on Crab and (later) The Upsetters' on Punch, for example. Aside from these few common threads, there seemed to be no rhyme or reason as to which discs were released on which subsidiaries.

By early 1969, then, Pama had five labels up and running: the main Pama label (which generally had blue [later purple] labels for soul releases and orange-and-red ones for rocksteady and reggae respectively), Nu-Beat, Unity,

Crab and Gas. By May 1969, Pama was of course firing on all cylinders when 'Wet Dream' charted. To cope with the sheer amount of music the company was putting out, it added another five subsidiaries to the roster between the middle and end of the year, namely Bullet, Camel, Escort, Punch and Success. It is uncertain, however, in which order they were launched.

Success, which was the UK counterpart of Rupie Edwards' label in Jamaica, was consistent in that it issued only his productions. Of the other four, Punch had a penchant for Lee Perry productions and Escort started off with quite a few Harry Johnson efforts. It's fair to say, however, that bar Success all of them were mixed-bag affairs.

With a name and label design possibly derived from Jim Bulleit's Nashville-based label of the late 1940s, Pama's Bullet label's first shot was an odd number (399) with Winston Shand's hypnotic 'Throw Me Corn', followed by a few Nicky Thomas numbers, which were scheduled but almost definitely not actually released. The featured producers during the early incarnation of the label were Harry Mudie (for The Ebony Sisters and Dennis Walks), AG Murphy (for The Kingstonians and The Fabions) and Ranny Williams (for Winston Shand and The Hippy Boys). Boss sounds indeed!

Camel started off with number CA 10 (what happened to the previous nine is a mystery) with The Techniques' 'Who You Gonna Run To', which, as mentioned earlier, was utilised over several compilations. Again, there was a short burst of Lee Perry wizardry with The Upsetters ('Taste Of Killing'/'My Mob' on CA 13), The Mellotones ('Facts Of Life' on CA 18) and The West Indians ('Strange Whispering' on CA 16, with lead vocals by Eric Donaldson). One particularly interesting sound is Winston Hinds' 'Cool Down' on the flip side of CA 20, which shows that producer Harry Johnson was using the same set of musicians as Coxson Dodd – the sound is a ringer for mid-1969 Studio One.

Escort is probably best known for having issued the first, unladen with strings, version of Bob And Marcia's 'Young, Gifted And Black'. Bob Andy recalls that it was something of a surprise to him (and Trojan) when Pama issued the record, and it is interesting that it was soon replaced on the same label and number by a rather lacklustre UK-produced version of the song by Denzil And Jennifer (with, strangely, a different flip side).

The sales were almost totally eclipsed by Trojan's cut, however, which had a strings arrangement by Johnny Arthey. What this showed was that Trojan was more willing to spend money on sweetening Ja tracks for possible success in the pop market. Escort had some good sides by Stranger Cole like 'Pretty Cottage' (ES 810) and the stop-start, proto-dub 'Remember' (ES 826).

Other highlights in the earlier stages included Sonny Binns' 'Boss A Moon' (ES 818, an organ cut to Derrick Morgan's 'Moon Hop'), Lloyd Charmers 'Soul Of England' (ES 820, with indecipherable cockney gibberish) and Martin Riley's 'It Grows' (ES 823, a very overlooked disc). For some reason the label's prefix changed to ERT around the time of release no. 827.

Of all the Pama label designs, Punch is probably the most striking, with its depiction of a fist smashing its way into a late 1969 top 20 chart, as if to say 'reggae music is breaking through'. The early part of the label concentrated, by and large, on classic skinhead reggae from Lee Perry. The 'official' follow-up to The Upsetters' 'Return Of Django' was 'Clint Eastwood' on Punch (PH 21), which almost charted but was hampered by apparent distribution problems. Lee Perry has gone on record as saying that he made a mistake in leasing the track to Pama since the company had much more difficulty in reaching the national market. The other Upsetters titles to sell really well were 'Return Of The Ugly' (PH 18) and 'Dry Acid' (PH 19), both of which were bought eagerly by West Indians and skinheads alike. One track – The Upsetters' 'Feel The Spirit' (PH 27B) – is one of the few Perry productions from this era not yet to have been reissued on CD. Again, there was some confusion when Dave Barker's 'Shocks Of Mighty' came out on both Punch and on Trojan's Upsetter subsidiary. Barker, although aware of Trojan's release of this record, was unaware of its Pama issue until interviewed for this book when the subject was brought up.

OPERATION ALBUMS

The company had also begun to issue compilation albums that collected the most popular singles from some of the subsidiary labels (notably Nu-Beat, Crab, Unity, Bullet and Camel); a few commendable individual artist efforts from Rudy Mills (*Reggae Hits*); Slim Smith (*Everybody Needs Love*); Derrick Harriott (*Sings Jamaica Reggae*); Laurel Aitken and Rico Rodriguez (*Scandal In A Brixton Market*); as well as two highly popular volumes of *Reggae Hits '69*.

Always one to look for sales potential in as many niche markets as possible, Harry Palmer also released albums featuring a rock 'n' roll revival outfit (The Milwaukee Coasters), a Welsh male voice choir, a holiday camp show band and a commemoration of the Prince of Wales' investiture (which the three Palmer brothers attended, and where they were the only black folk present). Acquiring the masters for such obscure material was also probably dirt cheap. The subsidiary labels package idea was an interesting concept which, for some reason, none of the other players in the market sought to emulate.

A virtually complete album listing can be found in the discography (see pp284–360), and it should be noted that the various prefixes (some of which make little sense) have not been defined. Logically the 'Special' series was initially part of the PMLP run (with an added 'SP' after it) and then became PSP (Pama Special). The company seemed to start off a series only for it to be supplanted by another. The Economy series (the first) was just that: an attempt to emulate Trojan's budget TTL series. Interestingly, though, at 15/6 (about 78p in today's money) Pama's albums were a shade more expensive than Trojan's 14/6 efforts.

While Pama reggae compilations are now highly sought after by collectors, a closer inspection reveals that many of the individual tracks – excellent though they are – were used on more than one LP (for instance, The Techniques' 'Who You Gonna Run To' was eventually included on four separate albums). Of course, there were often tracks that the potential buyer wouldn't have, or that weren't available on another album, and Pama's policy of duplicating tracks was merely a means of maximising profits on something it had already paid for. Curiously, a few albums contained the odd track that was never released as a single by the company. The strangest example is almost certainly Kent Walker's 'One Minute To Zero', a frenetic ska track from a long-gone obscure British label called Rymska which turned up on the third volume of *This is Reggae*. The aforementioned individual artist sets on the Economy series really are from the top drawer however and, justifiably, are still highly sought after.

The most desirable Pama album has to be *Boss Reggae*, which contains 12 Coxson Dodd-produced tracks, most (maybe all) of which were never released in the UK in any other form. Having said that, *Boss Reggae* does occasionally turn up in auction lists while the less desirable but equally collectable *African Melody* compilation has rarely been seen at all. One album of particular interest is Lester Sterling's *Bangarang* set, which features sleeve photographs of the interior of the 78 Craven Park Road shop with (possibly!) Harry Palmer's Jaguar outside.

One particular mystery surrounds the existence of a *Best of Escort* LP. It is certain that sleeves were printed but, possibly with the exception of a few test pressings, the set was almost certainly never made commercially available by the company.

RIVALS

'Boss Sounds from Pama – Party Music Specialists' was of course the phrase used on the singles sleeves designed by the company when at its Craven Park

Road address. Trojan/B&C had emerged as the biggest reggae company in the UK, while Pama had developed into a serious rival and almost certainly the number two reggae business. It had many of the same artists that appeared on Trojan labels, like The Kingstonians, The Ethiopians, Alton Ellis, Lloyd Charmers and The Upsetters, and had licensing arrangements with many of the same producers. Some Ja producers had in fact leased the same material to both companies, and there was an increasing number of cases of the same disc appearing on Pama and Trojan labels simultaneously. These were often 'covered up' through the changing of the title or the artist credit. All the same, this increased friction between the two companies and the producers involved. Often, the producers would explain away these incidents as mere oversights or clerical errors, or perhaps would just say 'So?', and the companies would get cheesed off and either give producer X a wide berth in future or offer him less money next time round. Certain artists would sell their own recordings to the companies direct. Sometimes this could be legitimate: they could have paid a particular producer to record the track, and ownership was with the artist. But, then again, if that producer had it on the end of one of his tapes…

At the end of the day, it was bad for the companies, bad for the distributors (who were often touting round copies of an identical title on two or three different labels) and bad for the punter. In the case of Trojan and Pama, it invariably meant that sales were split and that they had basically paid out for a particular tune to recoup only half of what they might have expected to make. In the case of the GG All Stars' 'Man From Carolina', for instance, the Pama (Escort) flip side was 'African Melody', which came out as a separate single on Trojan's Explosion subsidiary. So with the Pama release, buyers essentially got a two-in-one, double a-side deal. For a time, the two companies kept in regular touch with each other about what each was being offered, but the producers and artists were railing against this as they just wanted to make as much money as possible from their music.

Such duplicity merely strengthened the resolve of all the reggae companies in the UK to record and produce their music here in Britain, and therefore render the Jamaican producers superfluous. The simple truth, however, was that it was the Jamaican product that was doing most of the business with the fans.

The other big-league companies operating in 1969 were Junior Lincoln's Bamboo set-up, Graeme Goodall's struggling and soon-to-be-defunct Doctor Bird group and Melodisc's Fab label. None of these, however, could really compete with Pama, let alone Trojan. One of the likely reasons for Pama's proliferation of subsidiary labels is that it was competing directly against the supremacy of Trojan/B&C, which had in excess of 15 subsidiaries by that time. The logic was no doubt that the more subsidiaries a company had, the more its presence would be felt in the marketplace. In terms of radio play, it also helped the pluggers to be able to say to the DJs, 'Here's a new label for ya' – all, of course, to very little avail since reggae was hardly ever played on national radio anyway.

Pama also issued a few titles (Pat Kelly's 'How Long Will It Take' was definitely one) as 'Advance Release' labelled copies with deep blue writing and white backgrounds. These are likely to have been pressed in quantities of about 50 and are very hard to find now. Many Pama titles also came out on white or blank labels for sound system, DJ or promotional purposes, again probably pressed in batches of no more than 100. Unlike Trojan's GPW and TMX blank label series, however (which are listed in the book *Young, Gifted And Black*), it would be almost impossible to list all of those Pama sides made available in the blank format. It is known, though, that some of these were never given formal issue and others were made up of titles that did see release across perhaps two different singles.

Pama had a number of particularly strong sellers ('bubbling under' used to be the term) that year which stood a real chance of getting into the national charts. These were Pat Kelly's 'How Long Will It Take' (GAS 115), Owen Gray's 'Girl What You Doing To Me' (Camel CA 25), Tony Scott's 'What Am I To Do' (Escort ES 805), The Upsetters' 'Clint Eastwood' (Punch PH 21) and Derrick Morgan And The Rudies' 'Moon Hop' (Crab CR 32). Only 'Moon Hop' registered nationally (and only at a lowly Number 49 some three to four months after its initial release), with Owen Gray reaching a fairly respectable 29 in the *Melody Maker* chart. Trojan/B&C on the other hand, were breaking into the charts regularly by the end of that year with 'Return Of Django', 'Long Shot Kick The Bucket', 'Liquidator' and so on. Although 'Wet Dream' had beaten Trojan into the charts, Pama effectively failed to follow it up with any subsequent release bar 'Moon Hop'.

IT A-HAPP'NIN' INNA LONDON TOWN

Pama also decided to bring over a couple of its biggest-selling artists – namely Max Romeo and Stranger Cole – to do some recording with backing by either The Rudies or The Mohawks, with production duties generally undertaken by Derrick Morgan. With Max Romeo now in the public (or should that be pubic?) eye, he should have been well placed to score a follow-up hit to 'Wet Dream'. Unfortunately, his UK-recorded 'Mini Skirt Vision' floundered and the *A Dream* album definitely had its low points. During the Great Reggae

Package Tour, which lasted from the tail end of 1969 to the early part of 1970, a number of the artists involved laid down tracks in London. For example, The Upsetters recorded an album for Trojan (*The Good The Bad And The Upsetters*) and Stranger Cole also put down a few sides with backing by The Mohawks, which saw release on Escort. Sidney Crooks of The Pioneers would later settle here and become a producer for Pama, mainly using the Bullet imprint.

Stranger Cole, Owen Gray and Derrick Morgan also joined forces as The Clan and recorded 'Copy Cats' (Bullet BU 419). Aside from being an excellent record, the song (as evidenced by the title) seems to be about the 'reggae war' going on between Pama and Trojan in late 1969 and early 1970, when the latter issued Symarip's 'Skinhead Moon Stomp', and largely seemed to scupper Derrick's 'Moon Hop'. Unfortunately much of the precise nature of the lyrics to 'Copy Cats' is indistinct – there is mention of a 'Mister B', which is possibly the south London nightclub and/or its owner.

Joe Sinclair, manager of the Ridley Road Musicland store, which was one of a chain Trojan owned, recalls buying in its rivals' product, 'Musicland and Muzik City shops sold all reggae labels – Pama, Fab etc – but Pama would always cut the order back: if 25 copies were wanted then 10 would be delivered. I guess they didn't like us having too many of their records as they knew if it was a good tune we would shift them all.'

All the same, with the skinheads in full swing and all those great Jamaican artists over here for live dates, it really was an exciting time for reggae music.

Laurel Aitken, meanwhile, was continuing to bring out one skinhead classic after another on Nu-Beat and was developing his own roster of artists, including Tiger, Winston Groovy (whom he apparently discovered in the West Midlands) and King Horror (the latter two also had discs coming out on Trojan's Jackpot and Grape subsidiaries). Horror was actually Laurel on some sides but not others (it largely depended on which company he was leasing the material to and who was around in the studio at the time).

After 1969 and the change of label title to Newbeat, Laurel started singing more ballad-style material in a commercial vein. After his 'Mr Popcorn' (NB 048) and 'Reggae Popcorn' (NB 057) came out, subsequent releases like 'Baby I Need Your Loving' (NB 063) and 'Let True Love Begin' (NB 078) were not so eagerly bought by the skinheads. However, his 'Nobody But Me', tucked away on the flip side of the so-so 'Baby Please Don't Go' (NB 054) is a cracker and was the original cut to Tiger's 'Guilty' (Camel CA 70).

Laurel also brought Ian Smith's all-white Inner Mind reggae band to Pama's attention, and they not only had singles released on Newbeat and

Bullet but provided backing on a number of the company's UK productions. The Inner Mind played at the Apollo where they were billed as 'The Greatest White Reggae Band on Earth'. Dissatisfied with their treatment by Pama, however, Ian went his own way and established his own Hot Lead label in 1972 – the 'lead' in question referring to a newsman's scoop and not a reference to heavy metal. Ian is still alive, positively kicking and continues to work in the music business in his native Huddersfield.

It's also worth mentioning here that another all-white reggae band – Mood Reaction – had some material released on Pama, including an album of (mostly) cover versions of the big reggae chart hits.

'The band started in 1963,' says Wally (Alan Wallace) from Mood Reaction. 'Originally it was Ray [Sprawson – guitar], Clive [Sayer – bass/vocals] and Ernie [Green – guitar] who got together as The Concords and played locals pubs.' This was around the Medway towns in north Kent.

'I joined them sometime late '63 or early '64 on keyboards and we changed our name to "Mood Reaction". Paul [Dance – drums] came along then too.

'We played a mixture of pop and soul numbers, and did pretty well getting gigs around Kent. We tried most types of music – when rock was in we played that and we did psychedelic stuff too and Tamla. One day our roadie gave us a handful of reggae records that were big in the clubs at the time, and we decided that as we liked the sound we'd copy it – that's how we covered most records – we could copy almost anything.

'Soon we'd play a few reggae numbers in our sets and the crowd went for it, and from there on we'd play more and more reggae and less of anything else until we became a reggae band.'

This would have been around 1968 and Wally fondly recalls how Desmond Dekker unknowingly helped the band along: 'We'd been playing "Israelites" for some months (copied from a Ja import record) before it hit big for Desmond, and some people said they preferred our version to the one on the record.

'From there Laurel Aitken heard about us, came down to a gig and went back to Pama recommending us. Pama were not only interested in our music but because we were a white band playing reggae. They thought we'd have a good chance to break out of the reggae market into the pop audience.

By this time Mood Reaction were hot property with the reggae boom in full swing and their constant gigging country-wide. As Wally remembers, 'We were semi-pro by then and playing anywhere from Chichester to Leeds at weekends and more locally in the week. We were earning four times our daily wage in Mood Reaction but it was hard. I'd get in from work, eat, bath, change and back out the door in half an hour to get to that night's gig.

'We backed loads of artists live – Derrick Morgan couldn't believe how tight we were, and Desmond [Dekker], too, who said he would've preferred us to his own backing band as we were better.

'The strange thing with black as opposed to white gigs was that all the audience would sit and listen to you. We were used to the white kids jumping up and dancing, so to get almost no response for the whole set was pretty unnerving. After the set playing to West Indians, they would all crowd round and congratulate us on what a great sound we played…it seems they liked to listen and absorb the vibe rather than dance around the floor.

'We were one of the first bands to have a proper light show and we would appear out of a wall of dry ice with light playing across it, or sit behind the curtains in silhouette whipping up the audience. We always wore stage clothes, flashy shirts and bright slacks – the brighter the better – lime green was a favourite. We never dressed as the audience did (mainly skinhead styles in those days), and followed the path of people like The Pioneers, who always looked great in frilly shirts and things.

'Mood Reaction never backed anybody on record. We released a couple of singles and one so-called live album all through Pama, and like everybody else never saw much in the way of payment for our work.

'We recorded our singles at a small studio in Frant (a village south of Tunbridge Wells in Kent), and one day as we were going out of the studio The Marvels came in. Apparently they never got much payment for their records – and in fact Frant Studios complained to me that their bill was never settled either.'

The Pama-released album *Live At The Cumberland* was recorded at the Cumberland Club in Tunbridge Wells and then mixed at Frant Studios, with the master tape passed to Pama by Frant Productions.

The band were not particularly pleased with the finished album. 'The original sound wasn't too bad,' says Wally, 'but for some reason they overdubbed some instruments – notably the bass – and then speeded up a number of tracks. They must've thought it sounded better, but we weren't too happy at all.'

With the demise of the skinheads and the reggae boom, plus new family commitments, the various band members went their separate ways, with one forming a new band to play at weddings and parties.

Mood Reaction reformed recently and are again playing around Kent and occasionally venturing into the capital, still capturing the reggae groove like the old times and delighting audiences wherever they perform.

A NEW DECADE

Things began to change from the early part of 1970. It seems that a combination of several factors caused Pama to lose ground against Trojan/B&C – who were going from strength to strength – at this stage. There were accusations, notably from the Pat Kelly camp, that Pama's records were being poorly distributed and that 'How Long Will It Take' had been held back because of this. Owen Gray also complained that Pama had not pushed his 'Girl What You Doing To Me' sufficiently after it had showed in the *Melody Maker* top 30 ('They just collected their money', he said later in a 1975 *Black Music* magazine interview). While Trojan/B&C were to maintain key links with the big Ja producers, Pama seemed either to lose them or to accept an inferior product to that being offered to Trojan.

The first sign of trouble had come earlier in '69 when, according to one well-documented account, Bunny Lee gave Derrick Morgan's 'Seven Letters' to Trojan, who had in turn given it to Pama. The full story is not known and cannot reasonably be substantiated but, on the face of it, it seemed as though Lee and Morgan, possibly unbeknown to each other, were playing off both companies against one another. Trojan artists were complaining that they had no contracts with the company (it was the producers who were doing the business, they said), while certain Pama artists like Pat Kelly apparently did have contracts but still felt that they were being sold short. This was of particular importance to Pat as he had come to the attention of one or other of The Beatles, who wanted to sign him to their Apple label. Harry Palmer was apparently unwilling to release him from his contract, however. It was cloak-and-dagger stuff that very much emulated what was going on in Jamaica. Further animosity occurred between Trojan and Pama because of the 'Moon Hop' versus 'Skinhead Moon Stomp' fiasco.

Moreover, Pama had begun to suffer from having no deal with Leslie Kong, who had produced The Pioneers, The Maytals and Jimmy Cliff discs on Trojan, and was almost certainly Jamaica's leading producer and international hitmaker at that particular time. Nor did they have a deal with Duke Reid, who was undergoing a revival with his series of U Roy discs. One other important point was that Pama was attempting to make as much reggae as possible in this country rather than in Jamaica. This was always to be a pretty hit-and-miss affair, even with Trojan's similar forays; there was no doubt that it was often on the 'hit' side of hit and miss during the skinhead era, but after that cult had started to dwindle, making records directed specifically at the skinhead market became a less attractive proposition. Pama really came to be too dependent on UK-recorded material.

By the close of 1970, however, Pama still had lucrative licensing arrangements with Lee Perry, Lloyd Daley, Rupie Edwards, Alvin Ranglin, Lloyd Charmers and the up-and-coming Phil Pratt. Of these, Perry gave material to both Trojan and Pama, although he was ultimately to be a stronger force on the former due to its mighty Upsetter label. Daley went entirely to Trojan after 1972 but only for a year or so; after that, disillusioned, he quit music and returned to his electronics business. Edwards quit Pama in 1973 and had moved to Creole's Cactus label by the end of the following year. Ranglin offered Pama tracks that were also issued on some of Trojan's labels (notably Explosion and later GG) and was presently to establish his own GGs set-up in the UK.

Lloyd Charmers was to become an in-house producer for the Palmer brothers at about this time, staying with the company into 1972. He eventually parted with them amid much acrimony. In a late-1974 interview with *Black Music*'s Carl Gayle, he reported that in order to get out of his contract with the Palmer brothers and move over to Trojan, he was forced to agree to sign over all his Pama royalties, which he estimated to be worth around £12,000. Phil Pratt stayed with Pama until 1972 when, apparently disillusioned, he moved over to Trojan and then on to Russell Coke's new Magnet and Faith labels. He had set up his own shop (Terminal Records) in east London's Hackney area by 1976 and was issuing his productions on his Sunshot and Chanan-Jah labels. He now runs a West Indian eatery in Harlesden and continues to issue both old and new material, including a recent CD by Ambelique.

Derrick Harriott, Harry Mudie and Harry Johnson dealt exclusively with Trojan after the end of 1970, by which time that company had already launched the Song Bird, Moodisc and Harry J subsidiaries respectively to deal with its product. This must have been a significant loss to Pama at the time. The other major blow, of course, was that the Unity deal between Bunny Lee and the Palmer brothers had been discontinued at some point, probably around mid-1970, although Lee-produced discs continued to appear on Pama labels sporadically. Winston Riley used Pama for only a couple of releases after Trojan had set up the Techniques subsidiary for him in July 1970.

Looking at the positive aspects, however, Pama still had some big hits during 1970, which included The Viceroys' 'Chariot Coming' (a Sidney Crooks production on Bullet BU 441), Little Roy's 'Scrooge' (Camel CA 43), The Maytones' 'Black And White Unite' (Camel CA 47), The Ethiopians' 'Satan Girl' (Gas GAS 142), Lloyd Tyrell's 'Birth Control' (on Pama PM 792 – actually a far superior effort to Trojan's Byron Lee version), Pat Rhoden's 'Maybe The Next Time' (Pama PM 811) and Derrick Morgan's 'Return Of

Jack Slade' (Unity UN 546). The Rhoden disc was particularly successful for a UK recording.

Pama also continued to deal with small-time and up-and-coming/middle-ranking producers such as Eli Reynolds, Victor Griffiths and Willie Francis (in the first category), and Herman Chin-Loy, Charley Ace, Pete Weston, Stranger Cole and Ranny Williams (in the second). One producer particularly popular in the 1968–69 period – the mysterious Albert George Murphy – continued to have some product issued sporadically on Pama subsidiaries long after he had disappeared from other UK issuing labels. Pama's output had also been supplemented that year by short-lived deals from several big-name producers such as Coxson Dodd, Joe Gibbs and Sonia Pottinger. They were still releasing some good soul records too: Barbara Perry's 'Say You Need Me' on Pama (PM 795) is a stormer.

THE FINAL THREE

Pama set up a final three subsidiary labels at various stages during 1970, namely Ocean, Supreme and Pama Supreme. Ocean issued only two singles that October, both by black UK-based middle-of-the-road artists: 'Moon River' man Danny Williams and Louis Armstrong impersonator and *Desmond's* star Sol Raye (*Desmond's* was a sitcom set in a Caribbean-run barber's shop; it ran on Channel 4 in the UK from 1988 to 1994). It was however resurrected briefly in 1972 for one solitary issue. It is unclear whether there was ever supposed to be any substantive connection between Supreme and Pama Supreme, although the first release on each label was the same and carried the same catalogue number (Junior Byles' 'What's The World Coming To', more correctly titled 'Demonstration').

Supreme's first few issues were dated 1969 but, according to research, probably did not appear until around April 1970. These were excellent Coxson Dodd-produced sides that had somehow escaped release on Bamboo, which generally carried all Dodd's product for the UK market at that time. Otherwise, the label would issue material from Lee Perry, Lloyd Daley, Graham Hawk (for The Mohawks), Albert George Murphy, Victor Chin and Rupie Edwards, possibly after Pama had aborted the Success imprint. Basically, Supreme appeared to be just another pot-pourri with some 29 issues. Its biggest seller was undoubtedly The Mohawks' 'Let it be' (SUP 204). Others worthy of mention are The Emotions' wonderful 'Hallelujah' (SUP 209), Bob Marley's 'I Like It Like This' (aka 'Don't Rock My Boat' on SUP 216), and Dave Barker And The Charmers' smooth cover of The Temptations' 'Just My Imagination' (SUP 220). The latter also saw release on Trojan's Explosion subsidiary.

The third new subsidiary, Pama Supreme, was Pama's 'commercial' operation with most sides being by established UK-based artists such as Pat Rhoden, DD Dennis (aka Denzil Dennis), The Marvels and Owen Gray. To a large extent it was something like the main Trojan label of the time – lots of strings 'n' things courtesy of Norton York, who was Pama's answer to Trojan's Johnny Arthey. Production-wise, the two prime movers were Ranny Williams and Lloyd Charmers, both of whom had set up residence in London. Derrick Morgan, Sidney Crooks and Laurel Aitken formed the rest of the production team.

The biggest sellers on Pama Supreme were Max Romeo's 'Let The Power Fall' (PS 306), Winston Groovy's 'Free The People' (PS 323), which was also very big in West Africa, The Marvels' 'Rocksteady' (PS 338, also issued in Jamaica), Denzil Dennis's 'South Of The Border' (PS 350) and Cynthia Richards' 'Mr Postman' (PS 366, a Ja recording). Finally, there was Max Romeo's 'Everyman Ought To Know' (PS 385), which came among the last few releases on the label following an apparent policy decision to issue more Ja product on it.

Of these, the Romeo discs are pretty good and 'Rocksteady' was definitely The Marvels' finest moment. The British stable of artists was not, however, particularly popular among the younger West Indians who had grown up in the UK: 'South Of The Border', for instance, was definitely 'Big People Music'. Plenty of other stuff merely reggae-fied current pop hits: 'Candida', 'My Way', 'Crackling Rosie', and so on. Often, Trojan would issue a cover version of a pop or soul hit recorded in Jamaica (Eric Donaldson's 'Sylvia's Mother', for example) and, using one of its UK-based artists, Pama would then record and release a rival version of it for issue on Pama Supreme. The Jamaican effort from Trojan was generally superior, although in this case Winston Groovy imbued 'Mother' with a tongue-in-cheek charm.

As mentioned above, Denzil Dennis recorded some sides issued on Pama Supreme, with a couple of them being produced by Lee Perry: 'He [Perry] came to me,' says Denzil, 'to do a song called "I'm A Believer" that came out on Pama Supreme and that was a big seller. Then he came to me later to do "Woman And Money" that I did at Advision studios. I saw his name as writer, but he only came up with the title. He just had the rhythm and said just sing some lyrics, so I just went in and made it up. But he's good to work with – happy and positive. He recorded that with The Rudies then took the rhythm track to Jamaica, but the singer there couldn't handle it – if you listen to the record there's a scream at the beginning and that was from the session there, it wasn't me. So he came back to London and I did it. If you listen to "Woman

And Money" at the end, he was saying to me "ad-lib, y'know", so I sing "that's what I'm trying to do".'

Being so biased towards the pop/commercial end of the market, it should come as no surprise that Pama Supreme is Pama's least collectable label and is not particularly well regarded today. Members of the British Pama stable drifted off to other independent reggae labels in the mid-1970s (notably Third World and Jama) but still found substantial success hard to come by. Ranny Williams took the promising young Eugene Paul (another regular Pama Supreme recording artist) with him when he formed his own Rover Music label, and Winston Groovy found some success with Trojan, notably with his revived 'Please Don't Make Me Cry' in 1974. The Marvels went over to Trojan, where they were produced by Dandy Livingstone, as did Owen Gray, who found himself recording credible material in a roots and culture vein, such as his reggae Number One 'Bongo Natty' in 1975.

DAWN OF THE '70S: THE BEGINNING OF THE END?

The year 1971 was undoubtedly Pama's last golden one. The volume of the company's Jamaican product was beginning to dry up, almost certainly due to disagreements or bad feeling between the Palmer brothers and the producers concerned. Such a situation was clearly assisted by the benefit of producers having Trojan as an alternative outlet – and most producers dealing with Pama did indeed have Trojan as a second release source. More sides with misleading titles and erroneous artist credits were being put out than ever before by the companies, no doubt with the express intention of disguising the true identities of the tracks so that the producer – and other issuing companies – concerned would not catch on to their having been released. A lot of good material *was* being issued, but too often it was coming out on Trojan too.

Of his time with Trojan, the late Judge Dread once said that, 'people used to come in with a carrier bag full of tapes, go in, do their business, come out and then go up the road with another carrier bag and sell them again. They used to license them sometimes three times! So all of a sudden you'd find the same record out on Pama, you'd find it out on Bamboo, you'd find it out on Trojan – happened all the time...'. The 'people' Judge refers to are almost certainly the Jamaican producers, and interestingly he refers to 'going up the road'. The companies were indeed local to each other, with Trojan's Music House headquarters in Neasden only a mile or so from Pama's base in Harlesden. For the record, during 1971 and 1972 there were between 50 and 60 Pama-associated sides that also saw release on Trojan labels. Further friction with Trojan was caused when Pama issued a cover version of Dave & Ansel Collins' 'Monkey Spanner' (as mentioned earlier) with the obvious intention of cutting into sales of the original.

Despite all this, Pama's big hits during 1971 included The Gladiators' 'Freedom Train' (Camel CA 80), The Groovers' 'Bend Down Low' (Escort ERT 863, the last issue on the label), The Righteous Flames' 'Love And Emotion' (Newbeat NB 083), Max Romeo's aforementioned 'Let The Power Fall' on Pama Supreme, Pat Kelly's 'Soulful Love' (Punch PH 88), Dave Barker's 'Johnny Dollar' (Supreme SUP 228) and Max Romeo's 'Maccabee Version' (Unity UN 571). Around this time, the compilation albums were at their peak, with volumes of things like *This is Reggae*, *Straighten Up* (emulating Trojan's *Tighten Up* series but with even tackier sleeves) and *Hot Numbers* being issued on an increasingly regular basis. Perhaps this was an attempt to get even more mileage out of some of the more successful singles issued. Pama also allegedly put out some of these later albums on both cassette and the doomed eight-track format.

Pama was now issuing more UK productions than ever and during 1971 something approaching 40 per cent of the company's entire singles output emanated from these shores. Over the next two years, the shortfall in quality Ja product was also made good by reissuing and rehashing earlier material, such as Clancy Eccles' 'What Will Your Mama Say' (with added strings), Slim Smith's 'Spanish Harlem' and 'Slip Away', Alton Ellis's 'La La Means I Love You', a reworking of The Mohawks' 'The Champ', and Beverley Simmonds' 'You're Mine'/'What A Guy'. The company also reissued its in-house productions under alternate titles: for example, Les Foster's 'I'm The Nearest To Your Heart' was reissued a year later as 'The Man In Your Life'. By the end of 1971, Crab was issuing practically 100 per cent UK product and Success had already been wrapped up. In fact, none of Crab, Escort, Gas, Newbeat or Supreme were to see it through to 1972. That left only Bullet, Camel, Pama Supreme, Punch and the main Pama label as the company's issuing outlets (Ocean had pretty much been a non-starter).

Rather like Trojan in early 1973, Pama was undergoing a process of rationalisation as it went into 1972. The middle of that year saw some good news for Pama, however, with Winston Scotland's 'Buttercup' (Punch PH 100), a disc that up-and-coming producer Prince Tony Robinson had not given to Trojan. It was in fact so successful in the reggae market that Phonogram's Philips label picked it up for mainstream release. By the end of the year, Slim Smith's 'The Time Has Come' on the main Pama label was top of the company's best-sellers chart. While there's nothing particularly surprising about such a great tune hitting the top spot, the odd thing is that it was also Number One on Trojan's top 50 chart thanks to its release on that company's Explosion subsidiary.

How were the charts compiled, though? Did they reflect actual sales or were they instead intended to list titles that the companies wanted to 'promote' or thought should be at a higher position? This was one of the many mysterious machinations of the UK reggae business at that time. Pama's listings during 1972 often featured Max Romeo's 'Wet Dream' on Unity. How many people would have still wanted to buy it then? Was it actually still available even?

Among Pama's biggest hits in 1972 (in addition to 'Buttercup' and 'The Time Has Come') were Roy Shirley And Lloyd Charmers' 'Run Rhythm' (Bullet BU 502 – otherwise known as 'Mucking Fuch'), Max Romeo's 'Rasta Bandwagon' (Camel CA 85), BB Seaton's 'Lean On Me' (Camel CA 100 – a lovely version), Fermena Edwards' cover of Eurovision winner 'Come What May' (Pama PM 839), Charlie Ace And Fay Bennett's rude 'Big Seven', better known as 'Punanny' (Pama PM 853 – even issued in a picture sleeve) and Cynthia Richards' aforementioned 'Mr Postman' on Pama Supreme.

BANKRUPTCY OR POLICY CHANGE?

While the early part of 1973 saw Pama still having considerable success with 'The Time Has Come' and 'Big Seven', the year was to see the company issue only about 42 singles and one album. It did, however, create a new subsidiary, Star, which issued just one non-reggae single (Shelly's cabaret-style 'The Touch Of Love'); we'll return to that later. It was not unnatural to assume that Pama was either experiencing financial difficulties or had decided to reduce its output for some other reason. By this stage, a number of other reggae companies had been formed, notably Count Shelly, Lord Koos (which had links early on with Shelly's set-up) and Russell Coke's Magnet label. Both Shelly and Koos also had connections with Bunny Lee in Jamaica and began issuing his productions. With a wealth of material by top names such as Dennis Brown, The Heptones, Dillinger, Delroy Wilson and Alton Ellis, they couldn't really fail. Coke released a mixture of UK productions from people like Roy Shirley and Gene Rondo, together with Phil Pratt's productions from Ja.

The creation of these new companies (all but one of which were linked to retail shops) challenged Pama in what market it had left, although the trend whereby the different companies often issued the same disc sadly proliferated with the arrival of these and other new labels. Pama's biggest sellers during 1973 were Junior English's 'I Don't Want To Die' (Pama PM 866), Father Sketto's 'Big Nine' (Pama PM 877 – actually titled 'Murder In The Place'),

Pat Kelly's 'I Wish It Would Rain' (Pama Supreme PS 384), Max Romeo's 'Everyman Ought To Know' (Pama Supreme PS 385) and the same singer's 'Rent Crisis' (Unity UN 572) – a modest list indeed by previous standards.

As mentioned earlier, and explained more fully in the book *Young, Gifted And Black*, Trojan was undergoing some rationalisation by that time, with the steady closure of a number of its Muzik City shops and the scrapping of several subsidiary labels, although the company still seemed to have some two-thirds of the reggae business in the UK. Junior Lincoln's Bamboo and Banana imprints had been wound down, and he was by then running a slimmed-down operation with a second series of both the Ashanti and Ackee labels, distribution being handled by Trojan/B&C. Melodisc was pretty much out of the picture but was putting out some excellent Studio One material, some of it only on white labels. R&B Discs had by then withdrawn from issuing records. So, including Shelly, Koos and Magnet, that was pretty much the state of the UK reggae business around the mid- to late part of 1973.

The *London Gazette* dated 15 June 1973 carried the following winding-up notice:

> In the High Court of Justice (Chancery Division) – Companies Court. No. 001098 of 1973.
> In the Matter of Pama Records Limited and in the Matter of the Companies Act 1948.
> Notice is hereby given that a petition for the winding up of the above named company by the High Court of Justice was, on the 11th June 1973, presented to the said Court by the Commissioners of Customs and Excise of King's Beam House, 39-41 Mark Lane, London...

A further winding-up notice appeared in the same newspaper dated 22 February 1974 (no. 00341 of 1974), only this time the petitioner was not Customs & Excise but the Mechanical-Copyright Protection Society (MCPS for short).

From these two ominous notices it would certainly appear that Pama Records was in big trouble one way or another.

Around late 1973 or early 1974 (the latter is more likely since the last two Pama singles carried a 1974 release date) Steve Barnard of BBC Radio London announced on his *Reggae Time* show that Pama had gone out of business. It was likely that Harry Palmer had taken a policy decision to close down the records issuing side – probably because of the notices referred to above, and the other reasons already mentioned – then leased the retail premises to another unrelated concern (Sound Ville Records) but continued using the address as a business base. Without substantive information, this will have to remain somewhat speculative, but Harry Palmer returned to Jamaica in 1974 and started up other business interests. For him, the reggae world had become too much of a hard slog with plenty of aggravation and confrontation into the bargain. But, for whatever reasons, Pama released no new records for over a year.

MUSICAL RESURRECTION

If we fast-forward to October 1975, there is every reason to accept that bankruptcy was not in fact the issue. At that time, the youngest Palmer brother, Carl, gave an interview to *Black Music* magazine as part of an article looking at the emergence of several new labels (notably Klik, Vulcan and Sound Tracs), which were launched following Trojan's liquidation. In fact the article came some six months after the release of a number of 45s on the relaunched Pama main label and the Ocean, Bullet, Camel and Punch subsidiaries. These included Gregory Isaacs' 'Lonely Days' (which was issued on both Bullet and Camel) and 'Dance With Me' (Camel CA 2008), Pat Kelly's 'Sing About Love' (Pama PM 4000), Laurel Aitken's cover of Carl Malcolm's smash chart hit 'Fatty Bum Bum' (Punch PH 121), and reissues of Tiger's 'Guilty' and Ruddy And Sketto's 'Everynight'. Carl Palmer said that Pama had stopped issuing records simply because it didn't understand the way the music was going, particularly as regards the toasting/DJ phenomenon.

The interview reveals quite a lot about Pama's past. The questioner, Carl Gayle, put it to Carl Palmer that his label had, according to the artists and people involved with it, exploited them and had issued records without contracts or licensing agreements. Palmer completely refuted this, adding that everyone got their money; some artists even ended up owing Pama money (presumably after they had received advances bigger than the actual sales generated); and that some of those who had been involved earlier had even come back to the label. There was, however, controversy over Carl Malcolm's 'Miss Wire Waist', the follow-up to his UK hit 'Fatty Bum Bum'. The disc was issued by Birmingham's Black Wax label and by Pama, but Carl Palmer claimed his company had the rights to the tune and that there would be legal proceedings in respect of it. Of the split with Bunny Lee, Carl Palmer said that the producer had basically become a much bigger fish by the end of the '60s and that Pama could no longer afford to handle all his material.

Some of the 17 releases in this second phase were big sellers, particularly the two by Gregory Isaacs, Claudette Miller's 'Tonight Is The Night' (on Ocean, but also out on Jama) and Justin Hinds' 'Sinners Where Are You Going To Hide' (on Pama), which was one of the last productions by the late Duke Reid. There is in fact probably some credence to Carl Palmer's claim that people had come back to the label. Laurel Aitken was leasing material to them again, and contained among these new singles were productions by Alvin Ranglin and Phil Pratt.

An album on the main Pama label entitled *Reggae Hit The Town* (even the title is from another era!) was issued in mid-1975 and contained quite an array of material from the 1973–74 period by Derrick Morgan, Fermena and The Twinkle Brothers, together with some of the current 45s by Pat Kelly, Justin Hinds, Larry Marshall and Bill Gentles. Our guess is that Pama had scheduled the bulk of this for release some time in late 1973 or early 1974, but with its withdrawal from the market decided not to go ahead with issuing it. The sleeve also probably comes from this era since we're not aware that red-checked Oxford bags were still *de rigueur* in 1975. It was in fact a top five reggae album, and did particularly well since it was released at a time when, with Trojan in liquidation, few reggae compilations were coming out compared to a year or two earlier. After the Pama label pressing sold out, it was re-pressed on Star.

BANG UP TO DATE

After this flurry, however, there were no further new releases. Advertisements appeared in the newly launched *Black Echoes* early in 1976 re-promoting Gi Gi's soul dancer 'Daddy Love' and The Marvels' 'Rocksteady', two Pama Supreme releases from 1971. While they were probably original unsold discs rather than re-pressings, it was anybody's guess as to who'd want to buy them in such a time of dread culture. At this point, independent reggae labels were emerging on an almost weekly basis. For example, Buster Pearson's K&B set-up, Leonard Chin's Ital Music (which included both the Student and Nationwide? imprints), and Dennis and Castro Brown's Morpheus operation. These were just a few that sprung up in late 1975 and early 1976. Pama may have decided that, with this level of competition, any success it might have in releasing records was going to be harder fought than ever. At the same time big-league companies like Island and Virgin were signing up reggae artists and giving them, probably for the first time in their lives, some sort of reasonable deal.

Pama continued to dabble in the issuing side, however, and 1977 saw the release of a number of extended-play singles on its main label in the new 12-inch format. These comprised four tracks from the company's past, and Owen Gray, Stranger Cole and Tiger, among others, saw some of their greatest Pama hits repackaged. Similar issues by The Marvels and Pat Kelly appeared on 10-inch singles. That year, Pama's Star subsidiary scored a big reggae hit with Horace Andy And Tapper Zukie's 'Natty Dread A Weh She Want', a record that can still rock a revival dance to this day. Otherwise, there was a popular Pama 12-inch by Edi Fitzroy ('African Princess') and an album released by Tito Simon (*Love It Up*) around 1978, which had been co-produced by Harry Palmer. By the turn of the 1980s, the company issued sides by current DJ sensation Yellowman, including the 10-inch album *Operation Eradication*. However, there was no real consistency with its release schedule.

Basically, Pama – which had evolved into Jetstar Phonographics by 1978 – had became more and more involved in the distribution of reggae music during the late 1970s and throughout the 1980s, and its record releases were no longer crucial to the operation or success of the company. By this period, the business was largely in the hands of Carl Palmer and his wife Beverley (and this is probably where the 'Beverley Music' on some Pama labels comes from). In fact, it could have been inferred from the October 1975 *Black Music* article that Carl's two brothers were no longer involved in the record-issuing side at all. By way of background, the name 'Jetstar' was probably inspired by the small US Jet Star soul label, which had seen several of its recordings issued on the mauve Pama label at the end of the '60s.

The early to mid-1980s saw the reissue of certain key Pama albums, notably Slim Smith's *Everybody Needs Love*; *The Best Of Lee Perry And The Upsetters, Volumes 1 and 2* (basically reissues of the *Clint Eastwood* and *Many Moods Of The Upsetters* packages), and Winston Groovy's *Free The People*. Around 1986, The Mohawks' 'The Champ' became very popular again in the clubs and saw reissue on both 7-inch and 12-inch singles: bits of it had been 'sampled' in many hip-hop productions at the time, hence the revived interest in the original. The early 1990s even saw the release of decidedly limited re-pressings of the *Reggae To Reggae* and *Hot Numbers Volume 2* compilations, which had contained a smattering of Wailers material. As part of the trend towards 'revival' music, re-pressings of Tiger's 'Guilty' and Pat Kelly's 'How Long Will It Take' appeared in specialist shops several years ago, complete with facsimiles of the original labels. Exactly who was responsible for these is, however, open to speculation.

Nowadays, Jetstar is the most prominent reggae distributor in Europe, with large premises in West London's Park Royal. As late as 1992, there was still a retail outlet at 78 Craven Park Road (Spindle Records), although it is not known whether this was associated with Pama or Jetstar. Jetstar has long had its own label – Charm – and regularly issues the long-running series of *Reggae Hits* and other such compilations, as well as a lot of other material newly recorded at its own Cave Studio, so Pama can still be considered as a de facto reggae issuing company. Unlike Trojan, Pama has not really shown any interest in reissuing its back catalogue in any format, and it now looks unlikely it will ever do so. Vinyl re-pressings of the albums *The Champ* and *Moon Hop* have been seen in London, complete with original artwork and, by all accounts, Jetstar seems unperturbed by such activity.

Harry Palmer has lived in Jamaica since around 1975 and is involved with business activities away from the music field. The Palmer name is still connected to the Apollo Club, which, amazingly after all these years, continues to thrive as a nightclub venue. Into the new millennium, and Jetstar's day-to-day business is now handled by younger bucks who are more than likely pretty uninterested in what happened 30-odd years ago.

4 Straight To Trojan's Head

As detailed in both *Boss Sounds* and *Young, Gifted And Black*, reggae giant Trojan/B&C was seriously losing its way by 1974, following the scrapping of a large proportion of its producer-dedicated subsidiary labels, and was becoming increasingly reliant on issuing UK-recorded, string-loaded cover versions of current chart hits. Trojan manager Rob Bell gives his own and the company view of the sweetening of the releases with overdubs.

'To sweeten or not to sweeten? One lump or two? Raw cane sugar or saccharin? To a greater or lesser extent, this quandary existed before the '60s, and is certainly still present today.

'I think the key to understanding this dilemma is to take a long look at radio, and its role in selling records. As everyone is aware, radio play is of paramount importance in generating sales. The programme director/music director and, back then, the jock himself, had to dig the record before it was played. Thus a filter was put in place, a certain standard the aspiring hit had to match. The audience was deemed to be too sophisticated to want to listen to straight-ahead, down-in-the-alley music. So things got sweetened – some strings, maybe a horn arrangement.

'As this approach – with Trojan anyway – developed, the producers in Ja probably dug it. All they had to send over was pretty much a rhythm track and vocal. To be fair, the approach worked. As I remember, the artists did like it. I think they felt that Trojan going the extra mile to put arrangements on their records proved that the company was solidly behind their careers. And when it worked, and the record hit the charts, the artist was happy to see performance fees shoot up and some serious money come his way.

'Let's remember here that for most musicians, the bread comes from gigging, not record royalties. If you have a record on the chart and on radio, your price goes up. Sure, most of those guys dug what was happening at the time. The pop business being what it is, it is very hard to sustain that kind of success for more than a handful of years. So now, maybe three decades later, I can see that those involved have perhaps changed their attitudes. The money is long gone, but those recordings have endured. Now perhaps the arrangements sound dated or, with hindsight, the artist feels that bad decisions were made, both musically and career-wise. I don't really think Island and Trojan did anything that other companies would not have done. They went for the main chance, as they saw it, and that was that.

'However,' Rob adds significantly, 'on a purely personal note, I hated all that shit, all those strings and cheesy horn arrangements. Don't get me wrong – I love horns. When they are played with a groove and a feel, that is. My thinking, and this is why I have always been a renegade in the music business, is that, in the main, radio sucks. A whole lot of reggae tunes sold a whole lot of records without any sweetening. Listen to "007", "Israelites", "Return Of Django", "Liquidator", "Long Shot"…all these were straight-ahead tunes that connected because they were good *and* because they got play. Just like a decade or so before, when Little Richard, Fats Domino and those guys were hitting. They were getting play, and sales, with straight-ahead stuff.

'Then the awful Bobbies came along, with their godawful femme choruses, and strings and corny square gimmicks. They even got to Fats in the end! That shit got played because those who had the power to spin records decided the raw stuff was too hick, too out there for their audience.

'Perhaps they were right, but to me there has always been a kind of "emperor's new clothes" syndrome about popular music and radio: tell people that something is good for long enough, and they start to believe it.'

By this time, then, several small independent labels were already in operation, notably Count Shelly, Lord Koos, Magnet, DIP and Ethnic. Pama had, as we have seen, already stopped issuing music early that year.

Trojan/B&C now lacked the influence it had once exerted and the respect it had enjoyed at the height of its national chart successes between 1969 and 1972. With Pama off the scene, artists and producers were taking their product to Trojan largely because there were relatively few other outlets for them to go to. The existence of newly created independents clearly gave artists and producers other options to pursue, however, and since Trojan/B&C had also gained a reputation as an outfit that perhaps promised much but delivered little in the form of financial reward for those concerned, they were only too eager to take up those options.

On 24 March 1973, in his 'Black And British' reggae spot in the *NME*, Henderson Dalrymple reported that Byron Lee's Dragon imprint had been inaugurated in the UK by Island, with Trojan manager Graham Walker cited as 'representing Lee's interests, operating from offices in London's Willesden

High Road'. Trojan later took over the label, which was perhaps originally a joint venture, as at the time there certainly would have been a conflict of interests with Walker managing Trojan and also a rival company's new imprint.

Trojan boss Lee Gopthal tried to find a suitable buyer for the ailing company. After much to-ing and fro-ing, Marcel Rodd, a 62-year-old classical music aficionado and owner of the age-old Saga Records in Kensal Rise, agreed a deal with Gopthal that included the promise of better contracts for some of Trojan's producers and artists. Unfortunately for Trojan, two of Jamaica's key producers of the time – Bunny Lee and Lee Perry – had already thrown in their respective lots with a number of the new independents. Rodd, who'd made his fortune selling budget-priced classical music albums, admitted that he knew next to nothing about reggae music. Alas for him, he'd also largely lost Trojan's experienced workforce, who were quietly setting up their own independent labels. As was the case in Jamaica, the people involved in reggae music always had their irons in plenty of fires and were never keen to let the grass grow under their feet.

Rich back catalogue aside, Marcel Rodd had seemingly put his money into a lame-duck outfit largely devoid of new, decent material and know-how. The new Trojan essentially relied on a motley assortment of LP and 45 issues from its archives, a few new signings such as Jah Woosh, who were keen to try their luck over in the UK, and material from those tried and tested performers (notably John Holt and Ken Boothe) it could still hang on to. One by one, however, Jamaica's producers began to switch much of their allegiance from Trojan to the new independents. Without the life-blood of new reggae coming out of the top Kingston studios, Trojan looked unlikely to prosper again, particularly as other labels were better geared towards the ethnic market and, as became clear later on, were generally prepared to pay more to license tracks.

To return to those two key producers, Lee Perry had started placing his material with Larry Lawrence's Ethnic and Dennis Harris's DIP labels during the latter half of 1974, while Bunny Lee had done likewise with Lord Koos and Count Shelly, with whom he had especially close ties. At this time, little was known about any of these independents outside the grass-roots reggae fraternity: many sold large quantities via the specialist shops but, unlike Trojan, they could not boast truly national distribution or a high profile in the high-street record shops.

The key point here is that even before the arrival of the saviour Rodd, the rot had already well and truly set in for Trojan. The newly launched small labels were primarily concerned with issuing product aimed specifically at the West Indian market, while Trojan was still increasingly desperate to secure commercial, pop chart success at any cost.

These independents had begun to try their luck in a market that, by all accounts, was already revealing a window of opportunity by late 1973. When the individuals concerned were trying to get their cottage industries off the ground, they were in sharp competition with the fading might of Trojan/B&C. They were having to rely largely on word of mouth and the 'man with a van' route to promote their fledgling enterprises, for they lacked the hard cash for advertising space, and any sort of mouthpiece like expensive mainstream press ads for the music was non-existent. Ironically, it was said at the time of Trojan's crash that these earliest of independents had failed to build up sufficiently good reputations within the UK reggae business. Equally ironically, though, the Count Shellys of this world outlasted those operations launched in the immediate aftermath of Trojan's first phase.

SID BUCKNOR

Norman Bucknor, who is otherwise known as 'Siddy' or 'Sid', was enticed to London by the reggae boom. The renowned producer and engineer, who cut his musical teeth in the early 1960s at Studio One and went on to have a distinguished career working in almost every studio on the island, first arrived in the UK in 1974 and he soon became a resident sound engineer at Chalk Farm Studios. Once again, he found himself to be in hot demand elsewhere, too.

'I worked with Jimmy Cliff on remix sessions at Morgan Studio in Willesden, with Bob Marley And The Wailers at Island Studios, and on remix sessions with Aswad at Tony King's Studio in Hammersmith and Gooseberry Studio in Soho, to name a few. I never worked with The Rudies as a group, as they had disbanded before I started engineering in the UK. The Cimarons were the London group in ascendancy in the Chalk Farm Studios. The band was indeed self-contained, and at times they were discriminatingly averse to working with non-Cimarons band musicians,' he recalls.

An insight into life on the other side of the board at a typical recording session – how long would the basic rhythm track take to record, how long for the vocals, did you voice at the same session as laying the rhythm, how long would the mixing and overdub of strings (if required) take? – can be provided by Sid: 'The time it takes to record an acceptable backing track depends largely on the performers' competence and experience. Generally, the experienced session musicians could be very quick, and as a result got used more often by producers. It was not uncommon (understandably so, seeing that these players charged so much per completed rhythm track) to record three or four usable rhythm tracks in a three-hour session.

'In the mid-1960s when I started sound engineering [in Jamaica], voice-overs weren't an option. Constrained by the number of tracks available to record on to, we had to record vocals and accompaniments simultaneously. A mistake made seconds from the end of the piece and it's back to bar one for another take, sometimes ad nauseam. The Scully Electronics three-track recorder of the late '60s was a welcome bromide, especially for the session players. Out-of-tune singers could now record their parts at leisure later on.

'Strings overdubs were fairly unproblematic. The fiddlers were usually professionally trained musicians with perfect, or near-perfect, pitch sense – so much so that the session engineer sometimes had to use vari-speed correction techniques to ease their discomfort. Once everyone was happy with the sound, and the mandatory run-through for level balance and stereo imaging done, we are ready to roll. Three or four minutes later and we are listening to the playback of the take. If tracking [repeating the overdubs] is not needed or requested that job item is complete.'

How much input was taken from the artist, though? 'The Bob Andys of the era usually demanded, and got, their pound of flesh, sometimes with some blood, sweat and tears. However, they too occasionally had to eat humble pie. I bore witness to many a composition by veteran composer-singers being greatly enhanced by a change of cadence suggested by a session musician. On the other hand, the new kids on the block, understandably, initially just go with the flow. Most of them, after the baptism, usually went home feeling grateful and well pleased with the results.'

Did Sid try to replicate the Kingston sound, or did he acknowledge that London had its own vibe and sound? Indeed, did any artists/producers ask him to try and make the record sound like it was recorded in Jamaica? 'Getting that Kingston sound has always been the ambition of UK-based reggae groups. Personally, I never quite bagged that sound. Once or twice I went close to replicating the sound in Chalk Farm Studios, working with Jamaican session musicians who were passing through. The *Peek-a-Boo* album by Errol Dunkley for Count Shelly came close; so much so that to this day I still cannot convince some folks that the entire album was done in Chalk Farm Studios.

'I did so little work for Larry Lawrence and Pama Records I can't recall any of the titles. League-wise, these outfits resided in Division One. Overdubbing on Jamaica-recorded rhythm tracks was their forte.

'Trojan Records, on the other hand, was atop the Premier Division in terms of production work. Third World Records was also a Premier Division player, production-wise, albeit in the bottom half of the table. Not very many Jamaica-recorded backing tracks were used for melody overdubs. Occasionally, a producer would "try a ting" with some would-be Bob Marley or Marcia Griffiths. Most didn't convince for one reason or another.'

'I don't know how many reggae chart hits used Jamaican-recorded backing tracks. Judge Dread had one or two. Most reggae chart hits in the UK were melody completed in Jamaica and sweetened in the UK. [The rhythm tracks were] skeletally basic, some of them, especially when meaningful overdubs are envisioned for a targeted market. The knowledgeable producer always tried to get as tight a rhythm track as possible, using only the usual suspects: drums, bass, guitar, piano. Any subsequent additions to this combo are solely up to the producer, not infrequently with a friendly word of advice or warning from well-wishers that that last cow bell is clashing with the Agogo [general feel of the track].

'Acoustically, Chalk Farm Studios was about 80 per cent of what Jamaican studios were. DIY was very evident and in your face. A "back-a-yard studio abroad", someone once called the place.'

In the mid-1970s Chalk Farm Studios had the edge over its then Jamaican counterparts in the equipment area. Dynamic controllers, thin on the ground in Ja were varied and plentiful. Gear not already provided as standard in-house fare could be hired painlessly in for the job in hand. Fader riding was less stressful and hot mixes were more easily achievable. There were good days and bad days at the office in the heady Chalk Farm 1970s.

'One of my best memories,' says Sid, 'was the moment that my eccentric friend, Niney, of "Blood And Fire" fame, told me on returning to Ja from a visit to England, that sound engineers in the UK liked my sound. Words that confirm one's ego are always enjoyable and unforgettable!

'My worst memory is being threatened with a bowie knife for giving my opinion about a singer's performance in the studio. The irony was that the singer himself had asked me for an honest opinion. Although he was deeply apologetic the next day, the scare of the moment lingered for some time. It was rumoured that my criticism was too bluntly put in the presence of the girl the singer was trying to impress. He of course denied the assertion.'

THE FUNKY CROSSOVER

As Trojan started to sink into the string-laden musical ocean, one of its hopes of a lifebelt was covering popular soul and chart songs, done 'inna reggae stylee'. If it was a hit for Hot Chocolate then the hope was that Trojan could grab some of the fallout with a cover of the song.

Some, indeed, did make it big – in fact bigger than the original. A case in point is Susan Cadogan's Perry-produced cut of the Millie Jackson soul tune 'Hurt So Good', although unfortunately for Trojan by this time Upsetter was dealing with the new up-and-coming independents and Dennis Harris's DIP label scooped the gem. But it proved that it could be done – even if Harris had to license it on to the major label Magnet as he couldn't promote it sufficiently. 'Hurt So Good' hit Number Four in April 1975 and sold vast quantities for a reggae record.

Soul and reggae had always been close companions on the nightclub floor. Indeed, many ska numbers were based on R&B, blues, jazz or soul originals as the nearby USA influenced the Kingston studios. As the reggae era dawned, the UK's cosmopolitan nightclub scene cross-pollinated musical styles. James Brown's 'Popcorn' was a smash hit and forward-thinking producers quickly pulled the vibe into a reggae rhythm, in particular Laurel Aitken who had a hit with 'Mr Popcorn' and then 'Reggae Popcorn', using The Cimarons as his funky reggae band. Having already played soul in their stage shows, the band had no problem integrating the two musical styles.

Rufus Thomas scored a huge US hit with his 'Do The Funky Chicken'. Winston Groovy offered a British portion of 'Funky Chicken', again with a reggae lilt to the backing provided by The Cimarons.

This was during the skinhead era when many of the shaven-headed dancers took plenty of soul with their reggae, but as their numbers dwindled and the music continued to sweeten, the pop/soul covers became a stigma attached to reggae. Reviewers and radio jocks alike branded Trojan's output as the 'platters that didn't matter'.

By 1972 the roots reality sound had begun to emerge in Jamaica, while much UK reggae was still sweetly trying to recapture the chart action of three years before, not knowing that the majority of its audience was now going dread and checking the red, gold and green from Africa via Kingston.

So the funky and soulful reggae at the time was derided as insipid and copyist, with little or no dance floor action gained from a spin or two of the latest weak retread of an O'Jays or Barry White hit.

It wasn't all doom and gloom, though, as some artists took their inspiration from their American cousins and started to fuse the sweaty funk of The Fatback Band and Mr Brown with a sticky reggae rhythm, resulting in some of what are now regarded as the finest of cover versions.

US funk masters like Robert 'Kool' Bell's Kool And The Gang and the blues-tinged Ohio Players work was reinvented with a reggae beat for consumption in major city nightspots.

111

The Ohio's 'Skin Tight' was one of the first funk tracks to be reworked, although it wasn't to reappear for a couple of years after the original, and was more swing and dine than bump and grind.

The singularly most important black UK band of the early 1970s was Cymande. They pulled afro, funk and reggae rhythms together and infused the whole with Rastafarianism, thus creating one of richest and most creative bodies of work ever to come from a London recording studio. Cymande (the name means 'dove') had song titles such as 'Zion I', 'Rastafarian Folk Song', 'Sheshamani' and 'Bra' (hip-talk meaning 'brother'). They were the underground sound of London, driving home the Rasta message of peace and love a couple of years before it finally invaded the blues dances.

They called their sound 'nyah rock' and it was largely ignored within their home base of the UK, although they found favour in the USA and climbed the charts to almost-stardom, moving from the R&B chart to the mainstream at one point when their 'The Message' reached number 48 in the pop listing. A winning appearance at the famed Apollo, two US tours, the first as support to soul singer supreme Al Green and then latterly as the headline act, heralded their arrival. But after three great albums (plus one soul/disco affair recorded by a couple of group members under the Cymande name in 1981) and a handful of singles, they were gone by 1974, not to be rediscovered until the rare groove scene of the late 1980s whipped their records from the 50p dumpsters to top billing on the soul shops' wall display.

The band fragmented with just three members carrying on the Cymande name and issuing the previously mentioned disco album a few years up the road. One member, Mike Rose (not to be confused with Michael 'Black Uhuru' Rose of Waterhouse, Kingston, Ja), did carry on in the London music scene and became one of the finest session players on offer, playing brass with such luminaries as Aswad. He then toured in the 1990s with the big band sound of Jazz Jamaica, while still cutting copious sessions (and the odd solo album) for all and sundry.

Jamaican vocalist Tinga Stewart picked up on Cymande's biggest-selling single, 1972's 'The Message' (their only recording to receive any major club play in the UK), a song of togetherness and brotherly love, and infused the slinky, slippery feel of the original with a touch of reggae. Issued in the UK on the then Trojan Records subsidiary Dragon, at the time it left most people wondering why he'd bothered as they had all bought the Cymande original and could see no point in buying the same tune twice. Now it stands alongside the original as a very worthy version.

Other reggae producers tried their hand at more out-and-out funk. For example, London-based Mike Dorane with the previously mentioned 'Penguin Funk', issued on Junior Lincoln's Ackee label in 1972.

Dorane, or Michael Dan as he was to become later in the decade, was always interested in fusing styles and among his later work was his input, with Barry Ford, to the superb deep roots reggae band Merger (more on them later), and his board wizardry with Big Roy, which blended funk and steppers reggae to great effect on cuts like 'I'm Going To Ethiopia', issued on his own Movers label.

James Brown must surely have had the most profound effect on all forms of black music and as imitation is the sincerest form of flattery (although no doubt Mr Brown would prefer the royalty cheque), he was flattered to death by the Jamaican community. Acts running from lightweight Jamaican Hotel show band Llans Thelwell And The Celestials to skinhead DJ talkover artist King Horror wholeheartedly borrowed his work.

Jamaica's Chosen Few took the next step and recorded an entire album in Miami, surprisingly called *In Miami*, with King Sporty in the producer's chair. It was a funky soul album with some very worthy cuts and a long way from their sweet reggae roots. The Mighty Diamonds followed suit with an album cut in New Orleans, *Ice On Fire*, for producer-singer Alan Toussaint, although the blend wasn't to everybody's taste and it sold poorly.

In a mirror-image turn of fortune, the once derided funk copies are now the most highly prized items in many a DJ's collection, with records like that Matumbi lick of Kool's 'Funky Stuff', 'Reggae Stuff', now rocking many a dance – and so it should, as it was an excellent interpretation of the sweat-drenched original.

Sidney, George And Jackie's wah-wah-infused cover of The Temptations' 'Papa Was A Rolling Stone' again shows how good a reinterpretation can be, as they capture the cold heartlessness of the original. What's more these last two tracks were laid down in London, alongside gentler sounds like ex-Pioneer Jackie Robinson's version of The Chi-Lites' wistful 'Homely Girl'.

The soul catalogue was plundered to the extreme by the reggae business, which in its bleak years of the early 1970s hoped eternally for a chirpy reggae cover to pull it out of the doldrums – it didn't.

SHELLY REGGAE ROCK

Probably the first man to establish a small-scale record label during the early 1970s was Count Shelly (Ephraim Barrett). A giant of a man, Shelly came to the UK in 1962, starting work as a bricklayer. He set up his own sound system operation around 1967 as a sideline, but it was so successful that he became a full-time sound system operator two years later.

Shelly eased out of intensive sound system work in 1972 and formed his first label, logically called Count Shelly, that same year, although he still maintained a key residence at Dalston's Four Aces club for some years to come. Operating from his first record shop off Philip Lane in Tottenham, among his first few releases were The Soul Rebels' superb 'I'm The One Who Loves You' and Horace Andy's 'Jah Jah Children', both of which came out with label designs markedly different from those used after the fourth issue. There were also some first-rate compilation albums like *Feeling High, Return To Me, Look Before You Leap* and *All Stars*, and some dedicated artist packages like Alton Ellis's *Greatest Hits*, Max Romeo's *Everyman Ought To Know* and Honey Boy's *This Is Honey Boy*. Shelly soon moved his retail operation into a more central location in Dalston and, later on, Stoke Newington. North London, and the Tottenham area in particular, was always renowned as a Count Shelly stronghold and his releases sold particularly well in that part of the capital.

Much of the Count Shelly label's early product was provided by Bunny Lee, plus some early productions by Channel One (Stranger and Gladdy's 'Don't Give Up The Fight' was reputedly the first disc recorded at the studio), Prince Jazzbo (Linval Carter) and Jah Lloyd (Pat Francis). Particular hits included Sang Hugh's 'No Potion A Gal' and 'Rasta No Born Yah' (on which he was joined by The Lionlains), Leroy Sibbles' cover of The Stylistics' 'Break Up To Make Up', Scotty's 'Salvation Train' (also issued on the flip side to Lloyd Charmers' vocal cut on the rhythm, 'Free The People', on Trojan's Green Door imprint) and Roy Alton's soca-fied 'Carnival Night'. There was also a healthy supply of UK-produced music, much of which merely copied the original Jamaican hits (Honey Boy's do-over of Johnny Clarke's 'Everyday Wondering' and Bill Campbell's cover of Al Brown's 'Here I Am Baby' are two examples). In an August 1977 *Black Music* magazine interview, Shelly was honest enough to admit that, for these releases, he just went into the studio and copied the Jamaican sound as best he could.

Such was the success of these early releases that the Count Shelly label developed into the mighty Third World empire around May 1975. Surprisingly, the Third World label was originally owned by Sid Bucknor. 'I first used this label in Jamaica in 1973 and in the UK in 1975, administered by Shelly Records. Because I had registered it only as a label in the UK, Count Shelly, who owned and ran Shelly Records, subsequently registered it as a company in his name, unbeknown to me, when he liquidated Shelly Records.'

Third World distributed a number of labels for other producers as well as featuring a number of the Count's new subsidiaries, such as Penguin, Live and Love and Jamatel. In the former category was Paradise, whose first release, produced by guitarist Ranfold 'Ranny' Williams, was Ginger Williams' 'Can't Resist Your Tenderness', which went to Number One in the reggae charts and figured in the listings for much of the second half of 1974. This disc, so Shelly explained in the interview mentioned earlier, sold 54,000 copies with hardly any radio exposure or, of course, a consequent pop chart placing. It was later picked up for national release by Jonathan King for his UK label, which unfortunately seemed to promote it poorly. Records such as 'Tenderness' were now doing better than much that Trojan had on offer.

By 1977 Third World had become just about the biggest UK independent operation in the reggae market. As an independent, it had also made major inroads into the market for album releases, and its largely Bunny Lee-originated roster included The Ethiopians' *Slave Call*, Jackie Mittoo's *The Keyboard King* and *Thriller*, Delroy Wilson's double LP *Twenty Golden Hits*, Leroy Smart's *Get Smart* and Owen Gray's *Forward On The Scene*. The rousing *Rebel Rock* instrumental album, featuring Rico and Tan Tan Thornton, was recorded in London, and there were dub LPs by The Revolutionaries, The Third World All Stars and Bobby Ellis. Only the two multinationals, Island and Virgin, could really claim to top Third World's sales success.

Shelly always excelled at putting out decent albums. The half-dozen or so compilations on his Count Shelly label are rare today, and more often than not boasted superior track selections to anything Trojan was putting out at the time. Third World also maintained and developed its own stable of indigenous artists, including Winston Curtis, Raymondo, the Otis Brothers, Brenton King, Honey Boy and Gene Rondo, and mixed their tracks in with the authentic Jamaican product. The majority of the material by these artists was not to everyone's taste, though, and certainly seemed to mar many a good Third World compilation. On the other hand, some of it wasn't at all bad. Rondo did a credible job on his version of The Abyssinians' 'Declaration Of Rights' (flip side of Buggis's 'Buggis Mood' on TW 31) and Brenton King's 'Mama Say' on Penguin (PEN 1) is a beautiful record blessed with really superlative production.

In the singles stakes, Third World was certainly in the top flight. To name but a few: Devon Russell's elusive 'Race Track Riot'; Prince Jazzbo's 'Stealing'; I Roy's 'Mr Benwood Dick', 'Sister Maggie Breast' and 'Point Blank'; Gregory Isaacs' 'Slave Driver' and Cornel Campbell's cool 'The Investigator' are all of prime quality. These were all issued on the main Third World imprint: the hits came thick and fast on its subsidiary labels too. In 1979, Errol Dunkley, another Third World stable stalwart, had his 'OK Fred' leased to WEA's new Scope label, which took it into the UK top 20.

With such a high standard of releases, it's no surprise that Third World's success continued right into the 1980s. Early in 1978, the business moved its premises to 261 High Road, Tottenham, where Body Music is today. In reggae shop terms, it was almost supermarket-sized. That branch, and the Body Music chain of shops, is now run by Fitzroy Sterling, one-time Pama vocalist.

It is believed that Third World evolved into World Enterprise during the mid-1980s and shifted its base to Harlesden. Certainly, World Enterprise was responsible for reissuing a number of popular Third World album titles and, as far as we can tell, continued the Live and Love label. For reasons best known to himself, Count Shelly apparently emigrated to the USA during this time but still has business interests in the reggae scene, retaining connections with Bunny Lee to this day. Rarely has Shelly's name appeared in any reggae reference books, but his contribution to the music in the UK should not be underestimated. He worked doggedly to build up his enterprises in the face of daunting competition from the big reggae houses of the day, and it is only now that he is being recognised for his contribution.

KOOS IN FULL SWING

Another early indie pioneer was the late Lord Koos (real name Eric Scott). Koos was, like Count Shelly, a sound system operator of some considerable local repute, having established his set in Harlesden as early as 1964. He is quoted as saying in a March 1974 *Black Music* interview that his first production – 'Koos In Full Swing' by Keith Hudson – was recorded back in Jamaica in 1967 while he was on holiday there, but we can find no evidence that this track exists, or even that Hudson was recording as far back as that. Indeed, the story of the Lord Koos label is a muddled one and guaranteed to induce a migraine. Curiously, there was a record issued on a Lord Koos label in 1973 with that very title but it wasn't by Hudson!

Koos claims to have launched a fledgling Lord Koos imprint – and this could possibly have been as far back as the late 1960s – together with associate Danny Williams, distributing the label in London and Birmingham using a car and a van. He says that this never proved successful, however, and that no further releases were put out as a result. While we know that Koos placed his production of Owen Gray's 'Sincerely' with Pama in 1971 (the label issued it on its Punch subsidiary), our research has been unable to substantiate any Lord Koos label apart from the one he started around March 1973, which he again distributed himself, going as far as Manchester, Leeds and Huddersfield. We also know that some Koos material was released through Count Shelly's label early on, at around the same time as Koos was starting what we believe was his first and only label. There was also a link-up with Wolverhampton-based sound system and record retailer Sir Christopher, and two related 45s were issued on a label heralding 'Sir Christopher – From The Midlands'. All rather confusing.

As anyone who owns records on the Lord Koos label will testify, a number of sides also appear on other reggae labels but a lot of the titles and artists quoted (although certainly not all of them) are different. Early releases include Dennis Brown's 'Perhaps', Hubert Lee's 'Something On Your Mind' (also on Trojan's Down Town label), Jah Lloyd's 'Sunshine Girl', The Starlites' 'You Are A Wanted Man' (again, also on Down Town), Alton Ellis's 'Too Late To Turn Back Now' (also on Ackee) and 'Guiding Red' by Augustus Pablo (though credited to The Upsetters and titled 'Bring The Catch'). There was also a classic UK production from Clem Bushay – Tapper Zukie's 'Man A Warrior'.

Our own guess is that Koos had close dealings with a multitude of Jamaican producers, including Bunny Lee, Morice Wellington, Carlton Patterson and Pat Francis, who gave him certain 'specials' to air on his sound system. The tacit agreement may have been that they were happy for him to release limited pressings of these discs, and that is perhaps what he did. Singles on the Lord Koos label are few and far between, and many turn up on blanks. Whether it was ever any sort of 'official' label before the end of 1973 is therefore open to much speculation.

By the start of 1974, however, it had slightly modified its label design and began a more consistent and identifiable release schedule, with music coming from Johnny Clarke ('Enter Into His Gates With Praise'), Cornel Campbell ('Gun Court Law'), John Holt ('My Desire') and Derrick Morgan And Hortense Ellis ('Shirley Come Back To Me'), all from Bunny Lee's stable of artists. Alton Ellis's 'Alphabetically Yours' went to Number Two in *Black Music* magazine's charts in August 1974. The label in fact became quite a regular feature in the *Black Music* top 30.

There were also two excellent compilation LPs on Lord Koos, *Have A Grand Time* and *Send Request*, and a John Holt set, *Don't Break Your Promise*, all of which were issued during 1974 with marvellously DIY cover art. A mooted Slim Smith album, probably similar to Trojan's *In Memorial*, appears never to have seen the light of day. The *Send Request* set is interesting in that it contains some fine rocksteady numbers by The Viceroys originally put out on the Island label back in 1968.

Koos wrapped up his label in 1975 and, despite a few link-ups with Linval Thompson and Ossie Hibbert in the late 1970s (for the short-lived Thompson and Koos, and Ossie and Koos labels), appears to have eased out of issuing records. He passed away during the early part of the 1990s.

OUT OF ONE MAN

Larry Lawrence's origins as a UK producer were outlined in the *Boss Sounds* book, but much of his career fell outside its scope. We're pleased to have the opportunity to open things up a bit.

Larry's first retail outlets were in north London's Kensal Green and the Kilburn High Road area between 1973 and 1975 and, as previously noted, he'd been involved in UK production work since 1970 when his earliest sides were featured on a number of Trojan/B&C's subsidiary labels (notably Jackpot and Duke) and Eddy Grant's Torpedo set-up. Largely as a result of his working for Creole Records, Larry soon struck up a special relationship with Lee Perry. Larry's fledgling Ethnic label, which was initially administered through Creole in 1973, was to put out Scratch's excellent 'Fist Of Fury' and 'Mash Finger' 45s as well as Perry's production of Junior Byles' 'Mumbling And Grumbling', a fine sufferahs' tune.

Two further Perry outings on Ethnic were Leo Graham's 'Pampas Judas', one of the eccentric producer's first really esoteric efforts, and the popular 'To Be Your Lover' by the late great Earl 'George' Faith. Ethnic's other successes during this period were The Selectors' 'Rock Back' and 'Jenny Jenny' (with spiritually inspiring vocals courtesy of The Maytals' Jerry Mathias), Sidney Rogers' classic 'Miracle Worker', Jimmy Stratdan's 'So Long Baby', Winston Wright's 'Lucifer' and Larry's own 'King Boxer', which he did under the pseudonym Duke Larry. A couple of compilation albums allegedly saw the light of day, namely *Music Galore* and *Surprise Package*, the latter featuring the trombone talents of Rico Rodriguez, although we've never seen a copy of it.

Ethnic soon became synonymous with quality reggae, although it was often difficult to ascertain whether Lee Perry was on hand when a lot of Larry Lawrence's own (or so the labels stated) productions were laid. A sister label, Fight, emerged briefly late in 1974 and both this imprint and Ethnic were largely supplanted by Ethnic Fight in late 1975. A fair amount of Ethnic Fight's output was very good indeed and is now undergoing a full reappraisal by fans of 1970s reggae. Ones to watch out for are Junior Hibbert's (aka Delgado) 'Reaction' (but was it a Lee Perry or Larry Lawrence production?), Junior Byles' 'Bury-o-Boy', Dennis Alcapone's massive 'Brixton Hall' and

'Pressure In A Babylon', along with its original vocal cut 'Down Presser' credited to Booker T on the label, but actually Nathan Skyers, and the harsh 'Creation' by Joe Higgs.

There were also a number of now collectable dub albums on Ethnic Fight by The Ethnic Fight Band, the label's studio outfit: *Out Of One Man Comes Many Dubs*, *Gold Dust* (featuring one-time Rudies/Cimarons organist Sonny Binns) and *Music Explosion*, along with two compilations, *International Rockers* and *Various Artists Volume One*. By early 1976, Larry had moved his operations south of the river to 336 Coldharbour Lane, Brixton, where he was interviewed briefly by Carl Gayle for the *Aquarius* programme on British reggae. Ethnic carried on into the early 1980s, but its profile had largely diminished by then.

We are pleased to say that Larry is still alive and well and residing in Brixton, where he now runs a West Indian restaurant from his old retail premises. In recent years a number of 45s from his Ethnic empire have begun to appear on a 'Larry's' imprint. The range of titles available certainly shows that he was a key figure in providing both Jamaican and UK reggae for the British audience.

MAGNET RATTLER

Another independent of a reasonable size was Magnet Records, which was established late in 1973 and operated from two retail shops in London's Stoke Newington. There was absolutely no connection with the pop and soul label of the same name and era but it seems amazing that there could have actually been two at precisely the same time. This one evidently predated Pete Waterman's enterprise, as it proudly proclaimed itself 'Magnet – Mark One' in its magazine adverts of the time. The reggae Magnet was run by Russell Coke and, despite some 60 single releases, it was only ever mildly successful. As with Grounation, original ex-factory Magnet stock frequently turns up unplayed today and copies of many titles were being sold via mail order as recently as 1993. Sales-wise, its only real hot-shots in the reggae singles charts were Fay And Matador's 'Sex Grand National' and Denzil Dennis's 'I Had To Let It Out', during the closing months of 1974.

Up-and-coming Jamaican producer Phil Pratt had much of his artists' material released by Magnet before setting up his own shop and labels (Terminal, Chanan-Jah and Sunshot) in London's Hackney area. A lot of Pratt's output from this period was reasonable if, like the whole Magnet label itself, a tad inconsistent, and featured Al Campbell, Max Romeo and The Twinkle Brothers. The other Jamaican producer who had a lot of material out on Magnet was Willie Francis, who had formerly made a showing on several Pama label sides as both producer and singer. His style was very much in the vein of Lee Perry and he, like so many Jamaican production men, surely deserves a serious reappraisal.

UK productions were provided largely by the late Gene Rondo, Mr Coke himself (for two releases only), Carl Anderson, Mike (aka Martel) Robinson, the unknown 'G McTee' and Pete (aka Domino) Johnson. When looked at as a whole, however, the Magnet empire put out a relatively low level of UK product – little more than a third of its entire output, in fact – but still managed to flounder. Perhaps this goes to prove that having authentic Jamaican material is not necessarily a prerequisite for success.

The label did, however, put out some now quite collectable albums, including Keith Hudson's *Entering The Dragon* (easily the rarest), Joe White's Rupie Edwards-produced *Since The Other Day* set, Dennis Alcapone's *King Of The Track* and the mighty Derrick Morgan's *In The Mood*. Singles-wise on Magnet, Alcapone's 'England Here I Come' (which coincided with his successful UK tour of 1974) and Nora Dean's 'Judge Dread Is My Lover' are just about the most sought after, although both are pretty mediocre by all accounts.

Magnet's Faith subsidiary, launched in 1974, was rather better, however, and issued a spread of worthy Jamaican product from Pat Kelly (whose 'Summertime' hit big), Delroy Wilson ('Love Got Me Doing Things'), Bobby Kalphat (the Phil Pratt-produced melodica extravaganza 'Zion Hill') and The Heptones ('Party Time'), and made it through to 1976. Some of its tracks, like Linval Thompson's 'Girl You Got To Run', were apparently among the first sides recorded at Lee Perry's Black Ark studio and, with Scratch mania in full swing, have recently become collectable for that very reason. There is certainly a smattering of pretty good material on Faith but, as with the main Magnet label, you really need to know what to look for since even the Jamaican material can be a bit below par.

Original unplayed albums (but not the aforementioned collectable ones) were until fairly recently being sold in a record shop in Stoke Newington, which is, coincidentally, a short jaunt from the long since demolished Magnet premises. One other point of interest is that a Winifred Coke, very possibly related to the Magnet mainman, had a 12-inch 45 issued on Pama/Jetstar's Star label in the late 1970s. There was also a short-lived quasi-religious subsidiary run by Mr Coke, Trans-Universal, which came about after both the Magnet and Faith labels had folded.

Bang up to date and the Coke family and their Magnet label are once again in business, releasing contemporary material by the likes of Ambelique,

Peter Hunnigale and Lloyd Brown, and reissues such as Gene Rondo's 'Prisoner Of Love' and John Holt's 'Time And The River'. It's even got its own website. Sadly, however, Russell Coke passed away in 2003.

THE HOUSE OF EVE

One-time proprietor of DIP Records in Upper Brockley Road, near New Cross in southeast London, Dennis Harris is, in contrast to players like Count Shelly, Larry Lawrence and Russell Coke, pretty much an enigma. Harris started his working life as a mechanical engineer and as a sideline also organised large outings for West Indian people. By 1971 he had progressed to music and the record business.

His DIP (believed to stand for 'Dennis International Productions') label kicked off in late 1973 with a poorly pressed, strings and all, release by Roy Shirley entitled 'I Fancy You'. Roy had by then settled in London and was recording for Count Shelly, Magnet, Pama and Joe Mansano's Arrow label, and was also chancing his arm with Dennis Harris. This first release was perhaps indicative of a lot of what was to come from DIP: it wasn't quite from the top drawer. Although DIP's output may have been of variable quality, there's no doubt that a good market exists for it today.

Harris's empire showcased several different types of music alongside reggae, including comedy, calypso, doo-wop, R&B, soul and funk. His wife Yvonne, known also as Eve, was also heavily involved in the business. We say 'empire' since there were at one time some 13 labels under DIP's wing – the flagship label plus Black and White, Carifta, Counter Point, Happy Tone, I and I, Shebazz, Stop Point, Western Kingston, PEP, Lucky, Eve and House of Eve. The last two were of course named in honour of Mrs Harris.

Some of these subsidiaries, like Black and White and PEP, were actually imprints originated by certain Jamaican producers (in these cases Carlton Patterson and Rupie Edwards respectively), and their life span was limited to just one single each. This was perhaps an odd arrangement. But, hit and miss as it was, there was some cracking music on these labels, like Johnny Clarke's 'Don't Go' on PEP (utilising The Uniques' 'Out Of Love' rhythm), I Roy's 'I Man Time' on Lucky, The Royals' 'Promised Land' on the main DIP label, Dennis Brown's 'No More Will I Roam' on Sydna and Willie Williams' 'Magic Moment' on Untouchable.

Harris was certainly someone who dabbled in niche markets; he even leased an elderly (and rather good) track from blues legend Louisiana Red to fill out a half-baked compilation album. One of the main reasons that DIP is so eagerly collected today, though, is that it issued a run of Lee Perry 45s and albums. The LPs, hard to find today, were *Kung Fu Meets The Dragon* and *DIP Presents The Upsetter*. Perry provided the label with its biggest singles successes through Susan Cadogan's monster 'Hurts So Good' (which Harris promoted so heavily he almost bankrupted himself before leasing it on, whereupon it charted and sold 300,000 copies) and Junior Byles' classic 'Curley Locks', both of which were released initially on DIP and then licensed to the pop/soul Magnet label after they'd sold so well. 'Hurts So Good' reached Number Four nationally in May 1975 while 'Curley Locks' bubbled under the chart.

This would not be the last time that DIP nearly cracked the UK singles market. TT Ross, who as plain Joan Ross had recorded a worthwhile cover of Freda Payne's 'Band Of Gold' for Pama back in 1970, had a very strong seller on DIP's fledgling Lucky subsidiary with 'Last Date' late in 1975. This was also leased to another major label, this time Polydor. The problem of a lack of national distribution meant that, unable to cope with such strong demand for a particular title, the small independent was compelled to attract the attention of a major UK company. The viewpoint of the artists concerned, though, might be that the producer merely passed a tune on to a larger concern in order to reap even further financial reward from it, and there may be some justification for this opinion.

Aside from Lee Perry, DIP also put out material by producers Rupie Edwards, Niney (Winston Holness), Winston Edwards, Yabby You (Vivian Jackson), Alvin Ranglin, Bob Mack (alias George McLean), Roy Cousins, and Channel One's Joe Joe Hookim, credited as 'Joe Hokin'. On the UK side, the label featured producers such as Mike Dorane (or 'MJD'), Ranfold (Ranny) Williams and Gene Rondo. For Niney's weird 'Zuki-Zaki', which was little more than an instrumental version of Dennis Brown's 'Westbound Train' with strange nonsense singing over it, Harris put ads in *Black Music* proclaiming the arrival of 'a new dance'. This was creative thinking certainly.

More often than not, Dennis Harris was the console controller on the UK productions since, unusually for a small indie label, DIP had its own recording studio, Eve Studios, above its retail shop. In the best traditions of Coxson Dodd and Duke Reid in Jamaica, Dennis held Sunday-afternoon auditions there with the aim of attracting new talent and recording the successful acts on DIP labels. Some significant names in UK roots reggae laid down early tracks at Eve: I Jah Man Levi (the first, pre-Island, cut of 'Jah Heavy Load'), The Blackstones, Dennis Bovell And Matumbi and Steel Pulse. There were also some Eve Studios discoveries who just came and went, never to be heard from again, like George Williams (with a cover of Charlie Rich's 'Behind

Closed Doors'), Larry Knight ('You Can't Go'), Shirley ('The Harder The Battle') and Afro Connection ('African Woman').

Interviewed by Steve Barrow for *Black Echoes* in 1976, Harris spoke of I Jah Man's 'Jah Heavy Load' and the astounding dub side to the single: 'I helped to produce the thing...along with the other single "I'm A Levi", which is equally good in my opinion. He is an artist of immense talent, though whether he'll be able to make another "Jah Heavy Load" we shall just have to wait and see.' The wild dub side, he adds, was mixed by 'myself and Steve Wadey, who has always been my engineer. He's an English guy who is more in to reggae than anybody I can think of...I don't think there's anybody in this country as good. Most of the English-produced reggae hits were made through Steve – things like Ginger Williams' "I Can't Resist Your Tenderness" – Steve had a hand in that from the days when he had his own studio at Bury Street.'

Harris was by then concentrating on releasing UK recordings as opposed to continuing to buy in Jamaican product. 'The studio was primarily built because of my faith in the music of this country. I resented people coming over [from Jamaica] with bags of tapes, not realising how difficult it was to market in this country...we can produce our own. Moreover, there are lots of young singers and musicians who I felt needed a break, and who I felt could do as good a job as anyone. I therefore decided to look to England for the music, because when you consider that the average youth – 95 per cent don't know the West Indies – they are here, they are black, yet they are English as the man born within the sound of Bow Bells, and what a man's singing down Trenchtown really don't have any significance for them apart from the rhythm.'

There clearly must have been some animosity towards Harris from certain quarters: witness the Larry Lawrence-produced 'Straight To DIP Head Dub' on Ethnic Fight (EF 22b) by The Ethnic Fight Band, and The Blackstones' 'Straight To DIP Chest' on Sunshot (SS 10b), the latter perhaps echoing dissatisfaction with the label's treatment of the band in respect of their debut single, the rootsy 'Can't Get No Money' on Lucky.

The enterprising DIP also launched its own fan club from its shop – members' cards heralded 'You Are Now Entering DIP Country' – and issued around 20 albums, some of which came without custom sleeves and were pressed in decidedly limited quantities. Most of these are now considered among the finest roots and dub LPs of their era, particularly those by Jah Lloyd (*Herbs Of Dub*), Tommy McCook (*Reggae In Jazz*), Yabby You And The Prophets (*Ram-a-Dam*), Rico And The Upsetters (*Musical Bones*), and the Winston Riley-produced *Concrete Jungle Dub* on the label's Concrete Jungle subsidiary.

Beware, though, of a comedy effort by Charlie Hyatt (*Kiss Me Neck Again*) and a religious selection (*Sounds Of The Bibleway*). The most common LP on DIP is a one-side-soul/R&B, other-side-reggae compilation entitled *Only One Of Its Kind*.

By the middle of 1977, it had become rare to see DIP, its principal subsidiary Lucky and any of the company's other associated labels in the reggae singles listings. Harris was soon to capitalise on the burgeoning interest in lovers rock however, with his appropriately named Lover's Rock imprint. As usual, these productions were recorded economically at Eve Studios. Harris almost never utilised back-up singers, brass, organ or any other embellishments, which is why so much of what he produced sounds pretty sparse to say the least. With lovers rock groups, though, the harmony voices at least gave him the opportunity to fill out the sound. Dennis Bovell was often involved with these sessions, as was John Kpiaye, a brilliant UK session guitarist who had also laid down tracks for Magnet. In the *Black Echoes* interview, Harris named his studio band as 'session musicians – John [Kpiaye] on lead guitar, Ronnie on rhythm, Delroy on piano, and Bunny and Floyd from The Undivided Band on drums and bass. I've experimented with various permutations of these musicians on all my later records.'

Harris's new label hit paydirt immediately with the three-girl group Brown Sugar, a Sunday audition discovery that consisted of Pauline (surname lost to time), Carolyn Caitlin and Caron Wheeler, future star of '80s outfit Soul II Soul. Their 'I'm In Love With A Dreadlocks', a cover of Barbara Lewis's 'Hello Stranger' and the superb 'Black Pride' formed a hat trick of releases that all reached high positions in the reggae chart.

While Brown Sugar may have been the label's star act, Lover's Rock also scored significant hits with Carolyn (Caitlin) And Roland (covers of Larry Marshall's 'I Admire You' and Paul Anka's 'You're Having My Baby'), Cassandra (with 'If You're Not Back In Love By Monday') and TT Ross (with a cover of Ruby Winter's 'I Will'). The last two artists had moved over from the Lucky label, which had been wound up by that stage. All these titles are considered classics of their genre and have yet to see reissue on CD. 'It's a pity that people like myself have to resort to cover versions of soul hits only because of the lack of exposure in the media,' mused Dennis Harris. Our reggae [version] sells because a soul version is in the chart and getting airplay.'

While the Lover's Rock imprint had in many respects restored DIP to its 1974–75 status, Brown Sugar would express dissatisfaction with what royalties they had received from DIP in a September 1978 *Black Music* article. By mid-1978, the group had left Harris and decamped 50 yards down the road to

Joe Gibbs' Record Globe, a recently opened record shop managed by Gibbs' business associate Winston Edwards (who was also, as we shall see, a one-time business associate of Dennis Harris). Edwards ran his new Studio 16 label from there and a couple of Brown Sugar's Lover's Rock label releases were soon reissued on that imprint, although a fabled debut album never materialised. The group later recorded a one-shot 45 ('Our Reggae Music') for national label Decca without notable success.

Copying the Jamaican style of issuing a pre-release limited press of a record, Harris also launched a UK 'pre' label called Rama (taken from the name of a classic US doo-wop label). This was intended to provide a mechanism for promoting 'advance' copies of DIP material to hype up interest and, more significantly, to make the music appear as though it had originated in Jamaica. Dennis Bovell and Matumbi material appeared on this imprint using the *nom de plume* The 4th Street Orchestra. 'Ah Who Say? Go Deh!', 'Leggo, A Fe We Dis', 'Yuh Learn' and 'Scientific Higher Ranking Dub' were all big sellers in the reggae album charts, with punters unaware that the music was actually recorded in southeast London. In particular, 'Ah Who Say' was marketed in the sort of 'white label' minimal packaging normally associated with pre-releases.

It took Penny Reel, reggae correspondent of the weekly black music paper *Black Echoes*, to suss out what was going on and blow the whistle. There were also some Dennis Harris productions issued on Rama that later saw release on Lover's Rock. Brown Sugar's 'I'm In Love With A Dreadlocks' was pressed in the UK with a Rama label, Ja pre-style, and sold at a pre-release price, even though a few months later it could be bought on the formal Lover's Rock label for the price of a standard UK 45. This was by no means an uncommon practice, as Pama had run a 'Pama Pre-Release' series some six years previously.

DIP and its subsidiary labels seem to have disappeared from the reggae business by the end of 1978, and its apparent demise has never been properly explained. Its appeal enhanced by this aura of mystery, DIP is one of the most fascinating and appealing mid-1970s reggae indie labels to collect. For instance, in among gremlins like Sugar And Sweet's 'Indeed I Love You' on Lucky (which is as bad as the title suggests), D Miller's limp 'Faith Can Move Mountains' on Untouchable and Audrey Johnson's poor calypso 'Fire Fire' on Eve, you'll occasionally turn up really good things like Dillinger's 'Pack Up Your Troubles And Run' and George Dekker's 'They Cannot' (both on Concrete Jungle), Amigo's 'Judas A No Rasta' (on Lucky) and the stupendous 'Black Snowfall' and 'Soldier Round The Corner' by Jah Ali (both on DIP).

Look out, too, for the rocking R&B of male/female duo Sugar And Spice's 'Hey Jojo' on Stop Point: if it sounds dated, that's because it was recorded by Aladdin Records in Los Angeles in the mid-1950s, and its appearance on a DIP label is one of those enigmas that may now never be unravelled. So the music issued by Mr Harris's group of labels really is a bit of a lucky dip (no pun intended). It's all a matter of personal taste, of course, but some things you'll listen to and wonder how they were ever expected to sell. Others are moderate and some, particularly the Perry-produced sides, are rarely less than brilliant.

It isn't clear what happened to Dennis Harris since, like his DIP empire, he seemed to vanish without trace at the end of the 1970s. Usually, such people resurface somewhere or other on the reggae scene, as with the Coke family, but not so with this man. During a recent surf of the Internet, however, we stumbled across the transcript of an interview between Ranking Miss P and Dennis Bovell. Bovell specifically refers to the role that he, Dennis Harris and John Kpiaye played in defining the term 'lovers rock' and creating the label of the same name. Bovell also refers to Dennis Harris as 'dearly departed', so it seems that he is unfortunately no longer with us.

THE NEW BIG THREE?

This now brings us to the three labels that actually kick-started the new reggae explosion immediately after the collapse of Trojan: Vulcan (headed by ex-Ashanti and Bamboo boss Junior Lincoln together with Webster Shrowder, Trojan's ex-managing director), Klik (headed by two of Trojan's old hands, Des Bryan and Joe Sinclair, who had also been part of the Bush production team) and Sound Tracs (headed by Rupert Cunningham, formerly Junior Lincoln's right-hand man at Ashanti/Bamboo and a one-off singles artist for Trojan's Duke subsidiary in 1970). All three were launched during the second half of 1975.

So far as Lincoln was concerned, the collapse of B&C meant that he had no distribution for his Ashanti label. Having no formal distribution network for a reggae label – or any label – was a serious matter indeed. Therefore, together with Shrowder, ex-B&C man Bob Gilbert and Trojan's former PR director Chips Richards, he set about forming Vulcan (it was initially to be called Viking) in conjunction with major record company Phonogram, whose financial muscle and prestige in the marketplace gave Vulcan the clout it needed to do deals with the artists and producers it chose (since Phonogram also pressed Vulcan's discs, the quality of them was pretty good too). The main Vulcan label tended to concentrate on slightly more commercially slanted material with crossover potential, and had single releases out by Zap Pow,

Tommy McCook and Sharon Forrester. Ironically, though, its main claim to fame was to be Fred Locks' classic *True Rastaman* album, a set with real roots credibility.

Johnny Clarke and Cornel Campbell, two of the hottest talents in Bunny Lee's star-studded stable of artists, featured heavily on Vulcan's earliest releases. Both were prime exponents of riding Lee's innovative and influential 'flying-cymbals' rhythm, and Clarke had already enjoyed a massive reggae hit with 'Move Out A Babylon' (aka 'Move Up Rastaman') on the pre-Rodd Trojan's Harry J label, which by then no longer exclusively catered for Harry Johnson product. Similarly, Campbell was already an established performer who had recorded for Lee for several years. On the UK side, Vulcan signed The Cimarons from the old Trojan where they'd often been cajoled into recording do-overs of pop and soul hits under the aliases The Maroons and The Love Children. The group had really wanted to lay down some more rootsy material, however, and this was to come with the release of their *On The Rock* album, a small element of which was recorded at the Black Ark.

Vulcan's sister label, Grounation, dealt to a large extent with the roots side of the music, but ironically turned out to be the more successful of the two. Such success was, though, relatively brief and limited to only a dozen or so of its 45s (a seemingly inexhaustible unplayed supply of its many non-sellers can still be picked up with remarkable ease today). Aside from Bunny Lee, the bulk of Grounation's material was provided by Tommy Cowan, and by Norman Grant of The Twinkle Brothers.

Over 60 singles were issued on Grounation alone during a period of about a year (overkill at roughly five releases a month), and much of the material was surely several months old by the time it saw the light of day. In particular, Bunny Lee's flying-cymbals sound had become a bit dated by mid-1976 and the Channel One 'rockers' style had largely overtaken it in the popularity stakes. Junior Lincoln had obviously licensed a job-lot of the former and this, coupled with the fact that much of the label's music wasn't exactly from the top drawer anyway, meant that Grounation did not prosper for long. The company's album releases, however, notably the dub set *Grounation Dub*, Joe Higgs' *Life Of Contradiction*, The Twinkle Brothers' *Rasta Pon Top* and I Roy's *Truths And Rights*, are superb. By this time, though, Island and Virgin had begun issuing reggae in large quantities; Vulcan and Grounation appeared to flounder and were not to last beyond the early part of 1977.

On the whole, Lincoln's operation appears to have been the least successful of the three new companies when taking into account how much material it actually put out, and the quality of that music.

As for Klik, Joe Sinclair and Des Bryan certainly had a great deal of kudos within the UK reggae business. Both had been directors of B&C's Muzik City chain of shops (by then effectively defunct), had been partners in Bush Productions and, through Bush, had ties with Bunny Lee. Sinclair had also been involved with Junior Lincoln and Rupert Cunningham at Ashanti for a time. Sinclair and Bryan set up a small retail shop in Harlesden, and their big splash was the first album release – Big Youth's massive *Dread Locks Dread*, to which they had acquired the rights from Prince Tony Robinson in the face of strong competition from other labels. This was really quite a coup for Klik. 'That sold 50,000 copies by me mainly travelling round,' recalls Joe Sinclair. 'Unfortunately, *Negril* [another album Klik put out, which had distinct jazz overtones] didn't do well although I had major chart hopes for it.'

Running alongside the main Klik label were the Angen and Caribbean subsidiaries. The latter was a curious creature in that Count Shelly had administered a Caribbean imprint back in 1974, with a mirror-image label design that had also been utilised for a random handful of releases on his Count Shelly label. At a glance, the two Caribbean labels hardly look different from each other.

Klik was soon to do well with a series of Tapper Zukie 45s, which included 'MPLA' (the biggest by far), 'Ten Against One' and 'Pick Up The Rockers'. There were also sizeable hits with Susan Cadogan's Lee Perry-produced 'Congratulations' and Cornel Campbell's 'The Mighty Gorgon', one of a series of 'Gorgon' discs by the singer.

Klik's Angen subsidiary sadly faltered after hits by Cornel Campbell ('Talking Love') and The Admirals ('Natty Should Be Free') and made no real headway after that. Caribbean, on the other hand, had a very big seller (reggae top three) with John Holt's 'Winter World Of Love'. Other sizeable hits on the imprint were Max Romeo's 'Heads A Go Roll', Delroy Wilson's 'My Cecilia' and Trinity's 'Natty On The Banking'. There is also a bona fide curiosity, and rarity, on the label in the form of The Skatalites' 'Franco Nero', tucked neatly away on the flip side of I Roy's 'War And Friction'.

The bulk of Klik's LP releases maintained a very high musical standard, with titles released by Tapper Zukie (*MPLA*), John Holt (*Before The Next Teardrop Falls*), Cornel Campbell (*Natty In A Greenwich Farm*), Willie Lindo (*Far And Distant*), The Abyssinians (*Forward On To Zion*) and U Brown (*Satta Dread*). There were other, less high-profile, sets by a reformed Slickers (recorded in Tokyo), the previously mentioned Negril (including US jazz guitarist Eric Gale), The Equators and Bunny Scott. The label's *Klikers* compilation really does feature some of the best singles from the subsidiary labels, so the company certainly wasn't selling the punters short with that one. Bunny Lee and Lee Perry-produced material was quite abundant in Klik's initial release schedules, but dried up pretty quickly thereafter.

On the whole, Klik probably tended to be more successful in the albums market. This was lucrative if healthy sales were being generated on most titles but, LPs being relatively expensive to put out, there was a considerable financial risk involved for a small company like Klik. Unfortunately for Bryan and Sinclair, a number of the label's albums, particularly the Negril, Bunny Scott, Slickers, Judge Dread and Equators' sets, never exactly became blockbusters. In the singles market, it generally relied on just a few big-selling names.

Klik also made a failed attempt to enter the soul market with the issue of a number of UK-produced disco singles, which bombed completely. The label's last couple of releases were reissues by Tapper Zukie and The Abyssinians, which appeared on a newly designed label heralding 'Klik Chart Sounds 2001'; these were making a reappearance after only about a year. Klik was off the scene by the close of 1977. The following year, Virgin picked up Youth's *Dread Locks Dread* set but this is more likely to have come from Mr Buchanan himself rather than anyone associated with Klik.

The third label, Sound Tracs, was already established in both Jamaica and New York and was run jointly by producer Geoffrey Chung and Bob Andy of 'Bob And Marcia' fame. Cunningham was to run the UK arm of the label which, given its origins, not surprisingly featured 100 per cent Jamaican product. Cunningham was at the time still involved in the second series of the former Ashanti/Bamboo Tropical label, which he handled alongside Sound Tracs and two new subsidiaries, Second Tracs and Treble C. The distribution was by Ed Kassner's President Records, formerly a hit-making pop label but noted in the 1970s for offering good high-street distribution to a myriad of indie labels.

Album releases on Sound Tracs were limited to just three: Max Romeo's *Revelation Time*, Pablo Moses' *Revolutionary Dream* and Bob Andy's *The Music Inside Me*. All are classic, in-demand albums, and curiously the last two were also originally slated for release on Klik. Neither Sound Tracs nor its sister label Second Tracs had much luck in the singles market, however. Sound Tracs placed the funky 'Mango Walk' by The Crowd (a Geoffrey Chung production) and Carol Brown's 'Touch Me Baby' in the reggae top ten, while Second Tracs made only one significant impact with The Abyssinians' 'Tenayistillin Wandamae'.

Treble C had plenty of good material that seemed to get overlooked in the rush, including Shorty The President's 'Beast From The East', The Chantells' wonderful 'Eva', Augustus Pablo's 'Dubbing Pablo' and Dirty Harry Hall's 'Djamballa'. The imprint's only really big sellers were Pablo Moses' 'Blood Dunzer' and 'I Man A Grasshopper'.

With a strange irony, though, it was the already existent Tropical that did better than Sound Tracs and its new subsidiaries. Following its relaunch around mid-1974, its original palm-tree design replaced by a snappy yin-yang logo, Tropical had done notably well with several sides (most were produced by Geoffrey Chung), which included Hortense Ellis's great 'Woman In the Ghetto', Lloyd Parks' 'Ghetto Guns', Cedric Brooks' version of Hamilton Bohannon's 'South African Man' and Mikey Chung's 'Mr Shim'. In early 1976, Paul Davidson's 'Midnight Rider' became a UK top ten hit. The unknown Davidson was actually a white guy who seems to have come out of nowhere (though on a subsequent single he informed listeners that he was born and raised in poverty in Kingston), and the record, though reggae, displayed a strong white rock influence.

The national success for Tropical was not to last beyond this one tune, however, and Davidson sank back into obscurity. 'Midnight Rider' was just one of several reggae releases to do well in the UK that year. Others included Pluto Shervington's 'Dat' on NEMS' Opal subsidiary and Barry Biggs' 'Side Show' and 'Work All Day', both of which were on Creole's UK arm of Byron Lee's Dynamic label. Tropical also put out Augustus Pablo's groundbreaking debut LP *This is...*, which was slightly affected by Ja pre-release sales but still moved a good few units. Like Klik and Vulcan, though, Cunningham's Sound Tracs company disappeared after only a couple of years, although two of its three albums resurfaced later on another label: Different. It seems that Cunningham had shut up shop and relicensed the material to Different, a label that covered other musical forms as well as reggae.

RETURN OF THE HOUSE OF PAMA

Pama is covered earlier in this book, but needs a mention here since, through either ingenuity or sheer opportunism, it resurrected itself as a 'new' company during the year of Trojan's collapse and is therefore within the time frame of this chapter. The company maintained that it had never in fact gone away but had merely withdrawn from releasing reggae due to uncertainty over the direction the music was taking. It largely attributed this to the burgeoning DJ sounds of the early 1970s, and the difficulties it was having in dealing (double-dealing?) with Jamaican producers.

Pama's relaunch offered some top-flight sounds; for a few months it was almost like the old days of 1969–70 as record after record from the company hit home like a missile, notably 'Tonight Is The Night' by Claudette Miller (on Ocean), Gregory Isaacs' 'Lonely Days' (on the revived Bullet label), Pat Kelly's 'Sing About Love' and Justin Hinds' 'Sinners Where Are You Gonna Hide', both of which saw release on the main Pama label. Its new-found success was limited to only around six months, though, and the relaunch was probably seen as a stop-gap by the few producers, who seemingly leased material to it until something better materialised. Despite sporadic comebacks in the late 1970s with material by The Marvels, Tito Simon and Owen Gray, and a 12-inch reissue of Max Romeo's 'Wet Dream', Pama concentrated instead on distribution and evolved into Jetstar.

Although a few other, still smaller, labels briefly showed their heads above the parapet during the mid-1970s (who could forget Nationwide?, whose logo acknowledged the optimism of its name by putting a question mark after it), those were the major players of the era. What they all had on their side was that they were launched, or revived, immediately following the collapse of Trojan. All were able to blow their own trumpets more audibly than before in the media, for the profile of reggae had greatly improved since the early '70s, chiefly as a result of the new *Black Music* monthly magazine, launched to immediate acclaim in 1973, and later the equally popular weekly *Black Echoes*, which hit the news-stands in March 1976. Leaving aside Pama, the people involved had all, one way or another, been involved with Trojan or B&C, or both, and could claim to have some clout in the reggae business, and not just at grass-roots level either.

They were already waiting in the wings to swoop into the void left by Trojan's demise. No doubt the three newcomers felt able to say, 'We've been at the coal face, seen the problems and reckon we can do it better.' With the benefit of hindsight, however, we can see that, wary of a Trojan-type scenario, the cream of Jamaica's producers were cannily putting their eggs in more than one basket to avoid becoming reliant on one major UK outlet. They were certainly able to place their masters more widely this time and, as is apparent, there was a significant amount of, shall we say, cross-fertilisation going on (The Abyssinians actually appeared on all three of the new labels). Sound Tracs was probably the saddest loss since it never churned out the same old flying-cymbals sound but instead tried to be a tad more innovative and carried really authentic Jamaican music from the top drawer of the island's musical talent. Of all these labels, it offered the most killer and the least filler.

5 London's Reggae Rulers

By the 1970s, a community of reggae singers, players, writers and producers – and some who were all these things at once – had established itself in London. Their stories are often intertwined, as many of them played on each other's records, sang for other producers, produced other singers and so on. Some were already industry veterans; others rose to prominence and maintained long and distinguished careers; a few had careers that flickered brightly for a few months or years, only to wane thereafter. Between them, they raised the flag of UK reggae and kept it flying, often against all the commercial odds. In alphabetical rather than merit order, here they are...

LAUREL AITKEN

First and foremost, enter the great man Laurel Aitken. We've already covered much of his earlier days in the business in previous chapters but little of his 1970s career has been written about and it's well worth documenting.

After 1971 and the decline of the skinheads, Laurel's 'boss reggae' sounds pretty much fell out of favour and he began recording in a much sweeter style, often styling himself as Lorenzo. Seemingly leasing less material to Pama, he started doing more with Trojan where he had a near-miss in the national charts with 'It's Too Late (To Say That You're Sorry)' on the main Trojan label and a couple of singles on Big Shot. There was also a commercial one-off shot with EMI's outmoded Columbia label, namely 'Pretty Face (In The Market Place)', which sank without trace. He was involved too with Ian Smith and his Hot Lead label at various times between 1972 and 1974 and continued to be in big demand as a live act.

Laurel was continuing to record himself and other artists (often utilising Rico Rodriguez's talents) at his own studio sessions, leasing the tracks to Trojan or Pama, and pressing them up with blank labels to promote himself. The matrix for these was usually 'LA SP', and from our experience these blanks never generally gained formal release by any of the companies. Another blank label matrix associated with Laurel is 'PEP'. For one reason or another, his own label – apparently to be called Faith – never materialised, although a blank-label issue of Tiger's 'Guilty' did appear on it. In fact, it would be nigh on impossible to collect a complete set of Laurel's releases from this period as there were so many 'unofficial' waxings around. A particularly good one is Laurel And Girlie doing a thing called 'Hot Pants Parade' on an LA SP matrix.

In 1973 Laurel leased a number of tracks to Count Shelly, who was busying himself with launching his new Count Shelly empire during this time, and had an entire album issued on the label, *Maria Sophia*, and a stringsed-up single 'What Must I Do' (as Tony Lorenzo). A couple of his tracks also appeared on Shelly's *Return To Me* compilation album. Over the next few years, Laurel placed material with leading London independents like Jama and DIP. His biggest successes by far during this period were the 1969 recordings 'Saturday Night' (as Lorenzo) on Harry J, issued during 1974, and 'Baby Baby' (with Eva Marie) on DIP the following year.

Criticism has been levelled at both Trojan and Pama for never working to develop or properly market their artists, but merely sell their records. While some, like Winston Groovy and The Marvels, did have consistent runs of releases while at both companies, after Trojan and Pama had ceased operations it became even worse, since the smaller outlets were more or less working hand to mouth. That's essentially the situation in which Laurel found himself: placing bits and pieces here and there with this company or that. At that time, however, the older established artists like Laurel were having a hard time of it as the mid-1970s West Indian younger generation were more into The Mighty Diamonds, Carl Malcolm and Big Youth than the older artists. Laurel did his best, though, with a version of 'Fatty Bum Bum' (covering the hip Carl Malcolm on Pama's revived Punch label) and the answer tune 'Fatty Bum Bum Gone To Jail' (on Trojan's Horse subsidiary) – an odd case of putting two related tunes with two rival companies.

In 1977, Laurel once again looked like launching his own label, this time called Karlene, but a solitary issue, 'Rebel Woman', never seemed to get beyond the white label stage. A couple of lean years followed but, luckily, the close of the '70s saw the emerging Two-Tone explosion and its associated skinhead revival, and he was again in demand far and wide for club dates, as well as at last scoring a small, long overdue hit with 'Rudi Got Married'.

Thankfully it's stayed that way ever since. Across the whole of Europe, and further afield, Laurel still performs to packed houses and, now in his mid-70s, easily outdoes the younger bucks for sheer energy, verve and enthusiasm. His recording career really picked up again from around 1985 with releases featuring collaborations with Gaz Mayall and the Potato Five. A few of these, like 'Sally Brown' and 'Skinhead', have rivalled his vintage late '60s output in the popularity stakes.

DENNIS BOVELL

Dennis Bovell, also known as Blackbeard, is probably best known among reggae fans for his involvement with Matumbi, one of the UK's most successful reggae groups of the 1970s. But he was not merely a musician, he was also a noted producer and operated several independent reggae labels, later moving into more mainstream pop/rock production work. He was also involved in running the legendary Jah Sufferer sound system.

Matumbi formed in 1971, basically as a backing band to vocalist (and future lovers rock star) Tex Dixon. The south London band took their name from the African word meaning 'rebirth', and started their long career not only backing Dixon, but many other visiting and London-based reggae performers. The original line-up consisted of Dixon, Dennis Bovell on guitar, Errol Pottinger (guitar), Etan Jones (drums) and Bevin 'Bagga' Fagan, Glaister Fagan and Nicholas Bailey all taking vocal chores alongside Tex.

They recorded for Trojan during the 1972–73 period: 'Wipe Them Out' on Duke, 'Brother Louie' (complete with a rocking DJ version, which Joe Sinclair credits to Bovell on the microphone, on the flip) on GG and 'Reggae Stuff', a particularly inspired reading-in-reggae of Kool And The Gang's massive funk record 'Funky Stuff', on Horse. Trojan didn't, however, do the band any sort of justice, rejecting their self-composed material and compelling them to record mostly cover versions of chart hits. After Bovell had been released on appeal from a prison sentence (as the result of a trumped-up 'incitement to cause affray' charge), the group forged links with UK sound system operator, Lloyd Coxson.

With Coxson in the producer's seat, the lovers rock-inspired 'After Tonight' was to become an exclusive Coxson dub plate special for several months until it was eventually put out by Reg McLean's new label, Safari, in March 1976, after which it shot to Number One in the UK reggae charts published in the newly launched *Black Echoes*. With a keen eye on its back catalogue, Trojan reacted to the band's success by claiming that Bovell & Co were still under contract to them. Meanwhile, according to Bovell, Coxson had apparently been rather indifferent to the meteoric rise of such a classic tune – reggae's biggest-selling single of 1976 – and there followed a parting of the ways.

The band, feeling hard done by with Trojan, took to recording under various names such as African Stone, under which name they cut the excellent 'How Long Must I Wait' on DIP's Concrete Jungle imprint, and 'Run Rasta Run' for Buster Pearson's K&B label. Trojan, seeing through the subterfuge, agreed not to hold them to their contract.

Never a man to be messed about, Bovell established the aptly named 'Matumbi Music Corp' (MMC) imprint. 'Man In Me', a Bob Dylan composition ideally suited to a reggae treatment, was the follow-up to 'After Tonight' and another top ten reggae hit. Further successes on MMC came with 'Chain Gang' (the old Sam Cooke number) and 'Daughter Of Zion' (an original song by Matumbi member Bevin 'Bagga' Fagan). Trojan had also somehow gained the rights to both 'After Tonight' and 'Man In Me', and reissued them back to back, which must have cut into sales of the Safari and MMC originals. Alongside these Matumbi label releases, DIP's UK pre-release imprint Rama put out the band's first album *A Who Seh? Go Deh!* (as by The Fourth Street Orchestra) which gained top ten status in the reggae album charts. By this time Tex Dixon, Nicholas Bailey and Etan Jones had left the group and Lloyd 'Jah Bunny' Donaldson had come in on drums.

To make the point that UK bands could play roots to the same standard and with the same feel as their Kingston counterparts, Bovell/Matumbi recorded the suitably heavy 45 'Gimmie Gimmie African Love' and released it as The African Brothers on the Mainline label complete with a photocopied lyric sheet tucked in behind the single. It fooled many and was a very in-demand record about town, even after the deception was revealed.

At around this time (late summer 1977), Matumbi were signed by EMI's Harvest label, which soon saw them recording two albums. The first, *Seven Seals*, stands as one of the most accomplished UK-recorded roots reggae albums ever to see the light of day, its standout track being the long and dense 'Rock', which Harvest issued as parts one and two on a 45. By way of contrast, the swinging *Point Of View* mixed reggae with jazz, swing and other influences, and garnered plaudits from mainstream rock critics (the inner sleeve notes also gave the game away about the African Brothers single). Inevitably, though, this transition resulted in the band effectively losing much of its grass-roots following. The title track from *Point Of View* also reached the UK national top 40 and the band supplied the jaunty signature tune for the BBC's *Empire Road* series (set in Birmingham and originally transmitted at the end of 1978).

A couple of heavyweight 12-inch singles were also issued, showcasing the ease with which the group could move from tight lovers rock to the hardest roots reggae. 'Rolling Down The River' (credited to Dennis Matumbi) and the rockers' delight of the double-sided 'Guide Us Jah'/'Music In The Air' tore down many a dance and no doubt split a few bass bins with the patent Matumbi heavy bass work.

With the shift of band members, Matumbi moved on into the early 1980s where they had an album, *Testify*, issued on the Solid Groove label. It was an interesting album as the recordings took place both in London and at Channel One in Kingston. The band's line-up was also interesting, with Etan Jones reappearing on drums (alongside Jah Bunny), percussion and congos, supplemented by the rhythm twins Sly Dunbar and Robbie Shakespeare. Production credits were Etan Jones and Bevin Fagan, with Dennis Bovell just credited as taking a few guitar lines. The music itself was pure Matumbi with hard roots in the shape of 'Ethiopian', through current-style dancehall stepper 'In Brixton', to the taster single 'In Daylight', which emulated the swing of *Point Of View* and hoped for more than it achieved (something that could be said of the whole album, which few bought, but which certainly has its moments).

Bovell's exceptional musical talents were destined to go much wider than reggae and he soon aligned himself with the burgeoning punk/new wave movement, producing the likes of The Slits and The Pop Group. Alongside this, he was involved in running the new Tempus and More Cut labels, and was, perhaps prior to the arrival of Mad Professor Neil Fraser, considered the UK equivalent of Lee Perry with the visionary soundscapes he created.

Spring 1980 found him presiding over *I Wah Dub* on the More Cut label. A double album issued in 1982 by major label Philips, *Brain Damage*, found Bovell mixing styles from roots to soca and pop, with him declaring that he hoped it would 'fry a few crania'. The set was recorded at his own Studio 80 in south London; he not only sang on it but played almost all the instruments, from bass to viola, and of course wrote the whole thing.

Dennis was also instrumental in promoting the career of Linton Kwesi Johnson, the London based dub-poet, whose rebellious rhetoric the white new wavers went for in a big way. The new wave audience identified with LKJ's outspoken political stance, and he was elevated to the stage front of many gatherings and gigs in the post-punk era. Bovell supplied much of the deep and dense rhythm structure over which Johnson's doom-laden voice laid down some home truths for the appreciative rebel audience.

Today, Bovell fronts his own long-standing Dub Band, which is in demand here, there and everywhere. As it is, much of the music he made in the '70s remains to be reissued, leaving fanatics (and there are many, particularly in the Far East) to hunt down that elusive vinyl.

CASTRO BROWN

A larger-than-life character, Castro Brown started out as a DJ for Lloyd Coxson's sound back in 1965. Leaving Coxson in 1969, Brown then spent several years touring the UK as a DJ-cum-MC with the first line-up of The Undivided Band, and also worked as a freelance promoter of reggae shows and acts. During 1973, he took out a lease on the Georgian club in Croydon's Dingwall Road, presenting weekend reggae nights there. He then moved in to record retailing with a shop in nearby Thornton Heath, and launched his Morpheus label from there late in 1975.

Castro had had an earlier association with the unrelated Dennis Brown, possibly dating from the singer's 1974 UK tour. Since Castro was short of money as a result of his various fledgling business ventures, he asked Dennis whether he could help. In a splendid gesture of solidarity, the singer flew to the UK and played five nights at the Georgian – free of charge – and assisted in setting up Morpheus, providing Castro with several of his own tunes and productions for release on the new label. Among these early Morpheus issues were Dennis's own 'Life's Worth Living', Dennis's production of Junior Delgado's 'Every Natty' (credited to 'Jooks'), Michael Rose's pre-Black Uhuru cut of 'Guess Who's Coming To Dinner' (produced by Niney), I Roy And Jackie Brown's 'The Black Bullet' (produced by mid-ranking Jamaican producer Jackie Brown) and Gregory Isaacs' 'Rasta Business', 'Black A Kill Black' and 'Extra Classic'. As can be seen from this little selection, there is indeed some excellent music on Morpheus.

It is a sad irony, however, that such was the success of Morpheus that Castro was unable to cope with the hectic release schedule (issues weren't being sufficiently staggered), the sheer demand for many of the titles and a three-men-in-a-van distribution set-up that was allegedly busy purloining half the takings. In an attempt to take some of the burden off his own shoulders, Castro established a pressing and distribution arrangement with Charlie Gillett's Oval label. Unfortunately, this went pear-shaped after just four releases when Gillett discovered that Castro had also pressed up copies of the same titles on Morpheus – which he'd seemingly only done with the express intention of supplying the smaller specialist outlets himself, and to help try and dig himself out of a financial hole.

So it was, towards the end of 1976, that Castro called Dennis Brown again with a plea for help, and the two of them agreed to streamline and run down Morpheus over the course of the next year. Dennis had, of course, greater experience than Castro of both the record business and of running labels, and the deal was that a new label would ultimately handle all of

137

Dennis's music. With Dennis in Jamaica most of the time, setting up the deals, Castro would be the new label's mission controller back in the UK.

In the meantime, though, the record that really broke Morpheus more than any other on the label was 15-16-17's lovers rock classic 'Blackskin Boy'. The girly threesome (Sonya Williams with sisters Christine and Wraydette McNab) had performed at a talent night at the Georgian as 'The Gorgon Sisters' and, suitably impressed, Castro had recorded them with the assistance of Dennis Bovell. Their Morpheus debut, 'If You Love Me Smile', had pretty much bombed when issued at the end of 1976, but when 'Blackskin Boy' appeared in March 1977, it went right to the top of the reggae listings.

Similarly, the second Morpheus release of 1977 (and the last ever on the imprint) was Dennis Brown's classic 'Here I Come' single – another winner. It should be noted, though, that both of these were probably nominally the first releases on the new label, which was to be called DEB Music (after Dennis Emmanuel Brown) and was formally launched on 5 November 1977. The DEB imprint was at that time already up and running in Jamaica. The Morpheus shop then closed and the new DEB music store opened at 79 Battersea Rise, Clapham Junction.

DEB became synonymous with classic late '70s reggae. With the bulk of the material produced or overseen by Dennis, it was no wonder that it was voted UK Reggae Label of the Year by *Black Echoes* readers. Particular 45 hits included Dennis's own 'The Half' and 'Wolf And Leopards', Bob Andy's 'War In The City', 15-16-17's 'Suddenly Happiness' and Junior Delgado's ''Tition'. Album-wise, the label found its mark with Dennis's *Wolf And Leopards* set, Junior Delgado's *Taste Of The Young Heart*, Gregory Isaacs' *Mr Isaacs* and *Twentieth Century DEBwise* by The DEB Players (a dub album that really took off). A pressing and distribution deal with EMI ensured that DEB products could reach shops nationally. Also, there was a special link-up with music weekly *Black Echoes*, which saw a sampler LP – coincidentally titled *Black Echoes* – sold through the music weekly by mail order at a very low price. (This is well worth getting hold of – if you can find it – since it really did include some tasty 45 titles from the DEB catalogue.)

What a difference a year makes, and late in 1978 a licensing arrangement was forged between DEB Music and Alan Davidson's Lightning label, which saw the release of Dennis's 'Equal Rights', 'How Can I Leave' and the big UK chart hit 'Money In My Pocket'. Following that, Lightning set up the Laser imprint for the majority of its reggae output. Laser had Dennis's *Words Of Wisdom*, *Visions Of Dennis Brown* and *Joseph's Coat Of Many Colours* albums out, and the 'Ain't That Loving You', 'Should I' and 'So Jah Say' singles.

So what became of DEB Music? Basically, it seems to have run down its LP releases (putting them with Lightning/Laser instead) and continued issuing 12-inch 45s aimed largely at the ethnic market. What we were really seeing was Dennis's own material coming through a relatively high-profile label (Lightning had a distribution arrangement with WEA) and his various productions of Jamaican artists coming through DEB. Certain items successful on DEB, like Me And You's 'You Never Know What You've Got' and Black Harmony's 'Don't Let It Go To Your Head', were also leased to Laser in the hope of finding pop success.

DEB appears to have folded by the end of 1980, and the shop closed at about the same time. It isn't clear what happened to Castro in the grand scheme of DEB, but Dennis Brown, of course, continued to be the Crown Prince of Reggae right into the 1980s (although a contract with A&M did not live up to expectations). On the face of it, with the late Dennis's career in the ascendant, DEB seemed to have been rendered pretty superfluous.

Castro has bounced back, though. These days he is in the business of promoting revival sound clashes and the like. Most recently, he was involved with such a clash in Peckham featuring old-time sounds like Duke Neville, Duke Sonny (both among Birmingham's finest in their time), Sir Biggs, Sir Christopher, Neville The Enchanter and Lord Koos, revealing that these sets – or the spirit of them – continue today.

CLEMENT BUSHAY

Like many reggae producers, Bushay started out as an artist, with a single for President in 1972, 'Football Reggae', followed by another for Trojan the following year (a cover of The Small Faces singalong 'Sha La La La Lee' on Explosion). He also produced material for Trojan by Domino Johnson at this time, most notably 'Summertime', which was included on the company's third volume of the *Music House* album series and has since become something of a 'chillout' reggae classic. Bushay had links with Bunny Lee, who sent the wayward young DJ Tapper Zukie over to him during 1973. At least one landmark recording emerged from these sessions – 'Man A Warrior' – which saw release on Lord Koos. Bushay was a bit of an indie king and seemed to be licensing music to quite a few of them at one time or another: Count Shelly, DIP, Conflict and Kiss, for example.

In 1974, Bushay established his Summertime label with assistance and distribution from Count Shelly. The Realms' 'Happiness Is My Middle Name' had quite a bit going for it but pretty much bombed. Following this, a compilation album of his productions, *Dread In Session*, was issued towards the end of 1975, but Summertime was discontinued after that. Having seen some of his material by UK-based artists such as Paulette Williams, Owen Gray, Black Harmony and Junior English put out by Clive Stanhope's Burning Sounds empire, his production of Louisa Marks' 'Keep It Like It Is' on Trojan went into the UK reggae top ten in May 1977. Getting Marks on to his label was something of a coup after she'd left Lloyd Coxson's camp due, it is believed, to bad feeling of some sort. Also highly successful for Bushay at this time was Junior English's 'Never Lose Never Win' 45, and Trinity And Dillinger's *Clash* album on Burning Sounds, which was recorded in the UK.

Bushay set up his own Bushay's imprint in 1978 with the release of Louisa Marks' 'Even Though You're Gone' on a 12-inch disco 45. Distributed by Carib Gems, and with a label image of (presumably) Clement Bushay talking on the phone, Bushay's had a roster featuring most of the really good UK lovers rock artists of the era: Paulette Walker ('Mama Didn't Lie' and 'Is There A Place In Your Heart For Me'), Janet Kay And Rico Rodriguez ('Silhouettes'), Michael Black ('Out Of Love') and Louisa Marks with her superb 'Six Six Street', which he later licensed to Danny Ray's Robot label. There was also a smattering of worthy material by Jamaican artists like Trinity, Prince Jazzbo and Dave Robinson, laid down during spells over here. Clement added Bushranger as a sister label to Bushay's during 1979.

Despite such promising material, Bushay seems to have disappeared from the scene during much of the 1980s. After a gap of several years he released the *Super Power Volume 1* compilation album and another really first-rate selection of his late '70s tracks entitled *Collection Of Gold*, although with ten tracks a side some ruthless editing had obviously been needed to make them all fit. These days, Bushay still lives in London, in the Harlesden area.

BILL AND PETE CAMPBELL

The musical Campbell brothers arrived in Nottingham from Jamaica in the 1960s and formed a band called Mighty Sparrow (no relation to the noted Calypsonian), which built up a worthy reputation throughout the Midlands playing covers of soul tracks. Bill and Pete later moved to London and cut their first single, 'Come On Home Girl', for Trojan's Duke subsidiary in 1971. A number of other singles for Count Shelly followed over the next couple of years until, apparently dissatisfied with the lack of financial reward from their involvement with these labels, they started their own BB imprint in July 1975 ('BB' apparently stood for Bill (Campbell) and Barbara ('Ginger' Williams)). They also opened their own BB Records shop in Askew Road, Shepherd's Bush.

A real 'family and friends' set-up, the BB label was quietly successful over a considerable period and spawned a few really good sellers, including 'Is My Love Too Late?' by Honey Boy (the Campbells' cousin), Bill Campbell's 'Cool It' and Ginger Williams' 'I'll Still Love You'. The brothers added another few labels to their roster over the next couple of years, including Jumbo (believed to have been in association with Hunter Smith's Jumbo record shop in Leeds), Union and JUM (which was marketed as a Jumbo/BB 'pre-release' imprint, though the discs were pressed in Britain). All the tracks produced by the brothers were recorded in the UK and tended towards the easy-on-the-ear lovers rock. Jumbo had some reasonable sellers with Ginger Williams' 'I Must Be Dreaming' and Pete Campbell's 'Heavy Whiner'.

The Campbells' empire continued into the 1980s and the BB label evolved into Black Beat, presumably after Ginger Williams had dropped out of the picture. They also maintained a healthy presence in the Midlands and the north. In quite recent years, the brothers have run the World Sound Organisation label and put out CD releases of their early productions alongside more recent recordings from the likes of Tito Simon and Yvonne Curtis – big people music indeed! By tailoring their music to a limited but well-defined and faithful audience, they have been able to keep on keeping on for three decades while more aggressive, higher-profile labels have risen and fallen around them.

CLANCY COLLINS

Clancy Collins (aka Sir Collins) was a luminary of the UK scene from the very early days, when he ran a sound system and record stall in Petticoat Lane market selling ska and blue beat 45s. He started his Collins Down Beat label during the rocksteady era of 1967, utilising his own productions and those of Bunny Lee, with whom he had an association at this time. He also did a bit of singing himself, as on 'Dry The Water From Your Eyes'. It is not known, however, whether many of the tracks were laid entirely over here or merely used rhythm tracks recorded in Jamaica with the vocals being added in London. Apparently Bunny Lee was over here around this time too. Collins was for many years a regular sound system fixture at the annual Notting Hill Carnival where his effervescent, madcap personality certainly made the proceedings go with a swing.

A number of Collins Down Beat releases are exceptionally good – like The Uniques' 'I'm A Fool For You', Owen Gray's 'I'm So Lonely' and 'Hey Stella' and Lester Sterling with 'Sir Collins' Special'. The several Bob Stackie sides are an unknown quantity, however: we just don't know who this guy was apart from the fact that he was an organist. Collins also launched a very short-lived (one issue only) imprint, called Sounds of Jamaica, in 1968.

Collins Down Beat never made it through to the reggae era, and between 1969 and 1971 he placed product with Trojan, which put out a series of mostly excellent singles on subsidiaries such as Jackpot (including Vincent McLeod's 'Too Late'), Duke (Collins' own blistering 'Black Panther' and 'Brother Moses') and Smash (Merlene Webber's 'Hard Life' and Delroy Wilson's 'Satisfaction'). 'Hard Life', with its crunching rhythm, is perhaps Clancy's best-known production, as it found its way into thousands of homes upon its inclusion on Trojan's *Tighten Up Volume 4*. His studio bands at this time were The Earthquakes, The Diamonds and The Dials, featuring personnel unknown to the authors of this book. Also, during and after 1971, Collins briefly moved his material over to Junior Lincoln's Ackee label prior to establishing his Sir Collins Music Wheel (which we'll call SCMW for short) label in 1973.

SCMW had a big seller towards the end of 1973 with its first release, Collins' production of Honey Boy's 'Fight Life', which had largely been adapted from Delano Stewart's 1968 side 'That's Life'. Other SCMW titles came from Merlene Webber, Gene Rondo and Sir Collins And The Versatiles, and included two four-track extended-play singles – a novelty format for reggae at the time. There was also a compilation album, *Chapter 1*, featuring a fair few covers of then current pop songs voiced by some of his kids, including Leonie and Steve. By 1975, Collins had wrapped up SCMW in favour of the B&C Sound and Nice One imprints. Big Dread's 'Dread Man Music' saw heavy action on the former label.

He was still operating his sound system at the end of the '70s, but tragedy struck early in 1981 when his son Steve died in the New Cross fire. It was anticipated that he would be picking up the sound from his father. By all accounts, Collins was a broken man and, following the issue of a compilation album aimed at raising money for victims of the fire, he seemed to fade from the scene pretty much overnight. Of all the UK production men, precious little of his rich catalogue is available today. A re-press of 'Fight Life' did appear in London shops a couple of years back, and Trojan has reissued a few of the 1969 tracks for its *Skinhead Reggae* and *British Reggae* boxed CD sets.

SIDNEY CROOKS

Largely remembered as one third of The Pioneers, Crooks – more often known as 'Luddy' – settled in the UK with group members George Agard (George Dekker) and Jackie Robinson after the band had hit big with 'Long Shot Kick The Bucket', and established himself as a producer with Pama soon after.

The Pioneers continued recording for Trojan as a group, individual producers and solo performers, and provided a fair slice of the company's bread and butter during the entire 1969–75 period. Crooks was equally prolific for Pama, where he notched up some big sellers such as The Viceroys' 'Chariot Coming' (Bullet), Junior English's 'Jesamine' (Pama) and Eugene Paul's 'Farewell My Darling' (Pama Supreme).

In 1975, following Pama's withdrawal from the market and Trojan's collapse, Crooks leased some product to Eddy Grant's revived Torpedo label by artists including TT Ross, Gregory Isaacs and Tyrone Taylor. Following this seemingly stop-gap measure, Crooks then set up his own Pioneer label in 1976, soon followed by the Doctor and Golden Age subsidiaries (Golden Age was the name of Pioneer's music publishing company), working in particular with Danny Ray. This pair produced a significant seller in the relentless political manifesto 'Under Heavy Manners' by one Agro Pearson, who was in fact long-serving singer, producer and committed socialist Clancy Eccles. Sidney also established the Golden Age Music record shop in Harlesden.

Early in 1977, The Mexicano – actually Eddy Grant's brother David – shot to number one in the reggae top 30 with 'Move Up Starsky' on Pioneer, a production Crooks did jointly with Clement Bushay. Backed by a UK-laid rhythm track utilising Delroy Wilson's 'I'm Still Waiting', the toaster issued instructions in the latest Jamaican jargon about 'heavy manners and heavy discipline'. It was such a strong seller that it was picked up as a possible national hit by Pye's Baal label and subsequently reissued by Eddy Grant's Ice label. There was also a sister (or maybe brother) version on Doctor by UK DJ (Ranking) Superstar entitled 'Move Up Hutch', which shifted a few units around mid-1977.

Only Crooks' Pioneer label (renamed Pioneer International) was active by the early 1980s. He was also putting his album productions, notably Owen Gray's Hit After Hit series, with Adrian Sherwood's Carib Gems/Angstar outfit, which was located just around the corner from Golden Age. He then began issuing music in the USA in association with Alfred Abrahams, who would release it on his Abrahams' and Luddy's labels. Crooks' productions were by then largely of the medley variety and firmly aimed at the older West Indian market. This style culminated in a series of *Reggae For Lovers* LP volumes for Jeffrey Collins' Vista Sounds empire in the early '80s, which again saw him teamed with George Agard and Jackie Robinson.

Having operated his own UK studio for many years, Crooks returned to Jamaica a few years ago to take up the role of in-house producer and arranger at his old sparring partner Joe Gibbs' studio.

WINSTON CURTIS

Winston came to the UK from Jamaica in 1967 and settled in Nottingham. Prior to this, he had apparently sung with The Clarendonians. He spent several years with a band called The Favourites, and linked up with local brothers Bill and Pete Campbell. Moving to London, he cut his first singles for the Count Shelly and Cactus labels in 1973, 'Never Get Away' and 'Didn't You Know' respectively. Undoubtedly, he possessed a fine voice and his material was clearly aimed at the twenty- to thirtysomething West Indian audience. Some of it was self-penned but he specialised in reviving songs that were long-time favourites with his intended market. Together with Ginger Williams, Bill and Pete Campbell, Gene Rondo, Honey Boy, Denzil Dennis, Fermena Williams and numerous others, Winston formed part of a coterie of West Indian-born, UK-based reggae performers. Many of them either recorded or produced material for each other's various labels – it was a very incestuous business.

Winston produced a lot of his own material himself and tunes like 'Freedom Train', 'Send You' (both on Shelly's Penguin imprint) and 'Private Number' (on the Campbells' BB label) were big reggae hits during 1975. He also produced and recorded in collaboration with Honey Boy, with whom he also duetted on versions of the perennial favourites, Jerry Butler's 'Let It Be Me' and Doris Troy's 'What You Gonna Do About It'. Both discs hit the reggae top ten in 1976. The latter had been issued on his Empire label, which was part of Winston's new Empire Recording Co set-up. Empire also spawned the Diamond, Supreme, Jungle Beat and (in association with Les Cliff) Jah Lion offshoots.

Winston opened his Empire Records shop in Stoke Newington around early 1977 and over the next three years issued a series of albums by himself, Honey Boy and Samantha Rose. Many of the tracks were laid at the nearby Coach House Studio in Osbalderston Road; this studio was owned by Eddy Grant and increasingly competing with Chalk Farm Studios in terms of British-recorded reggae.

Empire seems to have closed its operations by the early part of the '80s. An Empire label did exist around 1983–84 but it is believed to be related to a non-UK concern. Sometime in the 1990s, Winston went on to run the Business Record Store in Dalston, which was later taken over by M&D Records when its shop in Dalston Lane was demolished. According to Keith Stone, Winston is now working as a London bus driver.

MIKE DORANE

One of black music's nearly men, who richly deserved success but never quite found it, Mike Dorane (sometimes known as 'MJD') is worthy of mention as a vocalist (falsetto a speciality), producer, session musician and multi-instrumental artist (he played practically everything), although he never really became a leading light in the British reggae business.

Born in the USA of Native American and Jamaican parentage, Mike started out with a soul band in the mid-1960s, which had two top ten hits in Germany. Having apparently blown all his royalties, he then came to the UK in the early 1970s, working as a session bassist for Pama. He also produced himself on a number of sides, the first being 'Funky Penguin' on Junior Lincoln's Ackee label early in 1972, on which he was accompanied by The Cimarons in their funk mode. Two major successes followed in 1974, when 'Loving You' and the similarly titled 'Loving You Just The Same' (both on DIP) hit the reggae top ten. He also recorded the wonderful but unrecognised wah-wah-fuelled 'The Ghetto' (on the second series of Lincoln's Ackee label). Seemingly hyperactive during this period, he teamed up with Gene Rondo to produce and record tracks for Magnet's *Reggae Desire* compilation album. Post-Magnet, he put a couple of overlooked and poorly marketed singles with Trojan's Horse label.

Disillusioned by the lack of financial reward from these records, Mike approached Island late in 1975 armed with a huge collection of self-produced material on master tapes. Island's people were suitably impressed with what they heard and gave him full access to their 24-track Basing Street studio, along with his own Rockers imprint. The label issued singles by local talent Fitzroy Henry ('Can't Take My Eyes Off You'), Carol Williams ('You Gotta Save All Your Love'), Big Roy ('In The Desert' and the superb funky rocker 'I'm Going To Ethiopia') and Mike Dorane himself (a cover of the Supremes' 'Stop In The Name Of Love'). Despite some good reviews, none made any measurable impact, particularly with the crossover audience at which they had primarily been aimed. His own album, *Reggae Time*, cut little ice either.

Mike had wanted to make Rockers into the British equivalent of Motown but despite worthy, commercially slanted material, combined with Island's financial muscle, it just never happened for him. Following the failure of Rockers and its similarly Dorane-dedicated sister label Movers (for his soul and disco productions), Mike then moved on to Pye's new Roots label, where he recorded under the *nom de disque* Jah Mike. Success there was even harder to come by, however. There was also a stop-gap issue on Robby Day's Trenchtown label with 'Police Try Fe Mash Up Jah Jah Children', recorded in response to the troubles at the turbulent Notting Hill carnival of August 1976.

Mike moved on to work with UK roots outfit Merger in the late 1970s, appearing on their excellent *Exiles In A Babylon* album (more of which later), and had a short-lived production career at Burning Sounds and also with Virgin Front Line producing The Twinkle Brothers (where he masqueraded as Dan Justice and Michael Dan respectively) at around that time. Despite continually reinventing himself and using various aliases, there was little apparent change in his fortunes. During the mid-1980s, he apparently used his multi-instrumental skills to move back into session work. He was undoubtedly a unique talent, and it is sad that his potential was never fully realised.

WINSTON EDWARDS

A business associate of Jamaican producer Joe Gibbs, Winston Edwards was himself also an apprentice record producer and had several sides issued through an arrangement with Dennis Harris and his DIP label during 1974. These included I Roy's 'Don't Get Weary Joe Frazier' (a cut of Tony Brevett's 'Don't Get Weary'), Big Joe's ultra-heavy 'Selassie Skank' and 'Weed Specialist', and The Gaylads' popular 'You Made A Mistake'. Two of Edwards' productions also appeared on Magnet at this time: Dennis Walks' cover of Ben E King's 'Don't Play That Song' and the unknown Wally Brown's 'Send Back The Rod'. These were not quite as top-drawer as the DIP output, however.

Edwards had initially started his own Fay Music operation from Jah Shaka's house in nearby Alpha Road, releasing the impossibly rare 'Stand By Me' by Albert Griffiths on the Jah Shaka label. Edwards' other business sideline at this time was to record material in Jamaica, press copies and then bring them over to the UK to sell to the shops as pre-releases. In 1974 he began his short-lived Stop Point imprint, also administered for him by Dennis Harris, and was quite successful with Gregory Isaacs' 'End Of The World'.

Late in 1975, Edwards opened his Fay Music record shop in southeast London's New Cross, just a short jaunt from DIP's premises, and started the label of the same name. He retained close links throughout with Joe Gibbs, and Fay Music's greatest triumph was undoubtedly the colossal *King Tubby Meets The Upsetter At The Grass Roots Of Dub* album, which remained for three months at the top of *Black Music*'s reggae chart and was eventually to become the UK's top-selling reggae LP of 1975. The album was produced by Edwards, and mixed by Tubby and Lee Perry. It proved to be a stepping stone to the wider acceptance of dub over here. Follow-ups, namely *King Tubby Surrounded By The Dreads At The National Arena* and *Natty Locks Dub* were not quite as successful, despite being fine albums of their ilk.

Successful singles on Fay Music included Augustus Pablo's 'Fort Augustus Rock', U Brown's charmingly titled 'Wet Up Your Pants Foot' and Leo Graham's

'Greedy Girl'. What let the generally fine quality of the music down, however, was the rather primitive nature of the pressings (believed to be from language specialists Linguaphone!), which were often marred by a fuzzy sound.

The label released no new products for much of 1976 and throughout 1977. Around the early part of 1978, Edwards closed down the Fay Music outlet and went on to manage Joe Gibbs' new Record Globe shop round the corner in Lewisham Way, from where he also issued his new Studio 16 label. The arrangement lasted until the start of the 1980s, and the shop seems to have folded at precisely the time Gibbs was apparently having various legal problems, which later saw him take a lengthy break from the scene.

Winston Edwards was something of an aspiring politician in Jamaica but it is not known whether he ultimately followed a political path. The Fay Music premises appeared to have been taken over by Jah Shaka in the early '80s and the small parade of shops there still houses West Indian-run businesses.

ROY FORBES

In the mid-1970s, Roy 'Hawkeye' Forbes (or Forbes-Allen) was another of Trojan's ex-employees who, seeing the way the wind was blowing, decided to set up business on his own account.

In late 1970, Roy had landed a job managing Webster Shrowder's Muzik City stall in London's Shepherd's Bush market, shortly acting in a similar capacity in the nearby Uxbridge Road branch. Forbes proved a good salesman – his keen eye for spotting pilferers was the origin of his nickname – and he soon established a network of contacts within the UK reggae business from working with one of Trojan's van-based salesmen. As a sideline to his work with Trojan, Roy imported and sold supplies of pre-releases sent direct by a cousin in Jamaica. As this cousin was apparently Manley Buchanan, aka Big Youth, these were of prime quality!

With Trojan's eventual collapse, Roy made tentative attempts to set up his own label, and acquired the UK rights to Jah Woosh's 'Set Up Yourself Dread', which he leased to Klik. This proved to be a less than satisfactory arrangement, however, and he decided that releasing discs on his own imprint was the only way he was ever going to see any money. He set up his own Hawkeye outlet near the 'the Bush', in Wood Lane, during 1975.

Roy's Hawkeye label was launched late in 1976 and was distributed initially by the late George Pecking's Studio One shop a mile or so away in Askew Road. Its first release was Dennis Brown's 'Whip Them Jah', which did extremely well for a first effort. The tune that really broke the label, though, was the Channel One-produced 'Pretty Looks' by The Jayes (credited to 'J Ayres' on the label), an updated version of The Heptones' 1968 Studio One rocksteady number. This went to Number Two in *Black Music*'s August 1977 reggae listings and Roy then moved up a few gears. Other notable successes on Hawkeye in the late 1970s were Gregory Isaacs' 'John Public', Enos McLeod's 'By The Look In Your Eye', Bim Sherman's 'Ever Firm', Augustus Pablo's 'Rockers' cut of 'East Of The River Nile' and The Immortals' 'Why Keep A Good Man Down'.

Hawkeye thrived into the '80s, having shifted its retail outlet a few miles north of the Bush to Harlesden. One of its biggest sellers, Sugar Minott's 'Good Thing Going', was picked up by RCA in 1981 for national release and became a UK top ten hit. These days, Roy Forbes occasionally reissues some of Hawkeye's key releases but appears not to be involved with new productions, although a trimmed-down version of the retail shop is still there at 2A Craven Park Road.

JUNIOR LINCOLN

We have already met Junior (first in Chapter 2). In fact, the Vulcan and Grounation labels really represent the nadir of his involvement in the reggae business – his Bamboo and Ashanti issuing outlets had proved much more successful and high-profile for him.

Starting off with a minor-league sound system in the late 1960s, the Indian-Jamaican Lincoln forged links with Coxson Dodd. During that time (from mid-1968 until around April 1969), Dodd's product was coming out through Trojan/B&C on the Studio One and Coxson subsidiaries, which the company had inherited from Island. Dodd ultimately seemed less than happy with this arrangement since he apparently believed Trojan was putting more effort into pushing its other titles at the expense of his. When the deal ended, he collaborated with Lincoln on launching Bamboo to cater exclusively for the issue of Studio One product in the UK. The first release – Ken Parker's 'My Whole World Is Falling Down' – came out around August 1969 and did big business.

Later in 1969, Lincoln launched another label, Ackee, to handle product from a hotchpotch of British and Jamaican producers – people like Stair McCallum, Clancy Collins, Larry Lawrence, Herman Chin-Loy and Laurel Aitken. Some of Ackee's titles, like The Harmonians' 'Music Street' and The Schoolboys' 'Do It Now', also appeared on the Junior label out of Birmingham, but it is not clear how these two labels were linked. What is certain is that, despite the name, Mr Lincoln did not run Junior Records: it belonged to Junior Bradley.

Largely overlooked at the time, Ackee was a strange animal, often featuring titles available elsewhere. For instance, Rupie Martin's frenetic 'Death In The Arena' came out on at least two other labels, and Dave Barker's 'Johnny Dollar' came out on Pama's Supreme imprint. There was an array of interesting material from some very obscure British artists like Sonny, Elijah, Tex Dixon (later to be Matumbi's vocalist), Mr Bojangles, Laurel Hardy (who may have been Eugene Paul), Paul Cooke (who was definitely Eugene Paul!) and Green Mango (a Tottenham-based band who later backed Ginger Williams). Ackee's biggest tune was undoubtedly Owen Gray's 'No More', which utilised an original Studio One backing track supplied by Coxson. Musically even better, though, were Larry And Alvin's 'Throw Me Corn', The Beltones' 'Soul People' (both of which were also from the Coxson stable) and Elijah's 'Selassie I', a nice early cultural piece produced by Clancy Collins.

Meanwhile, the main Bamboo label was putting out some really wonderful music from the likes of Ken Boothe ('Be Yourself' and 'Pleading'), Alton Ellis ('Better Example' and 'Tumbling Tears'), Sound Dimension ('Poison Ivy' and 'Doctor Sappa Too', the latter featuring DJ Sir Lord Comic) and the epitome of roots and culture, Burning Spear's majestic 'Door Peeper', which was hidden away on Jackie Mittoo's 'Money Maker' as a flip side. A couple of compilation albums appeared too, namely *A Scorcha From Bamboo* and *Natural Reggae*. Lincoln took great care in putting these together, often using Horace Ove's stunning ethnic photography. (Ove, incidentally, was to produce the film of the 1970 Caribbean Music Festival at Wembley, entitled *Reggae*.)

Despite releasing a stream of outstanding records in its first nine months or so, Bamboo seemed unable to eat into either Trojan or Pama's share of the market – not by a long chalk. Again, distribution may have been a problem, and the fact that Lincoln was aiming very much at the ethnic market was not conducive to reaching a wider (and white) audience; skinheads were not known for collecting Bamboo. About the only commercial shots from the label (strings and all) were The Heptones' version of 'Young, Gifted And Black', Marcia Griffiths' 'Shimmering Star' and Bob And Marcia's 'Really Together'.

Some time around the middle of 1970, Lincoln launched a sister label to Bamboo, namely Banana. The idea was to spread the music around to avoid releases getting 'lost' – as can happen when too many records come out on the same label, and that was certainly beginning to happen with Bamboo. Whereas Bamboo tended to showcase the tried-and-tested Studio One stalwarts – like Bob Andy, Marcia Griffiths, Ken Boothe, Jackie Mittoo and Sound Dimension/Brentford Road All Stars – Banana instead specialised in Coxson's largely 'new' roster of artists such as Horace Andy, Mad Roy (vocalist-cum-drummer Leroy 'Horsemouth' Wallace), Dennis Brown, King Cry Cry (later known as Prince Far I) and The Wailing Souls. As with Black Swan in the Island empire seven years before, Banana was very much a subsidiary label in terms of promotion, and issued many great records that sold in modest quantities.

The great music lasted on Bamboo until the close of 1970, after which the releases practically dried up and became rather less brilliant anyway. Banana continued apace with classics like Larry Marshall's 'Maga Dog', The Classics' (Wailing Souls) 'Mr Fire Coal Man', Freddy McKay's 'Picture On The Wall' and The Heptones' 'Freedom Line', but it was clear that Dodd was producing much less than previously and, without Dodd's constant stream of product, it was becoming difficult to run both Bamboo and Banana.

During 1972, a smattering of Studio One material was shunted across to Ackee, which had been supplemented a year earlier by two other subsidiaries, namely Ashanti and Tropical. Lincoln co-administered Ashanti with his business associate, Rupert Cunningham, for a short time. Even with a good tune or three, Ashanti was not really making an impression on the market. Tropical was co-administered, with Lincoln, by the little-known Jamaican-Chinese producer Ken Chang. Largely ignored at the time, this label is worth a second look, particularly Dennis Alcapone's 'Rude Medley' (which was about its only real success) and Lee Francis's 'Rising Of Another', a really solid rootsy tune.

The Banana release schedule was supplemented by productions from Larry Lawrence and Winston Riley, and the label soldiered on for a time. Bamboo just died, with only four releases in the entire 1971–72 period. It was a slow death, and so it was that Lincoln's Bamboo set-up was wound up. The Bamboo retail shop at 88 Stroud Green Road in Finsbury Park was rechristened Junior's Music Spot.

But Lincoln wasn't done yet. In what were obviously second series, revamped Ashanti and Ackee imprints were launched and continued side by side between 1973 and 1975 with financial input from Trojan and distribution by B&C. (Joe Sinclair states that Ashanti was partially set up on the money gained by the Shrowder/Bryan/Sinclair partnership from the Judge Dread chart singles they produced.) Both labels featured an array of top-quality Jamaican sounds: on Ackee there was Alton Ellis's 'Too Late To Turn Back Now', Charley Ace's 'Country Boy' and Prince Jazzbo's 'Kick Boy Face', while Ashanti blessed us with The Heptones' 'I Miss You', Sharon Forrester's proto-lovers rock 'Silly Wasn't I' and Dobby Dobson's near-hit version of the Brook Benton evergreen 'Endlessly'. The classic *Reggae Time* compilation appeared on Ashanti with a sleeve photograph showing Steve Barnard, host of Radio London's hour-long Sunday lunchtime show *Reggae Time*, in front of a pair of Mk 2 Garrard decks spinning the platters for the flared masses. Apart from the out-of-place 'Pup 'n' Temper' by Pete Weston (originally released in Jamaica with the malodorous label credit 'Chester And The Farts'), the selection is faultless.

Another fine Ashanti compilation album followed with *Ashanti Showcase*. A debut set by new Jamaican signing Sharon Forrester was aimed at the crossover market and, by reggae standards, it cost an absolute fortune to produce. Sadly, it did not reach its desired market or attract the sort of sales anticipated. An expensive mistake, perhaps, but it's a really fine album, which is only now being given the attention it deserved in the first place. It's certainly true to say that with B&C's involvement, Lincoln's labels were now much more high-profile than they had been back in the Bamboo days. An Ashanti business HQ was established directly across the road from his existing Junior's Music Spot in the early months of 1974.

Meanwhile, Trojan's Attack imprint put out two collections of singles that had appeared on Bamboo, Banana and the first series of Ackee, including a good showing of Studio One material. The first, *Big Bamboo*, was an all-Coxson affair while the second, *Rave On Brother*, featured only the last gasps of the various labels and is a thoroughly hit-and-miss affair. With stickered-out Bamboo catalogue numbers on their covers, both had clearly been destined for issue on that label. Both were also, by all accounts, poor sellers. Attack also re-released John Holt's *A Love I Can Feel* album, which had proved Bamboo's biggest-selling LP and which Trojan kept on catalogue for some considerable time afterwards.

Gradually, the scene shifted and, with it, the key producers who serviced Lincoln seemingly transferred their product elsewhere. The real death knell for both Ashanti and Ackee came, however, with the downfall of Trojan/B&C. Without distribution, the product could not get into the shops and the punter couldn't buy it. Planning release schedules was therefore hopeless since there could be no guarantee that the goods would reach the marketplace.

So Lincoln's labels were wound up in mid-1975. As outlined earlier, following the fallout from the Trojan collapse, he went on to form Vulcan, with Rupert Cunningham taking the by then defunct Tropical label (minus Ken Chang) with him to Sound Tracs. Junior Lincoln still lives in London but is not known to be actively involved in the music scene.

JOE MANSANO

What of Joe after those great skinhead reggae releases on Trojan and on Doctor Bird's Reggae label? How could the man possibly follow them?

Sadly, with the passing of the skinheads he wasn't able to. He placed a few of his 1970 sounds (particularly 'Trial Of Pama Dice') with Jack Price's new Sioux label for reissue and, although there is some uncertainty about this, he may have produced several singles on Fab by an outfit called Great Aces in 1972. Joe then established his Joe's Shack and Arrow labels in 1973, the first releases being cover versions of Jim Reeves' 'I Won't Forget You' by Ray Martell And The Champions and Peters And Lee's 'Welcome Home' by Roy Shirley And The Champions. That was pretty much the market he was targeting.

During this time, Joe was also operating a second shop around the corner from Joe's Shack in Atlantic Road. This one was in fact dedicated to Pama product, and the window display showed a selection of sleeves such as *Crab's Biggest Hits*, *This Is Reggae*, *Something Sweet The Lady*, and so on – a truly glorious sight. Joe was associated with another outlet (Vitronic) in Brooklyn, New York, but this seems to have been a short-lived venture. Early in 1974, he was also attempting to expand his operations by moving into the closed-down Muzik City shop in Balham Underground Station, but for whatever reason that just never happened.

In 1976, Joe again recorded Ray Martell, who had cut the wonderful 'She Caught The Train' for him six years previously. 'Sunny Soil', which came out under Martell's alter ego Martel Robinson, enjoyed strong sales on Arrow.

He also featured in a short interview for the 1976 *Aquarius* UK reggae programme, filmed in one of his shops. It provided a tantalising sight, with dozens of LP sleeves flapping in the racks.

Then, following an updated cut by The Twinkle Brothers of their 'It's Not Who You Know' in 1977, Arrow was wrapped up and Mansano withdrew from recording completely. He carried on running his Record Shack in Brixton's Granville Arcade until 1980 when he returned to his native Trinidad and Tobago.

He was last heard of in January 2003 in the role of Public Relations Officer for the Port of Spain Zone of the Trinidad and Tobago Table Tennis Association.

BUSTER PEARSON

Here's a man who served his musical apprenticeship at ground level. Buster played in various mainly unrecorded London bands during the 1960s, including The Astronauts, who recorded 'Syncopate' for Guyanese-born Count Hala's Halagala label, The Links and The In-Brackets, who were

Dandy's backing group for a time. On cutting a solo career for himself, he recorded 'Ain't It Groovy' for Trojan's Big Shot subsidiary in 1973. Utilising the backing of Jimmy Cliff's 'In The Good Good Old Days', this became a national breaker for the company and was popular enough to merit inclusion on *Tighten Up Volume 8*. A follow-up, 'Big Funk', was issued on Trojan's Action subsidiary but died a death, not least since the imprint lacked any real focus (was it soul or was it reggae?). Then came Trojan's collapse and, like so many artists associated with the label, Buster set up his own operation.

He opened his K&B record shop in Ilford around 1975 and started up the K&B label, which issued almost entirely UK-recorded music, including a re-release of 'Ain't It Groovy'; there followed Lynn Alice's 'Just Enough To Keep Me Hanging On', Dennis Curtis's 'Come With Me', African Stone's 'Run Rasta Run', DD MacDonald's 'I Believe' and John Christy And Jess Smith's 'One Man Woman'. The quality of this material is best described as variable, and several of the K&B roster seem never to have recorded for any other labels. To its eternal credit, however, K&B did put out Junior Ross And The Spear's 'Judgement Time', Ras Allah And The Spear's 'Bosrah' (originally titled 'Buzzrock' on Ja copies of the single) and Patrick Alley's 'Come See Yah' – three all-time classic roots tunes from 1976. Interestingly, some K&B material also appeared simultaneously on Eddy Grant's reactivated Torpedo label. Other K&B offshoots included ATA, Lion Sound and Lizzard, although the last two only managed one issue apiece. K&B is another UK indie that is well worth a listen and, with the exception of DD MacDonald and John Christy And Jess Smith, there are a few decent tunes in there.

Pearson's empire seemed to have ceased operation by 1978, and he was next seen managing the '80s group Five Star, whose personnel consisted entirely of his offspring. By all accounts, he ruled the band with a rod of iron and, while they made a lot of money in a short period of time, they spent it all very quickly on a lavish life of excess (or so the tabloids told us). When the hits dried up, they were soon bankrupt. Apparently, there is some sort of version of Five Star still on the road, but the good life is surely gone for ever.

PAT RHODEN

A veteran of the UK scene since the mid-1960s, Rhoden was another Jamaican male vocalist who had walked a well-trodden path: first to R&B Discs (specifically the Ska Beat label in 1965/66); then Trojan in 1968 (where he was produced by Dandy); then, for three years until 1973, Pama; then back to good old Trojan. Along the way, he had participated in a Jack Price-produced album for Mercury entitled *Let The Red Wine Flow* and recorded a one-off single for the Mary Lyn label, 'Time Is Tight'. His biggest success was undoubtedly with 'Maybe The Next Time' for Pama in the autumn of 1970, which was produced by Derrick Morgan and backed by The Mohawks.

After Pama took a temporary break from issuing records early in 1974, Rhoden moved back to Trojan for covers of Stevie Wonder's 'Boogie On Reggae Woman' and 'Living For The City'. It was during the autumn of 1975, following the collapse of Trojan, that he formed Jama with Tito Simon and Earl Martin.

'After Trojan went down,' explains Pat, 'the idea of starting a label came up. It was Earl Martin, who now runs "Miss Black UK", who introduced me to Johnny Johnson, whose real name was Johnny Euen and who was at the time selling insurance. Because of that he could get the finance we needed to start the label. The label name was Jama – short for Jamaica – and I was buddies with BB Seaton and Lloyd Campbell, who would supply some of the material.

'We quickly had some big hits like Claudette Miller's "Tonight Is The Night" and my own "Sweet Sunshine", which sold over 11,000 copies, and I recorded at Treasure Isle in Jamaica. We were doing very well, with everyone throwing material at us. Quite early on, around 1975, I started to go to Jamaica to record, and it was a great experience working with people like Sly And Robbie, Lloyd Parks etc. We had a real problem to emulate the Ja style here, and I felt I wanted to do more in Jamaica because of the feel – the Ja recording was mixed as it was being recorded while in the UK everything was flat, and then we had to remix it. Some of the Ja tracks that we took to London studios, the engineers thought they'd already been mixed so good was the recording in Kingston.

'We'd normally press up 1,000 copies as the tester, then press more if the record started to sell. The a-side was what we spent the most time on – the b-side we never spent so much time or money – we'd definitely differentiate between the two.

'I Roy's "Welding" sold very well for us, but with more DJ stuff coming after it, the music changed. Music sales took a dive and the business environment became very hard. We had two vans on the road at the time and sales dropped dramatically. In retrospect, Jama should've gone with the new styles, as the roots and culture music was supplanting the soft music that we released.

'So Jama was hit by finance problems, plus we could've done with better administration. We also had a problem internally and in the end I just walked.'

Jama soon spawned the Eagle and Love subsidiaries, and set itself up as a reggae distribution one-stop with a shop in Brixton. The ethos behind the company was that it was compact, personal (ie it had a close relationship with the artists), and was run by West Indians, who would have complete control over the music issued.

Largely overlooked until recently, Jama really did put out some good material, with some top-notch releases from Jamaican producers like Joe Joe Hookim, Lloyd Campbell and Glen Brown, and some often pale-by-comparison UK stuff, although to be fair some of it was almost as good. Pat's own 'Stop' and 'Sweet Sunshine' singles were particularly good sellers. The other prominent music people involved with the company at this point were BB Seaton, Les Foster, Eugene Paul, Norman T Washington and, need we add, Laurel Aitken, all of whom also had material issued through Pama at one time or another.

Alongside Jama, Rhoden was co-running the Earth International label with Les Foster and Denzil Dennis. He was also the main man associated with the Skip's label, which specialised in calypso and spouge music. Jama lasted until the start of the 1980s and Pat Rhoden, together with most of the other personalities mentioned earlier, seemed to fade from the scene.

SONNY ROBERTS

This enterprising retailer and producer has already been covered to some extent in the *Young, Gifted And Black* book, and in Chapter 1 of this one. In brief, he was one of the UK's earliest pioneers of West Indian music, establishing his Planetone and Sway labels in 1962 to issue music recorded at his own basement studio at 108 Cambridge Road in Kilburn Park, which later became the premises for Island Records' operations. When Island moved in, Sonny Roberts pretty soon moved out. It is believed he then started his Orbitone Record shop outside Willesden Junction station. This long-running shop was the first West Indian-owned specialist record store in Britain.

After the demise of Planetone, Sonny then concentrated on the retail side of the business for some years. He leased a couple of Sacred albums and a one-off Sacred single to Trojan in 1969, and these saw release on the company's Tabernacle and Blue Cat subsidiaries respectively. A few years later, he had product out on Trojan's Explosion label (The Orbitones' 'Memories Of Love') and on Count Shelly's eponymous imprint (Sonny's own 'Call Me').

Following this, Sonny launched his Orbitone label in 1973 and produced UK-recorded material by Tim Chandell, The Vaughans, Teddy Davis and Raymondo. Not all of it was reggae: Chandell's stock in trade was '50s-style sentimental R&B, which he performed admirably; The Vaughans were very much in Jim Reeves territory and Raymondo was sort of spouge with a bit of reggae thrown in. There were also some now highly sought-after afro-jazz albums from prolific session saxman Peter King and Nkengas. In 1977, Tim Chandell's *Loving Moods* album reputedly sold an astonishing 50,000 copies, largely to the older, sentimental West Indian buyer who had probably gone for Brook Benton a decade and a half earlier.

The Tackle subsidiary was added in 1974 with spouge king Roy Alton as the label's highest-profile artist, with other material coming from the likes of the Senators and Kalabash. Much of this was very popular with West Indians who had come to the UK from Trinidad, Barbados and Antigua. In 1975, the Affection imprint was established, seemingly to handle the lovers rock side of reggae, and was mainly focused on releases by Silver and by Bridie Stewart, whose 'Can't Let You Go', produced by Sonny, is an often overlooked tune. One rogue release on Affection was 'Can Be Done', which found the smooth Tim Chandell shaking free his ballad shackles and offering a slice of full-on funk.

In 1979, Sonny Roberts created the Cartridge imprint, which was notable for issuing Dandy Livingstone's cover of Dan Hill's 'Sometimes When We Touch'. Orbitone and Tackle, along with later subsidiary Sun Burn, continued issuing music right into the 1980s and their 12-inch 45s still turn up regularly today. Undoubtedly, 1986 was the big year for Orbitone when Judy Boucher's 'Can't Be With You Tonight' hit Number Two in the national charts. Boucher's follow-up, 'You Caught My Eye', was also a big national hit. Judy continued to be a big draw for the company over the next few years and is still singing today.

It is believed that Sonny Roberts went into the travel agency/shipping business (catering specifically for West Indians) in the late 1980s, and that the Orbitone shop closed several years later. According to a recent interview with Dandy, Sonny now resides in Jamaica and still operates his company from there. Other sources, though, suggest that Sonny passed away in the late 1990s.

CLIFF ST LEWIS

Not a great deal is known about Cliff, who was also known as Les Cliff. As Cliff St Lewis, he had a solitary, little regarded 45 out on Magnet's Faith subsidiary during 1974 ('Another Beautiful Night') and went on to form his own Saturn label the following year, issuing his own material and sides from Samantha Rose, Johnny Mahoney, Dennis Alcapone (who had now settled here), Jamaican veteran Neville Hinds and Aston Gayle. Most Saturn releases were UK-recorded, although Aston Gayle's 'Jah Will Help Us' may not be (and it's a very nice tune too). Sam Rose's 'My Only Chance' is worth picking up as it's good early lovers and is so obviously influenced by Susan Cadogan's 'Hurt So Good'.

Aside from Saturn, St Lewis teamed up with Samantha Rose as Sam And Les for '(I Can't Resist) Your Tender Lips' on DIP. Registering at mid-point in the reggae top 30 and popular with the old 'uns, it must be one of the least collectable records on the label despite its popularity at the time. He was also running the Jah Lion imprint in association with Winston Curtis during this period. By 1977, St Lewis was leasing material to Trojan by himself (specifically 'Banana' and 'Ching Lue') for release on Horse. Over in radioland, St Lewis was Tommy Vance's sidekick for his Saturday-night *TV On Reggae* show on London's Capital Radio.

He was still going in the early '80s when he covered Gregory Isaacs' 'One And Only Lover' on his KC (King Cliff) label, together with an album entitled *Vintage Point*. Although not a big player, and barely known even in reggae circles, St Lewis was one of those people that set up labels here and there, took some chances along the way, and formed a tiny part of the UK reggae jigsaw.

EPILOGUE (OR THOSE WE HAVEN'T MENTIONED)

Needless to say, there are a great number of UK players to whom we haven't been able to give detailed coverage in the space available here. It's also been difficult to know exactly who was behind certain labels or whether a certain imprint was operated by a particular individual at a particular time and then continued by someone else at a later date (the Live and Love label is probably a prime example of this). There is the added complication of distributors and whether certain labels simply handled product for individuals or were more actively involved in some other way.

A number of name-checks are definitely in order here, however, and we believe the following deserve at least a mention in this chapter: Philroy Matthias and David Tyrone (Venture Records); Mo Claridge (label operator and Mojo distribution kingpin); Ellis Breary (who produced Junior English's early material) and, last but not least, 'Mr Soul Of Jamaica' himself, Alton Ellis, whose short-lived Stonehouse label issued a massive reggae hit for Tony J Owens, 'Telephone Line', in 1977.

6 London To Birmingham...And Beyond

Some 120 miles northwest of London lies the UK's second city. It would be a gross oversight were it not to be mentioned here, since Birmingham was also the country's biggest reggae stronghold next to London and had the second-largest West Indian community. The Handsworth, Lozells, Soho and Small Heath areas were ethnic areas akin to, say, London's Brixton, Tottenham, Stoke Newington and Hackney. 'London To Birmingham' was also the title of a 1976 Jah Woosh single so the connection has already been immortalised on vinyl.

It was once said that the Midlands and the north missed out on the '60s and had them during the '70s instead, – there certainly seems to be some truth in this. Remember, too, that northern soul was flourishing in towns like Stoke, Cleethorpes, Wigan and Blackpool, and was just about to go 'overground'. London was no longer necessarily where it was at. Although there was no similarity between reggae and northern soul, both scenes were record-obsessed and awash with clubs. Furthermore, although skinheads may have largely died out in the south, they were still hanging on in the Black Country and far beyond. Even to this day, many original skinheads have an affection for northern soul.

However, it is interesting to hear Trojan manager Rob Bell's memories of selling records beyond London, 'I really have no recollection of any meaningful retailers in Wales or Scotland. HR Taylor's [of Birmingham] were our Midland and northern distributors during the mid-1960s possibly they had the odd account in those regions. Philips [later known as Phonodisc] took over distribution [of Trojan] by the late '60s – again, they probably had some kind of penetration in those areas.

'Really, we sold to primarily West Indian populations – the skinhead factor certainly kicked in on bigger sellers, but as that was more of a club-driven kind of thing, that brings you back to London, Bristol, Birmingham, Manchester, etc.'

As can be seen from a quick look through any mid-1970s issue of *Black Music* magazine's specialist record dealer ads, there was certainly a lot of reggae activity going on in Birmingham around this period. In fact, by the middle of 1975 there were at least ten shops serving the area. The region also had on its doorstep key reggae distributor, the aforementioned HR Taylor, which had handled Pama and Sioux at one time or another. There was also a tiny Birmingham independent – believed to be called Woolmac – issued by a shop in Heathfield Street, Lozells. It only ran to two singles, but it demonstrated that a sufficiently big market existed in the Midlands.

Junior Bradley ran Aquarius Records at 79 Soho Road, Handsworth, from where he issued his Junior imprint, of which some titles were simultaneously put out on Junior Lincoln's London-based Ackee label. That there were two men called 'Junior' involved in releasing the same titles is a great coincidence. Curiously, Ackee put out quite a few tunes from Herman Chin-Loy and his Aquarius set-up in Jamaica, and Aquarius was indeed the name of Bradley's shop. This again may just be coincidence.

There were some excellent tunes put out on Junior – if you can ever find them – by Laurel Aitken ('Think Me No Know'), Anthony King ('Let Them Talk') and the Soul Cats ('Land Of Love'). The distribution was probably decidedly local, with only a few hundred copies being sold around the Birmingham shops. Dating the label is also difficult since no issue year was ever quoted, although our guess is that it would probably have been between 1969 and 1970. Bradley is known to have moved back to Jamaica, where he set himself up in a profitable little business importing tyres and car batteries from the UK.

Atomic Records, headed by one Aaron Smith (known as 'English'), had two retail shops in the Small Heath area and administered two short-lived labels, namely Atomic, and Sun and Star. The main Atomic imprint put out just one tune, local singer Carlyle Rowe's romantic 'Darling', complete with publicity handout. Mr Rowe is apparently still singing and is known to have re-cut the song quite recently.

The first release on Sun and Star was The Loving Brothers' excellent 'Rule Ethiopia' – as the sound men used to say, 'if you don't know, get to know'. For the next release, and through some association with Doctor Alimantado, Sun and Stars issued his classic 'Best Dressed Chicken' single, recorded at the Black Ark in 1975. It was one of those tunes that seemed to have such erratic distribution that hunting down a copy even during its release period was a job in itself. In and around Birmingham, though, it was everywhere. The tune was such a good seller and made such an impression that three years later the Greensleeves label reissued it along with 'tado's other material from the time as the *Best Dressed Chicken In Town* album – probably still the company's best-selling LP over its 25-year release period. Always a frequent visitor to these shores, 'tado is believed to live in London these days, and issues and distributes his material on his own Keyman imprint. He can often be seen in the myriad record shops in and around Soho's Berwick Street area.

The Atomic set-up seems to have folded by 1977. Like Junior Bradley before him, Aaron Smith used the music business as a stepping stone to greater things. He returned to Jamaica, where he now operates a fleet of minibuses. A guy called Paul, who used to work for him, is now Dub Vendor's distributor in the Birmingham area.

BRIAN HARRIS: THE ICICLE SPEAKS

'If you bought reggae in Birmingham in the '70s, you knew me,' says Brian Harris as he sits within his office in Wylde Green near Birmingham, completely surrounded by Dexion framing groaning under the weight of rare ska and reggae vinyl. 'In those days I could walk into a dance and know 90 per cent of the people there.'

Brian is no braggart – he's just stating facts. A quietly spoken, neatly bearded man in his 50s, he's loved Jamaican music since his schooldays and has always made his living from it, as retailer, importer, wholesaler and distributor. Nowadays he operates the famed Icicle Records mail-order business, supplying the needs of oldies collectors worldwide.

Brian grew up in the Handsworth area of the city, listening to 'the usual rock 'n' roll stuff' until he became aware of the jumping Jamaican R&B favoured by the West Indian immigrants who were beginning to settle in the area. By the time he left school, there was only one career path for him: to become involved with music.

'I went to work for a Scottish chap named Dewar who had about four radio and TV shops around Birmingham, and of course in those days most radio shops sold records too. I alternated between the various shops until, round about 1964, Mr Dewar decided that he wanted to sell one of them, so I took it over. That was the shop at 104 Grove Lane, Handsworth. I stopped stocking radios and televisions, and set up as Brian Harris Records, which I later changed to Mango Records – that was before Island launched their Mango label. That was in the heyday of what we then called blue beat.'

In the '60s there weren't that many specialist record labels, so getting hold of stock was relatively easy. On occasion, Brian's Handsworth shop would be favoured with a visit from the boss of one the labels.

'Melodisc distributed the Blue Beat, Dice and Kalypso labels, and they would send their van up from London with the latest releases on board. Often Emil Shallit, who owned Melodisc, would come along; this tatty old van would turn up driven by Peter, Emil's driver, or sometimes by Emil's daughter, and Emil would be sitting on the van's floor because there was no seat in the passenger side. He was a nice little chap, always came into the shop with a huge Havana cigar, and I got to know him quite well.

'He'd had a remarkable life. He was in the CIA during the war and spoke ten or twelve languages fluently. He travelled all over the world on business; when he went to Jamaica he'd stay with Prince Buster, and he used to lease his Blue Beat releases through Buster. I think he must have looked after Buster quite well, which may be why the Prince stayed loyal to Melodisc instead of leasing his productions to lots of different labels.'

'There was one distributor in Birmingham, HR Taylor. I used to get Island Records from them in the earlier days of [the label], and they handled Melodisc as well. When they started up, Starlite was the very first label they handled and was the label that put out all the early Chris Blackwell productions.'

Perhaps surprisingly, since the shop was there during the heyday of mods and later skinheads, both prime consumers of West Indian music, very few of them would come into the shop. 'We'd get one or two, but most white kids would look inside the shop, see that it was absolutely packed with West Indians, and would decide to go and buy their records in the city centre,' recalls Brian.

'We had a few home-grown artists around at that time. There was The Locomotive, who did 'Rudy's In Love'; their singer Norman Haynes worked at HR Taylor's during the day. Ray King was a local black singer from over Oldbury way who made a few records, and of course Winston Groovy is a Birminghammie. His song 'Please Don't Make Me Cry', the original cut on Torpedo, was a huge hit for him in Birmingham. Later he moved to London and re-cut it for Trojan, then of course UB40 covered it and he made a large amount in royalties because he wrote the song.'

There was no shortage of live black music in the city. A man by the name of Tubby Stan made sure of that. 'He was a black guy who, as his name suggests, was big, and he was the local hot-shot promoter,' remembers Brian. 'He put on dozens of dances at Digbeth Civic Hall and at the Top Rank Suite on Dale End. He died just a few years ago. Some of the dances were just sound clashes, though they weren't called that then, when he'd bring a top sound system up from London to compete against the big local sounds like Duke Sonny, Duke Neville and, a bit later, Quaker City.

'There were literally dozens of smaller sound systems in operation, because of all the blues parties or shebeens held in private houses. Every Friday, Saturday and bank holiday, people would book a sound, set up their little bar in their house, and I'd get people dropping flyers into the shop, things like "Mrs So-and-so invites you to her blues party". They used to buy vast amounts of records to play at them too. It was a very big scene, but it's nearly all gone now.'

By 1975, the Midlands reggae scene was burgeoning as London's Blue Beat scene had a decade earlier. In that year, a group of former Handsworth school chums formed a band called Steel Pulse and issued their first single 'Kibbudu, Mansetta And Abuku' on London-based DIP's Concrete Jungle label. Reggae shops proliferated. In addition to those already mentioned, there was Tip Top Records in Handsworth's Rookery Road, GG Jeff's out on the Wolverhampton Road, WG Wyatt on the Dudley Road and Abi Records on the Coventry Road in Small Heath. London label operators like Count Shelly and Lord Koos sent a car or van full of records to the second city every week, reckoning they could sell more in Birmingham than they could in London.

A shop by the name of Don Christie's at 116 Ladypool Road in Sparkbrook had been run by a West Indian family since the '60s. One Dave McGinn took it over from the family, retained the name and was forever known as 'Don'. Dave operated his shop for many years before selling out to Ezra, the son of former Birmingham sound system man Duke Sonny. Ezra operated the shop until the old Bullring Centre was pulled down pending redevelopment. David/Don relocated to Miami where he unfortunately died of a heart attack while still in his 40s.

In 1975 Brian, too, took a major step forward when he launched his first record label, Mango. Unlike many label owners, he didn't produce any sides himself; instead, he licensed hot new platters from producers he knew in Jamaica. 'Yabby You was probably the first person I licensed anything from – that was Wayne Wade's "Black Is Our Colour". I'm not sure why I started a record label. It was just something that everyone was doing in the '70s!'

Meanwhile, over in the Lozells area of Birmingham, Keith Thornton had established his Black Wax shop, closely followed by the label of the same name. Its first release was Pat Kelly's 'Sunshine', which went to Number Two in the reggae listings in April 1975.

In about 1976 the two men amalgamated their businesses, giving Brian an input into the Black Wax label. Black Wax continued to make a strong showing, notably with Lee Perry productions and further classic Mighty

Diamonds sides such as the wonderful Channel One-produced 'Country Living', which went all the way to Number Two on the *Black Music* reggae listings during September 1975. Also huge at that time was Carl Malcolm's 'Miss Wire Waist'.

'The Perry connection started when we ran into Scratch's then wife Pauline Morrison,' recalls Brian. 'She was in England, and it was at the time when Prince Jazzbo's *Natty Passing Through* album was out in Jamaica, and she'd taken it to Island. Island didn't want it – it probably wasn't what they were looking for at the time – and she just gave it to us. That was in 1976, and after that we started putting a lot of Perry stuff out. We got on OK with Pauline.'

From Black Wax's headquarters, Brian Harris proclaimed himself the 'People's Number One Reggae and Soul Controller'. With a thriving mail-order business and a stupendous range of stock (both pre-release and UK released), if Black Wax didn't have it you probably couldn't get it. So successful was Black Wax that Brian and Keith soon launched a sister label, Locks, alongside it. Among Locks' first releases was the Mighty Diamonds' 'Right Time' – essentially the follow-up to 'Country Living' – which was a Marcus Garvey-inspired tune in Channel One's new 'Rockers' style. This again went all the way to Number One in the reggae singles chart in October 1975. Both discs ensured that The Mighty Diamonds would shortly become one of the first reggae outfits to be signed up by Virgin.

Brian and Keith soon realised that, packed out though the Handsworth and Lozells shops always were on a Friday and Saturday, the number of customers that could reach them was finite; so, since not everyone could come to where their records were, they resolved to take their records to the people. Thus was Vandisc born.

'Vandisc was the distribution company we set up in the mid-1970s. It was Keith, myself and Bobby Khouri, the son of the late Ken Khouri of Federal Records in Jamaica. Bobby had moved to England and lived over in Harborne. Keith had known him for some time, and of course Bobby had all the key contacts over in Jamaica. We had two vans at first, although later we found that one was enough. We imported records from Jamaica, and the van went all round the country distributing records; Bobby always went to London every week. By this time Keith and I had the absolute monopoly on pre-release sales in Birmingham, so we didn't sell to other shops within the city.' Of course at that time pre-releases were all the rage. A shrewd move, that: don't sell to your local rivals and you can preserve that hard-won monopoly.

Other Birmingham shops such as the Diskery (first in Hurst Street, then in Bromsgrove Street) and Summit, whose founder Winston established it in West Bromwich and which now has premises in the city centre and on the Dudley Road, would deal principally in UK releases. The Diskery, not exclusively a reggae shop but which always used to be a good place to find Jamaican sounds both old and new, has been going since the '60s, and Summit since the '70s. Meanwhile, Vandisc was making hay in the Home Counties sunshine.

'The van would go down south on a Monday, stay away all week and return half-empty. We had a pressing facility in Jamaica; if we wanted a particular title, we'd get in touch with Bobby, who would telephone (or Telex as it was in those days) Federal, give them our order, and within a week we'd have the records. There weren't many people who could compete with us. Vandisc went on successfully for about five years. Our very best seller was Delroy Wilson's "I'm Still Waiting" on the LTD label. We more or less had an exclusive on that one. We imported and sold thousands of copies, because no one released it in Britain until it was too late.'

However, as the decade drew to its end, a change was in the air. Brian, who had been in love with Jamaican music since he'd first heard it two decades before, was having a change of heart,

'In '79, reggae had lost all its direction. Roots had come to an end, new DJs were taking over, sales were diminishing, and Bobby Khouri was no longer involved with the business and later returned to live in Jamaica. I've spoken to him a couple of times, but I don't think he's involved with Federal, which has now been taken over by Tuff Gong, though it retains the same premises.

'After that we decided to deviate a little bit. So, still myself and Keith, we opened a shop in Birmingham city centre. There was a huge demand for punk and new wave music, and that's what Inferno Records specialised in. We had an Inferno label, too, which issued about six or seven records by local punk bands. Ours was the original Inferno label, the northern soul one came later.

'At first we ran the reggae shops alongside Inferno, but in 1980 the Lozells shop was due for demolition, so we closed that and it was pulled down shortly afterwards. The shop in Grove Lane went towards the punk side of things, and that finally closed down in the early '80s. We expanded Inferno and eventually ran three shops.'

About that time, Brian missed what, with the benefit of hindsight, must now be seen as a golden opportunity to enter the reggae oldies market – except that at the time such a market hardly existed.

'When Inferno was in Dale End, right opposite there was a branch of Tesco, and I remember going in there loads of times, and they had these circular bins full of all the Pama records that you could ever want, all mint, and they were 15 pence each. The albums were 50p or something like that. I could have come out with armfuls, but I didn't; I'd got the ones I wanted in my collection and so I wasn't particularly bothered about them. I used to look at them and think, hmm, those are cheap, and then walk past. When the various Tesco branches had sold all the copies they could, the records that were left, and there were thousands of them, were all collated together and put in a warehouse somewhere, and the warehouse burned down.'

Readers may wish to pause and dry their eyes at this point.

Ironically, a couple of years after that the ska and reggae oldies market began its rise and rise, and Brian relocated to a suite of offices in stylish Victorian Ruskin Chambers close to the city centre. From here, he ran Icicle Records, specialising in the retailing of original oldies and re-presses, and Ravensquire, which handled the wholesaling side of the business. He still yielded to the temptation of running record labels, too, with imprints like Plum Jam (remembered for the Jah Lloyd *Herbs Of Dub* LP), and later King Edwards, which issued six volumes of classic ska that Brian leased from the Edwards brothers, Vincent and George, on one of his business trips to Jamaica. He also continued his business association with Pauline Morrison, issuing a series of 45s on the Black Art label. When asked if he still issues records, Brian smiles and replies, 'Nothing at the moment', so don't bet against a new Harris-owned imprint hitting the shops some time.

Ravensquire imported Jamaican-pressed records in quantity, personally selected by Brian on those Jamaican visits. 'I used to go to Kingston twice a year. I stayed with Coxson's Mum, Doris Darlington, whom everyone called "Nanny" or "Miss D", and his son Junior. I'd known Junior for many years, because when I had the shop in Handsworth he lived nearby with his Mum, Coxson's first wife Una. He went back to Jamaica and invited me to stay at their place in Spanish Town where Doris had a record shop. She always used to sit in the shop even towards the end of her life. She died about four years ago; I think she was 87. I also met Prince Buster's Mum, Sally, a nice lady, who ran Buster's Shack for him. I seem to meet all their Mums!'

A couple of years ago, depressed by the increase in city centre rents and by the difficulty of parking within a country mile of Ruskin Chambers, Brian moved to his present premises in Wylde Green, within easy reach of his home and with free parking round the back. He's closed down Ravensquire, but Icicle remains a worldwide mail-order supplier of choice Jamaican oldies.

What goes around comes around, as the saying goes, and Brian Harris has probably had discs pass through his hands that he himself supplied through his shops back in the '70s. His importance in the development of the Midlands reggae scene should not be underestimated.

STEVE JUKES ON THE NOTTINGHAM REGGAE SCENE

With his slicked-back black hair and sideburns, Steve Jukes looks more like a rock 'n' roller than a reggae fan as he presides over his shop, Big Apple Records in Nottingham's Heathcoat Street, a never-ending source of vintage reggae vinyl. Indeed, he's one of the few people who love both rock 'n' roll and Jamaican music: Elvis Sun 45s nestle alongside black-and-silver Coxsons in his collection and in his shop. He puts this diverse taste down to his upbringing.

'Where I grew up, in Colwick, and over in Snenton, there were a lot of black immigrant families, so a lot of my mates when I was a boy were black and I heard their records – blue beat, early reggae. I used to go round their houses, and there'd be a shebeen, the older people would be in there playing the music and we'd be stood at the door listening. Meanwhile at home my elder brother was playing his rock 'n' roll records, and he also played guitar and sang, so I was exposed to rock 'n' roll too.'

Nottingham has had a black population for longer than most English cities – there was already a substantial immigrant community by 1958, when the regrettable race riots took place that would be overshadowed shortly afterwards by events in Notting Hill. Of course, with these settlers came a demand for their indigenous music, as Steve relates.

'One of the first, and in my opinion the biggest, sound system operator in Nottingham was a guy called Skylark, who went to school with Coxson Dodd in Jamaica. He's still around, in his 70s now. He arrived in England in the early '60s, set up a sound in Manchester, then brought it over to Nottingham about 1964. He played all the local venues for years – everyone knew Skylark. He had these huge record boxes that looked like treasure chests, all full to the top with vinyl. At that time, in the late '60s, early '70s, the best reggae gig in town was the Ad Lib Club in the Lace Market; they would have sound system sessions on Thursday nights, and live acts too. That was about the only big club, most of the sound sessions would be in pubs like the Bluebell in Foreman Street, which is still there but it's changed. At that time the DJ used to say, "Here is the one white record of the week, man" and he'd play "Return To Sender" by Elvis. Every single week. The rest of the music was 100 per cent black.'

Alongside the sound systems, specialist record shops sprang up to satisfy the needs of fans. 'The main one was on Union Road, between the back end of Mansfield Road and St Ann's [a major area of West Indian immigration]. I think it was run by a white lady and a black guy, and it was already there in the '60s, in the days of Blue Beat, Ska Beat, Studio One, strictly a Jamaican music shop although they sold only British releases, no imports. You can still find old records in Nottingham with the Union Road stamp on the sleeve; the funny thing is, the shop never had a name. There was a similar one down Arkwright Street in The Meadows, which again did only UK releases.'

Steve also has happy memories of a bookshop that sold reggae as a sideline. 'The Ace Bookshop was at the back of the Theatre Royal. It was a big bookshop, and upstairs was all records, UK-label records. They had a good stock of reggae, but it was rare that people used to buy it from there, so when they were virtually closing down, about 1972, they sold them off at two pence a time, and if you bought a load it was even less!'

In the early 1970s, Steve's elder brother turned to DJing, and Steve first learned the value of correct promotion. 'My brother would play Motown, all the stuff that was popular then, and I would do an hour's spot at each gig. I took along my reggae records because that's what I was mostly into at that time. I'd clear the floor every time! We were playing in pubs and places like the RAF Club in Arkwright Street, and when my spot came up, I got up there and played reggae. People would come up and say, "Not that bastard reggae stuff again! Play something we can dance to!" Because those weren't the right venues for the music: the session would be billed as soul and Motown, or whatever.

'So when I started to do my own gigs later on, me as The Duke and my mate Dave Forman as Blue Cat, I made sure there were posters and flyers advertising it as a ska and '60s reggae session. Advertising is the key to success – we used to pack venues like Bellamy's Wine Bar out at a pound a ticket. They'd run out of beer by ten o'clock and people would be dancing on the bar top!'

Unlike Birmingham, Nottingham has never had its own reggae record label, but it's not short of local artists, as Steve explains. 'There have always been ska bands, often more Two-Tone than vintage ska as far as their stage show goes. Perhaps the best-known local group is The Naturalites, and The Royal Roots also live in Nottingham. Bobby Melody, who did "Jah Bring I Joy", is Jamaican but he's lived in this area for years. He still performs, singing over his backing tracks, which are recorded on a CD.'

The lack of a local reggae record label is all the more surprising when we consider that in the late '60s and early '70s, brothers Bill and Pete Campbell, as members of Mighty Sparrow, and Winston Curtis, singing with The Favourites, all lived in the area. After moving to London, the Campbells would found the BB and Union labels, while Winston Curtis would run his Empire imprint.

Having promoted some local bands, by the '90s Steve, Blue Cat & Co reckoned that their city was ready for some bigger names. Their exploits, which led them to promote all-time greats like Laurel Aitken ('The local paper ran the story that he was flying in from Jamaica to sign a contract at the Big Apple Record Shop – actually he lives in Leicester,' recalls Steve) and Max Romeo to sell-out crowds in the '90s, are beyond our scope here. They show, however, that the Nottingham reggae scene, kick-started by Skylark 40 years ago, continues to thrive.

IAN SMITH AND THE WORKINGS OF THE INNER MIND

It is a fact that in the world of early reggae white people were not heavily involved. Dave Hadfield, Jack Price and Vic Keary were white reggae producers, certainly, but none was also known for fronting an active touring live band and establishing their own, back-of-a-shop record label as well. Ian Smith, however, managed to do all three.

The Inner Mind started out in West Yorkshire as a white soul/pop band playing Otis Redding and Wilson Pickett covers (they'd also been known as The Inner Circle at one time). Although the band's line-up changed over the years, the most stable of these consisted of Ian (lead vocals and keyboards), Finlay Topham (lead guitar), Dave Tattersall (bass) and Jimmy Walsh (drums).

Quite by chance, a guy by the name of Errol Babb, leading light of the Huddersfield West Indian Association, asked The Inner Mind to play at one of its dances and gave them a handful of rocksteady tunes to learn. Ian remembers these as probably being Buster's 'Shaking Up Orange Street', Jeanette Simpson's 'Watcha Gonna Do About It' and Laurel Aitken's 'I'm Still In Love With You'. Although they were the only white guys at the function, The Inner Mind went down a storm and the West Indian crowd demanded they play the rocksteady tunes they'd learned several times over, which was no problem at all since the band had all realised that this was the music they wanted to get into. From that point on, it was the West Indian sound all the way for The Inner Mind.

Playing rocksteady, and later reggae, the band became a big draw both locally and further afield. In fact, wherever there was a West Indian community they'd be booked to play. Notable club gigs were Sheffield's Shades (managed by one Max Omare, son of an African chief), where they had a residency,

Bristol's Bamboo (run by Tony Bullimore, he of champion yachtsman fame), Count Suckle's upmarket Q Club in London's Paddington, Huddersfield's Venn Street, Arawak and Palm Springs clubs, and the various nightspots with which the Palmer brothers were associated (notably Willesden's Apollo, Harlesden's Club West Indies/Club 31 and another one out in High Wycombe, possibly the Newlands). Later, the band would cut two instrumentals – 'Arawak Version' and 'Venn Street Rub' – in tribute to the two Huddersfield venues. Apart from performing their own original material, The Inner Mind would also back touring artists such as Laurel Aitken, Winston Groovy, Honey Boy, Alton Ellis, The Jubilee Stompers and Owen Gray.

Towards the end of 1970 Laurel Aitken, a regular visitor to the Huddersfield reggae venues, took one of The Inner Mind's acetates over to Pama records for demonstration purposes. Jeff Palmer was suitably impressed by what he heard. The acetate featured 'Pum Pum Girl', 'Freedom' and 'Dreams Of Yesterday', the first two of which saw issue on the company's Newbeat subsidiary, as did 'Witchcraft Man'/'Night In Cairo'. The following year, Pama's Bullet subsidiary put out 'Arawak Version'/'Cuffy Guffy' and 'Devil Woman'/'Venn Street Rub'.

Jeff Palmer had also wanted The Inner Mind to form part of the Pama session band team, doubling up with The Mohawks; but with no guarantee of a regular income from such work, neither Ian nor the others were attracted by the offer. Nor did they want to be based away from their northern fan base and Yorkshire roots. It is also worth bearing in mind that, apparently, neither Ian nor the band had received any money from the sales of their Pama singles.

Shortly after the release of 'Devil Woman', Ian tried a one-off shot with Rita and Benny King's R&B Discs in London's Stamford Hill. 'Witchfinder General'/'Deserted' was put out on the couple's new Hillcrest imprint and was issued under the moniker 'Smithy All Stars'. As with the Pama sides, 'Witchfinder General' was excellent skinhead reggae and, if skinhead reggae is up your particular street, this comes highly recommended. The arrangement with the Kings (who had by now legally changed their surname from Izons) was not entirely to Ian or the band's satisfaction, however, and there were no further releases.

So, having reaped no financial benefit from The Inner Mind's sojourn with two of the UK reggae majors, Ian opted to look at setting up his own label. The first was Shades, named after the Sheffield nightspot, which was actually financed by the aforementioned Max Omare. Its first release was a nice piano workout called 'Dreams Of Yesterday', a popular disc locally. A little while later, Pama clandestinely issued this track (it was on that initial acetate don't forget) as 'Breakdown Rock', crediting it to The Harlesden Monks. The second and final Shades release was the superb 'Jesse James Hits Back', the flip side of which, 'Let Me In', was penned by Laurel Aitken.

These tracks, and indeed all the previous Pama and R&B Discs output, had been recorded at a tiny studio (MAT) at the rear of H 'Matt' Matthias's audio shop at Colthorpe Yard, 38 King Street, central Huddersfield. Therein lies another story. Matt was something of an electronics wizard and developed a fine line in powerful amplifiers and top-drawer turntables, which were manufactured at a workshop in nearby Netheroyd Hill. Matt Amp products were in great demand by reggae sound system operators and are prized pieces of audio equipment today. The records themselves were made in somewhat primitive conditions, being taped direct to disc without any mixing down. This gave them a very raw, bass-heavy sound.

After Shades, Ian's next label venture in 1972 – which fortunately had a rather longer life than its predecessor – was Hot Lead (that's 'lead' as in 'lead bullet', not as in 'guitar lead' as has previously been suggested). He ran the operation from his house in far-flung Dewsbury, near Huddersfield. There wasn't a 'no. 1' release on Hot Lead as 'Jesse James Hits Back' effectively filled that spot, but the honours for inaugural issue went to Mr T Bones – alias John Noel – with 'Ruby'. John now lives in Leeds, and 'Ruby' sold a respectable 750 copies. Again, the sales were particularly strong at the regional level. For each release, 100 white-label copies, often just rubber stamped with the 'Hot Lead' logo and featuring handwritten credits, were pressed for promotional purposes.

After 'Ruby' came Alton (alias Aud/Audley) And The Groovers' 'Warm And Tender Love', a disc that, on the occasions it turns up, always seems to be in an extremely tired condition. Incidentally, Audley still lives in Huddersfield and is the lead vocalist you hear on The Groovers' 'Bend Down Low' on Pama's Escort label. A few releases later, Owen Gray turns in an excellent performance with 'Hurricane', a strong vocal with some nice accordion touches. Another local pair, The Dalton Brothers from Huddersfield's Dalton district, had a single issue with 'Farewell Don't Cry'.

The two Hot Lead releases that are the most common, in the south anyway, are The Groovers' cover of Roy And Paulette's 'Since You're Gone' and Smithy's 'Reggae Limits' (which is well worth picking up if you like the 'Apollo moon landing' series of records released around 1969). The only side not to have been recorded at the King Street studio was Superbad's 'Julie', which was produced by one D McIntosh at a studio in Birmingham. Incidentally, Superbad later became The JALN Band.

Despite its essentially local nature, Hot Lead did enjoy one really big seller – Smithy's 'Doggie Bite Postman'. It shifted around 22,000 and was a potential National Breaker – Ian just couldn't get copies pressed up fast enough. At various times and depending on which outfit had the available capacity, the record-pressing facilities of Orlake, Linguaphone (the foreign language specialists) and British Homophone were used. The latter also pressed records for Torpedo, Hot Shot and Crystal, and these can be identified by their deeply etched matrix numbers and raised rim. West Brothers of Mitcham, who printed labels and album sleeves for both Pama and Trojan, among others, were used for Hot Lead releases. The only copyrighted song on the label was 'Scarlet Ribbons', hence the stamp-sized 'Mecolico' paper stickers on the labels verifying that Castle Hill Music (Ian's publishing company) had paid a copyright fee for use of the tune (it is incredible that other reggae companies never seemed to use these).

Despite some strong sellers, Hot Lead as a regular issuing record label was finished by the early part of 1975, although a one-off maxi-single saw the light of day in 1976. This was in large part due to two particular labels/distributors taking, but never paying for, Hot Lead stock. Ian was unable to carry these debts himself, which meant he was effectively unable to press more discs. The Inner Mind also disbanded that same year for a combination of reasons. First, the burgeoning move towards the roots and culture side of the music meant that the UK's 'live' reggae acts, such as The Inner Mind, Winston Groovy and The Marvels, had begun to seem rather dated and unfashionable. It is also true to say that there was a general backlash against British-made reggae at that time, particularly as far as the younger elements of the audience were concerned.

Also, following the trend in the south, the north was now tending to feature only sound systems at venues: live acts were seen as a largely expensive and unnecessary overhead. Ian wrote to *Black Music* magazine in March 1976 to state his case about whether white bands could play reggae as well as black ones – they could and The Inner Mind had proved it. There was clearly a great sense of frustration during this time: the scene was changing, reggae was becoming more inward-looking and there was still no recognition for white players of the music. As the dread philosophy of the '70s increased as the decade wore on, fewer and fewer white musicians ventured into reggae music.

But The Inner Mind's glory period of 1968–74 is still fondly remembered by many people in and around Huddersfield, and their place in British reggae's history deserves to be documented. These days, Ian is still performing and producing in the area, although most of what he now does is outside the sphere of reggae. We are grateful to him for the many valuable reminiscences he has shared with us.

REGGAE UP NORTH

Shades and Hot Lead must have been the first reggae labels that were based outside the UK's inner cities and large African-Caribbean communities. Interestingly, even today there is a big demand in the West and South Yorkshire areas for UK-recorded 1970s reggae by the likes of Honey Boy, Gene Rondo and Winston Groovy. This is possibly because, with barely any specialist shops in that part of the country, fewer sound systems playing out and fewer blues parties, a lot of reggae was heard via touring artists such as these, and the punters were less hostile to a sound that was perhaps less ethnic than the music that was in fashion down south. Basically, they liked the sort of music they were hearing at live shows.

As Ian Smith's recollections reveal, there was a flourishing reggae scene in Yorkshire. Aside from The Inner Mind and The Groovers, Huddersfield bands Jab-Jab and The Big R Soul Band also backed artists at the various Huddersfield venues. Many top artists made the trip to those bleak climes, including the late Nicky Thomas, Dave & Ansel Collins, Johnny Nash, Eddy Grant, Matumbi, Desmond Dekker, Delroy Wilson, Bruce Ruffin and – the biggest draw of them all, would you believe – Millie Small. Apparently, there were queues round the block to see her when she played at premier venue the Venn Street Club. The second-contender award for the fullest house went to Gregory Isaacs.

Other local venues included the Shalimar Club in Sparrow Park, the Fartown International in Huddersfield's Fartown district near the football ground and the Leeds International further afield in Francis Street, Chapeltown. There were many other live venues in the area too.

In a depressing sign of the times, Matthias's audio shop and the MAT studio at 38 King Street were demolished around the end of 2001 to make way for a new shopping mall. The authors of this book were fortunate enough to visit the area just prior to the arrival of the wrecking crew, and by the look of things the studio must have been a pretty compact affair! Similarly, the Odeon-sized 1,000-capacity Venn Street Club was razed to the ground to make way for another shopping development. The Arawak Club in Upper Brow Hill was demolished some years back to make way for a small purpose-built block of modern flats. Only the Marillo Domino Club in Paddock now survives, although that was never actually a live venue as such. The Palm

Springs Club just round the corner from Venn Street is still there in the guise of the Parish Pump, but is now very much a modern watering hole.

In terms of specialist reggae outlets, there were just a handful in business north of the Midlands, and most of these shops must have got their records quite a bit later than their London counterparts since, given the distance, it was never that easy for a regular distribution network to operate there. The mid-point distribution-wise was Birmingham, where Brian Harris's Vandisc operation served the Midlands and the north very nicely for a time. However, with most of the reggae labels down in London, the capital's residents would always be able to buy the latest discs first.

By 1978, though, there was another key distributor: Mo Claridge's Mojo Distribution, with a one-stop operation in West Bromwich. Before Mo's arrival on the scene, you had to be very determined to acquire a decent stock of new reggae music in the north. The former owner of the Music Cave shop on Huddersfield's Bradford Road told us that he actually made regular trips in person to Ethnic, DIP, K&B, Trojan and other London reggae houses to buy records direct.

The only northern shops specialising in reggae that we're aware of were Hunter Smith's Jumbo Records in Leeds city centre (amazingly still there, but now handling all types of music), an outlet in Leeds' Chapeltown district co-owned by the late Lee Hyman (who also ran the Leeds International club) and those run by Sir Yank (or 'Yankee' as he was more commonly known), who operated a couple of shops in Chapeltown's Gathorne Street and the notorious red-light area of Spencer Place. The latter outlet specialised in pre-releases, and copies of Jamaican pre-releases still turn up with the 'Spencer Place' rubber stamp on them.

There was also a shop over in neighbouring Bradford, and another across the Lancashire border in Oldham, run by a guy known as Funky Chicken. Chicken carried product from Hot Lead and R&B Discs, which Ian used to distribute up north for Rita and Benny. Other than these outlets, it must have been a bit of a barren area if you wanted to buy reggae music on the independent labels. A punter could of course buy or order reggae product from the mainstream record retailers, but would have some trouble finding the latest releases on DIP, Jama or Ethnic Fight.

During the '60s and '70s, it was financially viable to sell reggae wherever there was a black community of a reasonable size, hence specialist shops were springing up all over the place. The situation then was rather different from that of recent times, in that the market for the music was definitely there, but finding the records in the overwhelmingly 'white' high-street shops was no easy thing. Today, though, such places would be unable to support similar operations since the last 15 years or so have seen the music regress into the position it was in at the very start of the 1960s, with just a few outlets flourishing in urban areas where West Indians heavily outnumber others. This is particularly the case in cities where the black communities have traditionally been small and confined to certain neighbourhoods, like Chapeltown in Leeds, St Paul's in Bristol and Toxteth in Liverpool.

The prime reason for this downturn has of course been the increasing influence of US rap, house, techno, garage, R&B (new style) and other forms of black dance music, which have appealed to black youth more than reggae or its latest incarnation, ragga. Basically, the black music arena has fragmented from the traditional 'plenty of reggae with a bit of soul chucked in'. As Brian Harris says, the reggae scene had become dominated by a new breed of DJs by the early 1980s. This, coupled with the prevailing topics of gun talk and slackness, led to a much smaller market for the music. In reggae's heyday, sales of a new single usually reached a couple of thousand and then some – now that figure could be as low as a couple of hundred. Those great days when you could walk into your local stockist in Chesterfield or Hertford and buy the latest Pama single off the shelf are no more.

7 Style And Fashion: Aprés Trojan

REGGAE GOES MAINSTREAM

By late 1976 two big companies, Chris Blackwell's Island and Richard Branson's Virgin, had largely supplanted Trojan in the reggae marketplace. The many independents existed alongside them, but there's no doubt that both Island and Virgin offered top-quality product from the top-rankin' Jamaican studios. The news had buzzed around Kingston late in 1975 that Virgin and Island were looking to sign contracts with the top producers, and that comparatively large advances were being offered to artists, with the possibility of royalties to come later. Figures rumoured to be in the region of £20,000 were mentioned but, as the saying goes, in Jamaica there is only rumour, not fact.

The Mighty Diamonds were among the first to be signed to Virgin and their debut LP for the label, *Right Time*, is an absolute classic. U Roy, The Gladiators (both through producer Prince Tony Robinson), Johnny Clarke (through Bunny Lee) and Keith Hudson were soon added to the roster – although the only album Hudson delivered to Virgin, *Too Expensive*, was a funk-rock offering that confused label and reggae buyers alike. As a result, Virgin dropped Hudson as quickly as it had signed him, and he headed off to the USA to record once again in a reggae vein. Island had signed Bob Marley And The Wailers in 1972 and was, of course, already very familiar with promoting reggae – after all, its owner Chris Blackwell had been producing Jamaican artists since the '50s. By June 1976, Marley was seeing UK album chart success with *Rastaman Vibration* and was just around the corner from the sort of international success hitherto unknown in the reggae world.

Meanwhile, Island also had an exclusive contract with Lee Perry, which meant that albums like The Upsetters' *Super Ape*, Max Romeo's *War Ina Babylon* and Jah Lion's (aka Pat Francis, aka Jah Lloyd) *Columbia Colly* were available nationally at the standard (ie non pre-release) LP price. Island's other scoops in 1975–76 were Burning Spear's *Marcus Garvey* and *Man In*

The Hills (Joe Sinclair had his eye on the former for his new Klik label, but Island beat him to it), Third World's *Third World*, The Heptones' *Night Food* and Toots And The Maytals' *Reggae Got Soul*. On the UK side, Island had signed young British-based reggae band Aswad, featuring fledgling actor-turned-musician Brinsley Forde of *Please Sir!* and *Double Deckers* TV fame.

Island did drop a clanger with Burning Spear's *Marcus Garvey* album, as it saw fit not only to tinker with the mix but also to speed up some of the tracks. Unlike Marley's *Catch A Fire*, which almost no one outside the Marley/Island circle had heard without the overdubs, the Marcus Garvey album was a very strong seller on Fox import, and tracks like 'Slavery Days', 'Resting Place' and the title track were selling in huge quantities on Ja singles through the import specialist shops, hence it was very obvious that Island had messed with the album.

Ian MacDonald in a piece entitled 'Public Service Announcements' in a November 1975 issue of *NME* tore apart the Island version of the album, even quoting the time differences in the supposedly identical tracks due to the speeding up. He also pointed out that the striking graphic of the Ja Fox label sleeve highlighting Marcus Garvey was tuned down to the point where Garvey's face had become a small two-inch sticker slapped randomly on the sleeve front.

With a drastically dropped-back bass and a rock-friendly remix, Island was obviously aiming to take Spear to the masses as it had Marley, and indeed the album did sell very well, but for the core reggae audience a slab of Jamaican vinyl was the only way to hear *Marcus Garvey*.

Island's only paltry defence of this messing was to say that, as the Ja original was in mono and as it wanted stereo, producer Jack Ruby had remixed it. Beyond that, Island refused to comment and, notably, Spear's follow-up album, *Man In The Hills*, was left well alone by the label and appeared in all its Kingston-roots glory.

Normally, then, Virgin and Island served reggae fans well, offering a good range of raw, undiluted reggae albums (*Marcus Garvey* aside) at good prices on top-quality vinyl aimed at a global audience. Some critics argued that the pressings were not as 'heavy' as their Jamaican counterparts – possibly true since many of the mixes were certainly different – and, a despicably elitist view, that the labels made the music too easily accessible: it had gone overground. These same critics also postulated that Virgin and Island threatened the existence of small independents. This was patently not true, since the independents continued to thrive and flourish.

What's more, neither Virgin nor Island attempted to dominate the reggae singles market (45s being the most purchased format at the time and the one on which most indie label releases came). It was usual for Virgin and Island to issue one single taken off each of their album releases, largely to whet one's appetite for the larger format. Unlike, say, April 1974 (a completely random date) when Trojan had 20 singles in *Black Music*'s top 30 reggae charts on its main label and various subsidiaries, Island and Virgin had maybe half a dozen between them in any one month by mid-1976. None the less, Island had some significant hits that year, such as Leroy Smart's tremendous 'Ballistic Affair', Junior Murvin's 'Police And Thieves' (eventually a national hit in 1980) and Jah Lion's DJ version of 'Police', entitled 'Soldier And Police War'.

Such was the success of its reggae albums that Virgin launched its specialist Front Line label, specifically for roots and culture music in 1978. There were, however, already rumblings of discontentment from Jamaican artists disappointed by what they perceived as unexpectedly poor royalty payments. Unfortunately for them, the advances paid by the two companies would often more or less match the sales achieved. There were also accusations from some that Island in particular had promoted Marley at the expense of their own material. Whatever the nature of these personal gripes, Virgin and Island probably offered Jamaica's top artists their best chance of making some decent money in the cut-throat world of reggae.

Two much smaller operations sprang up during the 1977/78 period to supplement what Island and Virgin were doing. Alan Davidson's Lightning label emerged in 1977 from a specialist record shop of the same name at the Harlesden end of Harrow Road. First selling a neat line in Jamaican pre-release albums, Davidson soon began licensing these albums for UK release on Lightning at standard prices. Lightning put out Culture's *Two Sevens Clash* set and the various chapters of Joe Gibbs And The Professionals' *African Dub* LPs several months after they had sold heavily on import. Following a short-lived arrangement with Marcel Rodd's Trojan/B&C, Davidson signed a distribution deal with Warner Brothers/WEA, which effectively meant that Lightning could reach shops nationally and had big company back-up. Further Lightning retail shops were also opened in Islington and far-flung Ruislip.

Lightning handled all Gibbs' productions in the UK and had national singles hits with Althea And Donna's 'Uptown Top Ranking', a UK number one in early 1978, and Dennis Brown's updated 'Money In My Pocket' the following year. Just prior to this, it had a considerable measure of underground success with Prince Far I's gruff 'Under Heavy Manners', Marcia Aitken's revival of Al Green's 'I'm Still In Love With You' and Trinity's 'Three Piece Suit' (the immediate precursor of 'Uptown Top Ranking'). Lightning also introduced a moderately successful sister label, Laser, which had a top 40

UK hit with Me And You's 'You Never Know What You've Got' (a Dennis Brown/Castro Brown production). Album-wise, it issued Dennis Brown's superb *Visions*, which had sold heavily on Ja Joe Gibbs, through a licensing arrangement with DEB Music.

Lightning had always dabbled in the burgeoning punk, new wave and disco markets with seemingly limited success, and it should come as no surprise, therefore, that it put out a lot of material that would not be appreciated by the reggae fraternity. Sadly, though, the label seemed to die a very sudden death around 1980, for reasons difficult to fathom. Being largely reliant on one Jamaican producer (Joe Gibbs) for material, however, was not an ideal situation by any means, and on the face of things, it looks as if this and other licensing arrangements ended, leaving Alan Davidson and Lightning floundering. Undeterred, he bounced back with the Old Gold subsidiary, which became a tremendously successful pop oldies label, issuing literally hundreds of revived 45s throughout the 1980s.

Sufferers Heights

The late 1970s reggae market was full of small UK-based labels issuing either home-grown product or licensed Jamaican goods. One label on which you could be sure of every issue being a classic track was Sufferers Heights. Joint label owner Dave Hendley reveals the label's origins.

'I was working for [the Marcel Rodd-owned] Trojan at the time, and was getting very frustrated with the system, and the fact they just didn't pay enough to the producers to get the top-drawer music. They weren't competitive, so all that we would get were the things other labels didn't want, or second-rate stuff.

'I used to take my lunch break in a pub over the road from Trojan and would chat to the production manager, Paul Wateridge, who also used to take his break there. Paul knew nothing of reggae, but knew everything about sales. So we hatched a plan to make a record label. I had the contacts having already been to Jamaica – I knew Jammy [producer Lloyd 'Jammy' James] – while Paul had the know-how to sell the records. I had no money for the project so Paul borrowed from a relative, I think, to get us started.

'The label name of Sufferers Heights had been kicking around in my head for a while. It was a biblical-type place in Jamaica – out of Kingston past Spanish Town. Steep, rocky place with a small shanty town built on a hillside. I said to the taxi driver we were with as we passed through, "Where's this?" and he replied, "Why, that's Sufferers Heights, man", and the name stuck with me. So we had a label name but no records.

'I went out to Jamaica in the January or February of 1979 with Mo Claridge and David Rodigan. I knew Rodigan from when I worked on the mail-order side of Dub Vendor and he had a market stall, selling reggae records, in Oxford. I was out there scouting for things to pick up for Trojan, and they had financed me going. At the same time I was looking around for the first release on Sufferers Heights. I met many people down at King Tubby's [studio], and Jammy played me "What A Great Day" by Lacksley Castell. I did a cash deal with Jammy for the tune with Lacksley lounging in the corner – he was only a young boy. Anyway, Jammy mixed it down from the four-track master tape for me one night.

'Sugar Minott had sold me his *Ghettology* album for Trojan, and he played me his own "Hard Time Pressure". I knew of the tune from the Captain Sinbad pre with him toasting over it and snatches of Sugar's voice in the background. The Sugar vocal was amazing and I did a deal on the spot. He brought the tape up to me a little while later when he was over here.

'We moved "Hard Time Pressure" up to be our first release and put the Lacksley Castell back as the second – even though the labels had been printed so in fact we released Sufferers Heights no. 2 before no. 1. Linguaphone pressed up 2,000 copies and they sold straight out. In fact, "Hard Time Pressure" was successful enough for Paul to leave Trojan and open an office. I have to say that Paul did all the donkey work – it would never have happened if it'd been left to me. I just looked after the artists side of things.

'Next, we put out "Youthman Promotion" by Ranking Joe backed up with "I Love Sweet Jah Jah" by Barry Brown – it did OK – it was a kinda stop-gap to keep us out there. Then in spring 1980, Paul and I met Mikey Dread [Campbell] in New York – I'd already met him in Jamaica in the February. I left Trojan and took a second trip to Jamaica in the July with Mo Claridge. We went for a month – Mo was out there to record The Royal Rasses' *Experience* album – the whole thing was done in a month.

'I went to Tubby's to meet Jammy and we got Earl Zero to recut "Please Officer" and got Augustus Pablo to blow on the other side. Well, King Tubby had this dub plate for sound system use only from Horace Andy, "Pure Ranking". He played it to me, and in the end I bought it. It needed mixing [for release on 12-inch] and I hassled Tubby to mix it; he did it in one take – 15 minutes, that's all! Everything was one take at Tubby's. Tubby was getting uninterested in mixing by this time and much of the stuff was done by Jammy. Well, "Pure Ranking" is one of the few records that did without doubt have a Tubby mix.

'Next we put out Rod Taylor's "His Imperial Majesty" backed up with "Behold Him", which we got from Mikey Dread, and I wanted a Mikey Dread dub album. He gave me a four-track, which Jammy mixed for me in a rush – in one take late one night. Mikey also gave us a separate tape of jingles, which we overdubbed back in London and added some reverb, speeding up and such.

'We had a Mikey Dread album, *African Anthem*, which was put out on our Cruise label. We wanted to keep it separate from Sufferers Heights and Mikey was getting a lot of media attention back then. The Cruise label design was more flashy – more disco – the album went top 60 in the Virgin chart. Mikey was asked to support The Clash on tour in 1980, but I wasn't interested so I just walked out of the thing. I'd had a very severe personal blow as well, which had spun me out, so I just let it all go. Paul put out one more Sufferers Heights 12-inch, but that wasn't anything to do with me.

'I did have one more go at a label with Pirate when my close friend Fatman [Ken Gordon] gave me Don Carlos's "Late Night Blues", which just sold and sold – it was such a great record. Linguaphone pressed that up and had a special offer on coloured vinyl – it was a few pence cheaper per record than black so I went for that. The next pressings were black as the special offer was gone.' Sufferers Heights releases sported many variations in label colours. This was 'Just for variety,' says Dave, 'to keep things fresh.'

'One thing I was always proud of with Sufferers Heights was our contracts. I was disgusted with the "in perpetuity" contracts that were around [where the artist signed away any rights to the work for ever]; all our contracts were for five years only, and only in the UK. They could release their work anywhere else in the world, and after five years the work was theirs again to do with as they pleased.

'I saw Sufferers Heights as a hardcore roots label, and we just made it up as we went along. I was only in my 20s and you just do things – they were great times.'

Reggae And Punk Fusion

One of the more interesting developments in the music during 1977 was the crossover between reggae and punk/new wave. Although light years apart in terms of sound, the two had much in common. Both genres were classified as 'underground', and were rebellious and anti-establishment in content. The punks and the Rastas formed part of the great dispossessed, and were drawn together as a result. Both types of music often came on to the market by way of DIY, cottage industry-type labels, produced on shoestring budgets and a flying-by-the-seat-of-their-pants philosophy. In 1979, reggae band Misty In Roots signed punk rockers The Ruts to their People Unite label, a perfect example of this ethos. And, like punk, reggae received little airplay. There was a hardness and 'reality' inherent in both genres, and a complete lack of any hype or commercialisation in their promotion.

The cross-pollination was sometimes musical as well as social. Among others, The Clash covered Junior Murvin's 'Police And Thieves' and Stiff Little Fingers did likewise for Marley's 'Johnny Was'. In between the three-chord thrash numbers, a punk outfit might slow things down with a few reggae licks and some thunderous bass lines. It all fitted in pretty well. You can hear the reggae/punk fusion going on in Public Image's eponymous debut single of 1978. And, as its title suggests, The Ruts' 'Babylon's Burning' has lyrics that fit well with both genres.

Geoff Travis's Rough Trade shop off London's Portobello Road was one of the first 'crossover' shops to begin stocking reggae early in 1977. A freelance music journalist, Travis had always liked the music and saw the affinities with punk. Honest Jon's further up Portobello Road soon became another such outlet.

Virgin's reggae albums were naturally available in its extensive chain of shops and sat alongside a wealth of other product: labels like Greensleeves, Magnum, Conflict, Third World, Melodisc, Klik, Grove Music, GGs and Studio One albums direct from Jamaica were all included, shrink wrapped, in Virgin's racks. This was unbelievable compared to the situation just a few years previously when most high-street stores wouldn't touch reggae. Virgin also kept a limited and slightly haphazard stock of reggae 45s although, as is the case today, 90 per cent of the company's business was in album sales. One particularly hip title was a pre-release of Augustus Pablo's 'Islington Rock' on the man's Rockers imprint – quite a startling find in a major store on your local high street.

It was rare, though, to see punks in any of the specialist shops in, say, Brixton or Tottenham. The reggae and punk cross-fertilisation tended to happen in the trendier parts of London like Notting Hill, Islington and Ladbroke Grove, where the punks would often be squatting in decaying Victorian properties. The great thing about the reggae/punk fusion was that you could now just walk into Virgin and pick up a copy of, say, Trinity's *Uptown Girl* or Tommy McCook And Bobby Ellis's *Blazing Horns* albums.

As it turned out, there were particular problems with Virgin's 'supermarket' concept since the product was intended to be taken direct from the shelf to the checkout. So as the vinyl was inside the sleeve, there was every incentive for the light-fingered just to wander out of the shop with it: this was before the days of security tags. Strangely, it always seemed to be the reggae and punk sections that 'walked'. Virgin was then loath to stock reggae but, talked into it by the distributors, was happy to make an exception and revert to a 'Master Bag' operation in the case of both musics.

Further bonds between reggae and punk came about as a result of the rise of the right-wing National Front during the late 1970s, as black and white united to join forces against fascists on the march. The Rock Against Racism (RAR) movement was very much the vibe of 1978, when punk bands shared the bill with reggae acts like Aswad, Steel Pulse and Misty at many a RAR benefit gig.

A particular turning point that year was the Front's march through the African-Caribbean areas of Peckham, New Cross and into Lewisham, an event at which things turned very nasty. Hatred towards the police intensified as they walked alongside the marchers to oversee the right to free speech and peaceful demonstration. It was easy to see the slowly burning tinderbox that eventually ignited oppressed ghetto areas of inner cities a few years later, by which time the UK had mass unemployment, a rapidly diminishing manufacturing industry and all the other unpleasantness that went hand in hand with living in Thatcher's Britain.

The Mojo Man

It would be unfair to leave out the role of the distributors in getting the music out to the masses. One key distribution outfit set up at the end of 1976 was Mo Claridge's Mojo Distribution. Sound system operator Mo had started out working at Pama's shop and, prior to establishing Mojo, had been on the road as a van salesman for Creole. With a few Barry Biggs hits under its belt, Creole started to move upmarket and Mo decided to move out and do his own thing, together with ex-Trojan van salesman Phil Xavier. Their underlying philosophy with Mojo was to get reggae into both the specialist shops and the high-street stores. It was Mojo that gained the interest – and trust – of big chains like Virgin and HMV, and secured the lucrative contracts to service them with reggae product from Island, Phonogram and leading reggae indies such as Hawkeye, D-Roy and Greensleeves.

With two vans on the road doing the rounds in London alone, Mojo was ahead of the game compared to the smaller indies that were just selling their own product. For Mojo, selling to Virgin and HMV was well worthwhile since they were well-resourced financially and had the cash. The obvious but uncomfortable truth is that it was always easier for a white guy than a black guy to sell to a white shop. The ethnic labels and their vans simply didn't go to white shops, or had given up doing so – so they were always going to be stuck in the same old routine, selling to the same old shops.

That said, the way reggae was sold didn't change: the music wasn't played on the radio, the prospective customer couldn't get to hear it, and the white shops' policy wasn't to have groups of youths milling around clamouring 'Play this one', 'Touch the flip side of this' or 'Nah, don't want that'. If they weren't buying it, they weren't wanted. The specialist shops carried on doing the business the way it was always done, and that was playing the music out in front of the customers. But Mo Claridge sold to both black and white shops, and was well respected for what he did.

Mojo also entered the record label game itself with Bam Bam (with releases from Alton Ellis and Ansell And The Meditations), Magnum (which later evolved into Ballistic) and Warrior. There was also a Mojo record shop just along from Pama's in Craven Park Road, Harlesden, and a reggae one-stop distribution centre, mail-order and retail outlet 130-odd miles away in West Bromwich: Hit Factory Records.

Some fine direct-from-yard music was issued on Ballistic/Magnum, including releases by Dillinger, The Royals, The Jolly Brothers, The Royal Rasses and Winston Jarrett And The Righteous Flames. Both labels also did their bit for the UK end of things with releases from London bands The Naturals and Psalms. Magnum was the product of a pressing and distribution arrangement with Pye (although Mojo of course handled distribution as well). That deal seems to have either lapsed or fallen through by April 1978, and Ballistic was set up through a similar arrangement with United Artists.

Mojo seemed to be everywhere until another distributor, Plastic Fantastic, came into the picture during 1978. This new outfit was linked to Pye, and distributed the various labels that company was associated with at the time, like Roots, Ultra, Manic and Pearl. Mojo stayed around for a couple more years but seemed to disappear around 1980.

CHANGING TIMES

Bob Marley's international success aside, three things began to hinder the sales of reggae records in the UK during the mid- to late 1970s and led to, at the very least, a slackening of demand. In spring 1977, the first UK-pressed reggae 12-inch 45s began to appear in the specialist shops. A few of the direct-from-yard variety had already been available but were prohibitively expensive and their impact had thus been fairly limited. These 12-inch 'disco 45s' had been popularised by the big US soul discos like Studio 54 around the middle of 1976 and, no doubt about it, the wider groove radius ensured that these discs boasted superior range and reproduction – and they played louder. It was always inevitable that they were going to catch on in a big way with sound system operators, but they took a while to get started in the reggae market, both here and in Jamaica.

Among the first British-pressed reggae 12-inch disco 45s available were Vivian Jackson's 'Chant Down Babylon Kingdom' on the Prophets label and Pat Kelly's re-done 'Talk About Love' on Phil Pratt's Chanan-Jah imprint, which had a great toast from Dillinger midway through. They cost about £1.50 each – the price of two conventional singles at the time – and it's unlikely that either was ever made available on the smaller format. At this early stage, there were probably no more than three or four 12-inchers in the reggae top 30, but this soon increased as more and more UK reggae companies got hip and responded to increasing demand. Obviously, it was more expensive to press disco 45s and, having more money tied up in them, an operator needed to be sure they'd be sellers. This is probably one of the main reasons why they were relatively slow in getting off the ground.

Cost was still a major disincentive. Prices got ridiculous after 12-inch disco 45s became really popular and the pre-12s from Jamaica were the things to have. By 1978, Dub Vendor's record stall in Clapham Junction's Northcote Road market was knocking out the latest Joe Gibbs And The Professionals titles for around £3.50 a throw – pure extortion – but no criticism is levelled at DV since the discs cost a fortune to buy wholesale in the first place. Some buyers no doubt found it quite annoying to have a good vocal track 'interrupted' by a DJ they didn't particularly like, or the inclusion of a slow, meandering dub workout (not everyone was into dub). These would previously have been tucked away on the flip side of a 7-inch where listeners could avoid hearing them if they preferred.

By the middle of 1978, a large proportion of reggae singles were still thankfully available in both formats, but there was a growing tendency to issue the 'Special Limited Edition Discomix With Brass Knobs On' variety, which weren't available at all on 7-inch. One absolutely stunning tune from this period is The Techniques' 1977 version of 'Love Is Not A Gamble' on a Carib Gems' 12-inch with Ranking Trevor doing his bit halfway through. But could it be found on a 7-inch single? By the early '80s only very strong sellers would be pressed on 7-inch. No doubt many will disagree about this, but the price of 12-inch singles really did seem to deter a sizeable proportion of people from buying the music and, with that, reggae started to lose some of its market. In particular, the slightly older thirtysomething punters, accustomed to just three minutes a side, simply had neither the time nor the money for such new-fangled things.

The second factor in the decline in sales – a well-documented fact this time rather than mere opinion – was the soaring popularity of Jamaican pre-release singles and albums during 1976 and 1977. Sales of pre-releases have of course always been an integral part of the reggae business – if it does well on pre, it's liable to get picked up for release by a UK company – but such was the intense level of sound system activity in the mid-1970s that everyone wanted the hottest sounds before anyone else. Absurdly, it soon became pretty much a no-no for a sound to play a released tune, despite the fact that it had gained UK release because fans liked it.

The reggae media soon introduced a pre singles chart, and it then became commonplace to see several pre titles appearing in the reggae album listings too. These were naturally being sold at the expense of British pressings and they often accounted for as much as 70 per cent of a specialist shop's business. By the middle of 1977, pre-release 45s retailed at about £1.20 each, against 70 pence for a UK single (pre-releases cost as much as 90 pence each to buy wholesale).

The 'pre versus released' battle was to a large extent temporarily resolved later that year when, as a result of ever spiralling inflation, the price of vinyl went up in Jamaica, which led to the cost of pre-releases in the UK going up to £1.40. UK 12-inch 45s cost little more and thus started to eat into the pre-releases' share of the market. Also, certain astute UK reggae operations were deliberately making their 45s appear like pre-releases so that they would attract a higher price. It became difficult to know what was and what wasn't the gen-u-ine Jamaican article.

The third and final sticking point was the lack of any *Tighten Up*-type compilations on the market. The budget prices of Trojan's TBL and TT series LPs had undoubtedly made reggae music accessible to a mass market seven or eight years previously, and thus helped promote the music to a wider audience. Trojan had started to go upmarket during 1972 by making incursions into full-price, or near full-price, stereo albums. Apart from a few final splutterings, its 99 pence each *Tighten Up* and *Club Reggae* series were wound up.

Island and Virgin did put out some good-quality, budget-priced LPs – especially *This Is Reggae Music* and *The Front Line* respectively – but these were clearly intended as mere samplers or promotional vehicles, and included tracks from existing or imminent albums by single artists. Good though they were, they never seemed to hang together quite as well as the Trojan and Pama efforts. Perhaps this was because those labels were able to include material by an array of different producers, and their compilations always seemed to be dictated by what had sold well and what the fans wanted to hear rather than what was dictated by current release schedules.

With pre-releases and 12-inch 45s having very much taken over the reggae marketplace, coupled with the lack of cheap compilations, the cost of buying the music had greatly increased since earlier in the decade. There are some contentious statements here, we know, but this is certainly how it appeared at the time. Also, as Brian Harris recalled in Chapter 5, by the close of the 1970s the roots phenomenon was largely over and sales had begun to decline as a result. As he was in the business of selling the music, you can certainly take his word for it.

LOVERS ROCK MOVES IN

As we have already seen, Ginger Williams' 'Tenderness' hit the top reggae spot in 1974 despite being recorded away from Trojan and its usual coterie of British-based reggae artists. It effectively broke the mould. UK independents produced even more reggae chart material after Ginger's breakthrough, some largely forgotten now: Honey Boy's 'In A Game' (Penguin), The Velvet Shadows' 'My Happiness Depending On You' (Sunbeam), Carl Bert's 'Loving Girl' (DIP), Leroy Housen's 'I Die A Little Each Day' (Third World) and Errol Dunkley's 'Letter To Myself' (Fat Man).

These records, all basically finely crafted love songs, were the precursors of the very British phenomenon that was to become lovers rock. As Kingston was rootsing-up, the London sound was dividing between the sweet love song and the incoming influence of Dread. Plenty of club-goers did not want to hear of sufferation, the red gold and green and Marcus Garvey all evening, especially if they were with a loved one who needed a bit of close body contact that night.

The kick-start in 1975 was undoubtedly the aforementioned 'Caught You In A Lie' from Louisa Marks, which sold so well as to be issued in Jamaica – quite a coup for a 14-year-old London girl. Her subsequent releases, such as 'All My Loving' and 'Six Six Street', repeated the success.

TT Ross, one of the few white female singers to break into reggae, struck gold with 'Last Date' for Dennis Harris on his Lucky imprint, and with the establishment of the Lover's Rock label by Harris the music had a tag and the genre had arrived. 'Last Date', indeed, sold so well that it was leased to major label Polydor and just missed the pop top 50.

The initial recordings in the new style were by young girls with voices shrill enough to shatter glass at 20 paces, bemoaning love lost or unrequited love, or celebrating love gained. Normally plucked from school, in their dinner hour they would voice these tear-jerkers before heading back for afternoon lessons.

From these somewhat makeshift beginnings, some exemplary singers emerged, such as the harmonious Brown Sugar trio. Their sweet but rhythmic reading of Barbara Lewis's soul gem 'Hello Stranger' set them on their way, with 'I'm In Love With A Dreadlocks' and the particularly good 'Black Pride' (with Dennis Harris at the helm) enhancing their reputation. The latter record signalled another sub-division in the reggae world – that of 'conscious lovers', as exemplified by Sandra Reid, Sandra Cross and Kofi (who updated 'Black Pride' for the Mad Professor) in the early 1980s.

Girl trio 15-16-17 hit home hard with 'Black Skin Boy', (Morpheus Records), an appreciation of the West Indian young man above all other races, which although not politically correct now, was a major lovers rock landmark. It certainly made its mark in Kingston judging by the number of UK-pressed copies that appear over that side of the Atlantic.

Into this arena of Kleenex, lost love and desertion came capable artists such as Caroll Thompson, an excellent singer with a voice way beyond schoolgirl shrillness, Joy Mack and the major chart-breaker Janet Kay. Her 'Silly Games', produced by lovers rock master Dennis Bovell, and originally issued on the Arawak label prior to major label Scope picking it up, struck the UK Number 2 spot in June 1979 (it hit again, reaching Number 22 in August 1990 on Arista, and Number 62 with a dance remix at the same time).

On the male side, singers such as Tex Johnson (on his own neatly named DiscoTex label), Trevor Hartley and rootsman Vivian Jones (more of him in the UK roots section on pp189–97) carried the swing. The biggest name in commercial terms was Trevor Walters, who climbed the charts with 'Love Me Tonight', which struck Number 27 in October 1981, the Lionel Ritchie song 'Stuck On You', which carried him to the Number Nine spot in July 1984, and a final brief chart flirtation at Number 73 for 'Never Let Her Slip Away' in December of the same year.

The lovers rock world was not, however, just singers and backing bands. The excellent self-contained band One Blood included within its members one Paul Robinson, who as his alter-ego Barry Boom would later crack the reggae charts both as a performer and as a producer, by propelling Maxi Priest high into the pop realms. One Blood's 'Get In Touch With Me' was picked up by major label Ensign and almost cracked the nationals as it moved from reggae clubs to mainstream dance floors in the mid-1980s.

One particularly notable group was north London's Instigators (not to be confused with the equally good Investigators from south of the river), who were the stepping stone to lasting success for UK rhythm twins Leroy and David Heywood, otherwise known as Mafia and Fluxy. Mirroring Kingston's Steely and Clevie, they spread a broad base of rhythm and production work, ranging from sweet lovers rock, through ragga, to working with visiting Jamaican roots artists like Max Romeo.

The D-Roy label hit hard with The Blood Sisters' version of Anita Ward's 'Ring My Bell', which was notable for an especially wild dub-mix on the flip.

The 1980s found two main labels carrying the swing as far as lovers was concerned. The first, Fashion, an offshoot of the London-based Dub Vendor record supplier (see pp218–19) hit immediately with Dee Sharp's 'Let's Dub It Up', and Ariwa, run by the aforementioned Neil 'Mad Professor' Fraser, who, with his bright production work, scored heavily with the likes of Deborahe Glasgow, Paulette Tajah, John McClean, Kofi and Sandra Cross (who was originally a member of The Wild Bunch, another Ariwa act).

Like any musical movement, lovers rock spawned numerous new labels of which only a noted few lasted longer than a couple of releases. These included Groove & A Quarter, which was run by an able group of guys known as The Administrators. Their own recordings, like the slinky 'Move Your Sexy Body' and Vivian Jones' 'Sugar Love', had a particular warmth to them, while Leonard Chin's Santic label captured the sublime Jean Adebambo, whose tour de force was 'Paradise'. The almost one-hit wonders, Harlesden's own Eargasm, whose personnel included white *Black Echoes* journalist Snoopy, held the top of the reggae charts in spring 1980 with the self-explanatory 'This Is Lovers Rock' on Venture Records before disappearing again.

The tender-voiced Peter Hunnigale also rose as the 1980s moved along. Although he built up an exemplary catalogue of work, which sold well, beyond the lovers/reggae circle he was an unrecognised talent until the 1990s. Then Jamaica acknowledged him when he was one of the UK artists chosen to play the major Reggae Sunsplash concert. Latterly he has been singing in a conscious style, albeit still in a sweet vein, and remains one of London's best-kept secrets.

Among others who have served are: Samantha Rose, whose soul cover 'Go Away Little Boy' is her best-known work; Victor Romero Evans, who made his initial impression with 'At The Club' before making it on to major label Epic for the excellent 'Miss Attractive'; Keith Douglas, who hit with 'Cool Down Aminia' and ex-Cimaron Winston Reedy with 'Dim The Lights' and the equally good but less recognised 'Daughter of Zion'. Visiting Jamaicans also took advantage of the lovers style as they passed through, one of the earliest being Lincoln 'Sugar' Minott, who recorded some very worthy love songs in London for issue on his UK-pressed Black Roots label, notably 1980's 'Lovers Rock'. Junior Delgado also applied his normally militant voice to an album for Fashion Records, which included some love songs.

ROOTSMAN IN THE UK

While the lovers rock fashion was in full swing, UK attempts at making roots music were also on the rise, starting in the mid-1970s. Delroy Washington was a pioneer of British roots reggae, as he cut a couple of bona fide early classics in 'Jah Man A Come' (tucked away on the b-side of a Carl Dawkins Lord Koos 45) and 'Freedom Fighters' on the tiny Axum label, which masqueraded as a Ja pressing with large centre hole, but was actually manufactured in London. Unfortunately most copies of the latter have a pressing fault and jump on the a-side, making it hard to appreciate Delroy's artistry to the full.

One oft-cited criticism levelled at black musicians brought up in the UK's ghetto areas was that they had no experience of the hardships, political rivalries and abject poverty going on back-a-yard and could not, as a result, reasonably expect their music to be taken seriously. As Keith Drummond, lead singer of Black Slate, said in a July 1977 *Black Music* interview, 'The sufferation in Jamaica, I think, depends on who's in power at any time. In this country, it doesn't matter who's in power – if you're black, you're going to go through sufferation. In my own case, over half my life so far has been in Jamaica – I was born there and stayed there 'til I was 13. So from my childhood, I know what life is. Like, a kid of 13 wouldn't know what a real rough life is the same way we do in Jamaica. We learned what struggle is, so when we combine the two influences together – half from here and half from Jamaica – we obviously won't have the same feel that they've got over there.'

Black youth in Britain was dealing with a similar, but inherently different, set of problems: police brutality, racism, stereotyping and severely limited job opportunities just because their faces happened to be the wrong colour.

To say that UK-recorded reggae had a somewhat quiet voice after the skinhead boom would be true, but as the red, gold and green of Rastafari swept through Jamaica, it was only a matter of time before artists in London would feel the new breeze blowing in from Africa. One of the earliest such bands, and the one that attained the highest profile, was Aswad. Courted by Island Records, and given the honour of supporting (along with Steel Pulse) and backing Burning Spear on his debut visit to these shores in 1977, Aswad were truly a black British roots band of the highest order.

Formed in West London in 1975, with a line-up of Brinsley Forde (guitar/vocals), George Oban (bass/percussion), Angus Gaye (drums/percussion), Courtney Hemmings (keyboards/vocals) and Donald Griffiths (lead guitar/vocals), they took the Arabic word for 'black' as the group's name. Aswad soon found favour with reggae audiences, particularly for their electrifying live dub workouts at the end of their songs, and within months had been signed by Island. Their debut single, 'Back To Africa' in 1976, was very mellow, very rootsy and very London, and heralded the arrival of the new young band.

Their playing was tight and impeccable, as demonstrated on the 1976 *Aquarius* programme on UK reggae where they are filmed backing Delroy Washington at that year's Notting Hill Carnival. In particular, Angus Gaye's drumming is superb, his tight rolls and crisp lickshots easily the equal of any Jamaican performer. He is still arguably the finest reggae drummer the UK has produced.

Their debut LP for Island, simply titled *Aswad*, contained some of their finest works, notably 'Natural Progression', where they take the 'live' dub playout from the concert venue on to vinyl. The album received the full Island treatment and came with a printed inner sleeve with 'roots style' pictures and a gorgeous, eye-catching outer jacket. *Hulet*, the follow-up album, may actually have been recorded before the first one. Issued on a joint Grove Music/Island label in 1978, it took the listener further into their London roots sound, and once again proved the power of the group with tracks like 'Behold Him'.

Bassist Oban left in 1980 to form the jazz-tinged reggae group Motion, and Tony Robinson, who had taken over from Courtney Hemmings on keyboards, now assumed bass duties.

Best known for the rousing instrumental 'Warrior Charge', Aswad were now complemented by a crisp horn section and expanded their sound courtesy of UK producer Michael 'Ruben' Campbell.

A move to CBS the following year brought forth the LPs *New Chapter* and its dub counterpart *New Chapter of Dub* in 1981 and 1982 respectively, but the band were by now moving towards a more universal sound, incorporating lovers rock as well as roots reggae, thereby losing the restless London 'dread roots' of their 1970s work. However, with the explosion of the new dancehall sound of the 1980s, Aswad moved with the times (and moved back to Island) and issued an album, *Live and Direct*, which was recorded at the 1983 Notting Hill Carnival.

From 1985 onwards, Aswad issued a handful of worthy singles on their own Simba label, starting with their own 'Bubbling' and notably including

'Promised Land' from Dennis Brown with, of course, backing by the band, before they managed to hit the national pop charts in a big way in 1988 with 'Don't Turn Around'.

If Aswad made it to the top, the career of vocalist Delroy Washington was the complete antithesis. The criminally underrated Washington was born in Jamaica in 1952 and came to the UK in the 1960s. He cut his teeth in the early 1970s Pama days, as noted in an earlier chapter, and then moved on to work at Island's Basing Street studios lending a hand, or rather voice, to the overdubbing work carried out on The Wailers' *Catch A Fire* album in 1973. He got no credit on the album sleeve for this work, but did receive encouragement from Marley when they met in the studio. Two singles followed, and then in 1976 he signed with Richard Branson's mighty Virgin Records.

The outcome of the signing was two fine albums. The first, *I-Sus*, released in 1976, included the 'Freedom Fighters' single, minus its jump this time, and the studio version of 'Jah Wonderful' as filmed live for the *Aquarius* UK reggae programme. The album was enhanced no end by the presence of the majority of Aswad on backing chores (this was possibly reciprocal, as he had sung backing vocals on their debut album). *Rasta* was issued the following year and continued in the same uncompromising vein, although sadly both albums were all but ignored by both reggae press and music buyers alike. After the *Rasta* album, Washington and Virgin parted company amicably due to them being unable to agree on the funding for a live band to tour with the singer.

Washington's main claim to fame remains the perennial blues dance favourite 'Give All The Praise To Jah', which Virgin issued on 12-inch and which is still a much appreciated work. It hints at the career Delroy might have had if fortune had smiled on him.

Another London-based group that did find fame was Black Slate, whose original band members comprised Anthony 'Tony' Brightly (keyboards), Keith Drummond (lead vocals), Desmond Mahoney (drums), Chris Hanson (lead guitar), Elroy Bailey (bass and vocals) and Cledwyn Rogers (rhythm guitar).

Formed a year before Aswad, in 1974, Black Slate trod the usual backing path before hitting hard in 1976 with the lyrically and musically vicious 'Sticks Man' (*Black Echoes*' Snoopy saw fit to dedicate an entire quarter-page to the single so well regarded was it). The anti-mugging single was issued on their own Slate label and hit home hard with its opening scat vocal intro and sound system-style bass. After a nationwide tour in 1978 and the setting up of another label of their own, TCD, they found limited success with the more subdued 'Mind Your Motion'. An album followed in 1979, *Black Slate*, which was picked up by Nigel Grainge's larger Ensign label and afforded a remix prior to its re-release the following year.

Slate's year of distinction was to be 1980, with their rise to Number 9 in the national charts with the simple but catchy 'Amigo', with the follow-up 'Boom Boom' making Number 51 in the December of the same year. Further albums and a handful of singles followed but the band never regained the incisive edge of 'Sticks Man'. Anthony Brightly moved on to found the Sir George label and produce some of the most satisfying lovers rock recordings of the 1980s, notably Sandra Reid's outstanding 1983 LP *If Dreams Were Real*, which encompassed both love and reality songs.

Another band of outstanding musical achievement, but little commercial success was Merger, which formed in the mid-1970s, with a line-up of Barry Ford (lead vocals/guitar), Winston Bennett (vocals/guitar), Ivor Steadman (bass), Mike Osei (drums) and Tony Osei (keyboards), with the two Osei brothers departing early on in the group's career. Their 1977 album debut, *Exiles In A Babylon*, featured the multi-instrumentalist Michael Dan (aka Mike Dorane), who also played bass (Steadman was noted on the sleeve but was unable to perform) and added vocals. He also co-mixed the album, on which Ford took over on drums.

The group's name, Merger, was originally intended to reflect the input of the various races present in the band and their differing musical styles (Dorane was half-Native American), but with the departure of the West African Osei brothers the group's sound hit the heavy roots groove and mixed in a London vibe courtesy of Dorane's keyboard work. Initially, the set was released in West Africa, and then in the UK on the one-off 'Sun Star Muzik Co' label, complete with a quality gatefold sleeve, following a remix.

Unfortunately, no one appeared to buy the album, which was a crime as it was without doubt one of the landmark UK roots reggae albums, with deep and heavy tracks like the title cut, '77' and 'Understanding' all catching the times perfectly. There was also a formative funk-reggae blend on 'Massa Gana' (written by Dorane), which he had originally cut as 'I'm Going To Ethiopia' by Big Roy for his own Movers label the previous year.

The album really was a tour de force by Dorane and Ford, both in terms of the writing and the playing. A 12-inch single followed, 'Biko', paying homage to South African martyr Steve Biko, and then the group appeared to split, with Ford moving on to a solo career and Dorane following his own idiosyncratic path (as detailed elsewhere in this book, see p113).

A London-based band that nearly made the big time were The Reggae Regular, whose 'Where Is Jah' was the debut release on the Greensleeves label

The Sunday Times Magazine, 4 February 1973

Pat Rhoden, London, 1963

Photograph courtesy of Pat Rhoden

Photograph courtesy of Pat Rhoden

Left to right: Johnny Johnson (Jama Records Director), Pat Rhoden, Tracy King (singer with The Meditations UK), and Ruddy And Sketto (one of Jamaica's first duos), 1975

BBC Radio London 'Reggae Time' DJ Steve Barnard rocks the crowd, 1973

REGGAE,
A Peoples' Music
Rolston Kallyndyr
Henderson Dalrymple

20p

The first book on West Indian music
to be written and published in the UK

The 'Hot Rod' Cimarons, circa 1974

Aswad: The Young Lions, circa 1976

Black Slate made a name for themselves with the anti-mugging single, 'Sticks Man'

Reggae Regular: live and direct, circa 1978

Photograph courtesy of Roy Shirley

Roy Shirley's distinctive vocal style ensured his continuing popularity in the world of West Indian music

Photograph courtesy of Noel Hawks

Dub Vendor stall in full swing, summer 1979

BLACK MUSIC

February 1974   25p/US one dollar

REGGAE SPECIAL!

Do black musicians get a fair deal?

An oasis in the sea of the rock press

Photograph courtesy of Noel Hawks

Dub Vendor, 155 Ladbroke Grove, London. (Left to right: John MacGillivary, Redman, Papa Face, Noel Hawks)

Black Wax, Birmingham, circa 1976

Photograph courtesy of Glenroy Oakley

Greyhound, circa 1971. (Back left to right: Danny Bowen Smith, Errol Danvers, Sonny Binns. Front left to right: Trevor Ardley White, Glenroy Oakley)

Photograph courtesy of Glenroy Oakley

Glenroy Oakley in full swing on *Top Of The Pops*, 1971

Photograph courtesy of Pat Rhoden

Photograph courtesy of Pat Rhoden

Lee Perry, London, 1967

Bunny Lee, London, 1967

Rupert Cunningham
headed up Sound
Tracs after leaving
Ashanti/Bamboo

Joe Sinclair, manager of
Klik, circa 1978

Flyer for DBC,
circa 1980

Photograph courtesy of Sid Bucknor

Vic Keary at the Chalk
Farm board, 1980

Bamboo and
Ackee boss,
Junior Lincoln,
circa 1978

Courtesy of Mike Pealing

DEB dance handbill, 1978

Rare Planetone label offshoot from 1963

A UK-pressed comment on the 1958 Race Riots

Major labels tested the ska water early on, as with this Decca issue of an album originally released by Rio (1964)

The best for Prince Buster ska (1964)

Ska and rocksteady gems galore (1967)

Pama Records gave Trojan some serious competition in 1969

I-Sus, a superb album from Delroy Washington with startling jacket graphics (1976)

Photograph courtesy of Virgin Records

Jamaican Blues vies with Owen Gray Sings (issued by Starlite) as the
first UK-pressed album to present the urban Kingston dancehall sounds
to London (1961)

in 1977. Their even more impressive 'Black Star Liner' (Greensleeves' fourth release) was issued in early 1978, and gained praise from all quarters. A 12-inch version of the two singles back to back, complete with dubs, was issued by Greensleeves (only the label's second disco issue) and quickly became a very desirable item among collectors as it offered both quality and quantity.

A shift of name to The Regulars and a change of label to the major CBS found them trying for a more accessible sound; whether this was their own or their new label's decision is unknown, but the *Victim* LP (1979), despite its 'free' 12-inch single and quality gatefold sleeve, just did not convince the reggae public to spend their cash, and the mainstream was not attracted to it either. From there it would appear that the band dispersed. Members Alan 'Kingpin' King and George 'Flea' Clarke went on in the reggae world, notably with the renamed Alan Kingpin releasing the indicting 'Letter From Jail' in the nu-roots 1990s.

A band who stuck to their principles was Misty In Roots. Formed around 1974 in Southall, Middlesex, on the fringe of Greater London, they always remained a collective concern, with band members coming and going around a core of the two Tyson brothers, Walford and Devlin. They consistently shunned major-label interest, preferring to run their own People Unite label for all their works and side projects.

They soon became known as a no-nonsense Rasta reggae band rocking audiences at colleges, open-air concerts and benefit gigs for various good causes, such as Rock Against Racism. Through these performances they became well known within the punk circle.

People Unite provided a place for all to come, to reason, to create and to compose. From this melting pot rose one of their first studio recordings, the double a-side 12-inch single 'Richman'/'Salvation'. The single and tracks from their debut 1979 album, *Live At The Counter Eurovision*, gained play on local radio, both pirate and legal. Radio 1 DJ John Peel, then as now a champion of rebel and minority music, was very fond of the band and they performed on his show a number of times in the early 1980s.

Their gigs alongside white punk bands and their tireless touring both in the UK and abroad had paid dividends, with a very racially mixed audience eagerly awaiting Misty's vinyl output and sending the LP high into the reggae charts. Encouraged, the band began work on a fresh album, which arrived in 1981. Entitled *Wise and Foolish*, it contained new material alongside studio cuts of some of the songs from *Live At The Counter*. This was a powerful album, dedicated on the inner sleeve by Misty to 'the freedom of Africa and all the oppressed peoples throughout the world'.

After much touring throughout England and further afield, two years later the LP *Earth* slipped out, to a surprisingly quiet response. In 1985 *Musi O Tunya* was released after Misty's return from extensive touring of Africa. It was seen as their strongest set, upholding the roots tradition forgotten by many of their Jamaican counterparts at the time. The whole album was their most fulfilled and complete, and was the last to feature Delvin Tyson, who died in 1987. The band made one more LP, *Forward*, in 1989, exhibiting a much crisper and brighter sound.

It was not only groups that proudly waved the roots banner in London, however. Three of the biggest tunes ever recorded in the genre were by solo singers: Vivian Jones's 'Who's Gonna Get Caught', Lion Youth's 'Rat A Cut Bottle' and Pablo Gad's 'Hard Times'.

Voted the most talented singer/songwriter in the UK by *Echoes* black music paper in 1981, Jones had come as a youngster to the UK from Ja in 1967. By 1976 he had worked in local west London bands such as The Spartans and The Mighty Vibes. An early roots-inspired single, 'Red Gold And Green', from 1976 credits 'V Jones and Dr Birds' as the performers.

A tie-up with the strangely named Virgo Stomach label (an offshoot of John Rubie's UK-based Freedom Sounds imprint – itself affiliated to the Ja version run by Bertram Brown and Earl 'Chinna' Smith) resulted in the heavy roots outing 'Who's Gonna Get Caught', which brought him to the attention of the reggae audience, along with the dancehall favourite 'Red Eye'. He followed this with the LP *Bank Robbery*, still retaining the hard roots feel, before he crossed to a gentler sound with the single 'Good Morning'. Jones had by then switched to the more tender climes of lovers rock, scoring with the excellent 'Sugar Love' in the 1980s and continuing a string of hits through the decade and on, notably 'Strong Love' from 1991. He is now back in the roots fold with hard-hitting works such as 'Big Leaders' and 'Aids In Africa'.

Very little is known about Lion Youth beyond that his real name was Clarence Williamson and his first record was 'I've Got To Go'. He then teamed up with Rubie (and his aforementioned bizarrely named Virgo Stomach label) and released the dance-rockers delight, 'Rat A Cut Bottle', which commented on strife and hard times in the land. With a voice very similar to that of Gregory Isaacs and a solid roots backing, the record hit the top of the reggae charts and stayed there for three weeks. The follow-up, 'Chant In A Dance', fared well and the Youth recorded an LP with producer Rubie, *Love Comes And Goes* (1982), which mixed roots and lovers themes. From then on, Lion Youth seems to have disappeared slowly from the scene, leaving us with his 'Rat A Cut Bottle', which is now regarded as a classic piece of UK roots.

If little is known about Lion Youth, then information about Pablo Gad is almost non-existent. Rising out of obscurity in 1980 with the harsh 'Hard Times' 12-inch, Gad continued to issue first-rate recordings such as 'Crisis Time', 'Oh Jah' and the accusing 'Blood Suckers'. An album, *Trafalgar Square*, was issued by Burning Sounds in 1980 to much acclaim and contained a selection of hard UK roots reggae tracks, notably the superb 'Jailhouse Pressure'. During the 1980s Gad's record output dwindled to nothing, possibly due to contractual problems, although he is now back in full swing recording for producer and record dealer Barry Isaacs' Reggae On Top label.

Many more London-based artists and bands served, but space does not permit them more than a brief but honourable mention here. 'Mad Professor' Neil Fraser's output from his Ariwa studio was prodigious through the 1980s, while Tradition stood astride the lovers and roots camps, as Trevor Bow and The Sons Of Jah very much affiliated with the red gold and green. Sharon Little recorded just one notable 12-inch for Jah Shaka, 'Don't Mash Up Creation', which remains a stalwart of the roots scene to this day.

Errol Bellott's 'Babylon' rocked many a dance, along with 'Jah Children Cry' from African Princess, while Tabby 'Cat' Kelly's 'Don't Call Us Immigrants' made no bones about his vision of Thatcher's Britain. This was while the Bovell/Matumbi-connected Guardian Angel sang of the 'China Gate' in 1979 inna true roots style, although their style would soon shift to disco-soul with the catchy 'Self Service Love' (1980) as their next release. Jimmy Lindsay, along with his group Dambala, had shown great promise with outings like the Jimmy solo 'Ain't No Sunshine' and the group effort 'Zimbabwe', but his *Where Is The Love* album (1979) for Gem failed to keep the momentum he'd achieved.

It should not be forgotten that major Jamaican talents also came to work in Britain at this time. First, The Twinkle Brothers' mainman Norman Grant who, at the end of his group's Virgin contract, tied in with Jah Shaka and continued to produce very worthy work both as The Twinkle Brothers and with other aspiring artists like ET Webster from London. Second, there was the superb visionary and vocalist Prince Lincoln Thompson, of Royal Rasses fame, who relocated to and recorded in London from 1983. Then there's Bim Sherman who, with the aid of Adrian Sherwood, who produced most of the tracks, issued the *Across The Red Sea* album in May 1982, and worked with Sherwood's On-U Sound label, and master singer-songwriter Bob Andy who forged links with London from his earliest travels on the back of the hit 'Young, Gifted And Black' in 1969. His I-Anka record label is still resident in the capital, although he is now back in Jamaica. So to say that London was the second home of roots reggae would be almost an understatement given the smattering of names listed above.

By the mid-1970s roots bands were springing up in every major city in England, with Birmingham's own Steel Pulse standing out from the crowd by virtue of a deal with Island Records that popped their debut album easily into record racks throughout the country.

Formed at Handsworth School in Birmingham around 1975, David Hinds (of perpendicular dreadlocks fame) was to be the central creator of the band, both as lead singer and writer. A period of establishing themselves in the Birmingham club scene was taken to new heights by the release of their debut single in 1976, 'Kibudu Mansatta Abuku' on the DIP Records subsidiary label Concrete Jungle. The dense and moody piece was a long way from the electric sound Steel Pulse are now know for, and gained an excellent review in *Black Echoes*. A sprightly 'Nyah Love' on Tempus followed late in 1977, before a support slot for Burning Spear on his first tour of the UK earned the band their contract with Island Records.

The Steel Pulse live show had always been invigorating, with the climax being them donning sinister white gowns and hoods to perform the accusing 'Ku Klux Klan' to rousing appreciation from the audience. It was this track that Island selected as the taster for the LP, and it was issued on both 7-inch and 12-inch formats. The album, *Handsworth Revolution*, followed in 1978 and was as good as everyone hoped, and Steel Pulse took centre stage both in the black music and rock music press.

The follow-up album, *Tribute To The Martyrs* (1979), was well received, as was *Caught You* (1980), but with a move to Elektra from Island they seemed to lose impetus, possibly due to the major label wanting them to shift away from their Rasta-fuelled stance to a more mainstream approach.

It is remarkable how few reggae acts have found success and happiness through a move to a big label. Despite their financial clout and media penetration, the big boys just don't seem to understand how to market the music – not in Britain, anyway. As interest in Steel Pulse dwindled in the UK, the new market of the USA opened and the group, minus a few members, spent increasing time that side of the Atlantic as the 1980s moved along, scoring a medium-sized hit with the *True Democracy* LP along the way.

Wolverhampton, an unlovely industrial town near Birmingham, produced Capital Letters, an eight-piece band picked up by Greensleeves Records, which issued their only album, *Headline News*, alongside two very worthy 12-inch singles, 'Smoking My Ganja' (an understandably popular title) and 'Natty Walk'. *Black Music* gave their album a rave review and four stars in its November 1979 issue, but they never scaled the heights of Steel Pulse or Aswad. Apparently the group were well thought of in the Netherlands, perhaps due in part to that 'Ganja' title, although they quickly faded from view.

Bristol contributed the superb Black Roots, who started out at the tail end of the 1970s, although they came more to prominence in the following decade, with their self-titled debut album, on their own Kick label, gaining both public and critical acclaim in 1983. A remix by DJ-cum-producer Jah Woosh of an album track, 'Juvenile Delinquent', was particularly strong and highlighted the band's roots outlook in the dancehall world of the mid-1980s. Black Roots toured ceaselessly countrywide, and the authors of this book can remember seeing them give an excellent performance locally in Tonbridge around the middle of the 1980s. They even recorded the signature tune for a BBC TV series, *The Front Line* (1984), with an LP of the same name appearing on the Kick label.

UK GEMS

So what were the top UK reggae records of the 1970s? The following are 50 examples of the genre that we consider to be classics in their own right, and equal – although intrinsically different – to what was coming over from Jamaica. They are listed in alphabetical order of labels and we have not therefore attempted to rank them in any sort of order of superiority.

Affection

Can't Let You Go/Version – Bridie Stewart (AFF 001) (Prod: Sonny Roberts) 1975

A forgotten classic, which seems to turn up quite frequently in London. It is vaguely reminiscent of Lee Perry's production on Susan Cadogan's 'Fever'. Moody and sultry.

BB

Is My Love Too Late?/This Love Version – Honey Boy (BB 009) (Prod: Bill Campbell) 1975

Most lover's rock was done by women, but this was probably an early approximation of it male style. In fact, the sort of sound that aimed to appeal to the ladies was largely Honey's stock in trade. His lyrics aren't too good (the line 'I'm going straight' presumably relates to an ex-con), but the music on this is really fine, with some great guitar licks courtesy of Ranny Williams.

This track was reissued in 1979 as the flip side of Honey And The Blackstones'
cover of 'Tracks Of My Tears' (Empire EMP 916).

Burning Sounds
In Loving You/Version – Junior English (Prod: Clem Bushay) 1978

Three years on from Honey Boy's BB effort, and Junior had come to define
the male sound of lovers rock. This is a beautiful track and was reggae Number
One over Christmas 1978.

Caribbean
I'm Going To Sit Right Down And Cry/Repatriation – Errol Dunkley (CB
03) (Prod: Sid Bucknor) 1974

Almost certainly recorded at Chalk Farm Studios, where Sid Bucknor was
resident engineer alongside Vic Keary. Errol settled in the UK late in 1973,
working initially for Count Shelly with local band The Pressure Shocks, and
has remained here more or less ever since. The flip is the one to go for – a
nice early cultural piece.

Circle International
I've Been Trying/Second Attempt – Clinton Grant (Prod: Dennis Bovell and
Clinton Grant) 1977

Grant has a falsetto voice, which works well on this anti-oppression number.
This was his best tune by miles.

Concrete Jungle
They Cannot/Version Cannot – GD/Jungle All Stars (CJ 753) (Prod: George
Dekker) (1976)

For some reason (contractual obligations with Trojan perhaps?), George
Dekker wanted to go undercover with his efforts on DIP, of which Concrete
Jungle was a subsidiary. A good self-composed number.

How Long Must We Wait?/Long Wait (instrumental) – African Stone And
The 4th Street Orchestra/4th Street Orchestra (CJ 600) (Prod: Dennis Harris)
1976

*Sufferers' time again, and Dennis Bovell undoubtedly had a hand in this.
African Stone were probably Matumbi using a different name for work they
placed with other producers, like Dennis Harris and Buster Pearson. The 4th
Street Orchestra were also Matumbi, probably augmented by session guitarist
John Kpiaye and a few assorted others.*

Congo
Nation Fiddler/Fire! – Makka Bees (CO 1) (Prod: Congo Music) 1977

*About people cheating the system, this should be in anyone's top ten of British-
produced roots reggae. This was the obscure Congo label's first release (the
second came six years later) and Birmingham DJ Macka Bee had nothing to
do with it.*

Count Shelly
Sweet Talk/One And Only Lover – Honey Boy/Junior English (CS 007) (Prod:
Lord Koos) 1973

*Just prior to forming his own label, soundman Koos was giving his early
productions to Count Shelly for release. On this one, Honey croons well over
an original rocksteady backing. A fine record. The flip is Junior's cover of
the song made famous by Gregory Isaacs.*

CTJ
Jah Life/Roots Life – Ranking Rueben with Winston Fergus And The Equators
(no issue number) (Prod: Equator) 1978

*Excellent DJ piece over a solid rocking rhythm. Rueben cut other music for
Trevor Bow's Natty Congo imprint, and Fergus and his Equators recorded
for other labels, notably Lightning and Klik.*

DEB Music
Black Starliner/Version – Reggae Regular (DEB 6) (Prod: Castro Brown) 1978

*Not sure why Reggae Regular chose to recut the tune they did first for
Greensleeves, which was tuff enough. This one seems heavier, though, with
a similarly heavy dub. RR later became The Regulars when they secured a
CBS contract.*

Ethnic
Miracle Worker/This Love – Sidney Rogers (ETH 22) (Prod: Larry Lawrence) 1974

Another winning release from one of the early '70s new independents, this went into the reggae top ten. A truly great song, and it's interesting that Sid seemed to stick with Lawrence for the duration of his solo career. His other notable record was 'Don't Throw Stones', which came out through Trojan on both Big Shot and Techniques. It isn't known what happened to him and why he had stopped singing by the end of the '70s.

Ethnic Fight
Cupid's Arrow/Cupid Rocker – Honey Boy/Ethnic Fight Band (EF 004) (Prod: Larry Lawrence) 1975

See Honey Boy's name on a record and think it's gonna be wimpy British reggae? We passed this up plenty of times thinking that, but it was a misguided view, as we discovered when we heard it. This is a do-over of Sam Cooke's 'Cupid' with a '60s rocksteady backing. Very nice.

Fat Man
Letter To Myself/Version – Errol Dunkley (FM 003) (Prod: Fat Man Hi-Fi) 1975

A Eugene Record-penned Chi-Lites song, the backing is solid and Errol's vocals rock nicely along. This went into the reggae top ten during mid-1975. Available on a re-press a few years ago due to 'Revive' demand.

Four Sixty
You Had Your Chance/Version – Joy Mack (FS 001) (Prod: Tony Washington) 1978

Joy was a great singer and this was a great song, very popular at the time. It falls between lovers and a reggae interpretation of Millie Jackson.

Golden Age
You'll Lose A Good Thing/Version – Christine Joy White (GAM 02) (Prod: Sidney Crooks and Danny Ray) 1977

An update of the Barbara Lynn number, long a favourite with West Indian audiences. A good production too from Crooks and Ray, both of whom had come to settle in the Harlesden area. The track was also featured on the label's Golden Age Of Reggae *album compilation. Annoyingly, many copies of the 7-inch single turn up with a damaged rim.*

Greensleeves
Where Is Jah?/Jah Is Here – Reggae Regular (GRE 001) (Prod: Lloyd Patten) 1977

The first ever release on the label, this was issued at a time when UK-produced roots music was beginning to be accepted by reggae audiences. A big hit.

K&B
Come With Me/Version – Dennis Curtis (KB 5518) (Prod: Dennis Curtis) 1976

A singer who came and went, Curtis's brother Bobby also recorded for K&B. This is a cultural piece that shows how these small labels could come up with worthwhile music. Matumbi are on here too.

Run Rasta Run/Version – African Stone (KB 5519) (Prod: Dennis Curtis) 1976

A song that bemoans the persecution of Rasta brothers in London by the police. Again, there's a Matumbi connection.

Love
Sympathy/Dub Sympathy – The Meditations (LOV 007) (Prod: Pat Rhoden) 1975

These were not Ansel Crigland's Meditations out of Ja, but a young combo from Brixton town who were Pat Rhoden's backing band. Some nice organ touches and a really good, heartfelt song. They had two more singles out on Jama's Love, the better one being 'Johnny', an excellent slice of UK roots.

Lover's Rock
I'm In Love With A Dreadlocks/Loving Dreadlock – Brown Sugar (CJ 613) (Prod: Brownie T) 1977

During the course of writing and researching this book, John Kpiaye (who was actually producer Brownie T) told us that in his view Lover's Rock was the most important British reggae label of the 1970s. Following Louisa Marks' successes with 'Caught You In A Lie' and 'All My Loving' the label, created by Dennis Bovell and Dennis Harris, defined the genre. It was just odd that it hadn't happened sooner and that somebody else hadn't already done it. 'Dreadlocks' was a great tune and these great girls had the greatest voices.

Hello Stranger/Stranger Version – Brown Sugar (CJ 614) (Prod: Brownie T) 1977

Issued almost simultaneously with 'Dreadlocks' in the late summer of 1977, this cover of Barbara Lewis's 1963 US hit was absolutely perfect for the Lover's Rock label.

Black Pride/Proud – Brown Sugar/Brownie T (CJ 619) (Prod: Brownie T) 1977

The last and best in a trio of superb Brown Sugar singles, this was issued not long before the group, apparently dissatisfied with their treatment on the part of Dennis Harris, decamped five minutes down New Cross Road to Winston Edwards' new Studio 16 set-up. After that, things went pretty much downhill for them. The tunes they cut for Edwards were all worthwhile, however, and the group re-cut 'Black Pride' for him under the title 'I'm So Proud'. After their departure to Winston Edwards' stable, Dennis Harris capitalised on his success with the group with an album release of their Lover's Rock label material, although its scarcity suggests it was either not given full issue or was withdrawn directly after release.

Lucky
Judas A No Rasta/Version – Amigo/Amigo Band (LY 6014) (Prod: Dennis Harris) 1976

A much overlooked and worthwhile roots-inspired single by an unknown outfit. With a name like Amigo, we wonder whether they might have been Black Slate, who hit with a tune called 'Amigo' in 1980. The group also had 'Jah A Go Bus Dem Shut' out on DIP's Organisation subsidiary.

Jah Heavy Load/Heavy Dub – I Jah Man Levi (LY 6016; also pressed with Concrete Jungle label) (Prod: Dennis Harris) 1976

Much better than the rather long version Levi cut after signing for Island. This is a roots and culture classic, which he performed acoustically on the Aquarius programme.

Magnet
Oh Sweet Africa/This Is Love – Gene Rondo (MA 28) (Prod: Gene Rondo) 1973

The late Gene Rondo really excelled himself on this cultural piece, and it was a theme he returned to later with 'Africa Is My Home' for Burning Sounds. Mike Dorane played on it too.

Main Line
Gimme Gimme African Love/Dub – African Brothers/Pure Roots (ML 1) (Prod: Bunny Donaldson) 1977

Matumbi again! Bunny Donaldson was sometime Matumbi sticksman and ran the Java Record Shack in Dalston, from where this label emanated. Again, this is solid UK roots.

Matumbi Music Corp
Man In Me/Man Size Rocker – Matumbi (MA 001) (Prod: Matumbi) 1976

Cheesed off with the deal they were getting from other labels, Matumbi launched their own label, doing everything themselves: recording, producing, engineering, mastering, pressing, getting the labels printed and even doing the man-in-a-van distribution. This was in the top ten listings from early 1977 right through to that June.

Daughter Of Zion/Version – Bagga (MA 002) (Prod: Matumbi) 1977

A heavy-duty roots outing from Matumbi's Bevin Fagan, alias Bagga.

Guide Us/Music In The Air – Matumbi (MA 004 – 12-inch only) (Prod: Matumbi) 1978

Considered by those in the know to be possibly the finest UK roots production ever. A compilation of Dennis Bovell material including gems such as this has been a long time coming.

Morpheus
Black Skin Boy/Blacker Version – 15-16-17 (MOR 6) (Prod: Castro Brown) 1977

This came out a couple of months before Brown Sugar hit the charts and was a huge hit. The group moved over to Dennis Brown and Castro Brown's new DEB Music label when they 'rebranded' from Morpheus. The pair had closed the Morpheus record shop at Thornton Heath and moved several miles north to open the new DEB Music shop in Clapham Junction's Battersea Rise. The three girls also worked behind the counter there.

Neville King
The Day Will Come/The Day Will Dub – The Sadonians (NK 6) (Prod: Lloyd T) 1978

Classic lovers rock by this seldom-recorded girl group, the Neville King label just brimmed over with quality. Also available on a rare compilation album on Warrior entitled For Lovers And Rockers.

Nice
Africa/Africa Is Our Home – Unity Stars/Big Dread And Unity Stars (NICE 1) (Prod: Clancy Collins) 1975

Veteran soundman and artist Sir Collins always came up with really hard UK rhythms and this was certainly one. Mind you, Clancy Eccles had recorded another tune called 'Africa' with pretty much the same sentiments as this a full five years earlier.

Paradise
I Can't Resist Your Tenderness/Little Boy – Ginger Williams (PR 01) (Prod: Ranny Williams) 1974

Already mentioned several times in this book, this needs no introduction here. Ranny Williams added more instrumentation to it on subsequent reissues which, sadly, detracted slightly from the original.

In My Heart There's A Place/He's My Honey Boy – Ginger Williams (PR 08) (Prod: Count Shelly) 1974

Shelly seemed to be producing Ginger just a few months after 'Tenderness'
so it might be assumed that all was not well in the Ranny Williams camp.
This was not actually the follow-up to 'Tenderness', which happened to be
a really mediocre thing called 'Your Love Driving Me Crazy' (PR 06) that
died a death. 'In My Heart' was pointing even more towards the lovers sound
that would have fully evolved by 1976.

Penguin

Mama Say/Stoke Newington Hop – Brenton King/Rico (PEN 1) (Prod: Count
Shelly) 1975

It is probably the flip side of this that really wins the plaudits. 'Mama Say'
has a good driving rhythm track but, depending on your personal taste, suffers
a bit as a result of having strings dubbed on. 'Stoke Newington Hop' uses
the same music with Rico doing his thing over the top. Penguin was launched
early in 1975 just as Shelly was rebranding his business as Third World.

Freedom Train/Version – Winston Curtis/Third World All Stars (PEN 03)
(Prod: Winston Curtis) 1975

Winston was a fine singer and this was one of his best. The backing is flying
cymbals all the way and may have been one of Bunny Lee's from Jamaica,
as it is known he was sending Shelly rhythms for his UK artists to voice over.
Based on the 'Train' series of tunes from around 1967–68, this one never lets
up. Sadly, most pressings are not up to scratch. Also check out Winston's
excellent version of '50s favourite 'Consider Me' on his Supreme label.

Pioneer

Move Up Starsky/When A Man Loves A Woman – The Mexicano/Harry
Hippy [Jackie Robinson] (PION 03) (Prod: Sidney Crooks and Clement
Bushay/Sidney Crooks) 1976

'When A Man Loves A Woman' was actually the a-side, but a decision must
have been taken at some point to flip this one over in favour of 'Starsky',
which just sold and sold. Everyone seemed to want a piece of it. The Mexicano
was Eddy Grant's brother David, and you can hear the similarity in the vocal
stylings. The track was later licensed for release on Pye's Baal subsidiary
(with 'Let Jah Be The One' on the b-side) and Eddy's Ice label. The track
itself was a novel piece of toasting over a UK cut (actually by Black Harmony)

of Delroy Wilson's 'I'm Still Waiting'. The UK producers and artists were at number one yet again.

Queen Bee
Rebel Woman/Version – Gene Rondo (QB 04) (Prod: Gene Rondo and Count Shelly) 1974

The second Rondo release in this list and another that is well regarded by collectors today. It is a good piece of earthy, soulful reggae over a solid UK backing.

RG
We Got A Good Thing Going/Ben (instrumental) – Zeita Massiah/no artist credited (RG 002) (Prod: Count Shelly/Sid Bucknor) 1974

Zeita (it's a he) was a regular sessioner at UK studios. Although this cover of a Jackson Five song got a few plays on Steve Barnard's Reggae Time *show, it ultimately did little business. It is, however, important inasmuch as it was far superior to the sort of cover versions of current hits that Trojan was putting out at the time. Sugar Minott got into the UK charts with the song seven years later.*

Robot
Six Sixth Street/Dub – Louisa Marks/The Bushrangers (RRS 2) (Prod: Clement Bushay) 1979

This put Louisa Marks back on top after a dry period following Trojan's 'Keep It Like It Is' in 1977. By the time this was released, 'Silly Games' had gone into the national listings. Also issued on a Bushay's 12-inch.

Safari
Caught You In A Lie/Caught Dubbing – Louisa Marks/Matumbi (SF 1105) (Prod: Lloyd Coxson) 1975

Louisa's cover of the Robert Parker song further defined the lovers rock genre and had some success in crossing over to the mainstream market. According to the press adverts at the time, this had sold 10,000 in the first fortnight of release. The usual lack of chart action was no doubt down to the usual non-chart-return shops doing most of the business.

After Tonight/Dub-In-Deh – Matumbi (SF 1112) (Prod: Lloyd Coxson) 1976

Reputedly the biggest-selling reggae single of 1976, it has only recently come to light that this was a Lloyd Coxson special on his sound for a fair while prior to formal release. They don't make them like this any more.

Sir Collins Music Wheel
Fight Life/Exodus – Honey Boy And Sir Collins/Sir Collins And The Versatiles (SC 02) (Prod: Clancy Collins) 1973

This was one of the first independents to make inroads into Trojan's dominance of the market during 1973. 'Fight Life' was based largely on Delano Stewart's 'That's Life'.

Slate
Sticks Man/Robber Man In Dub – Black Slate (KG 004) (Prod: Black Slate) 1976

This is a cornerstone of the British roots sound – an absolutely massive tune, which could never have come out of Jamaica. The message was also profound – the black 'sticks men' robbing their own brethren – and would be relevant today in the context of escalating 'black on black' crime. Unusually for a reggae single, it was still selling like mad a year or more after it was put out. An essential item for anyone's collection which, sadly, the group never bettered.

Stonehouse
Majority Rules/Ten Steps Forward – Caretaker/Ellis Band (SH 002) (Prod: Alton Ellis) 1976

A strange release by the equally strange Caretaker, 'Majority Rules' apparently uses an original Studio One backing track. This is very innovative, though (unless it was based on something we've not heard), and was treated very favourably by UK buyers.

Tempus
Jah Man/Jah – Errol Campbell (TEM 103) (Prod: Dennis Bovell) 1977

Another of the UK roots 45s from 1977 which proved that the British contingent could compare with what was coming out of Jamaica. A strident rockers beat on this tune had many people wondering if this was the product of Kingston or London. Campbell had other very worthy singles out during the mid-1970s, including 'Jah For I' (Concrete Jungle) and 'Wolves' (Shebazz).

Choose Me/Right Choice – African Stone (TEM 109) (Prod: Dennis Bovell) 1978

Far preferable to the version Dennis Bovell produced for Marie Pierre, which now seems to be lauded as a lovers classic even though it never climbed as high as this in the listings. Rootsy lovers with a dub-and-a-half on the flip.

Venture
Movin' On/Movin' Rockers – Tradition (VEN 7705) (Prod: David Tyrone) 1977

Tradition were a Harlesden-based band who for a couple of years, and with a contract with RCA in the bag, seemed almost on the verge of breaking through commercially. This was their first single for David Tyrone and Philroy Matthias's Venture label and a real beauty. Having signed with RCA, their 'Breezin' single in 1978 became a lovers favourite but was probably a little too close to the Young Rascals' 'Groovin' to really come across as convincingly original. Their albums Moving On, Tradition In Dub *and* Tell Your Friends About Dub *are well worth hunting down.*

Write Sounds
With You Boy/Dub You – Revelation (WTS 1003) (Prod: Write Sounds) 1978

This was everywhere during the summer of 1978 – a fine, fine piece of lovers music. Revelation later moved over to Burning Sounds where they were unable to produce anything nearly as good as this, although their Book Of Revelation *album is well regarded – and in particular the heavy roots track 'Survival'.*

8 The Dancehall: The Sound Systems, Reggae Radio, The Shops And The Printed Word

THE SOUND SYSTEMS

The single most important factor in breaking a record was the sound system, both in its native Jamaica and over in the UK. It was also enormously instrumental in testing an up-and-coming singer or DJ's metal, with the unforgiving crowd making him very much aware of their opinion of his work. The majority of Jamaican recording artists from the 1950s onwards have started out 'working the sound' before entering the recording studio.

The transition from live big band sounds to recorded music played over a primitive but very powerful PA system has been covered fully in several books on Jamaican music, including *Young, Gifted And Black*. Suffice to say that by 1955 after Duke Vin had relocated and set up his sound system in London, the record was king. Heady sweat-drenched US R&B rocked alongside pleading ballads initially, but as the Jamaican and UK offshoot recordings changed to shuffle and then ska, fledgling labels like Island and Blue Beat, which knew of the power of the sound system, were operating more like their Jamaican counterparts.

If a tune was big on a sound system in Kingston then a UK label would rush to issue the disc to capitalise on the demand this side of the Atlantic, after sometimes making available dub plates (acetates) of the recording to local sound men to boost interest in the disc. Word of a 'boss tune' would spread very quickly from a hot Kingston dance via visiting relatives, passing-through businessmen, aircrews, the London-printed version of *The Gleaner* (Jamaica's daily newspaper) and the like, to interested soundmen and dancers in the UK.

So West Indians in London, Birmingham and elsewhere would be very aware of the latest hot records being spun way over the sea, and would want to hear these delights for themselves. Once import or dub plate copies had arrived, the record label would gauge public reaction, and then after some wait to whet the music buyer's appetite the desired disc was pressed and issued.

Not only was the sound system gaining a foothold in the UK, newly arrived local talent was also eagerly climbing onstage to bring a little of sunny Jamaica to grey old London. Early arrivals on the UK scene – such as Rico, Pat Rhoden, DD Dennis, Owen Gray, Laurel Aitken, Jackie Edwards and Dandy Livingstone – all played live dates primarily in West Indian areas, as well as making fledgling UK recordings for Sonny Roberts, Rita and Benny King, Emil Shallit or Chris Blackwell.

Veteran UK singer Pat Rhoden recalls working 'all the town halls up and down the country' as a performer through the early 1960s. 'I think it was Bolton or somewhere like that, and people would come up and want to touch me as they'd never seen a black man before. Of course, down south and in the cities it was a different thing altogether – they were used to seeing black artists.'

As the 1960s turned into the 1970s, the sound system was fully installed across all the major cities of the UK. In addition, clubs were now established, venues like Count Suckle's Cue Club, the Flamingo, the Ram Jam and the Marquee playing Jamaican sounds and featuring live artists. The mods and then the skinheads had taken the Jamaican beat and pulled it nearer to the mainstream, to the point where reggae discs became national chart hits, as we have already seen.

Through the peak and the ensuing trough of reggae's impact on the nation's pop-pickers, the sound system remained constant – as ever, breaking new records and artists to the crowd. The retail shops certainly took a battering as reggae withdrew to its home bases once again, with the Pama and Muzik City chains closing, so if fans wanted to hear new releases it was the sound that carried the swing every time.

The roots 1970s saw new faces rising in the sound system stakes. These guys played the heavy roots and rockers sound that their young listeners demanded, with the top three shaking down to The Mighty Fatman (Ken Gordon), Jah Shaka (Neville Roache) and Lloyd Coxson (Lloyd Blackwood).

Exclusive bass-heavy dub plates were the order of the day for these system operators, with each of them moving from just playing records to producing and mixing their own exclusive recordings as the 1970s moved along.

Fatman

Fatman was born Ken Gordon and raised in West Kingston. He came to the UK in 1963 and soon became involved with the sound system scene in the Finsbury Park/Stoke Newington area of north London; he was a mike-man on the Sir Fanso set until the early 1970s when Fanso returned to Ja.

Fatman then built his own sound system, Imperial Downbeat, which soon changed its name to Fatman Hi-Fi.

By the mid-1970s, Fatman Hi-Fi had become the most popular sound in north London. He also began releasing records around the same time on the Fat Man, Boss and Godfather imprints, notable early releases being 'Easy Dreadlock' by John Brown, and 'Born Free' from Michael Rose/Black Uhuru, which was the first Prince Jammy production.

His strong links with the Waterhouse district of Kingston, and friendships with Bunny Lee, King Tubby and Prince Jammy, ensured that his sound had a steady supply of exclusive dub plates.

He began releasing records more seriously in early '80s with Hugh Mundell's 'Jah Fire Will Be Burning' and Junior Reid's 'Jailhouse' (12-inch singles on the J&F and KG Imperial labels respectively), which were both produced by Jammy. He also released the Johnny Osbourne LP *Fally Ranking* and the popular *Confrontation Dub – Fatman vs Shaka* set.

Fatman also produced the very popular 1980 hit 'Nice Time (Late Night Blues)' by Don Carlos, issued on Dave Hendley's short-lived Pirate label. He became one of the most respected and best-loved characters on the UK scene, and now runs a restaurant in north London, which acts as home from home for visiting Ja stars and UK-based artists.

He still dabbles in the music business on occasion, reissuing his back catalogue on the Fat Man label.

Jah Shaka

Named after an 18th-century Zulu king, Jah Shaka arrived in the UK at a tender age in the early 1960s and, after a brief flirtation with a small group and then a local sound system, started to build his own outfit. From humble beginnings, inspired by Rastafari and the prevailing mood of black awareness, he built up a strong following as the 1970s moved along, with the music played at ear-rending levels and interspersed with his trademark sirens – the hot steppers sound had found a champion. Unusually for a sound system operator, Shaka not only set up the system himself but also selected and played each personally picked tune, with his band of loyal fans simply helping him carry the hefty speaker boxes.

As the 1980s dawned, his brand of hard steppers sound gradually fell out of favour, but by then he had inaugurated his own record label, named after his sound, Jah Shaka King Of The Zulu Tribe. The label debuted in 1980 with his production of the rousing 'Jah Children Cry' from UK-based African Princess, which sold very well within the reggae fraternity. From humble beginnings Shaka's productions went from strength to strength as he issued a series of highly competent dub albums, while recording both UK talent and visiting Jamaican artists like The Twinkle Brothers, Willie Williams, Vivian Jones and Max Romeo.

A resurgence of interest in the patent Shaka-steppers in the late 1980s found him once again playing to full houses (with a much more cosmopolitan mix to the crowd), and his determination in sticking to the dub roots and culture brand of reggae has resulted in new followers turning to making music themselves. His inspiration can be heard in what is now termed 'UK dub', with names such as Conscious Sounds and The Disciples owing more than a passing nod to his unswerving vision of music.

Lloyd Coxson

Young Lloyd Blackwood followed a similar path to Shaka inasmuch as he too immigrated to London at an early age. In 1969 he set up his own sound system named after the mighty Sir Coxson of Kingston Jamaica. His rapid rise to fame was marked by a residency at the Roaring Twenties nightspot, which was celebrated by DJ I Roy on 'Coxson Affair' and the special one-off 'Coxson Time' (issued to the general public in the later 1980s) where Roy revoiced his mighty 'Blackman Time', both tracks being cut when the rapper was also resident at the club in 1973.

He set up his Intone record shop in Peckham Rye late in 1974 and on entering the production field his first issuing label appeared to be Ital Coxone, in association with Leonard 'Santic' Chin, whose debut release was the goodie 'Only For A Time' by The Royals in November 1974. His biggest impact, however, came via Reg McLean's Safari label and Louisa Marks' 'Caught You In A Lie', Matumbi's 'After Tonight' and the dub LP *King Of The Dub Rock*. He was also featured, speaking at length about the trials and tribulations of the reggae business, in BBC's 1976 *Aquarius* programme on UK reggae.

Helped by his legendary selector Festus, Coxson's sound went from strength to strength, and in 1975 he moved in to production with the lovers rock smash (many say it sparked the genre) 'Caught You In A Lie' by 14-year-old Louisa Marks. This song had first been recorded by New Orleans R&B singer Robert Parker – an illustration of how sound system men still listened with a keen ear to hot and hard-to-find stateside waxings.

In 1977 Coxson established his own Tribesman imprint with releases by Fabyenne Miranda, 'Prophecy' (then the mysterious 'Destiny'), Jimmy Lindsay with a cover of The Commodores' 'Easy', Fred Locks' roots anthem 'Love And Only Love' and The Creation Steppers in-demand 'Homeward Bound'.

Coxson's sound was rated the top UK system by *Black Echoes* readers at an awards ceremony in March 1978.

As the dancehall sounds moved in during the early 1980s, Coxson increasingly handed over the helm to younger members of the team (by then known as 'Sir Coxson Outernational') but, after a period of self-imposed retirement, he has now resurrected his sound, as a result of the recent revitalisation of interest in revival and roots and culture music.

Saxon

There was one sound system that was to rise through the ranks as the dancehall 1980s moved in. This was the Saxon sound, which became the second major player in the sound system stakes after supplanting the heavyweight roots of Sir Coxson. Saxon was much more in tune with Jamaican times than was Shaka, and ran a pile of hard dancehall dub plates over which premier UK MCs would strut their stuff.

As a launchpad for aspiring stars Saxon was the tops, with vocalist Maxi Priest being the featured singer prior to climbing into the hallowed top ten and becoming a top-popper. Saxon MCs also aspired to the mainstream, with Smiley Culture taking his Jamaican-cockney jive straight to the top with 'Police Officer' and then 'Cockney Translation' in the middle of the decade. Tippa Irie also held the microphone in many a Saxon dance prior to cruising up the silver ladder to success with the smooth 'Hello Darling' in 1986.

It was to be two of the lesser-known Saxon MCs, Philip Levy and Peter King, however, who were to lay the foundations of modern urban dance music.

Philip 'Papa' Levy really did take the coals to Newcastle in 1985 with 'Mi God Mi King' as he hit the Number One slot in Jamaica after topping the UK reggae charts with his rapid-fire chant in praise of Emperor Haile Selassie. This was a major triumph for UK reggae, as Kingston was finally convinced that authentic music could be created outside the Jamaican studios, and gave credibility to the notion that it was what was in a man's heart that mattered, not where he bared it.

The little-remembered Peter King digested the Jamaican rap style and formed a new hybrid, raising the speed of his commentary to unheard-of heights and firing off flashy remarks on all manner of subjects. The crowd was delighted by this new style, especially as, being a local boy himself, King's lyrics dealt directly with the trials and tribulations of his audience, so they could relate to his anger at joblessness or the injustice of the political system.

Tying in with King's new rap style was the digital revolution that had swept over Kingston, truly making the producer the main man and pushing musicianship out the window, as the Casio keyboard became king. No longer was a producer reliant on the bass man or drummer: all he had to do was touch a magic note and he was away, with metronomic bass and drums ready to do his every bidding. No tantrums, no argument and – best of all – no payment required. London, like Kingston, took to this brash, electronic minimalist sound. Soon, would-be producers were springing up in bedrooms across the capital, creating formative sounds that would later be tagged as techno, dance, house, jungle and, of course, ragga.

REGGAE RADIO

Except during reggae's magic period of the late 1960s to early 1970s, all the legal radio stations scorned the Jamaican beat, and it was only with the rise of the chart smashes that it forced its way on to *Top Of The Pops*.

The fizzy and sound-shifting pirates like Radio Caroline and Radio London had programmed ska and reggae, but grand old establishments like the BBC had no time for minority or 'ethnic' music as it termed it.

Cottoning on late, the BBC finally gave very limited airtime to those of its local radio stations it saw as having an ethnic (for which read West Indian) catchment area. BBC Radio London inaugurated *Reggae Time*, hosted by Steve Barnard, in 1970 in a ridiculously tight spot of 1–2pm on Sunday lunchtimes. Other major cities followed suit, with a tiny amount of airtime allocated to the fast-rising music style.

A few years later Steve was ousted, the show elongated to two hours (1–3pm), renamed in 1970s style as *Reggae Rockers* and Tony Williams was installed. Another young new DJ joined Williams in 1978, David Rodigan, and he and Tony were soon hosting on alternate weeks.

In London, competition reared its head in the shape of *TV On Reggae*, as forward-thinking independent Capital Radio took to the air in 1975. The show was hosted by rocker Tommy Vance (its title was a play on the name of his former pirate radio show *TV On Radio*), who was completely out of his depth fronting a reggae programme, although luckily his co-presenter Cliff St Lewis was reggae-wise and was a sometime reggae recording artist to boot. Vance soon decamped back to Harleys and leather jackets, and in 1979 David Rodigan switched stations and started chairing his own two-hour late-night *Roots Rockers* show on Saturdays for Capital.

Things improved as the 1980s rolled on, at least for those in reception range of the newly arrived London pirate stations. Notable among these were Kiss-FM, which programmed every conceivable strand of urban black music including copious quantities of reggae, and the legendary Dread Broadcasting

Corporation (DBC for short), whose very name indicated its DJs' musical predilections. DBC was run by Lepke, who is the brother of Miss P (a well-respected DJ in her own right) and who at one point fronted a reggae show on Radio 1; he now hosts a show on Radio London.

THE SHOPS

After hearing a record at a dance, the fan's next port of call would be the record shops to try and grab the slice of hot vinyl, if, of course, it was not still available only on tantalising dub plate. Just as the major sound systems had moved beyond merely playing records to making them, the same thing happened for the some of the main purveyors of the music. Three main reggae contenders covered the London area with a plethora of small and equally well-stocked shops, usually hidden away just round the corner from the high street. The 'big three' won, as they offered a mail-order service (as did Birmingham's Black Wax as we have already seen), which was invaluable to those who didn't live near enough to shop in person.

Daddy Kool

Keith Stone opened Daddy Kool in late 1975, having previously been a fire insurance assessor. In fact, while still in his former job, one of his early 'customers' had been Count Shelly, who Keith was to encounter again when he opened the shop and wanted to sell Third World records in his shop.

As a white man entering what was essentially a black man's business, opening the shop was certainly something of a challenge.

During the '60s Keith had been a mod and a regular visitor to the legendary Scene club. One of his sparring partners at this time had been the young Larry Lawrence, also then a mod. Keith became really interested in ska and rocksteady through visits to Dalston's Four Aces club. 'That was where it all started for me,' he says.

Initially, Keith saw Daddy Kool as an opportunity to enlarge his already vast collection of ska records at trade prices, not least since he would always keep a second-hand section going and would, of course, have the pick of anything people brought in. The first shop was in Hanway Street, a narrow thoroughfare running between Oxford Street and Tottenham Court Road. The small shop was packed to the rafters on Fridays and Saturdays, with punters regularly spilling on to the pavement outside. Just along from it was Contempo, which was to soul and funk what Daddy Kool was to reggae – though considerably more spacious once you had negotiated the narrow stairs.

Daddy Kool boomed right through the second half of the '70s, and throngs of black (and white) guys would come into central London especially to visit the shop. Apart from current material, Keith would scour disused warehouses and suchlike across the country to unearth unsold stock, which he'd keep in a basement-cum-cellar downstairs. He once had a particularly large Pama find from somewhere in Wales – literally thousands of singles – and was still selling these right into the mid-1980s. Defunct distributors and closed-down record shops were always a good source of stock, and Keith obtained a lot of old stuff from the Sir Yank outlet in Leeds.

Alongside the shop, Keith established a record label of the same name. Its first releases in late 1976/early 1977 were Cornel Campbell's 'I Heart Is Clean', Errol Dunkley's 'Enoch Power' and The Blackstones' 'We Nah Go Suffer'. The first two were produced by Niney and Tapper Zukie respectively, but all three were really classy roots tunes. Apart from, perhaps, 'Revolution Time' for Phil Pratt, The Blackstones in fact never really made a better record than 'Suffer'.

The label continued sporadically over the next eight years or so, and particular highlights were albums by Prince Far I And The Arabs (*Cry Tuff Dub Encounter Chapter 3*) and Jah Thomas (*Dance Hall Stylee*), and 12-inch 45s by Bob Marley And The Wailers ('Rainbow Country' and 'Natural Mystic') and The Majesterians ('So Many Times'). Daddy Kool's short-lived link up with Dub Vendor and Clapton's Regal Music Centre in 1978 saw Niney's production of Dennis Brown and Jah Bop's 'Tribulation' come out on a new and equally short-lived label named Three In One. Similarly, there would also be several collaborations with London sound system Silver Camel from around 1980.

During 1976–77, Keith also had to stay one step ahead of the competition in the pre-release business. In a *Black Music* interview from September 1977, he said, 'At the start, I had no intention of getting heavily into pre. But a couple of guys came in and we started getting friendly and they kept saying, "Why don't you stock pre?" So I went round to Lasco's [Lasco's Music Den in Dalston's Ridley Road, a big importer of pre-releases] and to my horror they were 70p wholesale. Anyway, I spent £90 and took them in the shop and to my amazement they went just like that. We got some more and that was basically how it built up.' In fact, pre-releases would at one point account for over 70 per cent of Daddy Kool's business, at least until the increase in Jamaican vinyl prices started to have an adverse effect on demand for them.

Into the early '80s, and Daddy Kool, Dub Vendor (by then with two shops) and Hawkeye were probably the premier reggae outlets in the London area.

Keith was soon to move the operation to another location in nearby Dean Street for several years until around 1989 when it was shifted a bit further away from Oxford Street to Berwick Street. He stocked the latest raggamuffin and dancehall sounds, but it seemed that the number of black punters travelling into central London to visit the shop had declined to a trickle. This was almost certainly symptomatic of the malaise that had by then set into the reggae scene: the music had changed and was selling to a smaller market, which was by and large focused around just a few predominantly West Indian areas. By this stage, Keith pretty much admitted that he no longer understood the music – a lot of old hands do find hardcore ragga pretty unintelligible – and decided to withdraw from this area to a large extent. In particular, the shop would no longer stock current ragga singles from Ja.

By the time of his move to Berwick Street in 1989, however, Keith had started selling more and more second-hand records. In fact, the Dean Street premises had been much too small to display all of the old singles stock, and the authors of this book recall vividly that on the first day of opening at the much larger Berwick Street shop, the frenetic buying activity resembled a Harrods sale, with people literally fighting over the multitude of record boxes. A day to remember.

Today, Daddy Kool sells an excellent range of CDs (and if Keith hasn't got it, he'll get it), second-hand vinyl, 7-inch and 12-inch re-pressings of vintage material and a selection of current 'Bashment' singles. Nearly 30 years after opening, it continues to thrive.

Greensleeves Records
A major force in the reggae marketplace, both as a label and record vendor, Greensleeves Records celebrated 25 years of trading in 2000.

In 1975 directors Chris Cracknell and Chris Sedgewick first opened a small shop in West Ealing selling soul, reggae and rock imports. Within a few months, they moved to Shepherd's Bush and decided to start a label as Jamaican import supplies were so erratic. A mail-order business was also established for those that couldn't venture to the shop door.

Chris and Chris dropped their soul and rock stock, and the now familiar Greensleeves label emerged in 1977, just as the punk movement was taking an interest in Jamaican sounds, and immediately began to score in the reggae charts with such top-flight artists as Dr Alimantado on the Ja front, and The Reggae Regulars UK-side. With high-quality mastering and crisp album sleeve designs – something of a rarity among reggae labels at that time – Greensleeves quickly rose to be one of the premier UK labels. Its distinctive disco sleeves graced many a fine record as the 12-inch gained prominence. The label always prided itself on offering a professional approach to the artists and producers it dealt with, which gave it high standing in the reggae community.

Linking up with ace producer Henry 'Junjo' Lawes really started the ball rolling at the end of the '70s. Junjo's production work with luminaries of the scene such as Eek A Mouse and Barrington Levi had the dancehalls rammed, and provided strong sales for Greensleeves on both album and 12-inch single.

There was even a flirtation with the pop charts, when a couple of surprise smashes were delivered by the DJ duo Clint Eastwood And General Saint, namely 'Another One Bites The Dust' and 'Stop That Train'. A series of top dub albums from King Tubby's disciple Scientist, resplendent in striking cartoon sleeves, further cemented Greensleeves as the premier label filling the market-leader void left by the demise of Trojan.

The forward-thinking Greensleeves picked up what was to be the pivotal record of the 1980s, Wayne Smith's 'Under Me Sleng Teng', in 1985 – the disc that heralded the dawn of new computer-generated rhythm tracks. Its influence still reverberates through ragga, techno and dance records, as much as King Tubby's dub mixes ushered in the remix engineer as an important contributor to the sound of reggae. With an eye to the swiftly moving fashions within reggae music, Greensleeves of all UK labels has kept abreast (or in front) of the swiftly changing Jamaican styles and now dominates the UK ragga scene with its brand new releases.

Dub Vendor

The much-loved emporium Dub Vendor celebrated its 25th year in the music business in 2002.

The reggae provider was started in 1977 by two school friends and long-time reggae and soul fans, John MacGillivray and Chris Lane (Chris had started in the music business as a journalist specialising in reggae for *Blues & Soul* magazine). Their aim was to extend and expand their passion for music into a business that sourced and delivered the cutting edge of Jamaican music to its core fans, the numerous sound systems in the UK and to all lovers of good music.

Starting with a Saturday-only market stall in Clapham Junction and a fledgling mail-order business run from the backroom of John's mother's house in Putney, the company established its reputation as the '70s drew to a close. Well-known names like Dave Hendley passed through the mail-order department, and it was quite likely that his north London voice would greet you when you called in search of some wonderfully exotic tune you'd heard the previous weekend. Stifled by the routine of packing and posting, Dave left, and soon Noel Hawks arrived on the scene. Already an avid devotee of the Jamaican sound, Noel brought not only his enthusiasm but his also his expertise to the expanding business. Noel, mainstay of Vendor for 20-odd years recalls, 'One of the major things was how hard it was for people to get [pre-releases], so with Dub Vendor we started being able to offer these.'

Chris left due to family commitments, but the business continued to expand and in 1980 the now world-famous Record Shack opened in Ladbroke Grove. Its manager was local celebrity Martin 'Redman' Trenchfield. In 1982, the Record Store was opened in Clapham Junction, managed by Donald 'Papa Face' Facey, DJ and selector with David Rodigan. This branch stocked not only reggae but the cream of US black music too. The rapidly expanding mail-order department was situated above the shop and managed by Noel.

John and Chris worked together again throughout the '80s and the '90s as Fashion Productions, a widely acclaimed label, studio and production company that gained Dub Vendor further credibility within the reggae business worldwide. Founded in the summer of 1980, Fashion quickly came to the fore alongside the other UK mainstay of the decade, Ariwa Records, run by Neil 'Mad Professor' Fraser. Both operations had a recording studio as well as a releasing label, thus cutting out the middleman to get their product to the streets more efficiently. The Fashion label hit the big time straight off with 'Let's Dub It Up' from Dee Sharp And The Instigators in 1980, and continued to record and hit with a multitude of UK talent as well as capturing the odd Jamaican visitor passing through London.

The A-Class Studio in the basement of Vendor's Clapham Junction shop opened in 1982, and provided a number of reggae hits for artists like Joseph Cotton, Cutty Ranks, Janet Lee Davis, Winsom and Barry Boom (aka Paul Robinson of the group One Blood). The label really struck DJ gold in 1984 with the aforementioned fast-rapping Smiley Culture and his humorous 'Police Officer', which peaked at Number 12 in the national charts in December, with the follow-up, 'Cockney Translation', issued in April the next year managing to hit Number 71.

Fashion has now closed its doors, but Dub Vendor continues to provide one of the only sources of Jamaican- and, latterly, US-pressed singles in the whole country.

THE PRINTED WORD

With the reggae boom at the tail end of the 1960s came the odd commentary in the music press of the day on this 'new Jamaican beat'. Photos of Desmond

Dekker riding on a London bus adorned the front pages of the likes of *Record Mirror* as he rode in on his 'Israelites' hit. The text, however, said little beyond crowing about this sunny new music coming out of the Caribbean, and hard facts or written appreciation of reggae were difficult to come by for the committed fan.

The pioneering *Blues & Soul Music Review* magazine, founded in 1967, was retitled in January 1970 as *Blues & Soul Music Review Incorporating Reggae*. It carried a 'ska and reggae' review page, and singles and LP charts. The pages appeared to focus mainly on Island/B&C/Trojan releases, but the section was dropped by readers' demand in May 1970 after lengthy letters were printed in which soul fans decried the coverage as irrelevant to their beloved US beat. Issue 31 of *B&S* actually carried a full-page debate entitled 'What You Say – Should Reggae Be In *Blues & Soul?*' with a resounding 'no' from the readers, with comments like 'I fail to see what reggae has got to do with B&S – it just leaves me cold' (Glyn Whiteoak, Keighley, Yorkshire), 'What do I think of reggae – scrub it…' (Richard Smith, Exeter) and Disgusted of Burnley, Lancs (aka Malcolm Willis), who says harshly, 'I'm just writing to express my disgust at finding a reggae section in your formerly great magazine…'. A lone voice cried, 'How dare you threaten to drop the reggae section in *B&S?*' (S Boothe, Brighton, Sussex), but to no avail.

The final word from the editor, John E Abbey, commented that *B&S* had hoped that fans of 'the reggae craze' would transfer their interest to soul once the boom had died out, but more damningly said, 'We also expected more support from the relevant [reggae] companies. During the 8 issues of *B&S* with Reggae we received just one solitary page of advertising.' Tellingly, that page was taken by major label MCA, then dipping its musical toes in Caribbean waters, not by a reggae specialist.

More harsh comment about the lack of support on the part of the very reggae labels *B&S* wanted to cover came in the final paragraph of the editor's comment: 'Another problem that we encountered was obtaining material for editorial and features. Most of the artists have little to say and the reggae record companies don't really sound too interested on whether they get editorial or not… However it comes as no surprise that Trojan Records are the most successful company in this sphere – they have some resemblance of commercial know-how and at least seem interested in selling their records.'

So the specialist soul readers didn't want reggae, and the general music press coverage was sporadic and quite often inaccurate, no doubt due to lack of hard-fact information from the record companies as commented on by John Abbey. In the reggae companies' defence, this problem was possibly due to the reggae labels receiving little information from the Jamaican artist or producer in the first place.

Reggae did, however, gain itself a few column inches and the occasional picture. The earliest regular music paper commentator was the 'amalgamously' named Brutus Crombie (Brutus was the skinheads' favoured brand of shirt, and a crombie was the sharp overcoat worn by the shaven-headed masses). The unlikely weekly, *Top Pops*, was also running a regular reggae column and chart in its mainly teenybop-slanted pages by 1969. Soon writers like Rob Randell appeared in the mainstream rock press. Randell's early 1970s interviews for the *NME* with the likes of Bob And Marcia, The Pioneers and Dave & Ansel Collins are forthright in their questions and knowledgeable in their commentary, showing that the writer had an appreciation of reggae sounds.

So it remained as the 1970s moved along with music papers' 'reggae corners' coming and going. At one point Judge Dread presided over a review section, Penny Reel (aka Scotty Bennett, aka Pete Simons) started to make comment and, in the *NME* throughout 1973, Henderson Dalrymple's 'Black and British' quarter-page reviewed a handful of releases and sometimes even showed a picture of a reggae artist or band.

A major coup for reggae was when *The Sunday Times Magazine* of 4 February 1973 carried a full-colour front-cover shot and main feature entitled 'Reggae Reggae Reggae' (as mentioned by Rico on p70), with an outsider's in-depth view of the London scene and plenty of glorious colour shots. No one can recall quite why such an organ as *The Sunday Times* decided to present a view of the reggae world London-side, but it was the first time the music had been acknowledged outside the music press – bar the reggae violence the tabloids associated with the skinheads – and was a breakthrough in terms of presenting the not-so-new West Indian culture in the UK to a mainstream readership. Sound systems, Rastafarianism and late-night blues were all intelligently observed and brought to the white middle-class over its Sunday-morning cornflakes. Sadly it was a one-off, and reggae remained firmly back underground now that the lack of crossover hits had drained away the interest from *Record Mirror*, *Sounds* and their ilk.

This dearth of good reggae writing was to change in November 1973 when the first issue of a new publication from major company IPC took to the news-stands. With a cover date of December 1973, *Black Music* magazine appeared. It was a monthly glossy crammed with articles on jazz and blues through to funk and soul, with a touch of afro and a pile of reggae, highlighted with crisp photos and succinct 45 and album reviews. Top writers covered all relevant genres and on the reggae tip, the best and most quoted of his era, Carl Gayle's intelligent and observant voice was first heard.

It was also the year that saw the first ever UK-written/printed book on reggae music: a slim 40-page A5 publication, *Reggae A People's Music* by Rolston Kallyndyr (surely the guy's name was 'Callendar') and old-hand *NME* reviewer Henderson Dalrymple. Priced at just 20p including postage from Carib-Arawak Publications of Willesden, it was a snip for every reggae lover, although the *Black Music* magazine review of it by Tony Cummings was less than complimentary, saying that it was inaccurate. It must be said, though, that Cummings was a soul expert, so why he was chosen to review a reggae book is something of a mystery. Dalrymple also penned an early appreciation of Bob Marley for the same publishers: *Bob Marley, Mystic Myth And The Rastas*.

Following on in soul tradition, the later 1970s saw privately printed small-format reggae magazines starting to appear sporadically, the best being *Pressure Drop*, which carried the very knowledgeable work of Chris Lane and the ubiquitous Pete Simons, alongside discographies and tantalising label shots.

Black Music magazine was an ideal vehicle for in-depth articles and album reviews, and carried a 'what's going on' section where performers' tour dates and venues were listed, and regular clubs could advertise forthcoming artists and events. However, being a monthly publication it suffered from long copy lead times. The black music scene was fast and snappy with a tune coming out and hitting before *BM* had time to write the copy, proofread it and have it set for the next issue. To fill this opening, *Black Echoes* arrived in January 1976. It was a weekly newspaper (coming out every Thursday) carrying the latest happenings in the USA, Ja and the UK, with dedicated reggae and soul review pages stocked with hot property straight from the labels.

The line-up of writers was a veritable who's who of black music journalists, with reggae luminaries such as Scotty Bennett/Penny Reel, Imruh Caesar, Sebastian Clarke (who would, in 1980, become the author of the second UK-written book on Jamaican sounds, *Jah Music*), Pat Griffiths, Steve Barrow (who reviewed the singles) and Mike Atherton (who was the blues correspondent at that point) being credited in a randomly selected issue dated 21 August 1976. It also carried a day-by-day breakdown of gigs happening through the week, a list of black music radio shows and a very lively 'What's the word' letters page. The inside back page was devoted to record shop advertising and all the new releases both on import and UK press were touted to the readers.

Black Music and *Black Echoes* sat happily next to each other through the 1970s as the glitterball disco sounds took over the nation's nightclubs.

Black Music, though, began to give reggae short shrift and, apart from the regular chart listings, no new releases were reviewed for some months, only picking up again around April 1977. The reggae singles chart was reduced from 30 discs to 20, and no longer credited any specialist shops as assisting in their compilation.

Black Music had became increasingly interested in jazz, and the new jazz-funk, to the extent that it retitled itself *Black Music And Jazz Review* in April 1978, changed format size slightly and downgraded its paper quality dramatically. The disco scene was also big and *BM* had determinedly broadened its scope to cover not only the hottest platters but the DJs' gear as well, with small features on turntables and light shows.

Reggae was still covered, albeit with more grainy pictures, as were soul and funk, but the magazine appeared to be cost-cutting. It stayed in this format (and the reggae coverage had perked up by 1980) until it eventually merged with its rival publication *Blues & Soul* in 1984, with the new magazine proudly saying that reggae coverage would not be affected and then promptly removing every trace of Jamaica from its pages.

Black Echoes, on the other hand, went from strength to strength as the voice of black music in the UK, and was avidly read by all and sundry. The proclamation of a good review in *BE* assured the lucky artist and label of a top seller, and if they were fortunate, a nice 'piece' on them too. The 'Black' was dropped from *Echoes* in 1980, and at the end of the century it reformatted to a monthly glossy, mirroring the original *Black Music* magazine (complete with time-lapse problems), which had started the ball rolling nearly 30 years before.

Epilogue: Reggae Music And Labels Into The 1980s

By 1982, Greensleeves was the dominant force in the reggae market and its releases would often account for around a quarter of the placings in the disco 45 chart. Other key players then were Hawkeye, Cha Cha, Fashion and Starlight. Starlight was run by ex-Trojan man Desmond Bryan, also known as Desmond Benup or 'Popsy', who had by then closed down his legendary Desmond's Hip City in Brixton (the riots couldn't have done much for business) and moved up to Harlesden. Starlight also had a couple of key subsidiary labels, namely Black Joy and Black Music. Of these, Black Joy had issued the massive *Rose Marie* album by Lone Ranger, which followed his eponymous disco 45. Starlight is still in business today, although it no longer has a label associated with it.

Of the other important labels active during this period, there was Black Roots (run by Sugar Minott), Copasetic (which put out the excellent *Disco Skate* album by Ranking Joe), Freedom Sounds (the UK counterpart of Bertram Brown's Jamaican operation), KG Imperial (run by Ken Gordon, alias Fat Man), CSA (operated by Clive Stanhope after he had left Burning Sounds) and Silver Camel (administered by the self-named London sound system, resident for a time at the 100 Club). Other labels, like Skynote/Carib Gems, GGs, Ethnic, Ital/Santic and Neville King, were old campaigners who still had a sizeable slice of the market.

Few of the newer concerns managed to maintain any lasting impact. Count among these Intense, Lovelinch (which had a shop tucked away in Brockley), Negus Roots, Oak Sound, Rockers Plantation, Rusty International, Selena and Sound City (out of Lee's Sound City at Deptford). Many were associated almost solely with releases by a certain Jamaican artist who would have arranged for the UK issue of their music through the particular outlet concerned. A case in point was the short-lived Orbit label, which came out of the equally short-lived Orbit record shop in Lozells, Birmingham. Its handful of releases were directly related to Jamaican singer Enos McLeod, and when the arrangement with him folded so did the imprint.

Of all the early '80s reggae labels, though, the strangest was without a doubt the Vista Sounds empire. Vista had metamorphosed from the obscure Echo imprint during 1980 and was operated by Jeffrey Collins. It began a haphazard policy of reissuing old material from all over the place. Early albums included Pablo's *Thriller* from Leonard Chin's Ital set-up, Gregory Isaacs' *The Sensational*, utilising early '70s material and some Rupie Edwards product that was slow and sentimental but marketed as 'lovers reggae'. Following this, material was leased from Larry Sevitt and Webster Shrowder's old Jamaica Sounds label (mainly reissued or repackaged material), Keith Hudson (for *Steaming Jungle* and *Black Morphologist of Reggae*), Owen Gray (for a long-running series of 'medley' albums where he sang it out with either Pluggy Satchmo or R Zee Jackson), and Sidney Crooks for some Pioneers' *Reggae For Lovers* volumes.

The other notable point about Vista was that literally 95 per cent of its output was in album format, not the 'traditional' reggae medium of the 7-inch or 12-inch disco 45. Its album sleeves were cheaply produced in France – economy was the name of the game – and often featured front-cover shots of darkened silhouettes of Bob Marley, Bunny Wailer and Peter Tosh.

Among Vista's subsidiaries (or at least labels that were related to it) were Culture Press, Dance floor (for largely disco-related material produced by King Sporty), Dance Hall Stylee (for live recordings of artists and sound system sessions), God Sent (material from Prince Lincoln Thompson of The Royal Rasses) and Sunsplash (for Reggae Sunsplash recordings). Bunny Lee seemed to provide Vista with most of its feedstock, and much of it was then in the prevailing 'showcase' style, with vocal tracks followed by dubs. Other material was sourced from Jah Thomas, Jah Life (Hyman Wright), Niney, Linval Thompson, Tad Dawkins (aka 'Tads'), Roy Cousins, Ernest Ranglin (for the *Kingston JA To Miami USA* album) and Martin 'Mandingo' Williams. For Cousins and Tads, Vista appeared to be merely supplementing identical albums that it was putting out on its own labels. There was also some Rasta-inspired music from Count Ossie, some calypso (from Explainer and The Nite Blues Steel Band) and two sets of *Reggae Masterpieces In Dub* albums by an outfit called Roots Rockers, which we have been advised are actually reissues of dub LPs first released on other labels back in the mid-1970s.

It would be impossible to give a blow-by-blow account of Vista – not least since over 100 albums were known to be issued on the main imprint alone – but there is a lot of good collectable material on there by the likes of Ranking Joe, Don Carlos, Earl Sixteen, Horace Andy and the Skatalites, mixed in with some average and some very poor. It's a fascinating label to collect (particularly several of the compilations) and much of the music deserves a second listen.

The early '80s, then, were a strange time for reggae music, and in particular the new 'dancehall' trend was supplanting roots and culture. The roots and culture crowd was still there, but the sounds coming from the likes of Toyan, Jah Thomas, Purpleman and 14-year-old DJ wonder Billy Boyo were not being made with them in mind. There were still some tunes that found favour with roots fans, often by people like Freddy MaGregor and the Wailing Souls, but the British reggae labels were by then focusing their release schedules on the newer, non-Rasta inspired audience. By and large, the Rastas were being cut adrift.

This change of scene needs also to be set against the mood of the times. By 1982, the UK was experiencing mass unemployment, much of it among young black youth; riots had taken place throughout many of the UK's major cities; the New Cross fire had happened and provoked the largest march throughout London by black people ever; racism was on the increase; Thatcher's right-wing policies were impacting on white and black working-class people; and for many people, particularly those out of work, life was bleak.

Jah Music was no longer uplifting a large proportion of reggae fans. Rather like a similar period during 1973–74 (with the oil price shock, three-day week, regular energy blackouts, trades union action, and so on), people started looking for things that would take them away from reality, things that did not even necessarily give them a vision of better times to come. The pop charts of that era were full of throwaway music by Mud, Slade, The Sweet and Gary Glitter. It bore no relation to reggae of any era, of course, but that's essentially what happened within reggae music during the early part of the 1980s.

Into the new millennium and pre-digitalisation dancehall is probably the last reggae genre to be finding a collector's market (nobody wants ragga yet). Interest in a lot of 1981–84 material, notably albums, is really starting to pick up. And since the market was so much smaller by then, copies are going to dry up far more quickly than they ever did for Trojan and Pama. As it is, however, there is still no great demand for early '80s 12-inch disco 45s. There are some exceptions certainly, but this is still a market waiting to be tapped. Listened to now, the dark and depressing days of the early '80s seem far far away.

Appendix 1: A Comprehensive Directory Of British Reggae Labels

The following list features mostly independent UK labels that were in operation during the period 1967 to 1979. While it is pretty exhaustive, it does not claim to cover absolutely everything. The primary focus is on the 1970s. Not all the labels were strictly reggae, but all were involved with music of a West Indian flavour. Trojan labels have already been included in the book *Young, Gifted And Black*, and Pama is dealt with separately elsewhere in this book. Headings are generally as follows:

Name: Label name.

Owner: The definition of 'owner' has to be very loose. Essentially, it means the principal person or persons involved with the label. We have also included any associated retail outlets.

Distributor: Of marginal interest to many, perhaps, but there were vitally important distribution networks for reggae labels. Distributors' details have therefore been inserted where known. It should be borne in mind, though, that many of the smaller labels tended to chop and change distributors pretty much as it suited them, so these networks were pretty flexible, informal affairs.

Period of operation: This information becomes a bit sketchy where labels extended into the early 1980s. Some labels, like Live and Love, continued for years using the same label design but often appeared to have no connection with the original 'owners'.

Comment: Important notes and relevant cross-references to other labels are quoted here. Where there is an abundance of subsidiary labels – such as is the case with DIP, Count Shelly and Third World – readers should refer to the main company entry for details.

This list has been updated and supplemented continuously over a period of about ten years and we are well aware that there are still some gaps, uncertainties and inaccuracies. We have tried our best! Any comments and suggested corrections would be gratefully received and may be sent to us care of the publisher (see the imprint page at the start of the book for their contact details).

You will see that some of the labels listed are definitely not 'independent' (ie they belonged to a major company) or are not from the '70s (eg Dees and Duke). Exceptionally, these have been included by virtue of the fact that we had information on them anyway; they had not, to the best of our knowledge, been listed elsewhere; and because, often, they contain some very worthwhile music.

A

Name: ABI
Owner: ABI Records, 402 Coventry Road, Small Heath, Birmingham **(retail outlet)**
Period of operation: 1975
Comment: Only one single issued on this label, Prince Jazzbo's 'Bag A Wolf', which also saw release on Third World.

Name: Achilles
Owner: David Sinclair (Tapper Zukie)
Distributor: House of Reggae
Period of operation: 1978
Comment: Possibly only one single issued on this label (Zukie's 'Liberation Struggle'), which had the 'Achilles' paper label pasted over a New Star one. See also Love and Unity, MER, New Star, and Youth and Youth labels.

Name: Affection
Owner: Sonny Roberts and Orbitone Records
Distributor: Creole Records
Period of operation: 1975–77
Comment: See also Cartridge, Orbitone **(for retail outlet details)** and Tackle labels.

Name: Akins
Owner: Honey Boy and Sol-Fa
Distributor: Shelly Record Co/Third World Recording Co
Period of operation: 1975
Comment: See also Collette, HB, Honey, Honey Boy and Sol-Fa labels.

Name: Alpine
Owner and distributor: President
Period of operation: 1976

Name: Amusicon
Owner: Not known
Distributor: Not known
Period of operation: 1967
Comment: A strange label with only two known issues, one of which ('Give Your Love To Me' by the Jamaican Jubilee Stompers) was reissued a short time later on Doctor Bird's JJ subsidiary with slightly different artist credits.

Name: Andinet
Owner and distributor: One Harmony Music, 20 Median Road, Clapton, London E5 (**retail outlet**)
Period of operation: 1978
Comment: Possibly administered by Leonard Chin and Ital Records.

Name: Angen
Owner: Desmond Bryan, Joe Sinclair and Klik Records
Distributor: Klik Records and President
Period of operation: 1975–76
Comment: See also Caribbean and Klik (**for retail outlet details**) labels.

Name: Arawak
Owner: Dennis Bovell and Arawak Records at 3 Library Parade, Harlesden, London NW10 (**retail outlet**).
Distributor: Not known for first few releases, but EMI Sales thereafter
Period of operation: 1978–84
Comment: Some issues used Radic label catalogue numbers after the first few releases as part of a licensing deal with EMI. See also Discovery, Matumbi Music Corp, More Cut, MR, Serious Business and Tempus labels.

Name: Aries
Owner: Not known
Distributor: Pye Records & Tapes
Period of operation: 1978

Name: A Rover
Owner: Ronnie (Ranny) Williams
Distributor: Rover Music and DL International
Period of operation: 1975
Comment: Some titles were pressed as well as distributed by DIP. See also Ronnie Williams and Style labels.

Name: Arrow
Owner and distributor: Joe Mansano at Joe's Record Shack, 93 Granville Arcade, Brixton, London SW9 (**retail outlet**)
Period of operation: 1973–77
Comment: See also Joe's Shack label.

Name: Ashanti
Owner: Junior Lincoln and Ashanti Records at 69 Stroud Green Road, Finsbury Park, London (**retail outlet**)
Distributor: Bamboo Records (1971–72) and Trojan/B&C (1973–75)
Period of operation: 1971–72 (first series) and 1973–75 (second series)
Comment: Trojan/B&C assisted Lincoln in resurrecting Ashanti after the first series failed as a result of the collapse of Bamboo and its associated labels (Ackee, Banana and the first phase of Tropical).

Name: ATA
Owner and distributor: Buster Pearson and K&B Records
Period of operation: 1977
Comment: See also K&B (**for retail outlet details**), Lion Sounds and Lizzard labels.

Name: Atomic
Owner and distributor: Aaron Smith and Atomic Records from addresses at 20 Coventry Road and 163 Kenelm Road in Small Heath, Birmingham (**retail outlets**)
Period of operation: 1975
Comment: See also Sun & Star label.

Name: Atra
Owner and distributor: Brent Clarke and Atra Records & Music Ltd at High Road Records, 388 High Road, Tottenham, London N17 (**retail outlet**)
Period of operation: 1973–1980s
Comment: See also Boss, Fat Man, J&F, Kiss, Mamba and M&M labels.

Name: Attack
Owner and distributor: Count Shelly (in association with Bunny Lee) and Third World Music
Period of operation: 1976
Comment: Possibly just one or two issues, both of which featured a Jackpot number. No connection whatsoever with the Trojan and Doctor Bird Attack labels.

Name: Axum
Owner: Delroy Washington
Distributor: Not known
Period of operation: 1975
Comment: One issue only (Delroy Washington's pre-Virgin cut of 'Freedom Fighters'), put out in very limited quantities.

B

Name: Baal
Owner and distributor: Pye Records & Tapes
Period of operation: 1976–78

Name: BAF
Owner and distributor: TRANCO Ltd
Period of operation: 1968–70
Comment: Most releases were pop-oriented, with only The Cats doing the reggae business (most notably with 'Swan Lake'). See also Pineapple label.

Name: Ballistic
Owner and parent company: Mo Claridge and Mojo Distribution in association with United Artists Records
Distributors: United Artists and Mojo Distribution
Period of operation: 1978–80
Comment: Company evolved from Magnum in April 1978. Mojo had its main retail outlet in London (Mojo Records at 94 Craven Park Road, Harlesden NW10) with a second in the West Midlands (Hit Factory Records) at 137 High Street, West Bromwich (**retail outlets**). See also Bam Bam, D-Roy, Magnum, Sunpower and Warrior labels.

Name: Bam Bam
Owner: Mo Claridge
Distributor: Mojo Distribution
Period of operation: 1977
Comment: See also Ballistic, D-Roy, Magnum, Sunpower and Warrior labels.

Name: Basilisk
Owner: Venues Music Co
Distributor: not known
Period of operation: 1978
Comment: Larry Knight of Lucky label fame was involved with this obscure label.

Name: BB
Owners: Bill Campbell and Barbara 'Ginger' Williams at BB Records, 197 Askew Road, London W12 (**retail outlet**)
Distributor: not known
Period of operation: 1975 to early 1980s
Comment: Label evolved into Black Beat in the 1980s, presumably when Ginger Williams dropped out. See also JUM, Jumbo and Union labels.

Name: BBJ
Owner: BB James
Distributor: Not known
Period of operation: 1976
Comment: Confusingly, there was apparently another BB James, a male vocalist who laid down a few UK-recorded tracks for Count Shelly in about 1973. The BB James on this label is a female, however.

Name: B&C Sound
Owner and distributor: Clancy Collins
Period of operation: 1975
Comment: Not to be confused with late '60s/'70s B&C label. See also Collins Down Beat, Nice One, Sir Collins Music Wheel and Sound of Jamaica labels.

Name: B&S
Owner and distributor: Philroy Matthias, David Tyrone and Venture Records
Period of operation: 1978
Comment: See also BPI, Culture and Venture (**for retail outlet details**) labels.

Name: Best of Everything
Owner: Not known
Distributor: Not known
Period of operation: 1978

Name: Big Chief
Owner: Marcel Rodd and Saga Records
Distributor: Saga Records
Period of operation: 1970
Comment: There was apparently a sister label to this, namely Apache.

Name: Big Five
Owner: Not known
Distributor: Big Five Records
Period of operation: 1979
Comment: Only one release found ('Confusion' by Alien).

Name: Bimbo Music
Owner: Not known
Distributor: Count Shelly Recording Co and Third World Recording Co
Period of operation: 1975
Comment: See also Count Shelly and Third World labels (**for retail outlet details**).

Name: Black Ark
Owner: Lee Perry
Distributor: Not known
Period of operation: 1973
Comment: It is unclear who administered this label for Perry, which may have had some connection with the Soul Food label. One possibility is that there was a link with Larry Lawrence. There were two known releases: U Roy's '006' and The Three Tops' 'Take Time Out', the latter of which also saw release on Pama's Bullet subsidiary.

Name: Black Art
Owner and distributor: Lee Perry in association with Dennis Harris and DL International
Period of operation: 1976
Comment: Only two substantiated releases (Merry Maker's 'Bag A Weed' and Jah Lloyd's 'I And I Fight For Survival'). The Lee Perry connection is tenuous. DIP is the most likely outlet since the pressings are very similar to those of its other subsidiaries at the time and it also had other 'Merry Makers' titles out (eg on Western Kingston).

Name: Black Jack
Owner: Danny Ray
Distributor: Not known
Period of operation: 1979–82

Name: Black Lion
Owner: Morice Wellington
Distributor: Not known
Period of operation: 1977–78
Comment: All issues found so far are in 12-inch format.

Name: Black Stag
Owner: Heptones and Barry Ford
Distributor: Not known
Period of operation: 1973
Comment: Only one known issue (Lloyd Vandel And The Heptones' 'Why Did You Leave?'). This label appeared during the year The Heptones toured the UK and licensed material to certain outfits, including Count Shelly and Sir Christopher.

Name: Black Star Music
Owner: Tony Mahoney and Black Star Music
Distributor: Not known
Period of operation: 1976–77

Name: Black Wax
Owner: Brian Harris and Keith Thornton at Black Wax Corporation, 23 Lozells Road, Lozells, Birmingham (**retail outlet**)
Distributor: Creole Records and Enterprise
Period of operation: 1975–78
Comment: See also Double LL, Locks, Mango and Taurus labels.

Name: Black and White
Owner and distributor: Dennis Harris and DL International
Period of operation: 1974
Comment: UK counterpart of Carl Patterson's Ja label, this had only one release (Larry Marshall's 'I Admire You'). See also DIP label (**for retail outlet details**).

Name: Blue Inc
Owner and distributor: WEA Records at 155 Church Street, Kensington, London W2
Period of operation: 1978–82

Name: Blue Mountain
Owner and distributor: Island Records
Period of operation: 1971–73
Comment: Although the label title might suggest otherwise, there were a fair few non-reggae releases on this Island offshoot.

Name: Blue Water Music
Owners: Winston Edwards and Fay Music in association with Clinton Grant
Distributor: Fay Music Inc
Period of operation: 1976
Comment: See also Fay Music (**for retail outlet details**) and T-Bone labels.

Name: BMB
Owners: Valentine Brown and Gene Rondo
Distributor: Not known, but probably Count Shelly/Third World
Period of operation: 1975
Comment: See also Saucy Boy and Skank labels.

Name: BOA
Owner: Tribesman band members
Distributor: Not known
Period of operation: 1978–79

Name: Boss
Owner and distributor: Brent Clarke, Fat Man (Ken Gordon) and Atra Records & Music Ltd
Period of operation: 1976–1980s
Comment: See also Atra (**for retail outlet details**), Fat Man, J&F, Kiss, Mamba and M&M labels. The history of the Boss label is not at all clear: no full printed labels seemed to appear after the first couple of issues in 1976 and Prince Jammy seemed to be associated with it from 1979.

Name: BPI
Owners and Distributor: Philroy Matthias, David Tyrone and Venture Records
Period of operation: 1976
Comment: See also B&S, Culture and Venture (**for retail outlet details**) labels.

Name: Brixton Sound
Owner: Bob Drumbago and Drumbago Music
Distributor: Not known
Period of operation: 1977
Comment: See also Karibs label.

Name: Burning Sounds
Owners: From 1976–83, Clive Stanhope and Burning Sounds Music at Burning Sounds Records, 379 Harrow Road and (later) 534 Harrow Road, London W9 (**retail outlets**). Administered by Stanhope from CSA Records at 101 Chamberlayne Road, Kensal Rise, London NW10 from 1983. Catalogue now in the hands of Trojan/Sanctuary Records.
Distributor: Burning Sounds Music, EMI Records Music (UK) and Trojan Record Sales Ltd
Period of operation: 1976 to date
Comment: Burning Sounds was largely discontinued by Stanhope after he had established his CSA label. It is now part of Trojan/Sanctuary, who have selectively reissued some material. See also Burning Rockers, Burning Vibrations and Dread Hot labels.

Name: Burning Rockers
Owner and distributor: Clive Stanhope and Burning Sounds Music
Period of operation: 1978–80
Comment: See also Burning Sounds (**for retail outlet details**), Burning Vibrations and Dread Hot labels.

Name: Burning Vibrations
Owner and distributor: Clive Stanhope and Burning Sounds Music
Period of operation: 1978–79
Comment: See also Burning Sounds (**for retail outlet details**), Burning Rockers and Dread Hot labels.

Name: Bushay's
Owner: Clement Bushay
Distributor: Not known
Period of operation: 1978–80
Comment: See also Bushranger and Summertime labels.

Name: Bushranger
Owner: Clement Bushay
Distributor: Not known
Period of operation: 1978
Comment: See also Bushay's and Summertime labels.

C

Name: Cactus
Owner: Bruce White, Tony Cousins and Creole Music/Creole Records Ltd at 4 Bank Buildings, High Street, Harlesden, London NW10 and (from mid-1978) 91–93 High Street, Harlesden (**retail outlets**)
Distributor: EMI Sales and Creole Records Ltd
Period of operation: 1972–78
Comment: See also Dinosaur, Dynamic, Jaguar and Rhino labels.

Name: Cancer
Owner: Webster Shrowder and Valdene Ltd
Period of operation: 1978
Distributor: CBS Records Ltd
Comment: See also Jamaica Sound label.

Name: Caribbean
Owner and distributor: Count Shelly and Shelly Record Co
Period of operation: 1974
Comment: There was a later reincarnation of this label by another operator (see below). Also, the Caribbean label design was used on several random Count Shelly label releases. See also Count Shelly label (**for retail outlet details**).

Name: Caribbean
Owner: Desmond Bryan, Joe Sinclair and Klik Records
Distributor: Klik Records and President
Period of operation: 1976–77
Comment: This had exactly the same label design as the aforementioned Count Shelly Caribbean imprint and it is a mystery why Bryan and Sinclair would want to reproduce it. See also Angen and Klik (**for retail outlet details**) labels.

Name: Carib Gems
Owners: Adrian Sherwood and Chips Richards
Distributor: Angstar and J&A Distribution
Period of operation: 1976–82
Comment: See also High Note, Hit Run and Sky Note (**for retail outlet details**) labels.

Name: Carifta
Owner and distributor: Dennis Harris and DL International
Period of operation: 1977
Comment: See also DIP label (**for retail outlet details**).

Name: Caroline
Owner and distributor: Virgin Records Ltd
Period of operation: 1974
Comment: LP releases only.

Name: Cartridge
Owner: Sonny Roberts and Orbitone Records
Distributor: Creole Records
Period of operation: 1979–80
Comment: See also Affection, Orbitone (**for retail outlet details**) and Tackle labels.

Name: Cha-Cha
Owner: Errol Dystant and Cha-Cha Records at Top Floor, 2A Craven Park Road, Harlesden, London NW10 **(retail outlet)**
Distributor: Hawkeye and Mojo Distribution
Period of operation: 1978–83
Comment: This label was the main UK specialist outlet for product from the Channel One studio.

Name: Chanan-Jah
Owner and distributor: Phil Pratt and Terminal Records
Period of operation: 1976–78
Comment: See also Phil Pratt, Sunshot and Terminal **(for retail outlet details)** labels.

Name: Charmers
Owner: Lloyd Charmers
Distributor: Not known
Period of operation: 1978
Comment: See also Plant Music and Sarge labels.

Name: Chek
Owner and distributor: Emil Shallit and Melodisc Records
Period of operation: 1962
Comment: One issue only (Owen Gray's 'Come On Baby'). See also D, Dee's, Downbeat, Duke and Top labels.

Name: CIR
Owner: Comedy International Recording Co Ltd, 143 Shoreditch High Street, London E1 6JE
Distributor: Not known
Period of operation: 1975
Comment: Very little is known about this short-lived label.

Name: Circle International
Owner: Reg McLean and Circle International Records Ltd at 89 Chiswick High Road, Chiswick, London W4 **(retail outlet)**
Distributor: President, WEA, CBS and Atlantic
Period of operation: 1977
Comment: See also Safari and Voyage International labels.

Name: Collette
Owner: Honey Boy in association with Norris Shears and Greenway Records
Distributor: Not known
Period of operation: 1978
Comment: See also Akins, Greenway, HB, Honey, Honey Boy and Sol-Fa labels.

Name: Collins Down Beat
Owner and distributor: Clancy Collins
Distributor: Not known
Period of operation: 1967–68
Comment: Some really good rocksteady on this label. See also B&C Sound, Nice One, Sir Collins Music Wheel and Sound of Jamaica labels.

Name: Concrete Jungle
Owner and distributor: Dennis Harris and DL International
Period of operation: 1976–77
Comment: Confusingly, the Concrete Jungle and Lover's Rock labels shared the same prefixes (CJ). See also Lover's Rock and DIP label **(for retail outlet details)**.

Name: Conflict
Owner: Ken Weston
Distributor: NEMS
Period of operation: 1977–78

Name: Congo
Owner: Congo Music
Distributor: Not known
Period of operation: 1977–83
Comment: The 1977 release was 'Nation Fiddler' by The Makka Bees, who had nothing to do with the Birmingham-based DJ and vocalist of 'Bible Reader' fame. Six years later, UK band Jah Lion's 'Melody For Negus' saw the light of day.

Name: Cool Rockers
Owner: Greensleeves
Distributor: Mojo Distribution and EMI Sales
Period of operation: 1979–81
Comment: See also Greensleeves label **(for retail outlet details)**.

Name: Cosmopolitan
Owner: AE Barnes
Distributor: Not known
Period of operation: 1977
Comment: Possibly related to Triumphant. See also Triumphant label.

Name: Cosmos
Owner: Not known
Distributor: Not known
Period of operation: 1975
Comment: See also Merry Makers label.

Name: Counter Point
Owner and distributor: Dennis Harris and DL International
Period of operation: 1976
Comment: See also DIP label (**for retail outlet details**).

Name: Count Shelly
Owner and distributor: Count Shelly and Shelly Record Co at 66–66b Summerhill Road, Tottenham, London N15 and 21/21a Stoke Newington Road, London N16 (**retail outlets**)
Period of operation: 1972–75
Comment: The Count Shelly empire mutated into Third World early in 1975 and, by and large, all its subsidiary labels simply mapped across to the renamed organisation. See also Akins, Bimbo Music, Caribbean, Honey Boy, Ital Coxone, Live and Love (first release), Paradise, Penguin, Queen Bee, RG, Saucy Boy and Third World (initial releases only).

Name: Crazy Plane
Owner: Not known
Distributor: Not known
Period of operation: 1979

Name: Creation Rebel
Owner: Adrian Sherwood and Neville Beckford (Jah Woosh)
Distributor: Not known
Period of operation: 1977
Comment: Administered by Sherwood but not believed to have been part of his Carib Gems group of labels. One single and an album release only (both by Jah Woosh).

Name: Crystal
Owner: Jack Price in association with President Records
Distributor: President Records
Period of operation: 1969–75
Comment: No reggae-oriented releases after 1971.

Name: CTJ
Owner and distributor: Cyril C Pinnock at CTJ Records, 198 Stroud Green Road, London N4 (**retail outlet**)
Period of operation: 1977

Name: Culture
Owner and distributor: Philroy Matthias, David Tyrone and Venture Records
Period of operation: 1978
Comment: See also BPI, B&S and Venture (**for retail outlet details**) labels.

D

Name: D Records
Owner and distributor: Emil Shallit and Melodisc Records
Period of operation: 1962
Comment: Probably only one issue, produced by Sir Dees, which also appeared on Blue Beat (Don Drummond's 'Twelve Minutes To Go'). This was probably a forerunner of Melodisc's Dee's label. See also Chek, Dee's, Downbeat, Duke and Top labels.

Name: D&E
Owner: Not known
Distributor: Not known
Period of operation: possibly 1978

Name: Daddy Kool
Owner: Keith Stone at Daddy Kool Records, 44 Hanway Street, London W1 (**retail outlet**)
Distributor: Dover Music
Period of operation: 1976–86
Comment: Daddy Kool is still operating as a revival/collectors' outlet in Soho's Berwick Street. See also Three in One label.

Name: DAN
Owner: Dave Bloxham and Dansak Productions Ltd
Distributor: Not known
Period of operation: 1975

Name: DEB Music
Owners: Dennis Brown and Castro Brown at DEB Music, 79 Battersea Rise, Clapham Junction, London SW11 (**retail outlet**)
Distributors: DEB Music and EMI Sales
Period of operation: 1977–80
Comment: Although the logo 'DEB Music' was featured on early Morpheus issues, DEB was in fact to become an entirely separate imprint. Some issues (from 1979) used Radic label catalogue numbers as part of a licensing deal with EMI Records. See also Morpheus and Olympic labels.

Name: Dee's
Owner and distributor: Emil Shallit and Melodisc Records
Period of operation: 1961–62
Comment: UK counterpart of Ja Dee's label, this is a rarely seen subsidiary of Melodisc. Most copies seem to turn up with water-damaged labels. See also D, Chek, Downbeat, Duke and Top labels.

Name: Dervia
Owner: Russell Coke
Distributor: Magnet Records Ltd
Period of operation: 1973
Comment: Featured soul recordings from USA but has been included by virtue of its being administered by Magnet. Only one issue (by Mark Holder). See also Faith, Magnet (**for retail outlet details**), Ray (first phase) and Trans-Universal labels.

Name: Diamond
Owner: Winston Curtis and Empire Records
Distributor: Not known
Period of operation: 1976–80
Comment: See also Empire (**for retail outlet details**), Jungle Beat and Supreme labels.

Name: Different
Owner: Possibly Rupert Cunningham
Distributor: Not known
Period of operation: 1978–79
Comment: May have superseded Rupert Cunningham's group of labels (Tropical, Tropical Sound Tracs, Second Tracs and Treble C) as some of Different's LP releases were reissues from his empire. Some releases were non-reggae.

Name: Dinosaur
Owner: Bruce White, Tony Cousins and Creole Music
Distributor: EMI Sales and Creole Records Ltd
Period of operation: 1973
Comment: Closely related to the Jaguar label. There is just one known issue on this label (Max Romeo's 'Everybody Watching Everybody'). See also Cactus (**for retail outlet details**), Dynamic, Jaguar and Rhino labels.

Name: DIP
Owner: Dennis Harris and DL International at 11/13 The Parade, Upper Brockley Road, London SE4, and additionally (for a brief period) 343–345 New Cross Road, London SE14 (**retail outlets**)
Period of operation: 1973–77
Comment: Eve Recording Studio was also housed at 11/13 The Parade. See also Black Art, Black and White, Carifta, Concrete Jungle, Counter Point, Eve, Happy Tone, House of Eve, I and I, Lover's Rock, Lucky, Organisation, PEP, Phoenix, Rama, Shebazz, Stop Point, Sydna, Teem, Untouchable, and Western Kingston labels.

Name: Discovery
Owner: Not certain, but had involvement from Dennis Bovell
Distributor: Not known
Period of operation: 1978
Comment: See also Arawak, Matumbi Music Corp, More Cut, MR, Serious Business and Tempus labels.

Name: Doctor
Owner and distributor: Sidney Crooks and Golden Age Music
Period of operation: 1976–77
Comment: See also Golden Age (**for retail outlet details**) and Pioneer labels.

Name: Double D
Owners: Len Dyke and Dudley Dryden from Dyke & Dryden, 43 West Green Road, Tottenham, London (**retail outlet**)
Distributor: Not known
Period of operation: 1967–68
Comment: Also issued a Gospel series. The label was a short-lived sideline to Dyke & Dryden's main business as a retailer of African-Caribbean cosmetics and toiletries.

Name: Double LL
Owner and distributor: Brian Harris, Keith Thornton and Black Wax Corporation
Period of operation: 1975
Comment: Strange label designed to look like a Ja pre. Probably one issue only ('Love Time' by Rastus And The Lovetouch Brothers). See also Black Wax (**for retail outlet details**), Locks, Mango and Taurus labels.

Name: Downbeat
Owner and distributor: Emil Shallit and Melodisc Records
Period of operation: 1960
Comment: Three issues, all R&B from the US Aladdin label. See also Chek, D, Dee's, Duke and Top labels.

Name: D-Roy
Owner: Delroy Witter in association with Mo Claridge and Ballistic Records at 5 Felixstowe Road, Kensal Green, London NW10 and (later) 36 Woodheyes Road, Neasden, London NW10
Distributor: Mojo Distribution, Pye Records & Tapes/Plastic Fantastic and United Artists
Period of operation: 1977–81
Comment: See also Ballistic, Bam Bam, Magnum, Niagara, Sunpower and Warrior labels.

Name: Dread Hot
Owner and distributor: Clive Stanhope and Burning Sounds Music
Period of operation: 1978
Comment: See also Burning Sounds (**for retail outlet details**), Burning Rockers and Burning Vibrations labels.

Name: Dread Wax
Owner and distributor: Not known, but possibly DIP
Period of operation: 1976

Name: Duke
Owner and distributor: Emil Shallit and Melodisc Records
Period of operation: 1961
Comment: Three issues from Ja, plus a mispress of US rock 'n' roll group The Hot Toddys' 'Rockin' Crickets', which also appeared, correctly credited, on Pye International. This label has no connection with Trojan/B&C's Duke imprint. See also Chek, D, Dee's, Downbeat and Top labels.

Name: Dynamic
Owner: Byron Lee in association with Bruce White, Tony Cousins and Creole Music
Distributor: EMI Sales and Creole Records Ltd
Period of operation: 1976–78
Comment: This was essentially a second series of the Trojan/B&C 1970–72 label administered by Creole. See also Cactus (**for retail outlet details**), Dinosaur, Jaguar and Rhino labels.

E

Name: Eagle
Owners and distributor: Pat Rhoden, Tito Simon, Earl Martin and Jama Music
Period of operation: 1975–77
Comment: See also Jama (**for retail outlet details**) and Love labels.

Name: Earth International
Owners and distributors: Les Foster, Pat Rhoden, Denzil Dennis and Full Moon Music
Period of operation: 1977–78

Name: Echo-Vista Records
Owner: Jeffrey Collins
Distributor: Not known
Period of operation: 1978–80s
Comment: Label's management handed over to Trojan Records circa 1986.

Name: EJI
Owner and distributor: Not known, but administered from 84 Mountgrove Road, Finsbury Park, London, N5 (**retail outlet**)
Period of operation: 1977–78
Comment: There was also a Ja counterpart of this label.

Name: Empire
Owner and distributor: Winston Curtis and Empire Records at 84 Dongola Road, Tottenham, London N17 and (from late 1978) 115 Stoke Newington Road, London N16 (**retail outlet**)
Period of operation: 1976–81
Comment: See also Diamond, Jungle Beat and Supreme labels.

Name: Ethnic
Owner: Larry Lawrence and Ethnic Records Ltd at 29 Hazel Road, Kensal Green, London NW10 (1973–74); 249 Kilburn High Road, Kilburn, London NW6 (1974–76); and 336 Coldharbour Lane, Brixton, London SW9 (1976–83) **(retail outlets)**
Distributor: Initially (1973–74) by Creole Records Ltd and Shelly Record Co, later by Ethnic Records Ltd
Period of operation: 1973–83
Comment: See also Ethnic Fight, Fight and Reggae labels.

Name: Ethnic Fight
Owner and distributor: Larry Lawrence and Ethnic Records Ltd
Period of operation: 1975–78
Comment: See also Ethnic **(for retail outlet details)**, Fight and Reggae labels.

Name: Eve
Owner and distributor: Dennis Harris and DL International
Period of operation: 1975–76
Comment: See also DIP label **(for retail outlet details)**.

F

Name: Faith
Owner and distributor: Russell Coke and Magnet Records Ltd
Period of operation: 1974–76
Comment: See also Dervia, Magnet **(for retail outlet details)**, Ray (first phase) and Trans-Universal labels.

Name: Fat Man
Owner: Ken Gordon and Fat Man Hi-Fi
Distributor: Atra Records and Music Ltd
Period of operation: 1975
Comment: See also Atra **(for retail outlet details)**, Boss, J&F, Kiss, Mamba and M&M labels.

Name: Fay Music
Owner and distributor: Winston Edwards (in association with Joe Gibbs) and Fay Music Inc at 21 Alpha Road, New Cross, London SE14 and (from late 1975) 324 New Cross Road, New Cross, London SE14 **(retail outlets)**
Period of operation: 1974–76
Comment: The premises at 324 New Cross Road were believed to be in the hands of Jah Shaka by the early 1980s and, interestingly, the first release on Fay Music had been by Shaka himself. See also Blue Water Music and T-Bone labels.

Name: Feelgood
Owner: Alan Blakely
Distributor: Not known
Period of operation: 1976–77

Name: Fiery
Owner: Silver
Distributor: Not known
Period of operation: probably 1975
Comment: There is only believed to be one release on this label (by Silver And The Magnets), which follows on from the Silver label numbering. See also Silver label.

Name: Fight
Owner and distributor: Larry Lawrence and Ethnic Records Ltd
Period of operation: 1974–75 and 1979
Comment: See also Ethnic (**for retail outlet details**), Ethnic Fight and Reggae labels. Although it might be assumed that Fight was later supplanted by the Ethnic Fight label, discs bearing the Fight imprint did appear sporadically after 1975. Albums in particular often made no distinction between Fight and Ethnic Fight.

Name: Flame
Owner: Not known
Distributor: Not known
Period of operation: 1977
Comment: This is not believed to be related to the Flames label.

Name: Flames
Owner: Ossie Thompson and Winston Jones
Distributor: Not known
Period of operation: 1976
Comment: See also Flamingo label.

Name: Flamingo
Owners: Ossie Thompson and Winston Jones
Distributor: Not known
Period of operation: 1977
Comment: One issue only ('Kissinger' by the Channel One All Stars). See also Flames label.

Name: Four Sixty
Owner and distributor: Tony Washington and Derrick's Record Village, 460 High Road, Leyton, London E10 (**retail outlet**)
Period of operation: 1977
Comment: See also Rite Sound and Write Sounds labels.

Name: Freedom Sounds
Owner: Bertram Brown at Freedom Sounds Records, 206 Church
Road, Willesden, London NW10 (**retail outlet**).
Distributors: Lightning Records and Mojo Distribution
Period of operation: 1977–80
Comment: Some discs pressed with White Rum and Red Stripe labels either side. See also
White Rum and Red Stripe labels.

Name: Front Line
Owner and distributor: Virgin Records
Period of operation: 1978–79
Comment: Definitely not an independent label!

G

Name: Galactic
Owner: Not known
Distributor: Not known
Period of operation: 1977

Name: Gales
Owner: Not known
Distributor: Not known
Period of operation: 1977
Comment: Believed to be one calypso-oriented release only.

Name: GG's
Owner and distributors: Alvin Ranglin and GG's Records at 60 Shenley Road and 5b
Addington Square, Camberwell, London SE5 (both of which were administrative addresses)
and 71 Queen's Market, Upton Park, London E13 (**retail outlet**); there is also believed to
have been a second shop at 4 Daneville Road, Camberwell
Period of operation: 1976–83
Comment: Some releases pressed with 'GG's Hit' label.

Name: Golden Age
Owner and distributor: Sidney Crooks and Golden Age Music Ltd at 180 Harlesden High
Street, London NW10 (**retail outlet**)
Period of operation: 1977
Comment: See also Doctor and Pioneer labels.

Name: Greensleeves
Owner: Greensleeves Records and Tapes at 57 The Broadway, West Ealing, London W13
and (later) 44 Uxbridge Road, Shepherd's Bush, London W12 (**retail outlets**)
Distributor: Mojo Distribution and EMI Sales
Period of operation: 1977 to date
Comment: No retail outlets operated since mid-1980s. Most 45s issued in 12-inch format
only after 1978.

Name: Greenway
Owner: Norris Shears and Greenway Records, 42 The Avenue, Tottenham, London N15
Distributor: Not known
Period of operation: 1977–78
Comment: Norris Shears ran Norris Music City in Brixton's Granville Market from one of Trojan/B&C's former branches of Musik City. See also Collette label.

Name: Grejam
Owner: Psalms' band members
Distributor: Not known
Period of operation: 1977
Comment: Only one known release by the Psalms ('Prophecy'), which was later issued on Magnum once the band had secured a recording contract with that label.

Name: Groove
Owner: Not known
Distributor: Not known
Period of operation: 1976
Comment: only one known issue, which was a disco version of 'Swan Lake' by a new line-up of The Cats.

Name: Grounation
Owner: Junior Lincoln and Webster Shrowder
Distributor: Phonogram
Period of operation: 1975–77
Comment: See also Vulcan label.

Name: Grove Music
Owner: King Sounds and Mikey Campbell at Grove Music, 425c Harrow Road, London W10 (administrative offices)
Distributor: Grove Music and, from 1980, Island Records
Period of operation: 1977–82
Comment: From around 1980, Grove Music became an Island Records imprint.

Name: HAM
Owner and distributor: M&M Music in association with Derrick's Record Village, 460 High Road, Leyton, London E10 (**retail outlet**)
Period of operation: 1974–75
Comment: Derrick's Record Village was, for a time, **distributor** of M&M's UK counterpart Harry Mudie labels, including Jungle and Moodisc (mid-1970s series). See also Jungle and Moodisc labels, which are related to HAM in that they also used the same prefix.

Name: Happy Tone
Owner and distributor: Dennis Harris and DL International
Period of operation: 1974
Comment: Only one known issue ('Reggae Samba' by the Mighty Falcons). See also DIP label (**for retail outlet details**).

Name: Hawk
Owner: Raymond Morrison at Hawk Records, 243 Finchley Road, London NW3 (**retail outlet**)
Distributor: Not known
Period of operation: 1978
Comment: Raymond Morrison had cut a few sides for Decca's Sugar label back in 1970.

Name: Hawkeye
Owner: Roy Forbes and Hawkeye Records, first at 4 Pavilion Parade, Wood Lane, London W12 and later (from early 1978) at 2A Craven Park Road, Harlesden, London NW10 (**retail outlets**)
Distributor: Mojo Distribution and Pecking's Studio One shop, 142 Askew Road, London W5 (**retail outlet**)
Period of operation: 1976–83
Comment: Record shop still in operation, but there is no new Hawkeye product.

Name: HB
Owner: Honey Boy
Distributor: Not known
Period of operation: 1976
Comment: Only one issue (by Honey Boy) which also saw release on Penguin. See also Akins, Collette, Honey, Honey Boy and Sol-Fa labels.

Name: High Note
Owners: Adrian Sherwood and Chips Richards
Distributor: Angstar and J&A Distribution
Period of operation: 1977
Comment: Only one issue on this label, which may originally have been destined for Sky Note. See also Carib Gems, Hit Run and Sky Note (**for retail outlet details**) labels.

Name: Hillside
Owner: Not known
Distributor: Not known
Period of operation: 1978
Comment: Only one issue found ('Free From Babylon' by Black Ivory Seven). Label may have been related to Hillside Studios.

Name: Hit-Me
Owner: Hit-Me Music
Distributor: Not known
Period of operation: 1978

Name: Hit Run
Owner: Adrian Sherwood and Peter Stroud
Distributor: Angstar
Period of operation: 1978–79
Comment: See also Carib Gems, High Note and Sky Note (**for retail outlet details**) labels.

Name: Honey
Owner: Honey Boy in association with Larry Lawrence and Ethnic Records Ltd
Distributor: Creole Records
Period of operation: 1973
Comment: Only one issue (Honey Boy's 'Sweet Cherrie'), which used an Ethnic catalogue number. See also Akins, Collette, Ethnic, HB, Honey Boy and Sol-Fa labels.

Name: Honey Boy
Owner: Honey Boy
Distributor: Shelly Record Co
Period of operation: 1975
Comment: Only one known issue (Honey Boy's 'River Of Tears'). See also Akins, Collette, HB, Honey and Sol-Fa labels.

Name: Hot Lead
Owner: Ian Smith and Hot Lead Records, 10 Victoria Road, Thornhill Lees, Dewsbury, West Yorkshire
Distributors: Hot Lead Records, Vandisc, R&B Discs and Atra
Period of operation: 1972–74 and 1976
Comment: Ian is still in the music business and the Hot Lead name is still a going concern (see www.fimusic.co.uk). The final Hot Lead release was put out in 1976.

Name: Hot Shot
Owner: Eddy Grant and Torpedo Records
Distributor: President
Period of operation: 1970
Comment: See also Torpedo label.

Name: House of Eve
Owner and distributor: Dennis Harris and DL International
Period of operation: 1976
Comment: See also DIP label (**for retail outlet details**).

I

Name: I and I
Owner and distributor: Dennis Harris and DL International
Period of operation: 1975
Comment: Only two releases on this label ('Faith Can Move Mountains' by D Miller on DR1, which also saw release on Untouchable, and 'Got You On My Mind' on DR2 by the same artist). See also DIP label (**for retail outlet details**).

Name: Ice
Owner: Eddy Grant
Distributor: Pye Records & Tapes
Period of operation: 1977 to present

Name: In-Line
Owner and distributor: President
Period of operation: 1975

Name: ISDA
Owner and distributor: Winston Thompson (Dr Alimantado) from 53 Eton Avenue, Swiss Cottage, London NW3
Period of operation: 1978–80
Comment: See also Vital Food label.

Name: Ital
Owner and distributor: Leonard Chin and Ital Records Inc/Ltd at 426a West Green Road, London N15 and, later, at 20 Median Road, Hackney, London E5 (**retail outlets**)
Period of operation: 1978–83
Comment: This label was almost certainly run from the 20 Median Road shop – formerly Phil Pratt's Terminal outlet. Ital was, however, primarily known as a **distributor** and retail outlet for Leonard Chin's group of labels, and only one 7-inch release bearing the Ital imprint has been found, although 12-inch issues were abundant after about 1980. See also Nationwide?, Santic, Stonehouse and Student labels.

Name: Ital Coxone
Owner: Lloyd Coxson and Leonard Chin/Santic Music
Distributor: Shelly Recording Co and Third World Recording Co
Period of operation: 1975
Comment: Only two known releases. See Count Shelly and Third World labels (**for retail outlet details**).

J

Name: J&F
Owner: Fat Man (Ken Gordon) in association with Prince Jammy
Distributor: Atra Records and Music Ltd
Period of operation: 1978
Comment: J&F probably stood for Jammy and Fatman. See also Atra (**for retail outlet details**), Boss, Fat Man, Kiss, Mamba and M&M labels.

Name: Jackpot
Owner and distributor: Count Shelly (in association with Bunny Lee) and Third World Music
Period of operation: 1976
Comment: Not related to Trojan's subsidiary. Confusingly, this used catalogue numbers very similar to those used for Justice. See also Justice and Third World (**for retail outlet details**) labels.

Name: Jade Music
Owner: Black Jade (reggae band)
Distributor: Not known
Period of operation: 1977–78

Name: Jaguar
Owner: Bruce White, Tony Cousins and Creole Music
Distributor: EMI Sales and Creole Records Ltd
Period of operation: 1973
Comment: UK counterpart of Ja Jaguar label. See also Cactus (**for retail outlet details**), Dinosaur, Dynamic and Rhino labels.

Name: Jah Lion
Owner: Les Cliff (aka Cliff St Lewis) in association with Winston Curtis and Empire Records
Distributor: Empire Records
Period of operation: 1975–81
Comment: See also King Cliff/KC and Saturn labels.

Name: Jama
Owners and distributor: Pat Rhoden, Tito Simon and Earl Martin at Jama Music, 1 Brixton Station Road, Brixton, London SW9 and later (from 1979) from premises in Clapham High Street (**retail outlets**)
Period of operation: 1975–81
Comment: See also Eagle and Love labels.

Name: Jamaica Sound
Owner: Webster Shrowder and Valdene Ltd, 297 Portobello Road, London W11 (**retail outlet**)
Distributor: CBS Records Ltd
Period of operation: 1977–79
Comment: Retail premises was formerly a branch of Musik City/Musicland, which Shrowder was involved with when he was managing director of the pre-Marcel Rodd Trojan. See also Cancer label.

Name: Jamatel
Owner and distributor: Count Shelly and Third World Recording Co
Period of operation: 1975–80
Comment: See also Third World label (**for retail outlet details**).

Name: Jamdown
Owner: Not known
Distributor: Not known
Period of operation: 1978

Name: JBC
Owner: Not known
Distributor: Not known
Period of operation: 1978

Name: Joe's Shack
Owner and distributor: Joe Mansano and Joe's Record Shack
Period of operation: 1973–74
Comment: See also Arrow label (**for retail outlet details**).

Name: JUM
Owners and distributor: Bill and Pete Campbell, and Jumbo Records
Period of operation: 1976
Comment: Only one release on what was essentially the Campbell brothers' 'pre-release' label. The disc concerned (Family Choice's 'As Long As You Love Me') would later see issue as a formal release on the BB label. See also BB (**for retail outlet details**), Jumbo and Union labels.

Name: Jumbo
Owner: Hunter Smith, possibly in association with Bill and Pete Campbell at Jumbo Records, 12a Queen's Arcade (The Balcony), Leeds LS1 and (from late 1974) 102 Merrion Centre, Leeds LS2 (**retail outlets**)
Distributor: Vandisc Sales
Period of operation: 1975–76
Comment: It is not known what, if any, connection the Campbell's had with Hunter Smith's shop – which exists in Leeds to this day – but the Jumbo label directly copied the logo from its advertisements. There may have been an association, but it might otherwise have been a bit of artistic licence on the brothers' part. The brothers also ran a shop in London's Shepherd's Bush area, however. See also BB (**for retail outlet details**), JUM and Union labels.

Name: Jungle
Owner and distributor: M&M Music and Derrick's Record Village, 460 High Road, Leyton, London E10 (**retail outlet**)
Period of operation: 1974–75
Comment: See also HAM and Moodisc labels.

Name: Jungle Beat
Owner and distributor: Winston Curtis and Empire Records
Period of operation: 1978
Comment: See also Diamond, Empire (**for retail outlet details**) and Supreme labels.

Name: Junior
Owner and distributor: Junior Bradley and Aquarius Records at 79 Soho Road, Handsworth, Birmingham (**retail outlet**)
Period of operation: 1969–70
Comment: Issued a number of titles that were also released simultaneously on Junior Lincoln's Ackee imprint.

Name: Junior
Owner: Neville 'Junior' McKenzie
Distributor: Not known
Period of operation: 1976
Comment: One issue only by TT Ross ('Taxation'), This was not linked to the Birmingham-based Junior label. However, TT Ross also went under the alias Nina McKenzie, so Junior McKenzie was possibly a relation.

Name: Justice
Owner and distributor: Count Shelly (in association with Bunny Lee) and Third World Music
Period of operation: 1976–86
Comment: Confusingly, this used catalogue numbers very similar to those used for the Jackpot label. Originally, it was used as Bunny Lee's 'pre-release' outlet and singles sold at a premium price. See also Jackpot and Third World (**for retail outlet details**) labels.

K

Name: Karibs
Owner: Bob Drumbago and Drumbago Music
Distributor: Not known
Period of operation: 1976
Comment: See also Brixton Sound label.

Name: Karlene
Owner: Laurel Aitken
Distributor: Not known
Period of operation: 1977
Comment: Only one known issue (Laurel's 'Rebel Woman') on white label only.

Name: K&B
Owner and distributor: Buster Pearson and K&B Records at 51 Ilford Lane, Ilford, Essex (**retail outlet**)
Period of operation: 1974–77
Comment: See also ATA, Lion Sounds and Lizzard labels.

Name: KIM
Owner: Not known, but possibly an association with Dennis Brown
Distributor: Jay Dee Enterprise Inc at 34 Peckham High Street, London SE15 (**retail outlet**)
Period of operation: 1978

Name: King Cliff/KC
Owner: Cliff St Lewis (aka Les Cliff)
Distributor: President
Period of operation: 1976 to mid-1980s
Comment: Only two issues have come to light on this label, the first on the King Cliff imprint and (after a long gap), another on the KC Records label. The latter was seemingly released in the mid-1980s and billed as a 'pre-import', whatever that was. See also Jah Lion and Saturn labels.

Name: King George
Owner: Anthony Brightly (aka Sir George)
Distributor: Not known
Period of operation: 1976
Comment: See also Slate label.

Name: King-Jam
Owner: Bunny Hylton
Distributor: Not known
Period of operation: 1977–83

Name: King Roy
Owner: Roy Shirley
Distributor: Not known
Period of operation: Not certain
Comment: See also Leroy, R&JJ, Shirley and Victry labels.

Name: Kiss
Owner: Barrington Dunn (Militant Barry) and Brent Clarke in association with M&M Music
Distributor: Atra Records & Music Ltd
Period of operation: 1975–76
Comment: See also Atra (**for retail outlet details**), Boss, Fat Man, J&F, Mamba and M&M labels.

Name: Klik
Owners: Desmond Bryan, Joe Sinclair and Klik Records, 2 Library Parade, Harlesden, London NW10 (**retail outlet**)
Distributor: President
Period of operation: 1975–78
Comment: A couple of later issues, including two re-releases, were pressed on the 'Klik Chart Sounds 2001' label (still using Klik catalogue numbers). See also Angen and Caribbean labels.

L

Name: Laser
Owner: Lightning Records
Distributor: WEA
Period of operation: 1979–80
Comment: A fair number of issues were non-reggae. See also Lightning label (**for retail outlet details**).

Name: Leroy
Owner: Roy Shirley
Distributor: Not known
Period of operation: 1974
Comment: See also King Roy, R&JJ, Shirley and Victry labels.

Name: Libra
Owner: Philip Fraser
Distributor: Not known
Period of operation: 1976

Name: Lightning
Owner: Alan Davidson, in association with Trojan/B&C and (later) WEA/Warner Brothers, at Lightning Records, 841 Harrow Road, London NW10; 398 St John Street, Angel, London EC1V 4NJ; and 108 High Street, Ruislip, Middlesex HA4 8LS (**retail outlets**)
Distributor: B&C and WEA
Period of operation: 1977–79
Comment: Shops opened in 1976. Alan Davidson had a licensing deal with Joe Gibbs, which gave Lightning much of its reggae output. Most of what it released, however, was punk and pop-oriented, and these tended to be issued on red versions of the same label design (the reggae issues were in green). There was also a Trojan connection in its formative period in that some early Lightning reggae releases were pressed with Trojan catalogue numbers. Lightning product was later the subject of a UK pressing and distribution deal with WEA. See also Laser label.

Name: Lion
Owner: Lloyd Campbell
Distributor: Not known
Period of operation: 1971
Comment: Only one issue found ('Mosi' by Sir Lloyd, possibly Lloyd Campbell himself). Very obscure.

Name: Lion Sounds
Owner and distributor: Buster Pearson and K&B Records/Folioworth Ltd
Period of operation: 1976
Comment: One issue only (Delroy Wilson's 'You Won't See Me', aka 'Honey Child'). See also ATA, K&B (**for retail outlet details**) and Lizzard labels.

Name: Live and Love
Owner and distributor: Count Shelly and Shelly Record Co/Third World Recording Co
Period of operation: 1974–89
Comment: This imprint seems to have been 'adopted' by Prince Jammy, with whom Shelly had an earlier association, during the mid-1980s, whereupon the label was operated by World Enterprise (basically the successor to Third World) from Klik's old premises in Harlesden. See also Count Shelly and Third World labels (**for retail outlet details**).

Name: Lizzard
Owner and distributor: Buster Pearson and K&B Records
Period of operation: 1976
Comment: One issue only (Pablo Moses' 'We Should Be In Angola'). See also ATA, K&B (**for retail outlet details**) and Lion Sounds labels.

Name: Locks
Owner: Brian Harris, Keith Thornton and Black Wax Corporation
Distributor: Creole Records and Enterprise
Period of operation: 1975–76
Comment: See also Black Wax (**for retail outlet details**), Double LL, Mango and Taurus labels.

Name: London (reggae series)
Owner and distributor: Decca Records Ltd
Period of operation: 1970 and 1972
Comment: No issues in 1971. Obviously not an independent, but never covered before. Featured a sizeable chunk of productions from Richard Khouri's Federal Records in Jamaica.

Name: Lonely I and I
Owner: Lee Francis and D Huntley
Distributor: Not known
Period of operation: 1978–81

Name: Lord Koos
Owner and distributor: Lord Koos (Eric Scott) at 7 Fortunegate Road, Harlesden, London NW10
Distribution: Enterprise
Period of operation: 1973–79
Comment: During the early part of this imprint, there were some tenuous links with Count Shelly's label in that Shelly's material often appeared on Koos' compilation albums and vice versa. See also Ossie and Koos, Sir Christopher and Thompson and Koos.

Name: Love
Owners and distributor: Pat Rhoden, Tito Simon, Earl Martin and Jama Music
Period of operation: 1975–77
Comment: See also Eagle and Jama (**for retail outlet details**) labels.

Name: Love and Unity
Owner: David Sinclair (Tapper Zukie) and Vego
Distributor: House of Reggae
Period of operation: 1978–83
Comment: See also Achilles, MER, New Star and Youth and Youth labels.

Name: Lover's Rock
Owner: Dennis Harris and DL International
Distributor: DL International and (during 1978) Plastic Fantastic/Pye Records & Tapes Ltd
Period of operation: 1977–78
Comment: This label shared its prefix and numbering system with the Concrete Jungle label, though there was also a series prefixed 'LBS' See also DIP **(for retail outlet details)** and Concrete Jungle labels.

Name: Lucky
Owner and distributor: Dennis Harris and DL International
Period of operation: 1975–77
Comment: Some of the earlier Lucky releases used DIP label catalogue numbers. See also DIP label **(for retail outlet details)**.

M

Name: M&M Records
Owner: Brent Clarke and Atra Records & Music Ltd
Distributor: M&M Records at 96 Craven Park Road, Harlesden, London NW10 **(retail outlet)**
Period of operation: 1978
Comment: It is not known whether this M&M bore any relation to the one associated with the UK counterparts of Harry Mudie's group of labels. All but one of the known releases were produced by Linval Thompson. See also Atra **(for retail outlet details)**, Boss, Fat Man, J&F, Kiss and Mamba labels.

Name: Magnet
Owner and distributor: Russell Coke and Magnet Records Ltd at 19 and 25 Rectory Road, Stoke Newington, London N16 **(retail outlets)**
Period of operation: 1973–75
Comment: This was not in any way related to the pop/soul label that had many chart hits during the 1970s and '80s. In fact, Russell Coke pointedly dubbed it 'Magnet Mark 1' in press adverts. See also Dervia, Faith, Ray (first phase) and Trans-Universal labels.

Name: Magnum
Owner and parent company: Mo Claridge in association with Pye Records & Tapes Ltd
Distributor: Pye Records & Tapes Ltd/Plastic Fantastic
Period of operation: 1977–78
Comment: Magnum evolved into the Ballistic label in April 1978. This may either have been because Claridge was dissatisfied with Pye's involvement, or because Pye pulled the plug. See also Ballistic and Bam Bam labels.

Name: Main Line
Owner: Bunny Donaldson at M&D Records, 36a Dalston Lane, Dalston, London E8 (**retail outlet**)
Distributor: Not known
Period of operation: 1978
Comment: M&D Records, formerly Java Record Shack, lasted into the mid-1990s until its premises were demolished. Bunny Donaldson ran the shops, and was associated with a number of British reggae outfits, including The Undivided and Matumbi. See also Peace label.

Name: Mamba
Owner: Brent Clarke in association with Keith Hudson
Distributor: Atra Records & Music Ltd
Period of operation: 1975
Comment: See also Atra (**for retail outlet details**), Boss, Fat Man, J&F, Kiss and M&M labels.

Name: Mango
Owner: Brian Harris at Mango Records, 104 Grove Lane, Handsworth, Birmingham (**retail outlet**)
Distributor: Creole Records and Enterprise, then (from 1976) Island Records
Period of operation: 1975–76
Comment: The Mango shop was formerly known as Brian Harris Records. In 1976, Mango was the subject of a pressing and distribution deal with Island Records. See also Black Wax, Double LL, Locks and Taurus labels.

Name: Manic
Owner: Vic Keary and Rob Hallett at 1a Belmont Street, London NW1 (Roundhouse Studios)
Distributor: Plastic Fantastic/Pye Records & Tapes Ltd
Period of operation: 1978–79

Name: Mary Lyn
Owner: Mary Lyn in association with Revolution Records
Distributor: Not known
Period of operation: 1970
Comment: Two known releases only, by Denzil Dennis and Pat Rhoden. See also Revolution label.

Name: Matumbi Music Corporation
Owner: Dennis Bovell and Matumbi
Distributor: Dover Music
Period of operation: 1976–78
Comment: See also Arawak, Discovery, More Cut, MR, Serious Business and Tempus labels.

Name: Melody
Owner: Not known
Distributor: Not known
Period of operation: 1968
Comment: Possibly a short-lived Melodisc offshoot, but nobody has so far sussed this one out.

Name: MER (Music of the Most High)
Owner: David Sinclair (Tapper Zukie) in association with Rough Trade
Distributor: Rough Trade
Period of operation: 1978
Comment: See also Achilles, Love and Unity, New Star, and Youth and Youth labels.

Name: Merry Makers
Owner: Not known
Distributor: Not known
Period of operation: 1975
Comment: Spouge and calypso rather than reggae. See also Cosmos label.

Name: Mich
Owner: Mike Dorane
Distributor: Not known
Period of operation: 1975
Comment: Only one known release ('Girl You Have Left Me' by Strecker Decker).

Name: Micron
Owner: Not known
Distributor: Not known
Period of operation: 1975
Comment: This was the UK counterpart of Pete Weston's Ja label, although only one issue has come to light (and that contained completely incorrect label credits).

Name: Militant
Owner: Mafiatone Hi-Fi
Distributor: Not known
Period of operation: 1977
Comment: Label originated from Birmingham.

Name: Mirto
Owner and distributor: see 'Comment'
Period of operation: 1973
Comment: One issue only, by The Messengers, which was given away as a freebie with Nutrament Energy drink. There is probably a connection with Lloyd Charmers since he was a member of The Messengers and producer of the record concerned. The discs were undoubtedly pressed by Phonogram.

Name: Moodisc
Owner and distributor: M&M Music and Derrick's Record Village, 460 High Road, Leyton, London E10 (**retail outlet**)
Period of operation: 1974–75 and 1978
Comment: Reactivated in 1978 and distributed by Big-Phil Records, which operated from London's Mill Hill area. See also HAM and Jungle labels.

Name: More Cut
Owner: Dennis Bovell in association with EMI Records
Distributor: EMI Sales
Period of operation: 1977–80
Comment: Some issues (in 1980) used Radic label catalogue numbers as part of a licensing deal with EMI Records. See also Arawak, Discovery, Matumbi Music Corp, MR, Serious Business and Tempus labels.

Name: Morpheus
Owner and distributor: Dennis Brown and Castro Brown at Morpheus Records, 11 Melfort Road, Thornton Heath, Surrey
(**retail outlet**)
Period of operation: 1975–77
Comment: The DEB Music imprint essentially succeeded Morpheus. See also DEB and Olympic labels.

Name: Motorway Sounds
Owner: Ray Williams
Distributor: Not known
Period of operation: possibly 1978
Comment: Mostly calypso and spouge type music, with a bit of reggae thrown in. See also Vasko label (**for retail outlet details**).

Name: Movers
Owner: Mike Dorane in association with Island Records Ltd
Distributor: Island Records Ltd
Period of operation: 1976–77
Comment: No known reggae releases, although it has been included by virtue of the Mike Dorane connection. See also Rockers label.

Name: MR
Owner: Matumbi band members in association with EMI/Harvest Records
Distributor: EMI Sales
Period of operation: 1979–80
Comment: Records issued using Radic label catalogue numbers as part of a licensing deal with EMI Records. See also Arawak, Discovery, More Cut, Serious Business and Tempus labels.

Name: MSR
Owner: Not known
Distributor: Not known
Period of operation: 1978
Comment: Nothing much known about this label, although there was certainly a Jamaican counterpart. 'MSR' stands for 'Mighty Soul Rebels'.

Name: Music Incorporation
Owner: Not known, but possibly related to Atra
Distributor: Not known
Period of operation: 1977
Comment: Printed labels with artist name and title rubber stamped on. A very curious operation.

N

Name: Nationwide?
Owner and distributor: Leonard Chin and Ital Music Inc/Ltd
Period of operation: 1975–80
Comment: See also Ital (**for retail outlet details**), Santic, Stonehouse and Student labels.

Name: Natty Congo
Owner: Trevor Bow
Distributor: Not known
Period of operation: 1978–83

Name: Neville King
Owner: Neville King and Neville King Hi-Fi
Distributor: not known
Period of operation: 1976–83
Comment: 12-inch singles only issued after 1978. There was also an early '80s sister label to this, namely NK.

Name: New Star
Owner: David Sinclair (Tapper Zukie)
Distributor: House of Reggae
Period of operation: 1977–78
Comment: See also Achilles, Love and Unity, MER and Youth and Youth labels.

Name: New Wave
Owner: Emil Shallit and Melodisc Records
Distributor: HR Taylor
Period of operation: 1968
Comment: One issue only ('Baby Please Come Home'/'Without You' by Donnie Elbert), which saw later issue on Deram and an R&B Discs' white label. See also Star label (Melodisc).

Name: Niagara
Owner: Delroy Witter and D-Roy Records
Distributor: D-Roy Records
Period of operation: 1979–80
Comment: See also D-Roy label. Niagara began following the ending of the various distribution deals with Mojo, Pye and United Artists.

Name: Nice One
Owner and distributor: Clancy Collins
Period of operation: 1976
Comment: See also B&C Sound, Collins Down Beat, Sir Collins Music Wheel and Sound of Jamaica labels.

Name: Night Owl
Owners: Dandy Livingstone and Dimples Hinds
Distributor: Mojo Distribution and Pye Records & Tapes
Period of operation: 1978
Comment: One issue only, an R&B-style LP by The Marvels.

O

Name: Observer
Owner and distributor: Winston Holness in association with Count Shelly and Third World Records
Period of operation: 1977
Comment: 12-inch releases only. See also Third World label (**for retail outlet details**).

Name: OCR
Owner: Orbach and Chambers Ltd
Distributor: Not known
Period of operation: 1978
Comment: Only one issue ('Cold Outside' by Fusion) has come to light on this label.

Name: Olympic
Owners and distributors: Dennis Brown and Castro Brown, and Morpheus Records
Period of operation: 1976
Comment: One stray issue only, which was issued with a Morpheus number. See also DEB and Morpheus (**for retail outlet details**) labels.

Name: One Stop
Owner and distributor: One Stop Records
Period of operation: 1979
Comment: Actually '1 Stop'. One Stop Records was a large London wholesaler.

Name: One Way
Owner: Locksley Mellow
Distributor: Not known
Period of operation: 1975
Comment: Publisher noted as 'AP Taylor'. See also Scarlet label.

Name: Opal
Owner and distributor: NEMS
Period of operation: 1975–76

Name: Orbitone
Owner: Sonny Roberts and Orbitone Records at 2 Station Offices, Station Road, Harlesden, London NW10 (**retail outlet**)
Distributor: Creole Records
Period of operation: 1973 to the 1990s
Comment: See also Affection, Cartridge and Tackle labels.

Name: Organisation
Owner and distributor: Dennis Harris and DL International
Period of operation: 1976
Comment: Only one known issue (Amigo's 'Jah A Go Bus Dem Shut') out of a possible four. See also DIP label (**for retail outlet details**).

Name: Ossie and Koos
Owner: Ossie Hibbert and Lord Koos
Distributor: Lord Koos
Period of operation: 1979
Comment: See also Lord Koos, Sir Christopher and Thompson and Koos labels.

Name: Oval
Owner: Charlie Gillett and Oval Records Ltd
Distributor: Virgin, Island, EMI Sales and Jama Music
Period of operation: 1976
Comment: Oval was an R&B-oriented label, which leased three Niney productions from Morpheus. Morpheus released them too!

P

Name: Pacific
Owner: Robby Day
Distributor: Dover Music
Period of operation: 1976–77
Comment: See also Trenchtown label.

Name: Paradise
Owner and distributor: Count Shelly and Shelly Record Co/Third World Recording Co
Period of operation: 1974–82
Comment: See also Count Shelly and Third World labels (**for retail outlet details**).

Name: Peace
Owner and distributor: Bunny Donaldson and M&D Records
Period of operation: 1977
Comment: See also Main Line label (**for retail outlet details**).

Name: Pearl
Owner: Tito Simon
Distributor: Pye Records Ltd/Plastic Fantastic
Period of operation: 1978
Comment: See also Splash label.

Name: Penguin
Owner and distributor: Count Shelly and Shelly Record Co/Third World Recording Co
Period of operation: 1975–78
Comment: See also Count Shelly and Third World labels (**for retail outlet details**).

Name: PEP
Owner and distributor: Dennis Harris and DL International
Period of operation: 1974
Comment: One issue only (Johnny Clarke's 'Don't Go'). See also DIP label (**for retail outlet details**).

Name: Phase One
Owner and distributor: Roy Francis at Phase One Records, 49b Grattan Road, Hammersmith, London W14
Period of operation: 1978 to date
Comment: UK counterpart of Francis's Ja label. Phase One still reissues its back catalogue.

Name: Phil Pratt
Owner and distributor: Phil Pratt and Terminal Records
Period of operation: 1978–85
Comment: LP and 12-inch releases only. See also Chanan-Jah, Sunshot and Terminal (**for retail outlet details**) labels.

Name: Phoenix
Owner and distributor: Dennis Harris and DL International
Period of operation: 1974
Comment: Probably only one (non-reggae) issue, namely Gene And Eunice's 'This Is My Story'/'Ko Ko Mo', a '50s re-release from the US Aladdin label. There was another unrelated Phoenix label administered by Bill Farley. See also DIP label (**for retail outlet details**).

Name: Pineapple
Owner and distributor: TRANCO Ltd
Period of operation: 1970
Comment: Only one known issue (the Trojans' 'The Trojan March'). See also BAF label.

Name: Pioneer
Owner and distributor: Sidney Crooks and Golden Age Music, 180, High Street, Harlesden, London NW10
Period of operation: 1976–86
Comment: See also Doctor and Golden Age (**for retail outlet details**) labels.

Name: Plant Music
Owner: Lloyd Charmers and Tony King
Distributor: Not known
Period of operation: 1979
Comment: See also Charmers and Sarge labels.

Name: Playboy
Owner and distributor: possibly Leonard Chin and Ital Music Inc Records
Period of operation: 1975

Name: Plum
Owner: Not known
Distributor: Not known
Period of operation: 1975

Name: PM
Owner: Pauline Morrison (on behalf of Lee Perry)
Distributor: Not known
Period of operation: 1978
Comment: Discs claimed to be pressed in Jamaica but are definitely from UK stampers.

Name: Precision Inc
Owner: Not known
Distributor: Not known
Period of operation: 1976
Comment: Possibly two issues only; this is a real mystery label.

Name: Prophets
Owner: Vivian Jackson
Distributor: Not known
Period of operation: 1976–77
Comment: UK counterpart of Ja label, Jackson (alias Yabby You) must certainly have had this administered by someone on his behalf.

Q

Name: Queen Bee
Owner: Bill and Pete Campbell in association with Count Shelly
Distributor: Shelly's Record Co/Third World Recording Co
Period of operation: 1974–75
Comment: See also Count Shelly and Third World labels **(for retail outlet details)**.

R

Name: Radic
Owner: EMI Records
Distributor: EMI Sales
Period of operation: 1979
Comment: Numbering system linked to several other reggae-oriented labels associated with EMI, including Arawak, DEB, More Cut and MR. Basically, EMI carried these labels under its Radic label as part of licensing deals.

Name: Rainbow Stepper & Kenton
Owner: Jah Larry (Larry Kenton)
Distributor: Not known
Period of operation: not definite, but probably 1979
Comment: Only one issue on this Southall-based label (Pat Kelly And Jah Larry's 'Carefree Girl') has so far come to light.

Name: Rama
Owner and distributor: Dennis Harris and DL International
Period of operation: 1976–78
Comment: This was initially a DIP 'pre-release' label but later began putting out full printed-label issues. See also DIP label **(for retail outlet details)**.

Name: Ranking Sounds
Owner: Fat Man Hi-Fi
Distributor: Not known
Period of operation: 1978

Name: Rapp
Owner: Roy Gee and Rapp Records
Distributor: Not known
Period of operation: possibly 1975
Comment: Only one issue has come to light on this label (Roy Gee's 'Children Of The Revolution').

Name: Ray
Owner: Ray Martell (aka Martel Robinson and Mike Robinson) from 36 Lilburne Walk, Pitfield Way, Stonebridge Park, London NW10
Distributor: Magnet (1973) and Creole (1977/78)
Period of operation: 1973–78
Comment: Only one issue in 1973, administered by Magnet, and no more until 1977. See also Dervia, Faith, Magnet (**for retail outlet details**) and Trans-Universal labels.

Name: Red Stripe
Owner: Bertram Brown and Freedom Sounds Records
Distributors: Lightning Records and Mojo Distribution
Period of operation: 1977
Comment: Records pressed with Red Stripe label on one side and White Rum label on the other. A potent brew! There was also another Red Stripe label in the early '80s, which is believed to have been connected to the Vista Sounds set-up. See also Freedom Sounds (**for retail outlet details**) and White Rum labels.

Name: Reggae
Owner: Graeme Goodall and Doctor Bird Records
Distributor: Trojan/B&C
Period of operation: 1969–70

Name: Reggae
Owner and distributor: Larry Lawrence and Ethnic Records Ltd
Period of operation: 1975–76
Comment: See also Ethnic (**for retail outlet details**), Ethnic Fight and Fight labels.

Name: Reggamite
Owner and distributor: Soulville Records
Period of operation: 1976
Comment: Administered from somewhere in Balham, London, this is another mystery label.

Name: Revolution
Owner: Dave Hadfield and John Harper (D&H Productions Ltd)
Distributor: Not known
Period of operation: 1968–70
Comment: This label had around five separate series – children's, pop, soul, rocksteady and reggae – with the latter two using the same prefix. It was operated by Andrew Loog Oldham and Tony Calder's pop label Immediate, going independent after that label ceased operating. See also Mary Lyn label.

Name: RG
Owner: See 'Comment'
Distributor: Shelly Record Co and Third World Recording Co
Period of operation: 1974
Comment: 'RG' may either have stood for Gene Rondo (initials transposed) or 'Ranny [Williams] and Gene'. See also Count Shelly and Third World labels (**for retail outlet details**).

Name: Rhino
Owner and parent company: Bruce White, Tony Cousins and Creole Music in association with EMI Records
Distributor: EMI and Creole
Period of operation: 1972–74
Comment: See also Cactus (**for retail outlet details**), Dinosaur, Dynamic and Jaguar labels.

Name: R&JJ
Owners: Roy Shirley in association with Mrs Johnson of R&JJ West Indian Restaurant, 10 Sandringham Road, Hackney, London E8 (**retail outlet**)
Distributor: not known
Period of operation: 1975
Comment: Probably one issue only (Roy's 'Heartbreaking Gypsy'). Roy Shirley also ran a retail outlet for a while from the rear of Mrs Johnson's eatery. See also King Roy, Leroy, Shirley and Victry labels.

Name: Rite Sound
Owner: Not known
Distributor: Derrick's Record Village, 460 High Road, Leyton, London E10 (**retail outlet**)
Period of operation: 1978
Comment: With only one issue, this label may in fact have been the result of a small typographical error and intended as a Write Sounds release (and the label design was indeed markedly similar to that of Four Sixty). See also Four Sixty and Write Sound labels.

Name: Robot
Owner: Not known, but had a Clem Bushay and Danny Ray connection
Distributor: Not known
Period of operation: 1979

Name: Rockers
Owner: Mike Dorane in association with Island Records Ltd
Distributor: Island Records Ltd
Period of operation: 1976–77
Comment: See also Movers label.

Name: Rock Soul
Owner: Kent Brown
Distributor: Not known
Period of operation: 1968
Comment: One known issue only (Kent Brown And The Rainbows' 'The High Priest'). Probably pressed in a quantity of no more than 99, possibly to be sold only at gigs.

Name: Ronnie Williams
Owner and distributor: Ranfold (Ranny) Williams and Rover Music
Period of operation: 1975
Comment: See also A Rover and Style labels.

Name: Roots
Owner: Not known
Distributor: Not known
Period of operation: 1975
Comment: One issue only (Johnny Clarke's 'I'm Alone'). Discs were pressed by CH Rumble Ltd, who pressed for many minor labels.

Name: Roots
Owner and distributor: Pye Records & Tapes
Period of operation: 1977–78
Comment: Featuring involvement from Mike Dorane, Norman Grant (of The Twinkle Brothers), Danny Ray, Jackie Edwards and Sidney Crooks, this may have been Pye's attempt to form a label dedicated to reggae.

S

Name: Safari
Owner: Reg Maclean and Circle International Records
Distributor: President, WEA, CBS and Atlantic
Period of operation: 1974–76
Comment: Not all of the releases on this label were reggae. There were a few poppy things among the 1976 issues, and by 1977 it had become solely pop and rock oriented. See also Circle International (**for retail outlet details**) and Voyage International labels.

Name: Santic
Owner and distributor: Leonard Chin and Ital Records Inc/Ltd
Period of operation: 1974–82
Comment: 1974 issue was an album, with 45s being released only from 1977. See also Ital (**for retail outlet details**), Nationwide?, Stonehouse and Student labels.

Name: Sarge
Owner: Lloyd Charmers and Sarge Records, 95, The Vale, London NW11
Distributor: Not known
Period of operation: 1978–82
Comment: See also Charmers and Plant Music labels.

Name: Saturn
Owner: Les Cliff (aka Cliff St Lewis)
Distributor: Not known
Period of operation: 1975–77
Comment: See also Jah Lion and King Cliff/KC labels.

Name: Saucy Boy
Owner: Gene Rondo and Valentine Brown in association with Count Shelly
Distributor: Shelly Recording Co and Third World Recording Co
Period of operation: 1975
Comment: See also BMB, Count Shelly (**for retail outlet details**) and Skank labels.

Name: Scarlet
Owner: Locksley Mellow
Distributor: Not known
Period of operation: Probably 1975
Comment: See also One Way label.

Name: Scope
Owner and distributor: WEA Records Ltd
Period of operation: 1979–80
Comment: WEA used Scope for issuing reggae it had leased from smaller companies like Third World and Jama, as well as some pop/soul.

Name: Sebastian
Owner: Lennie Cool
Distributor: Jama Music
Period of operation: 1975
Comment: Two issues, the a-sides of which also came out on Jama.

Name: Second Tracs
Owner: Rupert Cunningham
Distributor: President
Period of operation: 1975–76
Comment: See also Sound Tracs, Treble C and Tropical labels.

Name: Sensation Sounds
Owner and distributor: Rupie Edwards and Success Records at 31 Glenarm Road, Lower Clapton, London E5
Period of operation: 1977–78
Comment: Rupie Edwards still issues music from his record shop in Dalston's Ridley Road market. See also Success label.

Name: Serious Business
Owner: Dennis Bovell
Distributor: Not known
Period of operation: 1977
Comment: See also Arawak, Discovery, Matumbi Music Corp, More Cut, MR and Tempus labels.

Name: Shades
Owner: Ian Smith and Max Omare
Distributor: Not known
Period of operation: 1971–72
Comment: Omare was the owner of the Shades club in Sheffield. Despite the numbering used, there were only two issues on this label. See also Hot Lead label.

Name: Shebazz
Owner and distributor: Dennis Harris and DL International
Period of operation: 1976
Comment: Not clear whether this label actually had anything to do with Jamaican record producer Tony Shebazz. See also DIP label **(for retail outlet details).**

Name: Shirley
Owner: Roy Shirley
Distributor: Pinnacle
Period of operation: Not certain, but probably 1978–79
Comment: See also King Roy, Leroy, R&JJ and Victry labels.

Name: Silver
Owner: Silver
Distributor: Not known
Period of operation: possibly 1971
Comment: One issue by Silver And The Magnets. See also Fiery label.

Name: Silver Phoenix
Owner and distributor: Not known, but possibly Melodisc
Period of operation: c1962
Comment: Only one issue seen.

Name: Sir Christopher
Owner: Sir Christopher from Sir Christopher Records, 3 Salop Street, Wolverhampton **(retail outlet)**
Distributor: Enterprise
Period of operation: 1973
Comment: Sir Christopher was a Midlands-based sound system, whose record shop lasted several years after the label. The set-up had definite links with Lord Koos, however (both substantiated releases on the Sir Christopher label used Koos' KOO prefix and duplicated two of its already used issue numbers). See also Lord Koos, Ossie and Koos, and Thompson and Koos labels.

Name: Sir Collins Music Wheel
Owner and distributor: Clancy Collins
Period of operation: 1973–81
Comment: See also B&C Sound, Collins Down Beat, Nice One and Sounds of Jamaica labels.

Name: Sir Jessus
Owner: Morice Wellington in association with Sir Jessus Sound System and Record Shop, 186 Goldhawk Road, Shepherd's Bush, London W12 **(retail outlet)**
Distributor: Tropical in 1975 but not known thereafter
Period of operation: 1975–77
Comment: Initially administered by Tropical Records. One issue put out on 'Jessus' label (Junior Byles 'Know Where You're Going').

Name: Skank
Owner: Valentine Brown
Distributor: Not known
Period of operation: 1975
Comment: See also BMB and Saucy Boy labels.

Name: Skips
Owner: Pat Rhoden and Hill Top Music
Distributor: Not known
Period of operation: 1977
Comment: There was a Jamaican counterpart of this label administered by Rhoden, with involvement from Derrick Morgan, as early as 1970.

Name: Sky Note
Owners: Adrian Sherwood and Chips Richards at Angstar Records, 154 Rucklidge Avenue, Harlesden, London NW10 (**retail outlet**)
Distributor: Angstar and J&A Distribution
Period of operation: 1977–86
Comment: See also Carib Gems, High Note and Hit Run labels.

Name: Slate
Owner: Anthony Brightly (aka Sir George)
Distributor: Faith Productions
Period of operation: 1976–78
Comment: See also King George label (Slate issues have a KG prefix.)

Name: Slick
Owner: Slick Productions
Distributor: Not known
Period of operation: Not definite, but possibly 1977

Name: Soferno B
Owner and distributor: Soferno B Hi-Fi, 4, Granville Arcade, Brixton, London SW2
Period of operation: 1975–81
Comment: Initially distributed on behalf of Soferno B by Jama.

Name: Sol-Fa International
Owner: K Bailey and Honey Boy
Distributor: Third World Recording Co
Period of operation: 1975
Comment: See also Akins, Collette, Honey, Honey Boy and Third World labels (**for retail outlet details**).

Name: Solid Sound
Owner and distributor: Count Shelly and Third World Music
Period of operation: 1977
Comment: See also Third World label (**for retail outlet details**).

Name: Soul Breakers
Owner: Soul Breakers Productions
Distributor: Pye Records (Sales) Ltd/Plastic Fantastic
Period of operation: Not definite, but probably 1978
Comment: Interesting label with only one known issue. Although not a reggae release, it was by The Doyley Brothers And Blue Wonders who had a previous association with the music, hence its inclusion here.

Name: Soul Food
Owner: Lee Perry
Distributor: Not known
Period of operation: 1973
Comment: Believed to be one issue only ('High Priest' by U Roy). See also **comments** on Black Ark label, which may well be linked with this.

Name: Sound of Jamaica
Owner and distributor: Clancy Collins
Period of operation: 1968
Comment: One issue only ('Jamaican Bits And Pieces' by Lord Charles and his Band), which used a catalogue number from the Collins Down Beat label. See also B&C Sound, Collins Down Beat, Nice One and Sir Collins Music Wheel labels.

Name: Sounds News Studios
Owner: Sounds News Studios, 18 Blenheim Road, London W4 1ES
Distributor: not known
Period of operation: possibly 1979
Comment: Strange label emanating from independent recording studio in Notting Hill. Possibly one release only ('Blackbird' [parts 1 and 2] by The Duncans).

Name: Sound Track
Owner and distributor: Vince Record Shop
Period of operation: 1978
Comment: See also Vince label (**for retail outlet details**).

Name: Sound Tracs
Owner: Rupert Cunningham
Distributor: President
Period of operation: 1975–76
Comment: See also Second Tracs, Treble C and Tropical labels.

Name: Spencer International
Owner: Bill Spencer
Distributor: Not known
Period of operation: 1978
Comment: Spencer was a white musician and producer who dabbled in reggae, notably as producer for The Jah Lites.

Name: Splash
Owner: Tito Simon
Distributor: Pye Records Ltd/Plastic Fantastic
Period of operation: 1979
Comment: See also Pearl label.

Name: Staff
Owner: Not known
Distributor: Not known
Period of operation: 1978
Comment: One issue only (The Black Volts' 'Little Baby'). Publisher noted on label as 'Staff Music'.

Name: Star
Owner: Emil Shallit and Melodisc Records
Distributor: HR Taylor
Period of operation: 1969
Comment: One issue only (Sir Washington's 'Apollo 12'). This looks like a Pama group label, but has the words 'issued by Melodisc' at the bottom of the label as if it's an afterthought. See also New Wave label.

Name: Star
Owner and distributor: Pama Records/Jetstar at 78 Craven Park Road, Harlesden, London NW10 (retail outlet)
Period of operation: 1973 (Pama) and 1977–80 (Jetstar)
Comment: There was also an album release in 1975. Although this label would normally have been included in a Pama discography, given its very limited output it has been included here.

Name: Stonehouse
Owner: Alton Ellis in association with Leonard Chin and Ital Music Inc/Ltd
Distributor: Ital Records
Period of operation: 1976–77
Comment: See also Ital (for retail outlet details), Nationwide?, Santic and Student labels.

Name: Stop Point
Owner: Winston Edwards (in association with Dennis Harris and DL International in 1974 and Joe Gibbs in 1976)
Distributor: DL International (in 1974) and Fay Music (in 1976)
Period of operation: 1974 and 1976
Comment: There were essentially two separate phases of this label, of which there was also a Jamaican counterpart. It was administered for Winston Edwards by Dennis Harris/DL International in 1974 and, in 1976, by Edwards himself and Fay Music (ie after the Fay Music shop had opened). At least one of the 1974 releases was '50s R&B by the Gene And Eunice-related Sugar And Spice. See also DIP label (for retail outlet details).

Name: Student
Owner and distributor: Leonard Chin and Ital Music Inc/Ltd
Period of operation: 1975–76
Comment: See also Ital (**for retail outlet details**), Nationwide?, Santic and Stonehouse labels.

Name: Studio 16
Owner and distributor: Winston Edwards in association with Joe Gibbs at Joe Gibbs' Record City, 29 Lewisham Way, London SE14 (**retail outlet**)
Period of operation: 1978
Comment: This label supplanted Edwards' Fay Music operation.

Name: Style
Owner: Ranfold (Ranny) Williams and Rover Music
Distributor: Not known
Period of operation: 1975
Comment: One release only (Sedrick Isaacs' 'Jamaica Man'). See also A Rover and Ronnie Williams labels.

Name: Success
Owner and distributor: Rupie Edwards and Success Records
Period of operation: 1978–1980s
Comment: Only one 7-inch found (Ken Parker's 'I Wanna Be Loved'). Most of the material issued on this label consisted of Rupie's productions from the 1960s or 1970s, although some featured gospel music from Ken Parker, by then resident in the UK. See also Sensation Sounds label.

Name: Sugar
Owner: Charles Ross in association with Decca Records Ltd
Distributor: Decca Records Ltd
Comment: some interesting material, mostly in a commercial vein, but with a few solid Ja rhythms here and there.

Name: Summertime
Owner: Clement Bushay
Distributor: Shelly Recording Co for the first two issues only, and Clement Bushay for the subsequent releases
Period of operation: 1974–75
Comment: See also Bushay's and Bushranger labels.

Name: Sun & Star
Owner and distributor: Atomic Records, Birmingham
Period of operation: 1975
Comment: See also Atomic label (**for retail outlet details**).**Name:** Sunbeam
Owner: Sunbeam Music (1973–74) and Falcon Music (1975–76)
Distributor: Phonogram from early 1975; not known before that
Period of operation: 1973–76 and 1981 (one issue only)
Comment: Information regarding this label is vague to say the least, particularly as regards

who was involved with it at any one time. Laurel Aitken often used the 'Sunbeam Music' credit on his releases on other labels, so he may have been a prime mover, at least in the early stages. The one-off 1981 release was associated with Laurel and seems to support that theory.

Name: Sunpower
Owner and parent company: Jimmy Cliff in association with Mo Claridge and Ballistic Records
Distributor: Mojo Distribution, Pye Records & Tapes/Plastic Fantastic and United Artists
Period of operation: 1978
Comment: See also Ballistic, Bam Bam, D-Roy, Magnum and Warrior labels.

Name: Sunshot
Owner and distributor: Phil Pratt and Terminal Records
Period of operation: 1975–78
Comment: See also Chanan-Jah, Phil Pratt and Terminal (**for retail outlet details**) labels.

Name: Suntan
Owner: Not known
Distributor: Not known
Period of operation: 1978

Name: Supreme
Owner and distributor: Winston Curtis and Empire Records
Period of operation: 1976–78
Comment: See also Diamond, Empire (**for retail outlet details**) and Jungle Beat labels.

Name: Sydna
Owner and distributor: Dennis Harris and DL International
Period of operation: 1974
Comment: UK counterpart of US Andy's label, this had only two releases. See also DIP label (**for retail outlet details**).

T

Name: Tackle
Owner: Sonny Roberts and Orbitone Records
Distributor: Creole Records
Period of operation: 1974–78
Comment: Spouge-oriented label with the odd reggae issue thrown in. See also Affection, Cartridge and Orbitone (**for retail outlet details**) labels.

Name: Taurus
Owner: Brian Harris
Distributor: Creole Records and Enterprise
Period of operation: 1973–75
Comment: See also Black Wax (**for retail outlet details**), Double LL, Locks and Mango labels.

Name: T Bone
Owner and distributor: Fay Music
Period of operation: 1976
Comment: Possibly one issue only ('Sufferer's Heights' by the Black Starline Band). See also Blue Water Music and Fay Music (**for retail outlet details**) labels.

Name: Teem
Owner and distributor: Dennis Harris and DL International
Period of operation: 1974 and 1977
Comment: UK counterpart of Jah Lloyd's Jamaican label, there are just two substantiated issues only (one in each year), although it is not certain that the 1977 release was actually associated with DIP. See also DIP label (**for retail outlet details**).

Name: Tempus
Owner: John Francis and Dennis Bovell at Tempus Records, 21a Malvern Road, London W9 (**retail outlet**)
Distributor: 1977–79
Comment: See also Arawak, Discovery, Matumbi Music Corp, More Cut, MR and Serious Business labels.

Name: Terminal
Owner and distributor: Phil Pratt at Terminal Records, 25 Rectory Road, Stoke Newington, London N16 and (later) 20 Median Road, Hackney, London E5 (**retail outlets**)
Period of operation: 1975–78
Comment: See also Chanan-Jah, Phil Pratt and Sunshot labels.

Name: Third World
Owner and distributor: Count Shelly and Third World Recording Co at 113a Stoke Newington Road, London N16 and 261 High Road, Tottenham, London N15 (from April 1978) (**retail outlets**)
Period of operation: 1974–82
Comment: Third World essentially superseded the Count Shelly label early in 1975 and headed up Shelly's large group of labels. Like the Count Shelly label empire before it, Third World was also to be a key **distributor**. See also Attack, Bimbo Music, Caribbean, Ital Coxone, Jackpot, Jamatel, Justice, Live and Love, Observer, Paradise, Penguin, Queen Bee, RG, Saucy Boy, Sol-Fa and Solid Sound labels. The Third World shop at 261 High Road is now the Body Music record store.

Name: Thompson and Koos
Owners: Linval Thompson and Lord Koos (Eric Scott)
Distributor: Lord Koos
Period of operation: 1978–80
Comment: See also Lord Koos, Ossie and Koos and Sir Christopher labels.

Name: Three In One
Owner and distributors: a triumvirate of Daddy Kool Records, Dub Vendor at Northcote Road Open Market, Clapham Junction, London SW11 and Regal Music Centre at 92 Lower Clapton Road, Lower Clapton, London E5 (**retail outlets**)
Period of operation: 1978
Comment: Was initially to be called 'Skull Music'. Labels were printed up but apparently never used. See also Daddy Kool label (**for retail outlet details**).

Name: Timba
Owner: Not known
Distributor: Not known
Period of operation: 1978

Name: Tip Top
Owner and distributor: Tip Top Records, 276 Green Street, Upton Park, London E7 (**retail outlet**)
Period of operation: 1978

Name: Top
Owner and distributor: Emil Shallit and Melodisc Records
Period of operation: 1961
Comment: This was a UK counterpart of Sonny Bradshaw's Jamaican Top label. See also Chek, D, Dee's, Downbeat and Duke labels.

Name: Top Deck
Owner: Not known
Distributor: Not known
Period of operation: 1977
Comment: Not reggae. Only two issues have come to light by Tony And The Hippolytes/Hep-o-Lites, who toured West Indian venues in the mid-1970s and backed visiting US soul artists such as The Chi-Lites.

Name: Tops
Owner and distributor: Glen Darby and Tops Record Shop at 120 Acre Lane, Brixton, London SW2 (**retail outlet**)
Period of operation: 1976–78

Name: Torpedo
Owner: Eddy Grant in association with President Records
Distributor: President
Period of operation: 1970 and 1974–75
Comment: See also Hot Shot label.

Name: Trans-Universal
Owner: Russell Coke
Period of operation: 1977–78
Comment: Mainly religious material, with some 12-inch releases. Trans-Universal was not strictly a part of Coke's Magnet empire (it came after that). See also Dervia, Faith, Magnet **(for retail outlet details)** and Ray (first phase) labels.

Name: Treble C
Owner: Rupert Cunningham
Distributor: President
Period of operation: 1975–76
Comment: See also Second Tracs, Sound Tracs and Tropical labels.

Name: Trenchtown
Owner: Robby Day
Distributor: Dover Music
Period of operation: 1976–77
Comment: See also Pacific label.

Name: Tribal
Owner: Noel Bailey
Distributor: Not known
Period of operation: Possibly 1979
Comment: A roots-oriented label that may have surfaced in either the late 1970s or early 1980s.

Name: Tribesman
Owner: Lloyd Coxson
Distributor: Norris Musik City, 72 Granville Arcade, Brixton, London SW9 and (later) S&J Records, 4 Granville Arcade, Brixton **(retail outlets)**
Period of operation: 1977–82
Comment: See also Ital Coxone label.

Name: Triumphant
Owner: TL Barnes and PRS Publishers
Distributor: Not known
Period of operation: 1975
Comment: See also Cosmopolitan label.

Name: Tropical
Owner: Rupert Cunningham
Distributor: President and Record Corner, 27 Bedford Hill, Balham, London SW12 9EX **(retail outlet)**
Period of operation: 1974–76 and 1978
Comment: This was largely a continuation of the 1971–72 Bamboo subsidiary with which Cunningham was associated; 1978 release was an album reissue (Augustus Pablo's *This Is...*).

Name: Truth and Right
Owner: L Bent
Distributor: Not known
Period of operation: 1977–79

Name: Twylight
Owner: Not known
Distributor: Not known
Period of operation: 1976

U

Name: Ultra
Owner: Pye Records & Tapes
Distributor: Plastic Fantastic Ltd
Period of operation: 1977–78
Comment: Pye got quite involved in reggae in the mid- to late 1970s, launching labels (generally in connection with key individuals in the reggae market) such as Ice, Roots and Magnum. It also become a key **distributor** through its associated Plastic Fantastic operation. Ultra was another such label.

Name: Union
Owners and distributors: Bill and Pete Campbell, and BB Records
Period of operation: 1976–78
Comment: See also BB **(for retail outlet details)**, JUM and Jumbo labels.

Name: Untouchable
Owner and distributor: Dennis Harris and DL International
Period of operation: 1976
Comment: See also DIP label **(for retail outlet details)**.

Name: Upfront
Owner and distributor: Beacon Records Ltd
Period of operation: 1969–70
Comment: Reggae-inspired offshoot of Beacon. Also issued soul sides by Joyce Bond. There was also a US label with an identical design.

V

Name: Vasko
Owner and distributor: Ray Williams at Vasko Records, 219 Church Road, Willesden, London NW10 **(retail outlet)**
Period of operation: 1974–78
Comment: Most issues of a spouge nature. See also Motorway Sounds label.

Name: Venture
Owner and distributor: Philroy Matthias and David Tyrone at Venture Records, 994 Harrow Road, London NW10 (**retail outlet**)
Period of operation: 1974–81
Comment: Record shop was actually known as Gangsterville Music Arcade. See also B&S, BPI and Culture labels.

Name: Victry
Owner: Roy Shirley
Distributor: Not known
Period of operation: 1977
Comment: See also King Roy, Leroy, R&JJ and Shirley labels.

Name: Vince
Owner and distributor: Vince Record Shop at 643 Romford Road, Manor Park, London E12 (**retail outlet**)
Period of operation: 1978
Comment: See also Sound Track label.

Name: Vital Food
Owner and distributor: Winston Thompson (Dr Alimantado) and ISDA Records
Period of operation: 1978
Comment: See also ISDA label.

Name: Voyage International
Owner: Reg Maclean and Circle International Records
Distributor: President, WEA, Atlantic and CBS
Period of operation: 1979
Comment: Featured some reissues of material by Clinton Grant and Louisa Marks, which had been put out on Safari. See also Circle International (**for retail outlet details**) and Safari labels.

Name: V Rocket
Owner: Not known
Distributor: Mojo Distribution
Period of operation: 1979

Name: Vulcan
Owner: Junior Lincoln and Webster Shrowder at Vulcan Records, 49–53 Harrow Road, London W2 (**administrative offices**)
Distributor: Phonogram
Period of operation: 1975–76
Comment: Label title was originally slated as Viking. See also Grounation label.

W

Name: Wadada
Owner: Not known
Distributor: Not known
Period of operation: 1978

Name: Warrior
Owner and distributor: Mo Claridge and Mojo Distribution
Period of operation: 1979–80
Comment: This label was administered from Mojo Records at 94 Craven Park Road, Harlesden, London NW10 (**retail outlet**). See also Ballistic, Bam Bam, D-Roy, Magnum and Sunpower labels.

Name: Western Kingston
Owner and distributor: Dennis Harris and DL International
Period of operation: 1976
Comment: See also DIP label (**for retail outlet details**).

Name: White Rum
Owner: Bertram Brown and Freedom Sounds Records
Distributors: Lightning Records and Mojo Distribution
Period of operation: 1977–78
Comment: See also Freedom Sounds (**for retail outlet details**) and Red Stripe labels.

Name: Wildflower
Owner and distributor: Not known, possibly Brian Harris, Keith Thornton and Black Wax Corporation
Period of operation: 1976
Comment: UK counterpart of Ja label, this probably had just the one UK release ('Love Jah Jah Children' by Big Youth), the label of which states 'This copy only manufactured in United Kingdom'.

Name: Wind
Owner: Not known
Distributor: Not known
Period of operation: 1973, but not certain
Comment: UK counterpart of Winston Riley's Ja imprint.

Name: Wolf
Owner: Les Foster and Sylvan Williams
Distributor: Not known
Period of operation: 1974–77
Comment: There is no connection between this and the Ja Wolf label.

Name: Write Sounds
Owner: R Sinclair
Distributor: Derrick's Record Village, 460 Leyton High Road, Leyton, London E10 (**retail outlet**)
Period of operation: 1978–84
Comment: R Sinclair was Tapper Zukie's brother and also known as 'Blackbeard', although he had nothing to do with Dennis Bovell. See also Four Sixty and Rite Sound labels.

Y

Name: Youth and Youth
Owner: David Sinclair (Tapper Zukie)
Distributor: House of Reggae
Period of operation: 1977
Comment: Just one issue located (Freddy McKay's 'Marcia'). See also Achilles, Love and Unity, MER and New Star labels.

Z

Name: Zara
Owner and parent company: Spartacus R in association with President
Distributor: President
Period of operation: 1976–77
Comment: Calypso and West African music. Spartacus R was formerly of afro-rock outfit Osibisa.

Name: Zone
Owner: Not known
Distributor: Not known
Period of operation: 1978
Comment: Possibly a DIP-related label since copies were pressed by the same company DIP used and because the prefix is similar to the first release on the Untouchable label (ZO).

Appendix 2: Pama Discography

PAMA'S COLOSSAL OUTPUT: ANOMALIES AND ALL

The following discography – or, if you prefer, catalogue – is the result of many years of searching, collecting, buying, listening, pestering and sheer dedication. Our interest in the Palmer brothers' musical empire goes back even before that, to the very early '70s when we first heard gems like 'Say What You're Saying', 'The Horse', 'Scrooge', 'Return Of Jack Slade' and 'Bangarang' on a variety of colourful labels, all with the little circular 'Pama' logo on them. These truly were 'boss sounds'.

Like Trojan, after 1971 Pama put out a fair amount of less-than-top-drawer tunes. The catalogue does not feature anything the company issued post-1976, largely because such material was issued sporadically and is of much more limited interest.

In looking at your own collection or looking through the listings, you will find some definite anomalies, inconsistencies, contradictions and questions, and the following notes attempt to explain these.

NOTES ON THE DISCOGRAPHY

Glen Adams – On the face of it, it would seem that Adams, during his tour of the UK with The Upsetters, was also peddling material to Pama, which either he or Lee Perry could have laid claim to. For instance, 'Power Cut' on Gas (GAS 135B) was The Upsetters' 'Cold Sweat' but without Perry's spoken intro.

Gladstone Anderson – 'Judas' on Camel (CA 61A) had previously been issued on Blue Cat back in 1969.

Eric Barnet – It has already been established that a lot of Pama tracks credited to 'Eric Barnet' were actually by Theo Beckford's Group, but it hasn't been proved that literally all of them were. Barnett and his wife Dorothy were producers (or were folk who paid others to produce on their behalf) and Pama was in the habit of crediting records to such people whenever it suited it. GAS 130 in particular has noticeably different artists on each side. It may have been that the Barnetts supplied tapes or discs with no artist credits, leaving Pama little option.

Tony Brevett – 'So Ashamed' on BU 497A was also issued on Trojan's Green Door label as 'I'm Sorry' and credited to The Matadors. It is believed in this case that Pama had the issuing rights and that Trojan had been sold the tune by a third party under different credits. The track 'Long Island' on Pama Supreme (PS 350B) was a version of 'So Ashamed' with an organ overlay by **Graham Hawk** done in the UK.

Carl Bryan – A saxophonist who also went under the names **King Cannon** and **Cannonball King**.

Rad Bryan – The tracks on BU 463 are produced by Bryan but are probably not by him.

Cannonball King – See **Carl Bryan**.

Lloyd Charmers – See **Lloyd Tyrell**.

The Classics – Basically a UK session band consisting most times of Denzil Dennis and Milton Hamilton but sometimes featuring Les Foster or Eugene Paul. Delroy Washington also apparently joined for certain tracks after 1971. See also **Freedom Singers**.

DD Dennis – This is Denzil Dennis, who also went under the alias Alan Martin.

Roy Docker – See **Roy Smith**.

Winston Francis – 'Ten Times Sweeter Than You' may have been a self-production laid after he had moved to the UK but it uses a backing track from one of The Dynamites' tracks on Clancy Eccles' *Herbsman Reggae* album. On the other hand, it appeared in Jamaica on a Dynamic-related label where production credits went to Lynford Anderson.

Freedom Singers – Yet again, another UK session outfit named after a similar

Jamaican (Studio One) session team. The Freedom Singers mirrored **The Classics** (see them too). The personnel was broadly the same but there was an occasional extra in the form of Tiger, Lloyd Campbell or Laurel Aitken.

Bill Gentles – Gentles was a talented impersonator and could take off Desmond Dekker, Max Romeo, Derrick Morgan and probably a few others.

Hesketh Graham – See **Graham Hawk**.

Winston Groovy – His real name is **Winston Tucker**.

Gruvy Beats – Name The Cimarons used when working with Laurel Aitken and Winston Groovy.

Hammers – Another UK-based band, who may have done session work for Pama. They also had singles out on the President label.

Harry Harrison – Young Harry appears on the front cover of Lester Sterling's 'Bangarang' album, which was taken inside Pama's 'Soundsville' shop at the height of the company's greatness in 1969. He was also a vocalist and cut some sides with Fitzroy Sterling on Bullet and Escort.

Graham Hawk – Hawk was featured organist in a later (post-Hawkshaw) version of The Mohawks. It is believed that his real name was **Hesketh Graham**.

Alan Hawkshaw – Featured organist on the 1968–69 Mohawks Pama sides (ie the 'Champ' version of the band).

Dimples Hinds – Member of The Marvels and producer of a few Pama sides.

Ornell Hinds/Nellie Hinds – Member of The Marvels and responsible for 'I Who Have Nothing'/'You Send Me' (GAS 126) and 'Love Letters' (Pama PM 819B).

The Inner Mind – Billed as 'The Greatest White Reggae Band on Earth', Inner Mind leader Ian Smith still actively works in the music business in his native Huddersfield.

King Cannon – See **Carl Bryan**.

Tony King – See **H Robinson's** entry too. King was a white studio manager in London whose services and premises were used for a lot of UK-recorded and Ja remixed/remastered reggae in the late '60s and throughout the '70s. He was never believed to be an artist in his own right, however, although there was a Tony King who laid some US-recorded reggae in the late '70s. Ranny Williams frequently used King's studio, as did Derrick Morgan. All of the sides credited to him on various Pama label releases are almost certainly by someone else. Again, it was a convenient credit for either the Palmer brothers or the producers of the tracks to use.

Kurass – Probably a pseudonym for The Mohawks.

Lorenzo – An alias that Laurel Aitken sometimes used.

Melodians – 'Come Ethiopians' was issued on Trojan's Summit label as a Leslie Kong production, whereas Pama's Punch release credited the group as 'The Robinsons' and the production to Lloyd Daley. It does, however, sound more like Daley's work than Kong's (who never dealt with Pama), although it is possible that this could have fallen into Pama's hands by way of Tony Brevett, who was a Melodians' member who had many dealings with both companies.

Pacesetters – There was a UK reggae group called The Pacesetters who had an album issued on Saga records. The Escort release (ERT 829) may be by this group but could also have been by a Ja band with the same name, as the label credits 'G Murphy'. It could of course just be a Pama cover-up job. There is, however, a definite UK feel to these sides. GAS 130B sounds suspiciously like the same outfit, as does the backing band with Stranger Cole on Escort ES 819B.

Planets – There has been some speculation about whether the outfit on 'People Get Funny' on Bullet (BU 528) was actually The Maytones. It is very much in their style, but is not believed to be by them. The other tune that sounds like The Maytones is The Slickers' 'Coolie Gal' on Bullet (BU 449A), and it may be that the two Maytones (Vernon Buckley and Gladstone Grant) featured on backing vocals.

H Robinson – The identity of 'H Robinson' or 'Harry Robinson' is a bit of an enigma. In Jamaica, 'H Robinson' was apparently the owner of the Carib-Disc-Co record shop and label in Orange Street, and of Caribbean Record Distribution. In the UK, Harry Robinson was a white, middle-aged former jazz band leader in the 1950s, who ran a studio in London where his speciality was recording strings. I have it on good authority that Derrick Morgan used to take material there for mastering, remixing or whatever, and the credit 'H Robinson' often appears on Pama releases with which Derrick is associated. Until such time as further information comes to light on exactly where the 'H Robinson' sides emanated from, his name on records should be taken with a large pinch of salt.

Jackie Robinson – He may or may not be the vocalist on 'Heart Made Of Stone' on Punch (PH 50A). Producer Phil Pratt had Delroy Wilson voice this tune, but for some reason Pama, or perhaps Pratt himself, had another artist overdub the vocals. This does not sound like Jackie Robinson, who was the falsetto voice in The Pioneers and was a Trojan rather than a Pama man anyway.

Sidney Rodgers – A member of the Mk II version of The Mohawks for a time and later went solo, where he recorded for Larry Lawrence's Ethnic set-up. His real name was Sidney Bowrey.

Joan Ross – Later known as TT Ross, and also known as Silkie Davis and Nina Mackenzie.

Slickers – Some of the Bullet label sides credited to The Slickers and The Viceroys, and labelled as being produced by UK-based Pioneer Sidney Crooks are not all they seem. For a start, both band names were apparently used for whoever was around in the studio at the time so they will often sound completely different. Some were possibly UK-originated (like The Viceroys' 'Chariot Coming'), others definitely Ja. Some of the credits were incorrect, such as BU 453A, now known to be a Lee Perry production. A number of tracks, notably BU 449B and both sides of BU 454 also appeared under different artist and producer credits on Trojan's second volume of *Music House*.

Ian Smith – See **Inner Mind**.

Roy Smith – This was his real name but he also went under the aliases Junior Smith and Roy Docker. In order to try and preserve some consistency, however, we have kept his artist credits as they appear on the labels but production-wise have always used Roy Smith.

The Soul Cats – Again, another credit for different-sounding artists. The groups on the Camel sides (CA 23 and CA 24B) and 'Choo Choo Train' (Gas 109A) sound totally unalike. There *was* a Ja outfit called The Soul Cats, but they sounded nothing like any of these!

Winston Tucker – See **Winston Groovy**.

Lloyd Tyrell – See also **Lloyd Charmers**. Tyrell was Charmers' real name, which he usually used while doing his rude or organ instrumental sides. His 'Lloyd Charmers' alias was pretty much confined to his smooth vocal efforts.

Versatiles – Another band with different-sounding line-ups.

Viceroys – See **Slickers**.

Norton York – He was a strings arranger – Pama's equivalent to Trojan's Johnny Arthey.

Youth – 'The Youth' was Trevor Sutherland, who later became I Jah Man Levi. 'The Youth' was a genuine credit since Sutherland had issued a few singles under this guise on Deram and Polydor a couple of years previously. His single on Pama ('Fire Fire') was released on the Tower label in Ghana.

The vast majority of the catalogue items have been personally checked aurally and we have laboriously noted where 'record X is actually by artist Y', or the like, where record details are wrong. This may not be to everyone's liking but if you do come across a certain record with incorrect credits, these listings will give you the full picture. However, we have not necessarily split hairs and have taken it upon ourselves to correct some minor misspellings on labels.

If we have not substantiated a particular detail, it has gone down as 'unidentified' or left blank. 'NYT' means 'not yet traced'. Dates in brackets after a title signify the original year of issue of the particular recording. Where known, UK-recorded items have been noted as such after the production credit. Finally, as mentioned earlier, the Bunny Lee efforts on Unity are pretty difficult to pin down since, by most accounts, he was not always at the control panel but took the credits by virtue of being the session financer. His younger brother Don (or Don Tony Lee) was also involved in sporadic record production. It is quite possible, then, that quite a few of the Bunny Lee production credits are open to question.

BULLET

BU 399 Throw Me Corn/Darling Remember – Winston Shand And The Sheiks/Pat Edwards (Prod: Ranny Williams) 1969

BU 400 Madame Streggae/Stupid Married Man – Girlie/Laurel Aitken (Prod: Laurel Aitken (UK)) 1969

BU 401 Let Me Tell You Boy/Mannix – The Ebony Sisters/Rhythm Rulers (Prod: Harry Mudie) 1969

BU 402 Heart Don't Leap/I Am Sorry (1968) – Dennis Walks/The Clarendonians (Prod: Harry Mudie/Ken Lack) 1969

BU 403 Duba Duba/Running Alone – The Meditators/Cecil Thomas (actually Nicky Thomas) (Prod: Joe Gibbs) 1969 [PROBABLY UNISSUED]

BU 404 Work Boy Work/Girl Lonesome Fever – The Soul Rhythms/Cecil Thomas (actually Nicky Thomas) (Prod: Joe Gibbs) 1969 [PROBABLY UNISSUED]

BU 405 No Business Of Yours/Mash It Up – George Williams (Prod: Harry Mudie) 1969

BU 406 Festival Knocks (actually 'Greatest Scorcher')/Making Love (actually titled 'To Me') – The Tennors (Prod: Albert George Murphy) 1969

BU 407 Tribute To Don Drummond/Japanese Invasion – Rico Rodriguez (actually with Gene Rondo)/Rico Rodriguez (Prod: Bunny Lee and Rico Rodriguez) 1969

BU 408 Love Of My Life/Shady Tree – Dennis Walks (Prod: Harry Mudie) 1969

BU 409 I Am Just A Minstrel/Yesterday – The Kingstonians (Prod: Albert George Murphy) 1969

BU 410 V-Rocket/Smile (actually titled 'My Baby') – The Fabions/The Fabions (actually by The Tennors) (Prod: Albert George Murphy) 1969

BU 411 Matilda/Come To Me – Winston Shand/The Harmonians (Prod: Ranny Williams) 1969

BU 412 Hog In A Mi Minti/Lona Run (actually 'Lorna Run') – The Hippy Boys (actually with Winston Shand)/The Hippy Boys (actually with Ranny Williams) (Prod: Ranny Williams) 1969

BU 413 What's Your Excuse/Tell Me Tell Me – The Hippy Boys (actually with Count Sticky)/The Hippy Boys (actually with Winston Shand) (Prod: Ranny Williams) 1969

BU 414 Cat Woman/Selassie Serenade – Glen Adams/Peter Touch (actually Peter Tosh) (Prod: Bunny Lee) 1969

BU 415 Motherless Children/I Am Not Afraid – Willie Francis (Prod: Willie Francis) 1969

BU 416 Run Mr Nigel Run/Come Home – The Chuckles (actually with Nicky Thomas) (Prod: Derrick Harriott) 1969

BU 417 Black Is Soul/Always With Me (actually titled 'Emily') – The Imperials (actually with Horace Faith) (Prod: H Robinson) 1969

BU 418 NOT USED

BU 419 Copy Cats/Hot Lead – The Clan (actually Stranger Cole, Derrick Morgan and Owen Gray with The Rudies)/Bunny Lee All Stars (Prod: Derrick Morgan (UK)/Bunny Lee) 1970

BU 420 Each Time/Boss Walk – The Ebony Sisters With The Bunny Lee All Stars/Bunny Lee All Stars (Prod: Bunny Lee) 1970

BU 421 The Feeling Is Fine/Girl You're Killing Me – Freddie Notes And The Rudies (Prod: Derrick Morgan (UK)) 1970

BU 422 That's My Life (wrong title: possibly called 'Because You Lied')/Queen Of My Heart – Fitzroy Sterling (actually with The Rudies) (Prod: Fitzroy Sterling (UK)) 1970

BU 423 Phoenix (actually 'By The Time I Get To Phoenix')/Heartbreak Girl (1968) – Noel Brown (Prod: Derrick Harriott) 1970

BU 424 A Fistful Of Dollars/Crystal (1968) – The Crystalites/The Crystalites (actually with Bobby Ellis) (Prod: Derrick Harriott) 1970

BU 425 Come By Here/Somebody – Winston And Rupert (Prod: Harry Mudie) 1970

BU 426 Theme From 'A Summer Place'/Big Boy – Ranny Williams And The Hippy Boys (Prod: Ranny Williams) 1970

BU 427 Last Date/Cherry Pink – Hortense Ellis/Pat Satchmo (Prod: Tommy McCook) 1970

BU 428 Savage Colt/The Clean Hog – Ranny Williams (actually with The Hippy Boys)/The Eldorados (Prod: Ranny Williams) 1970

BU 429 Rome/Version Of Rome – Lloyd Jones/Rhythm Rulers (Prod: Harry Mudie) 1970

BU 430 Na Na Hey Hey Goodbye/Musical Bop – The Clan (actually Stranger Cole, Derrick Morgan and Owen Gray) With The Mohawks/King Stitt (actually by Count Sticky) (Prod: Derrick Morgan (UK)/Ranny Williams) 1970 [B-SIDE ALSO ISSUED ON ESCORT ES 807A AS WHITE LABEL]

BU 431 Pupa Live On High Top/Give Me Faith – The Reggae Boys (Prod: Glen Adams) 1970 [B-SIDE REISSUED FROM GAS 122B]

BU 432 NYT

BU 433 NYT

BU 434 Exposure/Baby Huey – Lloyd Tyrrell [Lloyd Charmers] (Prod: Lloyd Charmers) 1970

BU 435 Dollars And Bonds/Sounds Familiar – Lloyd Tyrell [Lloyd Charmers] (actually with The Hippy Boys) (Prod: Lloyd Charmers) 1970

BU 436 The Return Of Batman/In Action – Sidney All Stars (actually Sidney Crooks' All Stars) (Prod: Sidney Crooks (UK)) 1970

BU 437 Outer Space/Full Moon – Sidney All Stars (actually Sidney Crooks' All Stars) (Prod: Sidney Crooks (UK)) 1970

BU 438 Freedom Street/Freedom Version – Fitzroy Sterling/Fitzroy's All Stars (Prod: Fitzroy Sterling (UK)) 1970

BU 439 Reggae Sounds Are Boss/Goodbye My Love – Fitzroy [Sterling] And Harry (Harrison)/Fitzroy Sterling (Prod: Fitzroy Sterling (UK)) 1970

BU 440 Nice Grind/Nice Grind Version – The Rebels/Sidney Crooks' All Stars (Prod: Sidney Crooks (UK)) 1970

BU 441 Chariot Coming/Stackata – The Viceroys/Sidney Crooks' All Stars (Prod: Sidney Crooks) 1970

BU 442 Reggae A Bye Bye/Doctor Jekyll – Lloyd Tyrell [Lloyd Charmers] (actually With The Hippy Boys)/Lloyd Tyrell [Lloyd Charmers] (actually with Dave Barker) (Prod: Lloyd Charmers) 1970

BU 443 Oh Me Oh My/I Did It – Lloyd Tyrell [Lloyd Charmers] (Prod: Lloyd Charmers) 1970

BU 444 Power Control/Dip Dip (actually titled 'Vena') – The Viceroys/The Slickers (Prod: Sidney Crooks) 1970

BU 445 Keep Trying (actually 'Keep On Trying')/Keep On Trying (Version) – Little Roy/Little Roy (actually by The Matadors) (Prod: Lloyd Daley) 1970

BU 446 I Don't Want To Interfere/Preaching Love – The Maytones (Prod: Alvin Ranglin) 1970

BU 447 Second Pressure/Sammy Dead – Rhythm Rulers (Prod: Harry Mudie) 1970

BU 448 Set Back/Version II (actually titled 'Jack And Jill') – Gregory Isaacs/Biggie (?) (Prod: Rupie Edwards) 1970 [B-SIDE REISSUED ON BULLET BU 453B]

BU 449 Coolie Gal/Bawling Baby (aka 'Beef Balls And Gravy') – The Slickers/Biggie (?) (Prod: Rupie Edwards) 1970

BU 450 Come On Over/Version 2 – The Viceroys/Sidney Crooks' All Stars (actually by The Upsetters) (Prod: Lee Perry) 1970

BU 451 NYT

BU 452 Be Strong (actually 'Growing Up To Be Strong')/Wake Up In The Sunshine (actually 'Soft Lights And Sweet Music') – Solomon Jones (actually by unidentified male vocalist)/Solomon Jones (actually by Sidney Rogers and The Mohawks) (Prod: Lee Perry/Derrick Morgan (UK)) 1970

BU 453 Fancy Cloth (actually titled 'River To Cross')/Jack And Jill – The Viceroys/Biggie (?) (Prod: Lee Perry/Rupie Edwards) 1970 [B-SIDE REISSUED FROM BULLET BU 448B]

BU 454 I Wish (actually 'I Wish I Had Someone')/Black Is Black (aka 'Black Is Togetherness') – Basil Gail (actually by Glen Adams And The Hippy Boys)/Martin Riley (actually by unidentified male vocal group) (Prod: Glen Adams/Martin Riley) 1970

BU 455 Get Out Of This Land (actually 'Get Out Of This Thing')/Landmark (actually 'Get Out Of This Thing (Version)') – Sammy Morgan/Sidney Crooks' All Stars (Prod: Sidney Crooks (UK)) 1971 [ALSO ISSUED ON PUNCH PH 57]

BU 456 Knock Three Times/The Whealing Mouse – Carl Lewin (actually Carl Lewis)/Sidney Crooks' All Stars (Prod: Sidney Crooks (UK)) 1971 [ALSO ISSUED WITH A BLANK LABEL ON PAMA PM 821]

BU 457 Call Me/Call Me (Part 2) – The Cimarons (Prod: Cimarons (UK)) 1971

BU 458 Leave A Little Love/My Baby – The Cimarons (Prod: Cimarons (UK)) 1971

BU 459 Just Enough/Standing – David Isaacs/Roy Patin (actually Roy Panton) (Prod: Lee Perry) 1971

BU 460 Can't Reach You/Natural Woman – The Untouchables/Carl Dawkins (actually with The Upsetters) (Prod: L Perry) 1971

BU 461 All Combine (Part 1)/All Combine (Part 2) – The Upsetters (actually with Lee Perry) (Prod: Lee Perry) 1971

BU 462 My Love (aka 'Can't Hide The Feeling')/Stronger Love (actually 'My Love (Version)') – Rupie Edwards' All Stars (actually by The Gaylads)/Rupie Edwards' All Stars (Prod: Rupie Edwards And BB Seaton) 1971

BU 463 Shock Attack/Cuban Waltz – Rad Bryan (Prod: Rad Bryan) 1971

BU 464 Soul Town (actually 'Soul Town Reporter')/Let The Sun Shine On Me (actually 'Love Light Shining') – Bob Marley (actually with Charley Ace)/Bob Marley (Prod: Lee Perry) 1971

BU 465 Arawack Version/Cuffy Guffy – The Inner Mind (Prod: Ian Smith (UK)) 1971

BU 466 Blackman's Pride/Groove With It – Alton Ellis/Leroy Palmer (Prod: Sidney Crooks (UK)/Andell Forgie) 1971

BU 467 Nobody's Business/Standing By – Derrick Morgan (Prod: Derrick Morgan) 1971

BU 468 NYT

BU 469 NYT

BU 470 Rebel Nyah/Feel The Spirit – The Viceroys (Prod: Derrick Morgan (UK)) 1971

BU 471 I Wanna Be Loved/Get Back Together – Winston Groovy (Prod: Winston Tucker (UK)) 1971

BU 472 Peace Begins Within/Go Back Home – Nora Dean/The Slickers (Prod: Sid Bucknor) 1971

BU 473 Reggae In Wonderland/Wonder (Version) – The Charmers (actually by Byron Lee And The Dragonaires) (Prod: Lloyd Charmers) 1971

BU 474 Zion/Zion Version – Danny And The Flames (actually Danny Clarke And The Righteous Flames)/The Adisababians (Prod: Lee Perry) 1971 [ISSUE NOT CONFIRMED]

BU 475 The Same Thing For Breakfast/Sweeter Than Honey – Winston (Groovy) And Pat (Rhoden)/Winston Groovy (Prod: Winston Tucker and Pat Rhoden (UK)/Winston Tucker (UK)) 1971

BU 476 Never Love Another/Never Love Another (Version) – Busty Brown (Prod: Sid Bucknor) 1971

BU 477 There's A Train/Blue Moon – Speed (unidentified artist: possibly Earl George) (Prod: Earl George) 1971

BU 478 Mother Oh Mother/Drums Of Passion (actually titled 'Judgement Rock') – Max Romeo/Morgan's All Stars (actually by Charley Ace) (Prod: Rupie Edwards/Bunny Lee) 1971

BU 479 Let It Be Me/Dream Dream Dream (actually 'All I Have To Do Is Dream') – The Cariboes [MIS-CREDITED TO THE JAMAICA JUBILEE STOMPERS] (Prod: Laurel Aitken (UK)) 1971

BU 479 Let It Be Me/All I Have To Do Is Dream – The Cariboes (Prod: Laurel Aitken (UK)) 1971 [SECOND ISSUE WITH CORRECTED CREDITS]

BU 480 NYT

BU 481 NYT

BU 482 NYT

BU 483 Dandy Shandy Version 4/Go Back Version 3 – Impact All Stars (With Unidentified DJ) (Prod: Victor Chin) 1971

BU 484 NYT

BU 485 Don't Care/True Born African – Alton Ellis (Prod: Alton Ellis/Sid Bucknor) 1971

BU 486 Maga Dog/Bull Dog – Peter Tosh (actually with The Soulmates)/Third And Fourth Generation (Prod: Joe Gibbs) 1971

BU 487 NYT

BU 488 Sour Sop (actually 'Ripe Sour Sop')/Stranger Cole Medley – Stranger Cole (actually by Willie Francis)/Stranger Cole (actually with Patsy Todd) (Prod: Willie Francis/Stranger Cole) 1971

BU 489 Willie's Rooster/Willie's Rooster (Version) – Willie Francis (Prod: Willie Francis) 1971

BU 490 Devil Woman/Venn Street Rub – Ian Smith And The Inner Mind (Prod: Ian Smith (UK)) 1971

BU 491 So Far Away/So Far Away (Version) – Bel Teics (actually by The Hail Tones)/Brute Force And Ignorance (Prod: Raphael Gray) 1971

BU 492 One Night Of Sin/One Night (Version) – The Slickers (actually by Jackie Brown And The Gaytones)/The Slickers (actually by The Gaytones) (Prod: Sonia Pottinger) 1971

BU 493 Lick Samba/Samba Version – Bob Marley And The Wailers/The Wailers Band (Prod: Bob Marley And Lee Perry) 1971

BU 494 I'm Gonna Live Some Life/Rockin' – Rupie Edwards' All Stars (actually by The Ethiopians)/Rupie Edwards' All Stars (Prod: Rupie Edwards) 1971

BU 495 NYT

BU 496 This Tropical Land (aka 'This Beautiful Land')/Love I Bring – The Melodians/U Roy And Slim Smith (Prod: Tony Brevett/Rupie Edwards) 1972

BU 497 So Ashamed/My Only Love (actually 'My One And Only Lover') – Tony Brevett/Gregory Isaacs (Prod: Tony Brevett/Gregory Isaacs) 1972

BU 498 Three Combine/The Nearest Thing To Your Heart (aka 'The Man In Your Life') – Syd (Sydney Rodgers) And Joe/Les Foster (actually with Ansell Collins) (Prod: Ranny Williams (UK)/Derrick Morgan (UK)) 1972 [B-SIDE REISSUED ON CAMEL CA 102A]

BU 499 Beat Down Babylon/Babylon Version – Junior Byles/The Upsetters (Prod: Lee Perry) 1972

BU 500 Butter And Bread/Butter And Bread (Version) – Lloyd Young/Shalimar All Stars (Prod: Glen Brown) 1972

BU 501 High School Serenade/On The Track – Lennox Brown/Winston Scotland (Prod: Tony Robinson) 1972

BU 502 Rum Rhythm (actually titled 'Mucking Fuch')/Run Rhythm (Version) (actually 'Mucking Fuch (Version)') – (Roy) Shirley And (Lloyd) Charmers/Lloyd Charmers (actually by The Charmers Band) (Prod: Lloyd Charmers) 1972

BU 503 Aily And Ailaloo/Aily And Ailaloo (Version) – Niney And Max Romeo/Niney All Stars (Prod: Winston Holness) 1972

BU 504 Hard To Be Believe (actually titled 'Hard To Be Happy')/Softie – Gerry Meggie (actually by Beresford Hammond)/Max Romeo (Prod: Clancy Eccles/Lee Perry and Winston Holness) 1972

BU 505 NYT

BU 506 Pure In Heart/Clean Hands – Bill Gentles (Prod: Sir Derrick and A Silent) 1972

BU 507 Sad Movies/Movies Version – Barbara Jones/Sir Harry (Prod: B Brooks) 1972

BU 508 Oily Sound (actually 'Aily Sound')/Oily Version (actually 'Aily Version') – Lloyd Tyrell [Lloyd Charmers]/Lloyd Tyrell (actually by The Splash All Stars) (Prod: Lloyd Charmers) 1972

BU 509 Dub Up A Daughter/Daughter (Version) – Dennis Alcapone/Prince Tony's All Stars (Prod: Tony Robinson) 1972

BU 510 NYT

BU 511 Babylon Falling/Make It Love – Gaby Wilton And Charley Ace/Charley Ace (actually with The Youth Professionals) (Prod: Charley Ace) 1972

BU 512 Howdy And Tenky/Sprinkle Some Water – (Emmanuel) Flowers And Alvin (Ranglin)/Shorty Perry (Prod: Alvin Ranglin) 1972

BU 513 The King Man Is Back/The King Man Is Back (Version) – The Hoffner Brothers/Shalimar All Stars (Prod: Glen Brown) 1972

BU 514 I Miss My Schooldays/School Days Version – BB Seaton/The Conscious Minds (Prod: Lloyd Charmers) 1972

BU 515 For Once In My Life/Didn't I (actually 'Didn't I Always') – Cornel Campbell (Prod: Bunny Lee) 1972

BU 516 NYT

BU 517 NYT

BU 518 NYT

BU 519 Mr Parker's Daughter/On Top Of The Peak – Sir Harry And The Ethiopians/U Roy (Prod: Rupie Edwards/Alvin Ranglin) 1972

BU 520 Here Come The Heartaches/You'll Be Sorry – Delroy Wilson (Prod: Bunny Lee) 1972

BU 521 Hi-Jack Plane/Shower Of Rain – The Avengers (Prod: Kirk Redding (UK)) 1973

BU 522 Ben/Laughing Stock Version – Margaret Elaina/Ritchie And The Now Generation (Prod: Pluto Shervington/Val Douglas) 1973

BU 523 Place In The Sun (1969)/Burning Fire (actually titled 'Burning Desire') (1969) Slim Smith (Prod: Bunny Lee) 1973 [REISSUED FROM PAMA SUPREME PS 373A/UNITY UN 524B AND 508B RESPECTIVELY]

BU 524 The Word Is Black/Town Talk – King Miguel (Prod: Lee Perry) 1973

BU 525 Go On This Way/Santic Dub – Freddy McKay/Santic All Stars (Prod: Leonard Chin) 1973

BU 526 NYT

BU 527 Take Time Out/Just Like A Log – The Three Tops (Prod: Lee Perry) 1973

BU 528 People Get Funny/Funny Version – The Planets/Doc Bird All Stars (Prod: Dennis Brown) 1973

BU 529 Yama Skank (actually 'Yamaha Skank')/Doctor Run Come Quick – Shorty Perry/U Roy Junior (Prod: Rupie Edwards) 1973

Note: nos 530–49 were not used.

Second Series

BU 550 No Money, No Friend/Money Dub – Shelton Walks/Bob Mack All Stars (Prod: George Maclean) 1975

BU 551 NYT

BU 552 Step Right Up/Banjo Serenade – I Roy/Andy's All Stars (Prod: Roydale Anderson) 1975

BU 553 NYT

BU 554 Healing In The Balmyard/Healing (Version) – The Starlites/GG All Stars (Prod: Alvin Ranglin) 1975

BU 555 Lonely Days/Lonely Days (Version) – Gregory Isaacs (Prod: Gregory Isaacs) 1975 [ALSO ISSUED ON CAMEL LABEL CA 2004]

BU 556 NYT

BU 557 Nyah Chant (actually titled 'Fly Away Home')/Rasta Waltz – Sons Of Jah (Prod: Clive Davidson and RD Livingston [Dandy]) 1975

CAMEL

CA 10 Who You Gonna Run To?/Hi-There (actually titled 'Man Of My Word') – The Techniques/The Techniques (actually by Carl Bryan) (Prod: Winston Riley) 1969

CA 11 Down In The Park/Love Oh Love – The Inspirations (Prod: Lee Perry) 1969

CA 12 Can't Get No Peace/For A Few Dollars More – Eric 'Monty' Morris/The Upsetters (Prod: Lee Perry) 1969

CA 13 Taste Of Killing/My Mob – The Upsetters (Prod: Lee Perry) 1969

CA 14 Danny Boy/Reggae Happiness – King Cannon [Carl Bryan] (Prod: Harry Johnson) 1969

CA 15 Sad Mood/Give It To Me – Delroy Wilson (actually by Ken Parker)/Stranger Cole (Prod: Bunny Lee/Stranger Cole) 1969

CA 16 Strange Whispering/Hard To Handle – The West Indians/Carl Dawkins (Prod: Lee Perry) 1969

CA 17 Hold On Tight/A Hundred Pounds Of Clay – The Scorchers/The Royals (Prod: Lloyd Daley) 1969

CA 18 Facts Of Life/I'll Be Waiting – The Mellotones/The Termites (Prod: Lee Perry) 1969

CA 19 Everywhere Everyone/Go Find Yourself A Fool – The Techniques (Prod: Winston Riley) 1969

CA 20 Since You've Been Gone/Cool Down – Eric Fratter/Winston Hines (Prod: Harry Johnson) 1969

CA 21 Wonder Of Love/Cinderella – The Inspirations (Prod: Lee Perry) 1969

CA 22 Run For Your Life/When We Were Young – Carl Bryan/The Two Sparks (Prod: Harry Mudie) 1969

CA 23 Your Sweet Love/Keep It Moving – The Soul Cats/The Soul Cats (actually Withewan McDermott) (Prod: Ewan McDermott) 1969

CA 24 Midnight Spin/Money Money – Val Bennett/The Soul Cats (Unidentified Vocal Group) (Prod: Lee Perry?) 1969

CA 25 Girl What You Doing To Me/Woman A Grumble – Owen Gray (actually with The Rudies) (Prod: Derrick Morgan (UK)) 1969

CA 26 History (actually titled 'Wonderful World')/Just Be Alone – Harry And Radcliffe (Prod: H Robinson) 1969 [ALSO ISSUED ON PUNCH PH 8]

CA 27 Sentimental Reason/Lover Girl – The Maytones (Prod: Alvin Ranglin) 1969

CA 28 No More Teardrops/Love Me Or Leave Me – Eric 'Monty' Morris And The Maples (Prod: Ewan McDermott?) 1969

CA 29 Cat Nip (actually 'Yes Sah')/Cooyah (actually 'Cat Nip') – The Hippy Boys (actually with Lloyd Charmers) (Prod: Lloyd Charmers) 1969

CA 30 Confidential/House In Session – Lloyd Charmers (actually with The Hippy Boys)/Tommy Cowan (actually with Lloyd Charmers And The Hippy Boys) (Prod: Lloyd Charmers) 1969

CA 31 Warrior/Don Juan – Johnny (Osbourne) And The Sensations/Johnny Organ (actually by Boris Gardner And The Love People) (Prod: Winston Riley) 1969

CA 32 Power Pack/Throwing Stones – Winston Wright (actually with Mudie's All Stars)/The Two Sparks (Prod: Harry Mudie) 1969

CA 33 Beware Of Bad Dogs/Short Cut – The Soul Mates (actually by Glen Adams) (Prod: Glen Adams) 1969

CA 34 Don't Take Your Love Away/Two Lovers – Owen Gray And The Rudies (Prod: Derrick Morgan (UK)) 1969

CA 35 Nobody Knows/Somewhere – Junior English And Tony Sexton/Junior English (Prod: Harry Palmer (UK)) 1969

CA 36 Bongo Nyah/Dad Name (actually 'Bad Names') – Little Roy (actually with Don Carlos)/The Creations (Prod: Lloyd Daley) 1969

CA 37 Every Beat Of My Heart/Don't Cry – Owen Gray And The Rudies (Prod: Derrick Morgan (UK)) 1969

CA 38 Drink And Gamble/King Of The Road – Young Freddy (actually Freddie MacGregor)/Lenox Brown And Hue Roy (actually Lennox Brown And U Roy Junior) (Prod: Harry Johnson) 1969

CA 39 The Three Stooges/The Isle Of Love – Bunny Lee All Stars (Prod: Bunny Lee) 1970

CA 40 In This World/You Better Call On Me (actually titled 'Shocking Love') (1968) – The Federals (Prod: Derrick Harriott) 1970

CA 41 The Worm (actually titled 'King Of The Worm')/Afro – Lloyd Robinson/Neville Hinds (actually with The Matadors) (Prod: Lloyd Daley) 1970

CA 42 Gold Digger/The Mine – The Little Roys (actually by The Wailing Souls)/The Matadors (Prod: Lloyd Daley) 1970

CA 43 Scrooge/In The Days Of Old – Little Roy (Prod: Lloyd Daley) 1970

CA 44 London Bridge/Things And Time – Neville Hinds (actually with The Matadors)/The Scorchers (actually by The Wailing Souls) (Prod: Lloyd Daley) 1970

CA 45 Dark Of The Sun (actually 'Dark Side Of The Sun')/Dreader Than Dread – The Matadors (actually by Jackie Mittoo)/The Matadors (Prod: Lloyd Daley) 1970

CA 46 You Run Come/Skank King (actually 'Skank Me') – Little Roy (Prod: Lloyd Daley) 1970

CA 47 Black And White Unite/Jumbo Jet – The Maytones/Gloria's All Stars (actually by Charlie Ace And The GG All Stars) (Prod: Alvin Ranglin) 1970

CA 48 Jumping Dick/Newsroom – Gloria's All Stars (actually The GG All Stars) (Prod: Alvin Ranglin) 1970

CA 49 Since You Left/Bird Wing – The Maytones/Gloria's All Stars (actually The GG All Stars) (Prod: Alvin Ranglin) 1970

CA 50 Don't Sign The Paper/Packing Up Loneliness – Owen Gray (Prod: Derrick Morgan (UK)) 1970

CA 51 Bring Back Your Love/Got To Come Back – Owen Gray (Prod: Derrick Morgan (UK)) 1970

CA 52 Fight Them/Dreadlock – The Little Roys (actually by Little Roy)/The Matadors (actually with Count Sticky) (Prod: Lloyd Daley) 1970

CA 53 Catch This Sound/Suspense – Martin Riley (actually with The Uniques)/Martin Riley (Prod: Martin Riley) 1970

CA 54 Everyday Tomorrow/Lift Your Head Up High – Stranger Cole (actually with Gladdy Anderson) (Prod: Stranger Cole) 1970 [B-SIDE ALSO ISSUED ON GAS 152A]

CA 55 Feel It/Serious (actually titled 'Heppie Soul') – Sister (actually by Paulette And Gee)/GG All Stars (actually by Charley Ace) (Prod: Alvin Ranglin) 1970

CA 56 Everybody Bawlin' (actually titled 'Bawling For Mercy')/Mr Brown (actually Titled 'Mr Brown's Coffin') – Dennis Alcapone And Lizzy (Prod: Winston Holness) 1970

CA 57 Sellasie Want Us Back (actually 'Pack Up Your Things And Go')/Make It With You – The Little Roys (actually by The Overdrives)/Roy And Joy (actually Little Roy And Joy Lindsay) (Prod: Lloyd Daley) 1970

CA 58 1970s/1970s Version – Ron Sig (Prod: Ron Sig) 1970

CA 59 You Girl/Facts Of Life (1968) – Roy Edwards/Slim Smith And Roy Shirley (actually Roy Shirley And The Uniques) (Prod: Ron Sig/Bunny Lee) 1970

CA 60 Groove Me/No Other One – Owen Gray (Prod: Sidney Crooks (UK)) 1971

CA 61 Judas (1969)/Me Nah Tek You Lick (1969) – The Maytones (actually by Gladstone Anderson And The Followers)/The Maytones (Prod: Alvin Ranglin) 1971

CA 62 Donkey Skank/Donkey Track – Delroy And The Tennors (actually by Scotty With Delroy Jones And The Tennors)/Murphy's All Stars (Prod: Albert George Murphy) 1971

CA 63 Hold On Tight (Do It Right)/Cleanliness – Sister (actually by Paulette And Gee)/The Maytones (Prod: Alvin Ranglin) 1971

CA 64 I'll Never Fall In Love With You Again/La-Fud-Del – Winston Heywood (actually with The Fud Christian All Stars)/Fud Christian All Stars (Prod: Fud Christian) 1971

CA 65 Talk About Love/Love Music – Pat Kelly/Phil Pratt All Stars (Prod: Phil Pratt) 1971

CA 66 Black Equality/Big Thing (actually titled 'Reggae Is Tight') (1969) – Max Romeo/Winston Blake (actually by Lloyd Charmers And The Hippy Boys) (Prod: Pete Weston/Lloyd Charmers) 1971

CA 67 Heavy Load/Heavy (Version) – Pressure Beat (actually by Stranger Cole And Gladstone Anderson) (Prod: Joe Gibbs) 1971

CA 68 Rice And Peas (actually titled 'Dandy Shandy')/All The While (actually 'Dandy Shandy Version 2') – Dandy And Shandy (actually by The Ambassadors With The Impact All Stars) (Prod: Keith Chin) 1971

CA 69 Be My Wife/Hit Me Back Baby – Delroy Wilson/Joe Higgs (actually by Walter's All Stars) (Prod: Herman Walters) 1971

CA 70 Guilty/United We Stand – Tiger (Prod: Laurel Aitken (UK)) 1971 [FIRST PRESSING]

CA 70 Guilty/Funny Funny Man – Tiger (Prod: Laurel Aitken (UK)) 1971 [SECOND PRESSING]

CA 71 Silhouettes/That Did It – Winston Wright (actually with The Upsetters) (Prod: Lee Perry) 1971

CA 72 Crying (actually titled 'These Eyes')/It Must Come – Stranger Cole/Delroy (Wilson) And Dennis (Alcapone) (Prod: Byron Smith/Bunny Lee) 1971

CA 73 Nothing Can Separate Us/Girl I Want You To Understand – Owen Gray (Prod: Sidney Crooks (UK)/Harry Palmer (UK)) 1971

CA 74 This A Butter/This A Butter (Version) – Dennis Alcapone (actually with Pat Kelly)/Phil Pratt All Stars (Prod: Phil Pratt) 1971

CA 75 Running Back Home/Running Back Version – Rocking Horse/Soul Syndicate (Prod: H Thomas) 1971

CA 76 I Love You The Most/Love You The Most (Version) – Morgan's All Stars (actually by Lloyd Clarke And Derrick Morgan's All Stars)/Morgan's All Stars (Prod: Derrick Morgan) 1971

CA 77 When Will We Be Paid/He's Got The Whole World In His Hands – Martin Riley/Willie Francis (Prod: Martin Riley/Willie Francis) 1971

CA 78 Linger Awhile/Linger A While (DJ Version) – John Holt (Prod: Lloyd Daley) 1971

CA 79 Seven In One (Medley)/Seven In One (Part 2) – The Gaylads (Prod: Herman Chin-Loy and BB Seaton) 1971

CA 80 Freedom Train/Marcus Is Alive – The Gladiators/Willie And Lloyd (actually by Willie Francis) (Prod: Lloyd Daley/Willie Francis) 1971

CA 81 Spanish Harlem/Slip Away – Slim Smith (Prod: Bunny Lee) 1971 [REISSUED FROM UNITY UN 520 WITH A- AND B-SIDES REVERSED]

CA 82 The Coming Of Jah/Watch And Pray – Max Romeo And Niney (Prod: Winston Holness and Lee Perry) 1972

CA 83 Put Me Down Easy/I Want To Go Back Home – The Groovers (Prod: F Crossfield) 1972

CA 84 I Am Just A Sufferer (aka 'Send A Little Rain')/We Want To Know – Derrick Morgan (Prod: Derrick Morgan) 1972

CA 85 Rasta Bandwagon/When Jah Speaks – Max Romeo (actually with Lee Perry)/Max Romeo (actually by Lee Perry) (Prod: Winston Holness) 1972

CA 86 Public Enemy Number One/How Long Must We Wait – Max Romeo (Prod: Lee Perry) 1972

CA 87 Black Cinderella/Anniversary – Errol Dunkley/Phil Pratt All Stars (actually By Tropic Shadow) (Prod: Jimmy Radway/Phil Pratt) 1972

CA 88 Audrey/So Nice – Winston Shand (Prod: Ranny Williams) 1972

CA 89 Take Me Back/Where Do I Turn – Slim Smith (Prod: Bunny Lee) 1972

CA 90 Africa Arise/Holy Mount Zion (actually titled 'Zion 'Iah') – Laurel Aitken/Gi Ginri (Prod: Laurel Aitken (UK)/Gi Ginri) 1972

CA 91 Ain't No Sunshine/You Are Everything – Ken Boothe/Lloyd (Charmers) And Hortense (Ellis) (Prod: Lloyd Charmers) 1972

CA 92 The Ten Commandments Of Joshua/Only Love Can Make You Smile – Charley Ace/Gaby And Wilton (actually Gaby Wilton And The Cables) (Prod: Charley Ace And Glen Brown/Glen Brown) 1972

CA 93 NYT

CA 94 Wonderful World/Wonderful Version – Alton Ellis/Fab Dimension (Prod: Pete Weston) 1972

CA 95 My Confession/Daddy's Home (1968) – Cornel Campbell/Pat Kelly (Prod: Bunny Lee) 1972

CA 96 Darling Forever/Darling Forever Version – The Clarendonians/Stud All Stars (Prod: Peter Austin and Ken Wilson) 1972

CA 97 NYT

CA 98 Presenting Cheater/Official Trombone – Ansell And Elaine (actually Ansell Collins And Margaret Elaina)/Ron Wilson (Prod: Lloyd Parks) 1972

CA 99 Ten Times Sweeter Than You/Fat Boy – Tony Gordon (actually by Winston Francis) (Prod: Lynford Anderson) 1972

CA 100 Lean On Me/Samba Pa Ti – BB Seaton/The Now Generation (Prod: Lloyd Charmers) 1972 [FIRST PRESSING]

CA 100 Lean On Me/Black Heart – BB Seaton/U Roy (Prod: Lloyd Charmers) 1972 [SECOND PRESSING]

CA 101 Jamaica Song/Out Of Love – Lloyd Charmers (Prod: Lloyd Charmers) 1972

CA 102 The Man In Your Life/Man In Your Life (Version) – Les Foster And Ansell Collins/Ansell Collins (Prod: Derrick Morgan (UK)) 1972 [A-SIDE IS REISSUE FROM BULLET LABEL BU 498B UNDER DIFFERENT TITLE]

CA 102 The Man In Your Life/I May Never See My Baby (1968) – Les Foster And Ansell Collins/Derrick Morgan (Prod: Derrick Morgan (UK)) 1973 [SECOND PRESSING]

CA 103 Must I Be Blue/Blue Version – Owen Thompson (Prod: Owen Thompson) 1973

CA 104 NYT

CA 105 Room Full All Full/Room Full All Full (Version) – The Twinkle Brothers (Prod: Norman Grant) 1973

CA 106 Everyday Is The Same Kind Of Thing/Sweat Of Your Brow – Sister (actually by Paulette Williams)/Shorty Perry (Prod: Alvin Ranglin) 1973

CA 107 Rainy Weather (wrong title: Probably Called 'What Must Fari Do Fe Please You?')/Version – Roy And Joe (actually by unidentified male vocal duo)/The Den Brothers (Prod: Dennis Brown) 1973

CA 108 Baby Someday I'll Want To Know/Baby Someday I'll Want To Know (Version – Dennis Brown (actually by unidentified DJ – possibly U Roy Junior) (Prod: Dennis Brown) 1973

Second Series

CA 2001 Miss Wire Waist/Wire Dub – Carl Malcolm/Skin, Flesh And Bones (Prod: Clive Chin) 1975

CA 2002 Wolverton Mountain/Wolverton Mountain (Version) – Roman Stewart/Karl Pitterson All Stars (Prod: Karl Pitterson) 1975

CA 2003 Natty Screwface/Face Dub – Yvonne Harrison/Underground Express (Prod: Glen Adams) 1975

CA 2004 Lonely Days/Lonely Days (Version) – Gregory Isaacs (Prod: Gregory Isaacs) 1975 [ALSO ISSUED ON BULLET LABEL BU 555]

CA 2005 NOT USED

CA 2006 Everynight (1971)/Ethiopia (1971) – Ruddy (Grant) And Sketto (Richards) (Prod: Laurel Aitken (UK)) 1975 [REISSUED FROM SUPREME LABEL SUP 218]

CA 2007 La Vie En Rose/Spanish Eyes – Laurel Aitken (Prod: Laurel Aitken (UK)) 1975

CA 2008 Dance With Me/Dance Dub – Gregory Isaacs (Prod: Gregory Isaacs) 1975

CA 2009 Everybody's Somebody's Fool/Everybody's Somebody's Fool (Version) – Barbara Jones/The Sunshot Band (Prod: Phil Pratt) 1975

Note: CA 70 was issued again in 1975 (with 'United We Stand' as the flip side) as part of the second series.

CRAB

CR 1 Children Get Ready/Someone To Love (aka Lonely And Blue) – The Versatiles (Prod: Lee Perry/Bunny Barrett) 1968

CR 2 Fire A Muss Muss Tail/Blacker Black – The Ethiopians/The Ethiopians (actually by The Count Ossie Band) (Prod: H Robinson/Bobby Kalphat) 1968

CR 3 River To The Bank/Reggae Limbo – Derrick Morgan/Peter King (Prod: Derrick Morgan) 1968

CR 4 Reggae Hit The Town/Ding Dong Bell – The Ethiopians (Prod: H Robinson) 1968

CR 5 Spread Your Bed/Worries A Yard – The Versatiles (Prod: Lee Perry) 1969

CR 6 Reggae City/Mellow Trumpet – Val Bennett/King Cannon [Carl Bryan] (Prod: Bunny Lee/Derrick Morgan) 1969

CR 7 I Am A King/What A Big Surprise – The Ethiopians (Prod: H Robinson) 1969

CR 8 Seven Letters/Lonely Heartaches – Derrick Morgan/The Tartans (actually by The Clarendonians) (Prod: Derrick Morgan/Ken Lack) 1969 [RE-PRESSED IN 1971]

CR 9 Private Number/Another Chance – Ernest Wilson (Prod: Derrick Morgan/Lee Perry) 1969

CR 10 Run Girl Run/The Drifter – George Grossett/Dennis Walks (Prod: Harry Mudie) 1969

CR 11 The First Taste Of Love/Dance All Night – Derrick Morgan/The Tartans (Prod: Derrick Morgan/Ken Lack) 1969

CR 12 Work It/You Mean So Much To Me – The Viceroys/The Viceroys (actually by The Paragons) (Prod: Lloyd Daley) 1969

CR 13 Take Your Hand From Me Neck/Equality And Justice – The Viceroys/The Paragons (Prod: Lloyd Daley) 1969

CR 14 Please Please/The Destroyer -The Caribbeans/The Matadors (Prod: Lloyd Daley) 1969

CR 15 When There Is You/My Woman's Love – The Melodians/The Uniques (Prod: Winston Lowe) 1969

CR 16 Walking By/Promises, Promises – Vincent Gordon/The Viceroys (Prod: Lloyd Daley) 1969

CR 17 Freedom Train/You Should Never Have To Come (1963) – Ernest Wilson (actually with The Soulettes)/Stranger Cole (actually with The Baba Brooks Band) (Prod: Lee Perry/Duke Reid) 1969 [PRESSED IN BOTH STEREO AND MONO]

CR 18 Don't Play That Song/How Can I Forget – Derrick Morgan (Prod: Derrick Morgan) 1969

CR 19 Hold Down/Who Will She Be (1968) – The Kingstonians/Barry York (Prod: Derrick Harriott) 1969

CR 20 Tears On My Pillow/I'm Trapped – Rudy Mills (Prod: Derrick Harriott) 1969

CR 21 Just Once In My Life/Mighty Organ – Ernest (Wilson) And Freddie (MacGregor)/Glen Adams (Prod: Bunny Lee) 1969

CR 22 Mek It Tan Deh/Gimme Back – Derrick Morgan (Prod: Derrick Morgan) 1969

CR 23 Send Me Some Loving/Come What May – Derrick Morgan (Prod: Derrick Morgan) 1969

CR 24 A Heavy Load/Wholesale Love – Rudy Mills (Prod: Derrick Harriott) 1969

CR 25 Brother Ram Goat/What A Situation – Theo Beckford/The Starlighters (actually The Starlites) (Prod: Albert George Murphy) 1969

CR 26 Baff Boom/Feel Bad – The Tennors (Prod: Albert George Murphy) 1969

CR 27 Death A Come/The Sword – The Viceroys (actually by Lloyd Robinson)/The Matadors (Prod: Lloyd Charmers/Lloyd Daley) 1969

CR 28 Time Hard/Death Rides A Horse – Derrick Morgan/Roy Richards (Prod: Derrick Morgan/Stranger Cole) 1969

CR 29 True Brothers/Sign Of The Times – The Tennors (Prod: Albert GeorgeMurphy) 1969

CR 30 Man Pon Moon/What A Thing – Derrick Morgan And The Rudies (Prod: Derrick Morgan (UK)) 1969

CR 31 Long About Now/They Got To Move – Bruce Ruffin And The Techniques/Lloyd Robinson (Prod: Winston Lowe) 1969

CR 32 Moon Hop/Harris Wheel (actually 'Harry's Wheel') – Derrick Morgan And The Rudies/The Reggaeites (Prod: Derrick Morgan (UK)/Albert George Murphy) 1969

CR 33 Greater Sounds/Live The Life I Love – George Grossett (Prod: Harry Mudie) 1969

CR 34 Last Flight/Natural – Rupie Martin's All Stars (Prod: R Jackson) 1969 [WHITE LABEL ONLY]

CR 35 Long Lost Love/Uncertain Love – Rupie Edwards (Prod: Rupie Edwards) 1969

CR 36 I Want Everything/Cherry – The Tennors (Prod: Albert George Murphy) 1969

CR 37 Quaker City/Double Up – Eric Barnett (actually by Theo Beckford's Group) (Prod: Eric Barnett And Albert George Murphy) 1969

CR 38 Devil Woman/Nobody Cares – The Tender Tones (actually with Leslie Levy) (Prod: ?) 1969

CR 39 Without My Love/Here I Come Again – Little Roy (actually with Joy Lindsay)/Winston Samuels (Prod: Lloyd Daley) 1969

CR 40 Big Thing (actually titled 'Big Sin Thing')/Exclusively Yours (1966) – Winston Blake/Rupie Edwards (Prod: Rupie Edwards) 1969

CR 41 Never Miss/Redemption – Rupie Edwards' All Stars (actually with Winston Wright) (Prod: Rupie Edwards) 1969

CR 42 My Elusive Dream/Hee Cup – Ernest Wilson/Sir Harry (Prod: Lee Perry) 1969

CR 43 NOT USED

CR 44 A Night At The Hop/Telephone – Derrick Morgan And The Rudies/Derrick Morgan (actually with Jennifer Jones With The Rudies) (Prod: Derrick Morgan (UK)) 1970

CR 45 Sentimental Man/It's A Lie – Ernest Wilson (Prod: Bunny Lee) 1969

CR 46 Oh Babe/The Rat – Derrick Morgan/The Thunderbirds (Prod: Derrick Morgan (UK)) 1970

CR 47 Need To Belong/Let's Have Some Fun – Derrick (Morgan) And Jennifer (Jones) (actually with The Mohawks) (Prod: Derrick Morgan (UK)) 1970

CR 48 The Pill/Spring Fever – Bim, Bam And Clover/Tommy McCook (Prod: Derrick Morgan (UK)/Bunny Lee) 1970

CR 49 Immigrant's Plight/Bang Shang Along – Bim, Bam And Clover/Peter Austin And Hortense Ellis (Prod: Derrick Morgan (UK)/Bunny Lee) 1970

CR 50 (Too Busy) Thinking About My Baby/I Wonder – U B Barrett (actually with The Mohawks) (Prod: Derrick Morgan (UK)) 1970

CR 51 I Wish I Was An Apple/The Story – Derrick Morgan With The Mohawks (Prod: Derrick Morgan (UK)) 1970

CR 52 Take A Letter Maria/Just A Little Loving – Derrick Morgan And Owen Gray/Derrick Morgan (actually with Jennifer Jones And The Mohawks) (Prod: Derrick Morgan (UK)) 1970

CR 53 Rain Is Going To Fall/This Game Ain't Fair – Denzil Dennis (actually with The Mohawks) (Prod: Derrick Morgan (UK)) 1970

CR 54 Rocking Good Way/Wipe Those Tears (actually 'Wipe The Tears') – Derrick (Morgan) And Jennifer (Jones) (actually with The Mohawks) (Prod: Derrick Morgan (UK)) 1970

CR 55 Tenants/Western Standard Time – Jennifer Jones/Rico Rodriguez (Prod: Derrick Morgan (UK)) 1970

CR 56 Disgusted/Fire In Mi Wire – Bim And Clover (Prod: Derrick Morgan (UK)) 1970

CR 57 My Dickie/Brixton Hop – The Commentator (actually Derrick Morgan)/The Kurass (Prod: Derrick Morgan (UK)) 1970 [A-SIDE ALSO ISSUED ON PAMA PM 822B]

CR 58 I Can't Stand It No Longer/Beyond The Hill – D Morgan (Prod: Derrick Morgan (UK)) 1970

CR 59 Endlessly/Who's Making Love – Derrick Morgan (Prod: Derrick Morgan (UK)) 1970

CR 60 Having A Party/Man With Ambition – Denzil Dennis (actually with The Mohawks) (Prod: Derrick Morgan (UK)) 1970

CR 61 Band Of Gold/Midnight Sunshine – Joan Ross (TT Ross)/The Hammers (Prod: Derrick Morgan (UK)) 1970

CR 62 Hurt Me/Julia – Derrick Morgan (Prod: Derrick Morgan (UK)) 1970

CR 63 I Like The Way (You Kiss And Hug Me)/Tell Me Why – Winston Groovy (Prod: Winston Tucker (UK)) 1970 [ALSO ISSUED ON THIS NUMBER WITH BLANK (IE NO WRITTEN CREDITS) OCEAN LABEL]

CR 64 I've Got To Find A Way To Get Maria Back/Wanna Be There – Winston Groovy (Prod: Winston Tucker (UK)) 1971 [ALSO ISSUED ON THIS NUMBER WITH BLANK (IE NO WRITTEN CREDITS) OCEAN LABEL]

CR 65 In The Ghetto/Something Sweet – Rip 'N' Lan (actually by Zip And Len) (Prod: Laurel Aitken (UK)) 1971

CR 66 Birmingham Cat/Now You're On Your Own – The Invitations/The Invitations (actually Pat Rhoden And Denzil Dennis) (Prod: Laurel Aitken (UK)) 1971

CR 67 Searching So Long/Drums Of Passion – Derrick Morgan/Morgan's All Stars (actually by Bongo Herman) (Prod: Derrick Morgan (UK)/Derrick Morgan) 1971

ESCORT

ES 801 Hold The Pussy/Wha'ppen – Kid Gungo/King Cannon (actually by Sir Lord Comic) (Prod: Harry Johnson) 1969

ES 802 The Big Race [MENTO]/Calulo (actually titled 'More Callaloo') – Calypso Joe (actually by Lord Power) (Prod: Harry Johnson) 1969

ES 803 Shine Eye Girl/Who's Next – Vincent Foster (actually by The Jays)/King Cannon [Carl Bryan] (Prod: Harry Johnson) 1969

ES 804 Rich In Love (aka 'La La Always Stay')/Zumbelly – Glen Adams (actually by Glen Brown And Dave Barker)/The Woodpeckers (Prod: Harry Johnson) 1969

ES 805 What Am I To Do/Bring Back That Smile – Tony Scott (Prod: Tony Scott) 1969

ES 806 Early In The Morning/Mr Lonely – The Jamaicans (Prod: Harry Johnson) 1969

ES 807 My Love/Windsor Castle – Stranger (Cole) And Patsy (Todd)/Sweet Confusion (Prod: Stranger Cole) 1969

ES 807 Musical Bop/Where It Sore – Count Sticky (Prod: Ranny Williams) 1969 [DUPLICATE ISSUE ON WHITE LABEL ONLY. A-SIDE ALSO RELEASED ON BULLET BU 430B]

ES 808 Don't Let Me Down/Romper Room – Marcia Griffiths/The Reggaeites (actually by Peter Tosh) (Prod: Harry Johnson) 1969

ES 809 Elizabethan Serenade/Don At Rest – Sweet Confusion (Prod: Stranger Cole) 1969

ES 810 Pretty Cottage/To Me – Stranger Cole (actually with Gladdy Anderson) (Prod: Stranger Cole) 1969

ES 811 Why Did You?/Do You Remember – Stranger (Cole) And Patsy (Todd) (Prod: Stranger Cole) 1969

ES 812 Hotter Scorcher/Conquering Lion – Sweet Confusion (Prod: Stranger Cole) 1969

ES 813 Sad, Sad, Sad/Wonderful Light Of The World – Unidentified Male Vocalist/Stranger (Cole) And Gladdy (Anderson) (Prod: Stranger Cole) [ON WHITE LABEL ONLY]

ES 814 Please Stay/Voyage From The Moon – Lascelles Perkins/The Matadors (Prod: Lloyd Daley) 1969

ES 815 NYT

ES 816 Darling If You Love Me/Saturday Night (actually titled 'Prodigal Boy') – Tony Scott (Prod: Tony Scott) 1969

ES 817 Bandit/Family Man Mood – Errol Wallace/Aston Barratt (Prod: Aston Barratt) 1969

ES 818 Boss A Moon/Brotherly Love – SS Binns (actually by Sonny Binns And The Rudies)/Bunny Lee All Stars (Prod: Derrick Morgan (UK)/Bunny Lee) 1970

ES 819 Lena Lena/Nana, Na, Na, Nana (actually titled 'You Shouldn't Do It') – Stranger Cole And The Mohawks/Stranger Cole (possibly with The Pacesetters) (Prod: Stranger Cole (UK)) 1970

ES 820 Soul Of England/Shanghai – Lloyd Charmers (actually by The Jokers)/Lloyd Charmers (actually with The Hippy Boys) (Prod: Lloyd Charmers) 1970

ES 821 Mango Tree/The Removers – The JJ All Stars (actually with Winston Wright) (Prod: JJ Johnson) 1970

ES 822 Fight For Your Right/Soul Fight – Busty Brown (actually with The Upsetters/The Mediators (actually by The Upsetters) (Prod: Martin Riley) 1970

ES 823 It Grows/We Had A Good Thing Going – Martin Riley (Prod: Martin Riley) 1970

ES 824 Young, Gifted And Black [First Version]/My Cherie Amour – Bob (Andy) And Marcia (Griffiths)/Barry Biggs (Prod: Harry Johnson) 1970 [FIRST ISSUE]

ES 824 Young, Gifted And Black/I Am Satisfied – Denzil (Dennis) And Jennifer (Jones)/Owen Gray (Prod: Derrick Morgan (UK)) 1970 [SECOND ISSUE]

ES 825 Stampede/You Were Meant For Me (1968) – The Kurass/King Stitt (actually by Lee Perry) (Prod: Graham Hawk (UK)/Clancy Eccles) 1970 [B-SIDE REISSUED FROM PAMA PM 722B)

ES 826 Remember/Loneliness – Stranger Cole (Prod: Stranger Cole) 1970

ERT 827 Pop A Top Train/Doing The Moonwalk – Fitzroy (Sterling) And Harry (Harrison) (Prod: Fitzroy Sterling (UK)) 1970

ERT 828 NYT

ERT 829 Bits And Pieces/Nimrod Leap – The Pacesetters (Prod: ?) 1970

ERT 830 Little Things/Till The Well Runs Dry – Stranger Cole And The Mohawks (Prod: Stranger Cole (UK)) 1970

ERT 831 Everything With You/Picture On The Wall – Stranger Cole And The Mohawks (Prod: Stranger Cole (UK)) 1970

ERT 832 Pussy/Let Me In – Stranger Cole And The Mohawks (Prod: Stranger Cole (UK)) 1970

ERT 833 While There Is Life/Come On Over – Gregory Isaacs/Harry Young (Prod: Gregory Isaacs/) 1970

ERT 834 Midnight Sunshine (actually titled 'Mellow Moonlight')/You Are My Sunshine – Family Man (actually by Roy Docker And The Mohawks)/Gregory (Isaacs) And (Count) Sticky (Prod: Roy Smith (UK)/Gregory Isaacs) 1970

ERT 835 Man From Carolina/African Melody – GG All Stars (Prod: Alvin Ranglin) 1970

ERT 836 Ishan Cup/Soul At Large – Lloyd Charmers (actually with The Hippy Boys) (Prod: Herman Chin-Loy And Lloyd Charmers/Lloyd Charmers) 1970

ERT 837 Crock Iron/Memphis Bop – Ranny Bop [Ranny Williams] (Prod: Ranny Williams) 1970

ERT 838 Lonesome Feeling/Hop Scotch – Barbara Andrews/Ranny Bop [Ranny Williams] (Prod: Ranny Williams (UK)) 1970

ERT 839 Woman A Love In The Night Time/The World Is On A Wheel – Lord Spoon And David (actually by Mix Flour And Sugar) (Prod: Alvin Ranglin) 1970 [BOTH SIDES CALYPSO/MENTO]

ERT 840 Engine Number Nine/Do It (actually titled 'Don't Do It') – Moose/The Kurass (Prod: Ranny Williams? (UK)/Derrick Morgan (UK)) 1970

ERT 841 NYT

ERT 842 To The Rescue/Run For Cover – The Wailers (Prod: Tuff Gong) 1970

ERT 843 A Day Will Come/A Day Will Come (Version 2) – The Tartans (actually by The Clarendonians)/Robi's All Stars (actually by The Bunny Lee All Stars) (Prod: Bunny Lee) 1970

ERT 844 Work It/Good Lover – The Mellotones/Soul Man (Prod: Lee Perry) 1970

ERT 845 Man Short (actually titled 'Ten To One')/She Want It – Busty Brown (actually with The Gaytones)/Dave Barker (actually with The Gaylads) (Prod: Sonia Pottinger) 1970

ERT 846 Me A Tell Yuh/More Echo – The Victors/Lloyd (Daley's) All Stars (Prod: Lloyd Daley) 1971

ERT 847 I'm Gonna Knock On Your Door/Set Me Free – John Holt/Uriel Aldridge (Prod: Bunny Lee/Harry Johnson) 1971

ERT 848 Burn Them/Poor Boy – Willie Francis (Prod: Willie Francis) 1971

ERT 849 Chicken Thief/Tomorrow (actually titled 'Where Will You Be Tomorrow') – Lloyd Clarke/Stranger Cole (actually with Gladdy Anderson) (Prod: Derrick Morgan/Clancy Eccles) 1971

ERT 850 Yester Me, Yester You, Yesterday/Yes Sir – Little Roy/Matador All Stars (Prod: Lloyd Daley) 1971

ERT 851 My Love Come True (actually 'Love Me Tender') (1969)/This Feeling (1969) – Slim Smith (Prod: Slim Smith) 1971 [REISSUE OF UNITY UN 539]

ERT 852 Life Keeps Turning/My Conversation (1968) – Slim Smith (actually with unidentified male vocalist)/The Uniques (Prod: Slim Smith/Bunny Lee) 1971

ERT 853 Batchelor Boy/Colour Rites (actually 'Colour Race') – Bill Gentles/The Scorpions (Prod: Derrick Morgan (UK)) 1971

ERT 854 Love Brother/Love Brother (Instrumental) – Herman (Chin-Loy)/Aquarius (actually by Tommy McCook) (Prod: Herman Chin-Loy) 1971

ERT 855 One Woman/What Should I Do (actually titled 'Follow Your Heart') – Lloyd Charmers/Dave Barker And The Charmers (Prod: Lloyd Charmers) 1971

ERT 856 NYT

ERT 857 Peace Treaty/Brainwash – The Conscious Minds (Prod: BB Seaton) 1971

ERT 858 Girl Tell Me What To Do/Be Careful – Fitzroy Sterling (Prod: Sidney Crooks (UK)) 1971

ERT 859 My Girl/Plus One – Slim Smith/Rico Rodriguez (Prod: Slim Smith/Sid Bucknor) 1971

ERT 860 Rasta Never Fails/Rasta Never Fails (Version) – The Charmers (Lloyd Charmers And Ken Boothe)/The Charmers Band (Prod: Lloyd Charmers) 1971

ERT 861 Love And Unity/Wha No Dead – Cynthia Richards/The Maytones (Prod: Lloyd Daley/Alvin Ranglin) 1971

ERT 862 African Museum (actually titled 'Jah Picture')/Version (actually 'Jah Picture (Version)') – Sounds Combine (actually by Winston Wright) (Prod: Errol Dunkley) 1971

ERT 863 Bend Down Low/The Burning Feeling – The Groovers (Prod: Derrick Morgan (UK)) 1971

GAS

GAS 100 The Horse/Action Line – Eric Barnett (actually by Theo Beckford's Group)/Eric Barnett (actually by The Versatiles) (Prod: Eric Barnett/Lee Perry) 1968

GAS 101 Gimme Little/Trip To War Land – Junior Smith (actually with The Rudies) (Prod: Roy Smith (UK)) 1968

GAS 102 Got To Play It Cool/Jezebel – Fitzroy Sterling (actually with The Rudies) (Prod: Roy Smith (UK)) 1968

GAS 103 Reggae In The Wind/Try Me One More Time – Lester Sterling/The Soul Set (actually by Stranger Cole And Gladdy Anderson) (Prod: Bunny Lee/Stranger Cole) 1968

GAS 103 Reggae In The Wind/Blowing In The Wind – Lester Sterling/Max Romeo (Prod: Bunny Lee) 1969 [DUPLICATE ISSUE ON WHITE LABEL ONLY. B-SIDE ALSO ISSUED ON NU-BEAT NB 022A]

GAS 104 Long Life/Oh Tell Me – Bill Gentles/The School Boys (Prod: H Robinson/Bunny Barrett) 1969

GAS 105 Diana/English Talk (actually titled 'Some Talk') (1968) – Alton Ellis (Prod: Alton Ellis/Alton Ellis And Johnny Moore) 1969 [B-SIDE ALSO ISSUED ON PAMA PM 707B]

GAS 106 Te Ta Toe/Lonely And Blue – Eric Barnett (actually by Theo Beckford's Group)/Milton Boothe (Prod: Eric Barnett) 1969

GAS 107 Pictures Of You/Searching For My Baby – Nola Campbell (Prod: Harry Palmer (UK)) 1969 [BOTH SIDES SOUL]

GAS 108 Ring Of Gold/You've Got It – The Melodians (Prod: Winston Lowe) 1969

GAS 109 Choo Choo Train/The Load (actually titled 'Swinging For Joy') (1962) – The Soul Cats (actually Unidentified Vocal Group)/The Soul Cats (actually by The Count Ossie Band) (Prod: (UK)/Harry Mudie) 1969

GAS 110 Workman Song/Never Give Up – Pat Kelly (Prod: Bunny Lee) 1969

GAS 111 The Weight/Tell Me Now – Stan Hope/Marcia Griffiths (Prod: Coxson Dodd) 1969

GAS 112 1,000 Tons Of Megaton/Musical Resurrection – Roland Alphonso (actually with Derrick Morgan)/Roland Alphonso (Prod: Derrick Morgan) 1969

GAS 113 Soul Call/Musical Gates – The Soul Rhythms (Prod: Joe Sinclair) 1969

GAS 114 Walking Proud/Why Baby – Martin Riley/Lloyd Charmers (Prod: Winston Lowe) 1969

GAS 115 How Long Will It Take/Try To Remember – Pat Kelly (Prod: Bunny Lee) 1969

GAS 116 Personally Speaking/Trouble Trouble – The Melodians/Lloyd Robinson (Prod: Winston Lowe) 1969

GAS 117 Ain't Too Proud To Beg/Love And Devotion (1968) – The Uniques (Prod: Bunny Lee) 1969

GAS 118 Wanted/I'll Always Love You – Baba Dise (actually Pama Dice)/The Sensations (Prod: Winston Riley) 1969

GAS 119 Never Gonna Give You Up/Let Me Remind You – The Shades (actually by The Techniques) (Prod: Winston Riley) 1969

GAS 120 Throw Me Corn (Instrumental)/Temptation – Ranny Williams/The Hippy Boys (Prod: Ranny Williams) 1969

GAS 121 Janet/Believe Me – Tony (actually unidentified male vocalist) And The Hippy Boys/The Harmonians (Prod: Ranny Williams) 1969

GAS 122 Phrases/Give Me Faith – The Reggae Boys (Prod: Glen Adams) 1969 [A-SIDE REISSUED ON GAS 141B. B-SIDE REISSUED ON BULLET BU 431B]

GAS 123 Unchained Melody/You're My Girl – Honeyboy Martin/Sammy Jones (Prod: Harry Johnson/Jack Price) 1969

GAS 124 Festival Time/Festival Time (Part 2) – Pat Kelly (Prod: Bunny Lee) 1969

GAS 125 If It Don't Work Out (actually titled 'Then You Can Tell Me Goodbye')/I'm Coming Home – Pat Kelly (Prod: Bunny Lee) 1969

GAS 126 I Who Have Nothing/You Send Me – Nellie (Hinds) (Prod: Derrick Morgan (UK)) 1969

GAS 127 NOT ISSUED

GAS 128 Look What You Are Going To Do/Hold On To What You Got – Vincent Brown (Prod: Vincent Brown) 1969 [ISSUED ON WHITE LABEL ONLY]

GAS 129 People Are Wondering/Long Time – The Show Boys (Prod: Rupie Edwards) 1969

GAS 130 Pink Shark/Swing Free – Eric Barnett (actually by Different Unidentified Vocal Groups) (Prod: Eric Barnett And Albert George Murphy/) 1969

GAS 131 When I Am Gone/She Brings Me Joy – The Clarendonians (Prod: ?) 1969

GAS 132 The Vow/Why Didn't You Say – Slim Smith And Doreen Shaeffer/James Nephew (Prod: Bunny Lee) 1969

GAS 133 Stagger Back/The Creeper – Cannonball King [Carl Bryan] (Prod: Albert George Murphy) 1969

GAS 134 Waking The Dead/Got What You Want – Cannonball Bryan [Carl Bryan]/Trevor And Keith (Prod: Harry Mudie) 1969

GAS 135 Ba Ba (actually titled 'What Is This?')/Power Cut (Cold Sweat) – The Slickers (actually by The Reggae Boys)/Glen Adams (Prod: Lee Perry and Glen Adams) 1969

GAS 136 Too Much Loving/Roaring Twenties – Mood Reaction (Prod: Theo Loyla (UK)) 1969

GAS 137 King Kong/Please Stay – The Desectors (Prod: ?) 1970 [POSSIBLY UNISSUED]

GAS 138 Sail Away/Fight A Broke – The Marvels (Prod: Derrick Morgan (UK)) 1970

GAS 139 Someday We'll Be Together/The Rhythm – The Marvels/The Mohawks (Prod: Derrick Morgan (UK)) 1970

GAS 140 NYT

GAS 141 Leaving On A Jet Plane/Phrases – Glen Adams And The Reggae Boys/The Reggae Boys (Prod: Glen Adams) 1970 [B-SIDE REISSUED FROM GAS 122A]

GAS 142 Satan Girl/The Pum – The Ethiopians/The Matadors (Prod: Lloyd Daley) 1970

GAS 143 Change Of Heart/Runaway Man – Mood Reaction (Prod: Theo Loyla (UK)) 1970 [REISSUED ON GAS 148 (WHITE LABEL RELEASE)]

GAS 144 Tammy/I'm Not Your Guy – Pat Kelly (Prod: Pat Kelly) 1970

GAS 145 Striving For The Right/When A Boy Falls In Love – Pat Kelly (Prod: Pat Kelly) 1970

GAS 146 Something Sweet The Lady/Love Letters – Dora King And Joe Marks With The Pete Weston Band/Bim, Bam And Clover (Prod: Pete Weston/Derrick Morgan (UK)) 1970

GAS 147 Bumper To Bumper [HI-LIFE]/Fat Turkey – Eric Barnett (Both By Different Unidentified Instrumental Outfits) (Prod: Alvin Ranglin) 1970

GAS 148 Something On Your Mind/I Need Love – Errol Dixon (Prod: Errol Dixon (UK)) 1970

GAS 148 Change Of Heart/Runaway Man – Mood Reaction (Prod: Theo Loyla (UK)) [DUPLICATE ISSUE (WHITE LABEL ONLY) AND REISSUE OF GAS 143]

GAS 149 NYT

GAS 150 What Kind Of Life/It's All In The Game – Slim Smith/Martin Riley (Prod: Slim Smith/Martin Riley) 1970

GAS 151 Suzie/Denver – Alton Ellis And The Flames (Prod: Alton Ellis) 1970

GAS 152 Lift Your Head Up High/Everyday Tomorrow, Version 2 – Stranger Cole (actually with Gladdy Anderson)/Stranger Cole (actually with Tabby And The Diamonds) (Prod: Stranger Cole) 1970 [A-SIDE ALSO ISSUED ON CAMEL LABEL CA 54B]

GAS 153 So Alive (actually titled 'The Young Folks')/Mercy Mr DJ – GG All Stars (actually by Keelyn Beckford) (Prod: Alvin Ranglin) 1970

GAS 154 I Love You Madly/Greatest Love – Busty Brown (actually with Lloyd Charmers)/Busty Brown (Prod: Lloyd Charmers) 1970 [REISSUE OF PUNCH PH 38 WITH A- AND B-SIDES REVERSED]

GAS 155 Pipe Dream/Suck Suck – Ranny Williams (Prod: Ranny Williams) 1970

GAS 156 Daddy Daddy Don't Cry (actually 'Don't Cry Daddy')/I Like It – Tony King (actually unidentified male vocalist) And The Hippy Boys/Tony King And The Hippy Boys (actually unidentified female outfit) (Prod: Ranny Williams (UK)) 1970

GAS 157 I Just Don't Know What To Do With Myself/Laura (actually titled 'Lorna (What's He Got That I Ain't Got)') – Pat Kelly (Prod: Bunny Lee) 1970

GAS 158 Teach Me (actually titled 'Beverley')/Sea Breeze – Pat (actually by Earl George)/Rhythm Rulers (actually by Cedric Brooks And David Madden) (Prod: Earl George) 1970

GAS 159 It's Christmas Time Again/If I Could See You – Norman T Washington (Prod: Derrick Morgan (UK)/Harry Palmer (UK)) 1970

GAS 160 To The Other Woman/Raindrops – Hortense Ellis/The Music Blenders (actually The Mohawks) (Prod: Winston Riley/Harry Palmer (UK)) 1970

GAS 161 Lord Deliver Us/Originator – Alton Ellis/Neville Hinds (actually with The Matadors) (Prod: Lloyd Daley) 1970

GAS 162 Hotter Than Scorcher/Someday Could See You (actually titled 'Someday You're Gonna Cry') – The Hammers (Prod: Tom of Brixton (UK)) 1970

GAS 163 Work Out (actually titled 'Sweet Like Candy')/Too Long (actually titled 'Work Out') – Donald Lee (actually by Winston Williams And Pat Kelly)/Donald Lee (actually by Jeff Barnes And Pat Kelly) (Prod: Bunny Lee) 1970

GAS 164 Back To Africa/Delivered – Alton Ellis/Neville Hinds (actually with The Matadors) (Prod: Lloyd Daley) 1971

GAS 165 Greedy Boy/Please Stay (1968) – Nora Dean/Keith (actually by Slim Smith) (Prod: Bunny Lee) 1971

GAS 166 La La La (actually titled 'I Shall Sing')/Stand By Your Man – Hortense Ellis (Prod: Winston Riley) 1971

GAS 167 Blood And Fire/33-66 – Niney/Roland Alphonso (Prod: Winston Holness/Bunny Lee) 1971

GAS 168 What You Gonna Do About It?/Halfway To Paradise – Ernest Wilson/Dobby Dobson (Prod: Rupie Edwards) 1971

GAS 169 Give It To Me/Why – Ken Boothe (Prod: Phil Pratt) 1971

GAS 170 NYT

GAS 171 Love (actually titled 'He Ain't Heavy, He's My Brother')/With All Your Heart (actually titled 'The Prophet') – Pat Kelly (Prod: Bunny Lee) 1971

NU-BEAT/NEWBEAT

NB 001 Train To Vietnam (actually 'Train To South Vietnam')/Skaville To Rainbow City – The Rudies (Prod: Palmer brothers) 1968

NB 002 Rain And Thunder/Swing Baby Swing – The Soul Tops (Prod: Dickie Wong) 1968

NB 003 Cover Me/Darling – Fitz (actually Fitzroy Sterling) And The Coozers (Prod: Jeff Palmer) 1968

NB 004 Rocksteady Cool/I Have Changed – Frederick Bell/Carlton Alphonso (Prod: Carl Bradford) 1968

NB 005 Engine 59/My Girl – The Rudies (actually with Dandy) (Prod: Jeff Palmer) 1968

NB 006 This Festival '68/I Really Love You – Clancy Eccles (Prod: Clancy Eccles) 1968

NB 007 Rhythm And Soul/True Romance – Bobby Kalphat (actually with The Caltone All Stars)/Bunny And Ruddy (Prod: Ken Lack) 1968

NB 008 Hey Boy, Hey Girl/If Music Be The Food Of Love – Derrick (Morgan) And Patsy (Todd)/Derrick Morgan (actually unidentified male vocalist) (Prod: Derrick Morgan) 1968

NB 009 Easy Snapping/My Lonely Days – Theo Beckford/Eric 'Monty' Morris (Prod: Clancy Eccles) 1968

NB 010 I Can't Stand It/Tonight (actually titled 'Feeling Inside') – Alton Ellis (Prod: C Bough) 1968

NB 011 On The Town/Simple Simon – Bunny And Ruddy/Eric 'Monty' Morris (Prod: Ken Lack/Clancy Eccles) 1968

NB 012 Young Love/Days Like These – The Imperials (actually with Horace Faith) (Prod: H Robinson) 1968

NB 013 Bye Bye Love/My Lonely Days – Alton Ellis/Eric 'Monty' Morris (Prod: Clancy Eccles) 1968 [B-SIDE REISSUED FROM NB 009B]

NB 014 La La Means I Love You/Give Me Your Love – Alton Ellis/Alton Ellis (actually with David Isaacs) (Prod: Alton Ellis/C Bough) 1968 [RE-PRESSED ON NEWBEAT LABEL IN 1971]

NB 015 Blue Socks/Solas Market – Rico Rodriguez (Prod: Harry Palmer) 1968

NB 016 I Love You/Searching – Derrick Morgan/Junior Smith (Prod: Derrick Morgan/Roy Smith (UK)) 1968

NB 017 Push Push/Girls – The Termites (actually by The Hi-Tones) (Prod: Eric Barnett) 1968

NB 018 My Argument/Foey Man – Lloyd Charmers/George Dekker (Prod: H Robinson) 1968 [ISSUED ON WHITE LABEL ONLY]

NB 019 Rhythm Hips/Deltone Special – Ronald Russell/The Soul Rhythms (Prod: Eric Barnett) 1968

NB 020 Mini Really Fit Them/Soul Train – The Soul Flames (actually Alton Ellis And The Flames) (Prod: Alton Ellis) 1968

NB 021 Let's Have Some Fun/Making Love – Devon (Russell) And The Tartans (Prod: H Robinson) 1969

NB 022 Blowing In The Wind/Money Girl – Max Romeo/Larry Marshall (Prod: Bunny Lee/Ken Lack) 1969 [A-SIDE ALSO ISSUED ON GAS 103B (WHITE LABEL ISSUE)]

NB 023 Mr Ryha/After Dark – Lloyd Tyrell [Lloyd Charmers] (Prod: Winston Lowe) 1969

NB 024 Woppi King/Mr Soul – Laurel Aitken (Prod: Laurel Aitken (UK)) 1969

NB 025 Suffering Still/Reggae '69 – Laurel Aitken And Girlie/Laurel Aitken (Prod: Laurel Aitken (UK)) 1969

NB 026 Another Heartache/Come On Little Girl – Winston Sinclair (actually by Gregory Isaacs)/Winston Sinclair (Prod: Winston Sinclair And Gregory Isaacs/Winston Sinclair) 1969

NB 027 I'll Do It/Give You My Love – Derrick And Paulette (Morgan) (Prod: Derrick Morgan) 1969

NB 028 You've Lost Your Date/Little Girl (actually titled 'Stars') – The Flames (actually The Righteous Flames)/The Eternals (actually with Cornel Campbell) (Prod: Coxson Dodd) 1969

NB 029 Rescue Me/Unity Is Strength – The Reggae Girls (actually by The Ebony Sisters)/The Soul Mates (actually by Lester Sterling) (Prod: Harry Mudie/Bunny Lee) 1969

NB 030 Rodney's History/Tribute To Drumbago – Carl Dawkins/The Dynamites (Prod: Clancy Eccles) 1969

NB 031 My Testimony/One Dollar Of Soul – The Maytals (actually by The Ethiopians)/The Johnson Boys (actually The JJ All Stars) (Prod: JJ Johnson) 1969

NB 032 Haile Selassie/Blues Dance – Laurel Aitken/Laurel Aitken And Girlie (Prod: Laurel Aitken (UK)) 1969

NB 033 Lawd Doctor/Big Fight In Hell Stadium – Laurel Aitken And Girlie/Laurel Aitken (Prod: Laurel Aitken (UK)) 1969

NB 034 Crimson And Clover/What A Situation – The Uniques (Prod: Winston Lowe) 1969

NB 035 Run Powell Run/A Message To You – Laurel Aitken/Rico Rodriguez (Prod: Laurel Aitken (UK)) 1969

NB 036 Splash Down/Finders Keepers – The Crystalites (Prod: Derrick Harriott) 1969

NB 037 I'll Make You Love Me (actually 'I'm Gonna Make You Love Me')/Lover's Prayer – The Uniques (Prod: Winston Lowe) 1969

NB 038 Buss Your Mouth (aka 'Contention')/Rough Rough Way Ahead – The Ethiopians/Glen Adams (actually by Keith Blake And The Hi-Tals) (Prod: JJ Johnson/Glen Adams) 1969

NB 039 Save The Last Dance For Me/Walk Right Back – Laurel Aitken (Prod: Laurel Aitken (UK)) 1969

NB 040 Don't Be Cruel/Sloop John B – Laurel Aitken (Prod: Laurel Aitken (UK)) 1969

NB 041 Island In The Sun/Work It Up – Winston Groovy (Prod: Laurel Aitken (UK)) 1969

NB 042 Josephine/Champagne And Wine – Winston Groovy (Prod: Laurel Aitken (UK)) 1969

NB 043 Shoo Be Doo/Babylon Gone – Laurel Aitken (Prod: Laurel Aitken (UK)) 1969

NB 044 Landlords And Tenants/Everybody Sufferin' – Laurel Aitken (Prod: Laurel Aitken (UK)) 1969

NB 045 Jesse James/Freedom – Laurel Aitken (Prod: Laurel Aitken (UK)) 1969

NB 046 Pussy Price/Gimme Back Mi Dollar – Laurel Aitken (Prod: Laurel Aitken (UK)) 1969

NB 047 Skinhead Train/Kent People – Laurel Aitken/The Gruvy Beats (Prod: Laurel Aitken (UK)) 1969

NB 048 Mr Popcorn/Share Your Popcorn – Laurel Aitken/The Gruvy Beats (Prod: Laurel Aitken (UK)) 1970 (**Newbeat label**)

NB 048 Benwood Dick/Apollo 12 – Laurel Aitken (Prod: Laurel Aitken (UK)) [DUPLICATE ISSUE – WHITE LABEL ONLY]

NB 049 I've Got Your Love/Blue Mink – Laurel Aitken/The Gruvy Beats (Prod: Laurel Aitken (UK)) 1970 (**Newbeat label**)

NB 050 Scandal In A Brixton Market/Soul Grinder (actually titled 'Madame Streggae') – Laurel Aitken And Girlie/Girlie (Prod: Laurel Aitken (UK)) 1969 (**Nu-Beat label**) [B-SIDE ALSO ISSUED ON BULLET LABEL BU 400A]

NB 051 Frankenstein/I Can't Stand It – King Horror/Winston Groovy (Prod: Laurel Aitken (UK)) 1970 (**Nu-Beat Label**)

NB 052 Souls Of Africa/Dallas Texas – Tiger (Prod: Laurel Aitken (UK)) 1970 (**Newbeat label**)

NB 053 Standing At The Corner/You Send Me – Winston Groovy (Prod: Laurel Aitken (UK)) 1970 (**Newbeat label**)

NB 054 Baby Please Don't Go/Nobody But Me – Laurel Aitken (Prod: Laurel Aitken (UK)) 1970 (**Newbeat label**)

NB 055 Yellow Bird/For Your Love – Winston Groovy (Prod: Laurel Aitken (UK)) 1970 (**Newbeat label**)

NB 056 I'll Never Love Any Girl (The Way I Love You)/The Best I Can – Laurel Aitken (Prod: Laurel Aitken (UK)) 1970 (**Newbeat label**)

NB 057 Reggae Popcorn/Take Me Back – Laurel Aitken (Prod: Laurel Aitken (UK)) 1970 (**Newbeat label**)

NB 058 Here Is My Heart/Birds And Flowers – Winston Groovy (Prod: Laurel Aitken (UK)) 1970 (**Newbeat label**) [A-SIDE REISSUED ON PAMA SUPREME PS 364B]

NB 059 Election/Tomorrow's World – The Freedom Singers (actually Denzil Dennis, Eugene Paul And Laurel Aitken) (UK)/Flece And The Live Shocks (Prod: Laurel Aitken (UK)) 1970 (**Nu-Beat label**)

NB 060 Pick My Pocket/Freedom – The Versatiles/The Freedom Singers (UK) (Prod: Laurel Aitken (UK)) 1970 (**Nu-Beat label**)

NB 061 Same Old Feeling/So Much Love – The Classics (UK) (actually Denzil Dennis And Milton Hamilton) (Prod: Laurel Aitken (UK)) 1970 (**Newbeat label**)

NB 062 Nobody Else But You/Version Of Nobody – Joel Lace/The Live Shocks (Prod: Laurel Aitken (UK)) 1970 (**Nu-Beat label**)

Note: all releases from this point on were on the Newbeat label.

NB 063 Baby I Need Your Loving/Think It Over – Laurel Aitken (Prod: Laurel Aitken (UK)) 1970

NB 064 Musical Scorcher/Three Dogs Night – Tiger (Prod: Laurel Aitken (UK)) 1970

NB 065 Sex Machine/Since You Left – Laurel Aitken (Prod: Laurel Aitken (UK)) 1970

NB 066 Groovin'/Sugar Mama – Winston Groovy (Prod: Laurel Aitken (UK)) 1970

NB 067 Witchcraft Man/Night In Cairo – The Inner Mind (Prod: Ian Smith (UK)) 1970

NB 068 NYT

NB 069 Pum Pum Girl/Freedom – The Inner Mind (Prod: Ian Smith (UK)) 1970

NB 070 NYT

NB 071 History Of Africa/Honeybee – The Classics (UK) (actually Denzil Dennis And Milton Hamilton) (Prod: Laurel Aitken (UK)) 1970

NB 072 Pachanga/Pachanga (Version) – Laurel Aitken (Prod: Laurel Aitken (UK)) 1970

NB 073 Tennessee Waltz/Old Man Trouble – Winston Groovy (Prod: Laurel Aitken (UK)) 1970

NB 074 Your Testimony/Train Coming – The Freedom Singers (UK) (actually Denzil Dennis, Milton Hamilton, Lloyd Campbell And Tiger)/The Freedom Singers (actually Denzil Dennis, Milton Hamilton And Lloyd Campbell) (Prod: Laurel Aitken (UK)) 1971

NB 075 African Beat/Blackman Land – Tiger (Prod: Laurel Aitken (UK)) 1971

NB 076 Give It To Me/Hot – The Versatiles/Tiger And The Versatiles (Prod: Laurel Aitken (UK)) 1971

NB 077 Ganja (?)/The Funky Mash – Pama Dice/The Gruvy Beats (Prod: Laurel Aitken (UK)) 1971 [ISSUED ON WHITE LABEL ONLY]

NB 078 Let True Love Begin/The Best I Can – Laurel Aitken (Prod: Laurel Aitken (UK)) 1971

NB 079 Only Heaven Knows/Freedom Psalm – Sheila/(Ruddy) Grant And (Sketto) Richards (Prod: Laurel Aitken (UK)) 1971

NB 080 Monkey Spanner/Monkey Spanner Version 2 – Larry And Lloyd (actually by Denzil Dennis And Pete Campbell)/Lloyd And Larry's All Stars (actually by The Gruvy Beats) (Prod: Laurel Aitken) 1971

NB 081 Co Co/Hey Girl Don't Bother Me – The Marvels (Prod: Sidney Crooks (UK)) 1971

NB 082 Blackman (actually 'Know Yourself Blackman')Tell The People (wrong title: possibly called 'How Did You Know?') – Rupie Edwards' All Stars (actually By The Meditators)/Rupie Edwards' All Stars (actually by unidentified male vocalist) (Prod: Rupie Edwards) 1971

NB 083 Love And Emotion/Love (Version 2) – The Righteous Flames (actually with Winston Jarrett) (Prod: Derrick Morgan) 1971

NB 084 Mary/Soldier Boy – The Jamaicans/The Conscious Minds (Prod: Tommy Cowan) 1971

NB 085 NYT

NB 086 Walk A Little Prouder/Walk Version – Carl Dawkins/Youth Professionals (Prod: Max Romeo) 1971

NB 087 Mother Radio/Little Deeds (actually 'Each Little Deed') – Joe Higgs/Dawn Sharon (actually Sharon Emmanuel) (Prod: Rupie Edwards) 1971

NB 088 Have You Ever Been Hurt/Our Day Will Come – Tiger (Prod: Laurel Aitken (UK)) 1971

NB 089 I Can't Stop Loving You/El Paso – Laurel Aitken (Prod: Laurel Aitken (UK)) 1971

NB 090 Hold Them One (actually 'The Great Roy Shirley (One)')/Two Three Four (actually 'The Great Roy Shirley (Two, Three, Four)') – Roy Shirley (Prod: Roy Shirley) 1971

NB 091 Three In One/One In Three – Errol Dunkley/Rupie Edwards' All Stars (Prod: Rupie Edwards) 1971

NB 092 Valley Of Tears/Because I Love – Cock And The Woodpeckers (Prod: Laurel Aitken (UK)) 1971

NB 093 Everyday And Everynight/I Fall In Love Everyday – Cock And The Woodpeckers (Prod: Laurel Aitken (UK)) 1971

NB 094 I Will Never Let You Down/This Magic Moment – Lorenzo (actually Laurel Aitken) (Prod: Laurel Aitken (UK)) 1971

NB 095 Iron Sound/Iron Sound Part 2 – Lester Sterling/Coxson's All Stars (Prod: Lloyd Blackford) 1971 [PROBABLY UNISSUED]

OCEAN

OC 1001 Welcome Stranger/Until Then – Sol Raye (Prod: Danny Williams) (UK)) 10/70

OC 1002 Fare Ye Well Separate Ways/A Girl Like You – Danny Williams (Prod: Danny Williams) (UK)) 10/70

OC 001 Little Green Apples/Little Green Apples (Version) – Dennis Brown/Sound Dimension (Prod: Coxson Dodd) 1972

OC 002 NYT

OC 003 Wet Dream (1968)/She's But A Little Girl (1968) – Max Romeo (Prod: Bunny Lee) 1975 [REISSUED FROM UNITY LABEL UN 503]

OC 004 Can't You Understand/Locks Of Dub – Larry Marshall/King Tubby (Prod: Carlton Patterson) 1975

OC 005 Tonight Is The Night/Night Dub – Claudette Miller/The Conscious Minds (Prod: BB Seaton) 1975

OC 006 Dreadlocks Power/Black Lash – Carlton Patterson (Prod: Carlton Patterson) 1975

OC 007 Never Found A Girl/Never Found A Girl Version – Denzil Dennis/The Inmates (Prod: Denzil Dennis (UK)) 1975

OC 008 NYT

OC 009 It De Hay (actually 'It Deh Yah')/Dub Deh Yah – Freddie McKay/Phil Pratt All Stars (Prod: Phil Pratt) 1975

Note: also issued with an Ocean label were Winston Groovy's 'I Like The Way (You Kiss And Hug Me)'/'Tell Me Why' with the number CRAB 63 and 'I've Got To Find A Way To Get Maria Back'/'Wanna Be There' with the number CRAB 64.

PAMA

Note: discs marked * are soul.

PM 700 Where In This World/Peace Makers (actually titled 'Groove To The Beat') – Carlton Alphonso (Prod: Roy Bennett) 1967

PM 701 What Will Your Mama Say/Darling Don't Do That – Clancy Eccles (Prod: Clancy Eccles) 1967 [A-SIDE REISSUED ON PAMA SUPREME PS 332A WITH ADDED STRINGS]

PM 702 Let's Get Married/Around The World – Little John And The Shadrocks (Prod: Palmer brothers (UK)) 1967

PM 703 Western Organ/Mother's Advice – The Clancy Set/The Clancy Set (actually by The Inspirations) (Prod: Clancy Eccles) 1967 [PREFIX ON THIS ISSUE IS ACTUALLY PMB]

PM 704 Bad Minded People/My Heart Is Aching (actually titled 'Witch Doctor') – Miss Jane (actually by The Trials)/The Trials (actually by The Coolers) (Prod: Clancy Eccles) 1968

PM 705 NOT ISSUED

PM 706 Soul Man/It's Not Unusual – Rico Rodriguez (Prod: Palmer brothers (UK)) 1968*

PM 707 The Message/Some Talk – Alton Ellis (Prod: Alton Ellis/Alton Ellis and Johnny Moore) 1968 [B-SIDE REISSUED FROM GAS 105B]

PM 708 NOT ISSUED

PM 709 NOT ISSUED

PM 710 Bang Bang Lulu/I Never Knew – Lloyd Tyrell [Lloyd Charmers]/Mrs Miller (Prod: Lynford Anderson) 1968 [PREFIX ON SOME ISSUES IS PMB]

PM 711 Heartbeat/Birds Of The Air – Ernest Ranglin/The Coolers (Prod: Clancy Eccles) 1968 [PREFIX ON THIS ISSUE IS ACTUALLY PMB]

PM 712 The Fight (actually 'The Big Fight')/Great – Clancy Eccles (Prod: Clancy Eccles) 1968

PM 713 NOT ISSUED

PM 714 NOT ISSUED

PM 715 Tenderfoot Ska/Memories – Rico Rodriguez (Prod: Palmer brothers (UK)) 1968

PM 716 Mr Pitiful/That's How Strong My Love Is – Beverley Simmons (Prod: Harry Palmer (UK)) 1968*

PM 717 My Time Is The Right Time/Tribute To Sir Alex – Alton Ellis/Johnny Moore (Prod: Alton Ellis and Johnny Moore/Johnny Moore) 1968

PM 718 Back To School/They Wash – The Joyce Bond Show (Prod: Carl Palmer (UK)) 1968

PM 719 The Champ/Sound Of The Witchdoctors – The Mohawks (Prod: Alan Hawkshaw and Harry Palmer (UK)) 1968*

PM 719 The Champ/Baby Hold On – The Mohawks (Prod: Alan Hawkshaw and Harry Palmer (UK)) 1968* [SECOND ISSUE]

PM 720 Fiddlesticks/Please Stay – Tommy Mckenzie Orchestra/Lascelles (Perkins) And Yvonne (Harrison) (Prod: Harry Palmer (UK)/Clancy Eccles) 1968 [A-SIDE REISSUED ON PAMA SUPREME PS 327B]

PM 721 Say What You're Saying/Tears In Your Eyes – Eric 'Monty' Morris (Prod: Clancy Eccles) 1968

PM 722 CN Express/CN Express, Part 2 (actually titled 'You Were Meant For Me') – Clancy's All Stars (actually Clancy Eccles, Lee Perry And Count Sticky)/Clancy's All Stars (actually by Lee Perry) (Prod: Clancy Eccles) 1968 [B-SIDE REISSUED ON ESCORT ES 825B]

PM 723 Soul Food/Music Flames – Lyn Taitt And The Jets/Soul Boy (Prod: Lynford Anderson) 1968

PM 724 NOT ISSUED

PM 725 I Know It's Alright/I Surrender – The Crowns (Prod: Harry Palmer (UK)) 1968*

PM 726 Afro Blue/Empty Little Shadow – Diana Landor (Prod: ?) 1968*

PM 727 NOT ISSUED

PM 728 Don't Change Your Mind About Me/Anytime Man – Anthony Deeley (Prod: David Osborn) 1968*

PM 729 Push It Up/Two Of A Kind – The Termites/The Termites (actually by Clancy Eccles And Cynthia Richards) (Prod: H Robinson/Clancy Eccles) 1968

PM 730 Same Thing All Over/You've Been Cheating – Norman T Washington (Prod: Carl Palmer (UK)) 1968*

PM 731 You're Mine/What A Guy – Little Beverley (Simmons) (Prod: Harry Palmer (UK)) 1968* [REISSUED ON PAMA SUPREME PS 380]

PM 732 I Have A Dream/Top Of The Mountain – Dr Martin Luther King (Prod: Berry Gordy for Gordy Records (USA)) 1968*

PM 733 Treat Me Nice/Sick And Tired – The Milwaukee Coasters (Prod: Harry Palmer (UK)) 1968*

PM 734 Lament To Bobby Kennedy/If You Were My Girl – Knights Of The Round Table (Prod: ?) 1968*

PM 735 Broadway Ain't Funky No More/I Met My Match – Bobby Patterson And The Mustangs (Prod: Jetstar Records (USA)) 1968*

PM 736 Jerking The Dog/Keep Me Going – The Crowns (Prod: Harry Palmer (UK)) 1968*

PM 737 NOT ISSUED

PM 738 Show Me The Way/What Can I Do – The Termites/The Termites (actually by Carlton Alphonso with unidentified female vocalist) (Prod: H Robinson/Roy Bennett) 1968

PM 739 Baby Hold On/Baby Hold On, Part 2 – The Mohawks (Prod: Alan Hawkshaw and Harry Palmer (UK)) 1968* [A-SIDE ALSO RELEASED ON DUPLICATE ISSUE OF PM 719B]

PM 740 How Come (actually titled 'I Come')/Oh My Lover – Mrs Miller (actually by Lee Perry And The Gaylets)/Clancy (Eccles) And Cynthia (Richards) (Prod: Lynford Anderson/Clancy Eccles) 1968

PM 741 Tip Toe/Don't Hang Around – Norman T Washington (Prod: Palmer brothers (UK)) 1968*

PM 742 If I Love You/Losing You – The Buttercups (Prod: Harry Palmer (UK)) 1968* [A-SIDE REISSUED ON PAMA PM 760B]

PM 743 The Good Ol' Days/Don't Be So Mean – Bobby Patterson And The Mustangs (Prod: Jetstar Records (USA)) 1968*

PM 744 Dr Goldfoot And His Bikini Machine/Where Do I Go From You? – The Beas (Prod: Harry Palmer (UK)) 1968*

PM 745 She Ain't Gonna Do Right/I Need Your Loving – The Crowns (Prod: Harry Palmer (UK)) 1968*

PM 746 Beverley/Wait For Me Baby – Eldridge Holmes (Prod: Allen Toussaint for Sansu Records (USA)) 1968*

PM 747 NOT ISSUED

PM 748 Only Your Love/I Feel Good All Over – Betty Lavette (Prod: Don Gardner For Calla Records (USA)) 1968*

PM 749 Jumping Jack Flash/Spinning – Norman T Washington (Prod: Harry Palmer (UK)) 1968* [B-SIDE REISSUED ON PUNCH PH 11B]

PM 750 When/Go – Roy Docker (Prod: Roy Smith (UK)) 1968*

PM 751 Sweet Soul Music/Hip Jigger – The Mohawks (Prod: Alan Hawkshaw and Harry Palmer (UK)) 1968*

PM 752 Lulu Returns/I Feel The Music – Lloyd Tyrell [Lloyd Charmers]/Junior Smith (Prod: Lynford Anderson/Roy Smith (UK)) 1968

PM 753 Peace On Earth/Love Is A Message – Premo And Joseph/The School Boys (Prod: H Robinson/Bunny Barrett) 1968

PM 754 Busy Busy Bee/Sweet Taste Of Love – Bobby Patterson And The Mustangs (Prod: Jetstar Records (USA)) 1968*

PM 755 I Just Can't Help Myself/One Way Loser – The Volumes (Prod: American Artists Records (USA)) 1968* [PROBABLY ISSUED ON WHITE LABEL ONLY]

PM 756 Everyday Will Be Like A Holiday/I'm An Outcast – Roy Docker (Prod: Roy Smith (UK)) 1969*

PM 757 Monty Monty/Pepsi – The Mohawks (Prod: Alan Hawkshaw and Harry Palmer (UK)) 1969*

PM 758 Ride Your Pony/Western Promise – The Mohawks (Prod: Alan Hawkshaw and Harry Palmer (UK)) 1969*

PM 759 Call Me/Since You Been Gone – The Crowns (Prod: Harry Palmer) 1969*

PM 760 Come Put My Life In Order/If I Love You – The Buttercups (Prod: Harry Palmer (UK)) 1969* [B-SIDE REISSUED FROM PAMA PM 742A]

PM 761 I Need Your Love So Bad/I'm Coming Too – Billy Bass (Prod: Stan Watson for Philly Groove Records (USA)) 1969*

PM 762 Underdog Back Street/Just Like A Woman – Warren Lee (Prod: Wardell Quezergue for Tou-Sea Records (USA)) 1969*

PM 763 TCB Or TYA/What A Wonderful Night For Love – Bobby Patterson And The Mustangs (Prod: Jetstar Records (USA)) 1969*

PM 764 NOT ISSUED

PM 765 Sock It To 'Em Soul Brothers/Sock It To 'Em Soul Brothers (Instrumental) – Bill Moss (Prod: Bill Moss for Bell Records (USA)) 1969*

PM 766 Walk On Judge/Lose The One You Love – The Soul Partners (Prod: Bill Justis and Bill Moss for Bell Records (USA)) 1969*

PM 767 Action/What Would It Take – The Showmen (Prod: Moses Dillard for Amy Records (USA)) 1969*

PM 768 You Don't Know/Ode To Billy Joe – Anna Walker And The Crownettes (Prod: Randy Irwin for Amy Records (USA)) 1969*

PM 769 Oh Happy Day/Can't Get Along Without You – The Conroy Cannon Mission (Prod: Golden City Records (USA)) 1969 [GOSPEL]

PM 770 PROBABLY UNISSUED [ISSUED ON PM 771 INSTEAD]

PM 771 Mr Pitiful/Let's Get Married – Joyce Bond/Joyce Bond And Little John (Prod: Harry Palmer (UK)) 1969*

PM 772 The Sun Gotta Shine In Your Hearts/I Only Have Eyes For You – The Persians (Prod: A Bay-Wes Production for ABC Records (USA)) 1969*

PM 773 My Thing Is Your Thing/Keep It In The Family – Bobby Patterson And The Mustangs (Prod: Jetstar Records (USA)) 1969*

PM 774 Who's Got The Ball Y'all/Half Time – Roosevelt Grier (Prod: Chips Moman for Amy Records (USA)) 1969*

PM 775 A Shot Of Rhythm And Blues/I Am Not Going To Work Today – Clyde McPhatter (Prod: Rick Hall and Bob Montgomery in association with Amy Records (USA)) 1969*

Note: PM 776 to PM 783 were not issued.

PM 784 C'mon Cupid/High Society Woman – Roosevelt Grier (Prod: Chips Moman For Amy Records (USA)) 1969*

PM 785 Let's Get Together/Little Girl – The Other Brothers (Prod: Dale Hawkins for Amy Records (USA)) 1969*

PM 786 Karate/I Got To Have Her – The Emperors (Prod: Mala Records (USA)) 1969*

PM 787 NOT ISSUED

PM 788 NOT ISSUED

PM 789 Give Peace A Chance/Theme From 'She' – The Rudies (actually with Freddie Notes)/The Rudies (Prod: Derrick Morgan (UK)) 1969

PM 790 Come Dance With Me/You've Danced With Me – Stranger Cole (Prod: Stranger Cole) 1970?

PM 790 Dancing Time/Love Locked Out – The Soul Tones/Bunny Barrett (Prod: Bunny Barratt) 1970? [DUPLICATE ISSUE]

PM 791 NYT

PM 792 Birth Control/Return To Peace (actually titled 'Overproof') (1969) – Lloyd Tyrell [Lloyd Charmers]/Val Bennett (actually by Carl Bryan) (Prod: Lloyd Charmers/Lynford Anderson) 1970

PM 793 You Turn Out The Light/Good Humour Man – Clifford Curry (Prod: Buzz Cason for Elf Records (USA)) 1970*

PM 794 I'm A Poor Man's Son/That's How Much I Love You – Spencer Wiggins (Prod: Quinton Claunch and Rudolph Russell for Goldwax Records (USA)) 1970*

PM 795 Say You Need Me/Unlovable – Barbara Perry (Prod: Quinton Claunch and Rudolph Russell for Goldwax Records (USA)) 1970*

PM 796 Number One/Landscape – Bill Moss/The Mohawks (Prod: Bill Moss for Bell Records (USA)/Alan Hawkshaw and Harry Palmer (UK)) 1970*

PM 797 I Can't Get A Hold Of Myself/Ain't No Danger – Clifford Curry (Prod: Buzz Cason for Elf Records (USA)) 1970*

PM 798 Skinhead Shuffle/Red Cow (actually 'Bridgeview Shuffle') – The Mohawks/Rico (actually by Don Drummond) (Prod: Graham Hawk (UK)/Coxson Dodd) 1970

PM 799 Close Shave/Prisoner Of Love (1968) – Kirk Redding/The Untouchables (Prod: Kirk Redding/Enos McLeod) 1970

PM 800 Down On The Corner/Who Is That Stranger? – Sid (actually Sidney Rodgers) And Joe And The Mohawks (Prod: Graham Hawk (UK)) 1970

PM 801 What A Woman/Sleepy Cat – Bill Gentles And Bunny Lee's All Stars (Prod: Bunny Lee) 1970

PM 802 Jeff Barnes Thing/Lover's Mood – Jeff Barnes And Bunny Lee's All Stars/Lennox Brown (Prod: Bunny Lee) 1970

PM 803 Annie Pama/Mr Magoo – Bunny Lee's All Stars (Prod: Bunny Lee) 1970

PM 804 Reggae And Shout/The Green Hornet – The Black Beatles (actually Derrick Morgan And The Mohawks)/Lennox Brown (Prod: Derrick Morgan (UK)/Bunny Lee) 1970

PM 805 Take Back Your Necklet/Blueberry Hill – Ferdinand (Dixon) And Dill (Bishop) (actually with The Mohawks)/Ferdinand And Dill (actually by Ferdinand Dixon With The Mohawks) (Prod: Derrick Morgan (UK)) 1970

PM 806 Hound Dog (actually 'How Much Is That Hound Dog In The Window?')/Black Girl – Sketto Richards (Prod: Derrick Morgan (UK)) 1970

PM 807 Confusion/We Got To Have Loving – Noel And The Fireballs (Prod: Derrick Morgan (UK)) 1970

PM 808 Can't Turn You Loose/Skinny Legs – Noel And The Fireballs (Prod: Derrick Morgan (UK)) 1970

PM 809 True True Train/Give And Take – Bill Gentles/Jeff Barnes (actually with The Bunny Lee All Stars) (Prod: Bunny Lee) 1970

PM 810 Sugar Dumpling/I Don't Know Why – Owen Gray (Prod: Sidney Crooks (UK)) 1970

PM 811 Maybe The Next Time/Got To See You – Pat Rhoden With The Mohawks (Prod: Derrick Morgan (UK)) 1970

PM 812 Here Comes The Night/Jaded Ramble – Solomon Jones (actually with The Marvels And The Mohawks)/Rico Rodriguez (Prod: Derrick Morgan (UK)) 1970

PM 813 Love One Another/Falling Rain (actually titled 'Rhythm Of The Rain') – The Marvels With The Mohawks (Prod: Derrick Morgan (UK)) 1970

PM 814 Soul And Inspiration/Stand By – The Blossoms (Prod: Bill Medley for Bell Records (USA)) 1970*

PM 815 Choking Kind/Chocolate Candy – Sonny Cox (Prod: Richard Evans) 1970*

PM 816 Got To Get You Off My Mind/So High, So Wide, So Low – Shel Alterman (actually with The Mohawks) (Prod: Harry Palmer (UK)) 1970

PM 817 Don't Let Him Take Your Love From Me/A Little Smile – The Marvels (Prod: Derrick Morgan (UK)) 1970

PM 817 Don't Let Him Take Your Love From Me/La La La – The Marvels (Prod: Derrick Morgan (UK)) 1970 [DUPLICATE ISSUE ON PURPLE LABEL WITH DIFFERENT B-SIDE]

PM 818 Mary's Boy Child/Mary's Boy Child (Version) – Laurel Aitken/The Gruvy Beats (Prod: Laurel Aitken (UK)) 1970

PM 819 Oh Lord, Why Lord/Love Letters – The Marvels/Nellie Hinds (Prod: Derrick Morgan/Dimples Hinds (UK)) 1970

PM 820 My Sweet Lord/Darling That's Right – Fitzroy Sterling (Prod: Sidney Crooks (UK)) 1971

PM 821 Knock Three Times/The Whealing Mouse – Carl Lewin (actually Carl Lewis)/Sidney Crooks' All Stars (Prod: Sidney Crooks (UK)) 1971 [ON BLANK LABEL ONLY. OFFICIAL RELEASE ON BULLET BU 456]

PM 822 Love Bug/My Dickie – Derrick Morgan (Prod: Derrick Morgan (UK)) 1971 [B-SIDE IS REISSUED FROM CRAB CR 57A]

PM 823 Heaven Help Us All/Can't Do Without Your Love – Winston Groovy (Prod: Sidney Crooks (UK)) 1971

PM 824 Fire Fire/Jesus Keepeth My Soul – The Youth [I Jah Man Levi] (Prod: Jeff Palmer (UK)) 1971

PM 825 No More Lonely Teardrops/My Mama Told Me – Joan Ross [TT Ross] (Prod: Harry Palmer/Les Foster (UK)) 1971

PM 826 Grooving Out On Life/Grooving Out On Life Version – Hopeton Lewis/The M Squad (Prod: Winston Blake and Byron Lee) 1971

PM 827 Don't Break My Heart/How Long Will This Go On? – Winston Groovy (Prod: Sidney Crooks (UK)) 1971

PM 828 Jesamine/The Flash – Junior English/Sidney Crooks' All Stars (Prod: Sidney Crooks (UK)) 1971

PM 829 Oh What A Mini/Mini (Version 2) – Willie Francis (Prod: Willie Francis) 1971

PM 830 Sex Education/Soul Flash – The Classics (actually Denzil Dennis And Les Foster)/The Power (actually The Mohawks) (Prod: Harry Palmer (UK)) 1971 [B-SIDE ALSO ISSUED AS WHITE LABEL ON PAMA SUPREME PS 314B]

PM 831 NOT ISSUED [PROBABLY ISSUED ON PAMA PM 829]

PM 832 Do You Know You Have To Cry (actually titled 'Didn't You Know You Have To Cry Sometime?')/Love Power – The Marvels (Prod: Harry Palmer (UK)/Dimples Hinds (UK)) 1971

PM 833 You Don't Care/Must Care – Lloyd Parks/Prince Tony's All Stars (Prod: Tony Robinson) 1972

PM 834 Living In Sweet Jamaica/Living In Sweet Jamaica Version – Jackie Brown/Prince Tony's All Stars (Prod: Tony Robinson) 1972

PM 835 Way Down South/Take Warning – U Roy/Billy Dyce (Prod: Alvin Ranglin) 1972

PM 836 Night Angel (Maxi-Single): Wet Dream – Max Romeo (Prod: Bunny Lee)/Bang Bang Lulu – Lloyd Tyrell [Lloyd Charmers] (Prod: Lynford Anderson)/Birth Control – Lloyd Tyrell [Lloyd Charmers] (Prod: Lloyd Charmers)/Sex Education – The Classics (UK) (actually Denzil Dennis And Les Foster) (Prod: Harry Palmer (UK)) 1972

PM 837 NYT

PM 838 Beautiful Sunday/Take Care Son – Eugene Paul (Prod: Ranny Williams (UK)) 1972

PM 839 Come What May/Come What May (Version) – Fermena (Edwards)/Fermena (Edwards) And Ranny (Williams) (Prod: Ranny Williams (UK)) 1972

PM 840 Girl I've Got A Date/Eat Bread – Alton Ellis (Prod: Alton Ellis (UK)) 1972

PM 841 Miss Playgirl/Once In My Life – Junior English (Prod: Ellis Breary (UK)) 1972

PM 842 Rocket Man/I'm All Broke Up – The In-Flames (Prod: Ranny Williams (UK)) 1972

PM 843 You've Lost That Loving Feeling/Feeling Version – The Heptones/Rupie Edwards' All Stars (Prod: Rupie Edwards) 1972

PM 844 Shake It Loose (actually 'Help Me Make It Through The Night')/Shaking Version – Ken Parker/Ken Parker And Tommy McCook (Prod: Duke Reid) 1972

PM 845 I'll Always Love You/3x7 Rock & Roll (1966) – John Holt/Slim Smith (Prod: Bunny Lee/Stranger Cole) 1972

PM 846 I'm Feeling Lonely/Lonely Version – The Maytones (actually by Vernon Buckley)/The Maytones (actually by The GG All Stars) (Prod: Alvin Ranglin) 1972

PM 847 This Is My Story/Caldonia – The Clarendonians/Val Bennett (Prod: Bunny Lee) 1972

PM 848 The House Where Bombo Lives/Our High School Dance – Stranger Cole/Stranger Cole (actually with Patsy Todd) (Prod: Bunny Lee) 1972

PM 849 NYT

PM 850 The Time Has Come/The Time Has Come (Version) – Slim Smith/Rico And The Aggrovators (Prod: Bunny Lee) 1972

PM 851 Feel Good All Over/Dangerous – Phil Pratt All Stars (actually by Horace Andy)/Keble Drummond (Prod: Phil Pratt) 1972

PM 852 Pledging My Love/I Will Know What To Do – John Holt/James Brown (Ja) (Prod: Bunny Lee) 1972

PM 853 Big Seven (actually titled 'Punaany')/Ace And The Professionals Version (actually 'Punaany Version') – Charley (Ace) And Fay (Bennett)/Charley Ace And Youth Professionals (Prod: Charley Ace) 1972

PM 854 Cowtown Skank/Cowtown Skank Version – I Roy/Augustus Pablo (Prod: Augustus Clarke) 1973

PM 855 NOT ISSUED

PM 856 Good Hearted Woman/What Happens – The Clarendonians/Cornel Campbell (Prod: Bunny Lee) 1972

PM 857 Fever/Soul Sister – Junior Byles/The Groovers (actually by The Heptones) (Prod: Lee Perry) 1972

PM 858 NOT ISSUED – RELEASED ON PM 863 INSTEAD [SECOND ISSUE]

PM 859 At The End/Goodnight My Love – Shenley Duffas (Prod: Lee Perry) 1972

PM 860 Sound Doctor/Doctor Skank – Bobby Floyd/Young Dillinger (Prod: Lee Perry) 1972

PM 861 NYT

PM 862 The Godfather/Some Day – Jerry Lewis/Alton Ellis (Prod: Bunny Lee) 1972

PM 863 Big Eight (actually 'White Rum And Pum Pum')/Lightning Stick – Lloyd Tyrell (actually by Lloydie [Lloyd Charmers] And The Lowbites)/Lloyd Tyrell (actually Unidentified DJ) (Prod: Lloyd Charmers/) 1973 [FIRST ISSUE]

PM 863 Big Eight (actually 'White Rum And Pum Pum')/Auntie Lulu – Lloyd Tyrell (actually by Lloydie [Lloyd Charmers] And The Lowbites)/Junior Byles (Prod: Lloyd Charmers/Lee Perry) 1973 [SECOND ISSUE]

PM 863 Big Eight/Instrumental Version Of Big Eight – Winston Reedy/Ranny Williams' All Stars And The Classics (Prod: Ranny Williams (UK)) 1973 [THIRD ISSUE]

PM 864 I Want Justice/Justice (Version) – BB Seaton/Rupie Edwards' All Stars (Prod: Rupie Edwards) 1973

PM 865 NYT

PM 866 I Don't Want To Die/Land Of Sea And Sand – Junior English (Prod: Ellis Breary (UK)) 1973

PM 867 NOT ISSUED – PROBABLE ISSUE ON PAMA SUPREME PS 382

PM 868 NOT ISSUED – PROBABLE ISSUE ON PAMA PM 869

PM 869 Daniel/Perfidia – Junior English (Prod: Ellis Breary (UK)) 1973

PM 870 NYT

PM 871 All Over The World People Are Changing/Dubwise (actually 'Changing World (Dubwise)') – The Maytones/Volcano (actually by The GG All Stars) (Prod: Alvin Ranglin) 1973

PM 872 Dedicated To Illiteracy/Dub – Stranger (Cole) And Gladstone (Anderson) (actually with Shorty Perry)/GG All Stars (Prod: Alvin Ranglin) 1973

PM 873 True Believer/Water Your Garden (actually Version Cut) – Larry Marshall/The Flames (actually by Winston Jarrett And The Righteous Flames) (Prod: Lee Perry) 1973

PM 874 Woman Smarter/Standing On The Hill – Billy Dyce/Shenley Duffas (Prod: Lee Perry) 1973

PM 875 Pussy Watchman/You Are My Sunshine – Max Romeo/Cornel Campbell (actually by Roman Stewart) (Prod: Bunny Lee) 1973

PM 876 Village Ram/Push It Inna – The Twinkle Brothers (Prod: Norman Grant) 1973

PM 877 Big Nine (actually titled 'Murder In The Place')/Old Lady – Father Sketto (actually Sketto Richards)/The Untouchables (actually by Rico Rodriguez And The Mohawks) (Prod: Ranny Williams (UK)) 1973

PM 878 Education Rock/Nobody Knows – Junior Byles/Ken McKay (Prod: Lee Perry) 1973

PM 879 Wonderful Dream (Erestu)/Wonderful Dream (Version) – Fermena (Edwards)/Fermena (actually by Ranny Williams' All Stars) (Prod: Ranny Williams (UK)) 1973

Second Series

PM 4000 Sing About Love/Sing About Love (Version) – Pat Kelly/Pat Kelly (actually by The Phil Pratt All Stars) (Prod: Phil Pratt) 1975

PM 4001 Sinners/If It's Love You Need – Justin Hinds And The Dominoes (Prod: Duke Reid) 1975

PM 4002 Darling It's You/Car Pound – Bill Gentles (Prod: Bill Gentles) 1975

PAMA SUPREME

PS 297 What The World Is Coming To (actually titled 'Demonstration')/Live As One – King Chubby (actually Junior Byles) (Prod: Lee Perry) 1970 [ALSO ISSUED ON SUPREME LABEL WITH SAME NUMBER]

PS 298 Do What You Gotta Do/Crying Won't Help – Pat Rhoden (Prod: Ranny Williams (UK)) 1970

PS 299 I Am In Love Again/I Am In Love Again (Version) – Owen Gray/Ranny Williams (Prod: Ranny Williams (UK)) 1970

PS 300 Why Can't I Touch You?/You Can't Turn Your Back On Me – Laurel Aitken (Prod: Laurel Aitken And N Bell/Laurel Aitken (UK)) 1970

PS 301 My Way/Happy Days – DD (Denzil) Dennis (Prod: Laurel Aitken (UK)/Derrick Morgan (UK)) 1970

PS 302 Candida/When Will I Find My Way – Owen Gray (Prod: Sidney Crooks (UK)) 1971

PS 303 Don't Let The Tears Fall/Another Saturday Night – Eugene Paul (Prod: Sidney Crooks (UK)) 1971

PS 304 Painful Situation/Nothing Has Changed – DD (Denzil) Dennis (Prod: Ranny Williams (UK)) 1971

PS 305 I Found A Man In My Bed/So Many Things – Eugene Paul (Prod: Sidney Crooks (UK)) 1971

PS 306 Let The Power Fall On I/The Raid (actually titled 'Club Raid') [1969] – Max Romeo (actually with The Hippy Boys)/Max Romeo (actually with The Rudies) (Prod: Derrick Morgan/Derrick Morgan (UK)) 1971

PS 307 POSSIBLE ISSUE ON ESCORT ERT 853

PS 308 Crackling Rosie/Little Deeds Of Kindness – Lloyd Jackson/Lloyd Jackson And The Scorpions (Prod: Derrick Morgan (UK)) 1971

PS 309 Cheer Me Up/The Clock – The Mohawks (Prod: Don Lawson (UK)) 1971 [BOTH SIDES SOUL]

PS 310 You Gonna Miss Me/I Hear You Knocking – Owen Gray (Prod: Sidney Crooks (UK)) 1971

PS 311 Nothing Can Separate Us/Girl I Want You To Understand – Owen Gray (Prod: Sidney Crooks (UK)/Harry Palmer (UK)) 1971 [ISSUED ON WHITE LABEL ONLY – OFFICIAL RELEASE ON CAMEL CA 73]

PS 312 NOT ISSUED – PROBABLE RELEASE ON PAMA PM 825 INSTEAD

PS 313 NOT ISSUED – PROBABLE RELEASE ON PAMA PM 824 INSTEAD

PS 314 Whole Lotta Woman/Soul Flash – Eugene Paul/The Power (actually The Mohawks) (Prod: Sidney Crooks (UK)/Harry Palmer (UK)) [WHITE LABEL ONLY. A-SIDE ISSUED ON PS 317B. B-SIDE ISSUED ON PAMA PM 830B]

PS 315 NYT

PS 316 NYT

PS 317 Farewell My Darling/Whole Lotta Woman – Eugene Paul (Prod: Sidney Crooks (UK)/Harry Palmer (UK)) 1971 [B-SIDE ALSO ISSUED AS WHITE LABEL ON PS 314A]

PS 318 Don't You Weep/Weeping Version – Max Romeo/Max Romeo (actually by Morgan's All Stars) (Prod: Derrick Morgan) 1971

PS 319 The First Time/Not Now – Winston Groovy (Prod: Winston Tucker (UK)/Winston Tucker And Norton York (UK)) 1971 [ISSUED ON WHITE LABEL ONLY. A-SIDE ISSUED ON PMP 2011 (SIDE 2 OF ALBUM) AND B-SIDE ON PS 323B]

PS 320 NYT

PS 321 John Crow Skank/Give Thanks – Derrick Morgan (Prod: Derrick Morgan) 1971

PS 322 NYT

PS 323 Free The People/Not Now – Winston Groovy (Prod: Winston Tucker And Norton York (UK)) 1971 [B-SIDE ISSUED AS WHITE LABEL ON PS 319B]

PS 324 Then You Can Tell Me Goodbye/Up And Down The Highway – The Mohawks (Prod: Harry Palmer (UK)) 1971

PS 325 Summer Sand/Something To Remind Me – Owen Gray (actually with The Groovers) (Prod: Derrick Morgan (UK)/Harry Palmer (UK)) 1971

PS 326 NYT

PS 327 Eastern Promise (1968)/Fiddlesticks (1968) – Tommy Mckenzie Orchestra (actually by Earl St Joseph)/Tommy Mckenzie Orchestra (Prod: Palmer brothers (UK)) 1971 [REISSUED FROM PAMA LP PMLP-SP3 AND PAMA SINGLE PM 720A RESPECTIVELY]

PS 328 Ginalship/Ginalship (Version 2) – Max Romeo/The Upsetters (Prod: Lee Perry) 1971

PS 329 Somebody's Changing My Sweet Baby's Mind/Hard Minded Neighbour – Eugene Paul (Prod: Ranny Williams and Norton York (UK)) 1971

PS 330 I'm A Believer/I'll Make The Way Easy – DD (Denzil) Dennis (actually with The Carols) (Prod: Ranny Williams and Norton York (UK)/Ranny Williams (UK)) 1971

PS 331 Piece Of My Heart/Right On The Tip Of My Tongue – Mahalia Saunders (actually Hortense Ellis) (Prod: Lee Perry) 1971

PS 332 What Will Your Mama Say (1967)/United We Stand – Clancy Eccles/Tiger (Prod: Clancy Eccles and Norton York/Laurel Aitken (UK)) 1971 [A-SIDE REISSUED FROM PAMA PM 701. B-SIDE ALSO ISSUED ON CAMEL CA 70 (FIRST PRESSING)]

PS 333 Greatest Hits Part 1/Greatest Hits Part 2 – Owen Gray (Prod: Ranny Williams (UK)) 1971

PS 334 Send Me Some Loving/I'm Lost (1968) – Slim Smith/Slim Smith (actually with The Uniques) (Prod: Bunny Lee) 1971

PS 335 Daddy Love (Vocal)/Daddy Love (Instrumental) – Gi Gi (Prod: Charles Hodges For Sweet Records (USA)) 1971 [SOUL] [RE-PROMOTED BY PAMA IN JANUARY 1976]

PS 336 NYT

PS 337 I Stayed Away Too Long/Country Boy – Manley Patterson (Prod: Manley Patterson And Norton York (UK)) 1971

PS 338 Rocksteady/Be My Baby – The Marvels (Prod: Lloyd Charmers) 1971 [RE-PROMOTED BY PAMA IN JANUARY 1976]

PS 339 Shaft/Harry's Mood – Lloyd Charmers (Prod: Lloyd Charmers) 1971

PS 340 Red Head Duck/Jingle Jangle (wrong title: possibly 'Cindy, Cindy') – Lloyd Tyrell [Lloyd Charmers] (Prod: Lloyd Charmers) 1971

PS 341 NYT

PS 342 NYT

PS 343 NYT

PS 344 NYT

PS 345 Pray For Me/Pray For Me (Version) – Max Romeo/Max Romeo (actually by The Gaytones) (Prod: Sonia Pottinger) 1972

PS 346 Show Business/Gloria (actually 'Reggae In Wonderland (Version 2)') – Lloyd Charmers/Debby And Lloyd (actually by Byron Lee And The Dragonaires) (Prod: Lloyd Charmers) 1972

PS 347 Moon River/I Can't Find Out – Alton Ellis (Prod: Alton Ellis (UK)) 1972

PS 348 What A Hurricane/If You Love Her – The Marvels (Prod: Norton York/Dimples Hinds (UK)) 1972

PS 349 What You Gonna Do/Why Did You Leave – Winston Groovy (Prod: Winston Tucker (UK)) 1972

PS 350 South Of The Border/Long Island (So Ashamed Version) – DD (Denzil) Dennis/Graham Hawk (actually with Brevett's All Stars) (Prod: Ranny Williams and Denzil Dennis (UK)/Graham Hawk and Tony Brevett) 1972

PS 351 Time/Harlesden High Street – Owen Gray/Graham Hawk (Prod: Ranny Williams (UK)) 1972

PS 352 Rock Me Mr Pingwing (actually titled 'Travelling On')/Breakdown Rock (actually titled 'Dreams Of Yesterday') (1971) – The Harlesden Monks (actually by Lloyd Charmers)/The Harlesden Monks (actually by The Inner Mind) (Prod: Lloyd Charmers/Ian Smith (UK)) 1972

PS 353 Gonna Give Her All The Love I've Got/As Long As You Love Me – Pat Kelly/The Maytones (Prod: Ranny Williams/Alvin Ranglin) 1972

PS 354 That Wonderful Sound (1970)/That Wonderful Sound (Version) – Dobby Dobson/Dobby Dobson (actually by Rupie Edwards' All Stars) (Prod: Rupie Edwards) 1972 [REISSUED FROM SUCCESS RE 913A]

PS 355 Desiderata/Desiderata Music – Lloyd Charmers And The Now Generation/The Now Generation (Prod: Lloyd Charmers) 1972

PS 356 Throw Away Your Gun/Sad Song – Busty Brown And The Warners/The Twinkle Brothers (Prod: Sid Bucknor) 1972

PS 357 I'll Take You There/Beautiful Baby – Eugene Paul (Prod: Ranny Williams (UK)) 1972

PS 358 Hail The Man/I'll Follow You – Owen Gray (Prod: Ranny Williams (UK)) 1972

PS 359 Are You Sure/Va Va Voom – Max Romeo/Carl Masters (Prod: Rupie Edwards/Glen Brown) 1972

PS 360 Amazing Grace/Don't Stay Out Late – Owen Gray And Graham Hawk/Sketto Richards (Prod: Ranny Williams (UK)/Derrick Morgan (UK)) 1972

PS 361 Working On A Groovy Thing/Working On A Groovy Thing (Version) – Alton Ellis/Harlesden Skankers (Prod: Alton Ellis (UK)) 1972

PS 362 And I Love Her/Storm – The Mohawks (Prod: The Mohawks (UK)) 1972

PS 363 NYT

PS 364 Sylvia's Mother/Here Is My Heart (1970) – Winston Groovy (Prod: Winston Tucker/Laurel Aitken (UK)) 1972 [B-SIDE IS REISSUE FROM NEWBEAT NB 058A]

PS 365 Breakfast In Bed/Guitar Shuffle – Winston Reedy/Ranny Williams (Prod: Ranny Williams (UK)) 1972

PS 366 Mr Postman/Mr Postman Version – Cynthia Richards/Skin, Flesh And Bones (Prod: Cynthia Richards And Irving (Al) Brown) 1972

PS 367 Save The Last Dance For Me/Save The Last Dance Version – The Heptones/The Heptones (actually by The Joe Gibbs' All Stars) (Prod: Joe Gibbs) 1972

PS 368 NOT ISSUED – PROBABLE RELEASE ON PAMA SUPREME PS 384

PS 369 Look What You Done For Me/Look What You Done For Me (Version) – Ken Boothe/Lloyd Charmers (Prod: Lloyd Charmers) 1972

PS 370 NYT

PS 371 NYT

PS 372 NYT

PS 373 A Place In The Sun (1969)/Stranger On The Shore (1969) – Slim Smith (Prod: Bunny Lee) 1973 [A-SIDE IS REISSUED FROM UNITY UN 524B/ BULLET BU 523A]

PS 374 Sweet Caroline/Eleanor Rigby – BB Seaton (Prod: Lloyd Charmers) 1972

PS 375 Mama We're All Crazy Now/A Lady Is A Man's Best Friend – Denzil Dennis/Roy Shirley (Prod: Derrick Morgan (UK)/Ranny Williams (UK)) 1973

PS 376 Cherry Pink/The Champ [1973 RE-CUT] – The Mohawks (Prod: Graham Hawk/Graham Hawk And Harry Palmer (UK)) 1973

PS 377 NYT

PS 378 Out Of Time/Put A Little Rain Into My Life – Pat Rhoden (Prod: Ranny Williams (UK)) 1973

PS 379 Twelfth Of Never (1969)/5,000 Watts – Pat Kelly/Jerry Lewis (Prod: Bunny Lee) 1973 [A-SIDE REISSUED FROM UNITY UN 511A]

PS 380 You're Mine (1968)/What A Guy (1968) – Beverley Simmons (Prod: Harry Palmer (UK)) 1973 [REISSUE OF PAMA PM 731]

PS 381 Garden Party/Keep The Faith (actually titled 'Reach For The Sky') – Junior English/Derrick Morgan (actually by Rico Rodriguez And The Charmers' Band) (Prod: Ranny Williams (UK)/Lloyd Charmers) 1973

PS 382 Power To All Our Friends/Wicked And Dreadful – Eugene Paul/Ranny Williams' All Stars (Prod: Ranny Williams (UK)) 1973

PS 383 Hide Away/Sweet And Gentle – Max Romeo/The Soul Syndicate (Prod: Victor Chin) 1973

PS 384 I Wish It Would Rain/Hallelujah – Pat Kelly/The Pat Kelly Singers (Prod: Phil Pratt) 1973

PS 385 Everyman Ought To Know/Everyman Ought To Know (Version) – Max Romeo/Max Romeo (actually by The Impact All Stars) (Prod: Keith Chin) 1973

PS 386 NYT

PS 387 I'll Never Give Up/I Who Have Nothing – Derrick Morgan (Prod: Bunny Lee) 1973

PS 388 NYT

PS 389 NYT

PS 390 Thanks We Get [DIFFERENT CUT TO THAT ISSUED ON UPSETTER LABEL]/Oppression –The Heptones (actually by The Versatiles)/The Heptones (actually by Delroy Butler) (Prod: Lee Perry) 1974

PS 391 Woman And Money/Ten Cent Skank – DD (Denzil) Dennis/The Upsetters (Prod: Lee Perry) 1974

PUNCH

PH 1 The Burner/Juckie Juckie – The Dynamics (actually with Vincent Gordon)/The Dynamics (actually by Tommy McCook And Carl Bryan) (Prod: Lloyd Daley) 1969

PH 2 Mix Up Girl/Qua Kue Shut (actually titled 'Ketch Him Shut') – The Creations (Prod: Lloyd Daley) 1969

PH 3 Jump In A Fire (actually titled 'I'm Righteous')/Give To Get – The Viceroys/The Viceroys (actually by Winston Samuels) (Prod: Lloyd Daley) 1969

PH 4 Strange/Your New Love – Dobby Dobson (Prod: Rupie Edwards) 1969

PH 5 Too Experienced/Mule Jerk – Winston Francis/Jackie Minto (actually Jackie Mittoo) (Prod: Coxson Dodd) 1969

PH 6 Can't Take It Anymore/Anyway – David Isaacs/Lloyd Douglas (Prod: Lee Perry) 1969

PH 7 Trying To Be Free/I've Got It Bad – Martin Riley (Prod: Martin Riley) 1969

PH 8 History (actually titled 'Wonderful World')/Just Be Alone – Harry And Radcliffe (Prod: H Robinson) 1969 [ALSO ISSUED ON CAMEL LABEL CA 26]

PH 9 Hello Dolly/Never Get Away – Pat Satchmo/Eric Donaldson (Prod: Lee Perry) 1969

PH 10 Broken Heart/Tribute To A King (actually titled 'King Of The Trombone') – Busty Brown (Prod: Lee Perry) 1969

PH 11 Oh Happy Day/Spinning [SOUL] – Norman T Washington (Prod: Harry Palmer (UK)) 1969 [B-SIDE IS REISSUED FROM PAMA PM 749B]

PH 12 The Masquerade Is Over/Love For Ambition – Dobby Dobson (Prod: Rupie Edwards) 1969

PH 13 The Bigger Way (actually titled 'The Big M Way')/Chatty Chatty – Winston Blake/The Itals (Prod: Rupie Edwards) 1969

PH 14 Love Is The Key (actually titled 'Love Is The Foundation Of The World')/High Tide (1968) – Lloyd (Robinson) And Devon (Russell)/The Virtues (actually With Val Bennett) (Prod: Rupie Edwards) 1969

PH 15 Herbert Spliffington/Oh Lord Why Lord – Winston Blake/The Itals (Prod: Rupie Edwards) 1969

PH 16 Goosy/Soul Stew – Pat Satchmo/The Upsetters (Prod: Lee Perry) 1969 [PROBABLY ON BLANK LABEL ONLY]

PH 17 Games People Play/Serious Joke – The Upsetters (Prod: Lee Perry) 1969 [PROBABLY ON BLANK LABEL ONLY]

PH 18 Return Of The Ugly/I've Caught You – The Upsetters/The Upsetters (actually with Count Sticky) (Prod: Lee Perry) 1969

PH 19 Dry Acid/Selassie – The Upsetters (actually with Count Sticky)/The Reggae Boys (Prod: Lee Perry) 1969

PH 20 Prisoner Of Love/Soul Juice – Dave Barker/The Upsetters (actually with Busty Brown) (Prod: Lee Perry) 1969

PH 21 Clint Eastwood/Lennox Mood – The Upsetters (actually with Lee Perry)/Lennox Brown (Prod: Lee Perry) 1969

PH 22 You Betray Me/Will You Still Love Me Tomorrow – Dave Barker (Prod: Lee Perry) 1970

PH 23 Ram You Hard/Soul Stew – John Lennon And The Bleechers (actually by The Bleechers)/The Mediators (actually by The Upsetters) (Prod: Lee Perry) 1969

PH 24 Wonderful World/Purple Mast (actually 'Purple Mist') – Pat Satchmo/The Virtues (Prod: Rupie Edwards) 1970

PH 25 Shock Of Might (actually 'Shocks Of Mighty')/Part 2 – Dave Barker (actually with The Upsetters) (Prod: Lee Perry) 1970

PH 26 Sweeter Than Honey/1,000 Pearls – Norman T Washington (Prod: Harry Palmer (UK)) 1969

PH 27 The Result (actually 'Touch Of Fire')/Feel The Spirit – The Upsetters (Prod: Lee Perry) 1970

PH 28 In The Mood/Slide Mongoose (actually titled 'Sly Mongoose') – Pete Weston And His Band/Aston Barratt (Prod: Pete Weston/Aston Barratt) 1970

PH 29 I Am Proud Of You/I Am Proud Of You (Version) – Victor Griffiths/King Victor All Stars (Prod: Victor Griffiths) 1970

PH 30 Artibella/Version Of Artibella – Ken Boothe/Phil Pratt All Stars (Prod: Phil Pratt) 1970

PH 31 Last Goodbye/Mother's Pride – Norman T Washington (Prod: Harry Palmer (UK)) 1970

PH 32 Smile/Musical ID – Ranny Williams (Prod: Ranny Williams) 1970

PH 33 Morning/Morning (Version) – Ken Boothe/Phil Pratt All Stars (Prod: Phil Pratt) 1970

PH 34 Scandal/Song Of The Wise – U Roy/U Roy And The Paragons (Prod: Lloyd Daley) 1970

PH 35 Serious Love/Musical Combination – The Maytones/Keelyn Beckford (actually by Charley Ace) (Prod: Alvin Ranglin) 1970

PH 36 Oh My Darling/Ball Of Confusion – A Boyne (actually by Audley Rollen)/Dennis Smith (actually Dennis Alcapone) (Prod: Keith Hudson) 1970

PH 37 Mr Car Man/Chiney Man – Eli Reynolds (Prod: Eli Reynolds) 1970

PH 38 Greatest Love/I Love You Madly – Busty Brown/Busty Brown (actually with Lloyd Charmers) (Prod: Lloyd Charmers) 1970 [REISSUED ON GAS 154 WITH A- AND B-SIDES REVERSED]

PH 39 Roll On/True Love – Roland Alphonso And The Upsetters/Carl Dawkins (Prod: Lee Perry) 1970

PH 40 It's Party Time/Peace And Love – The Cybermen (Prod: Ranny Williams (UK)) 1970

PH 41 The Ark/False Reader (wrong title: possibly called 'I've Got To Move') – Trevor And Keith/The Minna Boys (Prod: Alvin Ranglin) 1970

PH 42 Reggae Meeting/Soul Bone – Dave Barker/Martin All Stars (actually by Rico Rodriguez And Martin Riley) (Prod: Martin Riley) 1970

PH 43 Death In The Arena/Man Cometh (actually titled 'Julius Caesar') – Rupie Martin's All Stars/Charley Ace (actually with The Upsetters) (Prod: R Jackson/Charley Ace) 1970

PH 44 For Our Desire/For Our Desire Version – Hugh Roy (actually by King Sporty)/Winston Wright And Tommy McCook (Prod: Byron Smith) 1970

PH 45 Bye Bye Happiness/Sufferation We Must Bear (actually titled 'Bongo Man') – The Modifies (actually by The Linkers) (Prod: Fud Christian) 1970

PH 46 Son Of Thunder/Only If You Understand (actually titled 'Do It Madly') – The Punchers (actually by Lee Perry And The Upsetters)/The Punchers (actually by Chuck Junior) (Prod: Lee Perry) 1970

PH 47 NYT

PH 48 My Heart Is Gone/My Heart Is Gone (Version) – John Holt/Phil Pratt All Stars (Prod: Phil Pratt) 1970

PH 49 Silver And Gold/Bump And Bore (actually titled 'The Chalice') – Charley Ace/Phil Pratt All Stars (actually by Charley Ace) (Prod: Phil Pratt) 1970

PH 50 Heart Made Of Stone/I May Never See My Baby – Jackie Robinson (actually by unidentified male vocalist)/Bob Taylor (actually by Horace Andy) (Prod: Phil Pratt) 1970

PH 51 NOT ISSUED – PROBABLE ISSUE ON SUPREME SUP 209

PH 52 NOT ISSUED – PROBABLE ISSUE ON SUPREME SUP 210

PH 53 Book Of Books/Musical Dove – Charley Ace/Winston Harris (Prod: Phil Pratt) 1970

PH 54 Fight The Good Fight/Fight Beat Version – Bill Gentles/Bill Gentles (actually by Gentles' All Stars) (Prod: Bill Gentles) 1970

PH 55 Hold The Ghost (actually 'To The Fields')/Duppy Dance (actually 'To The Fields (Version)') – Herman Chin-Loy/The Aquarians (Prod: Herman Chin-Loy) 1971

PH 56 What Do You Fall In Love For? (actually 'Chariot Coming (Version 2)')/Too Much – The Agro's (actually by Unidentified DJ)/The Slickers (Prod: Sidney Crooks (UK)/Sidney Crooks) 1971

PH 57 Get Out Of This Land (actually titled 'Get Out Of This Thing')/Landmark (actually 'Get Out Of This Thing – Version') – Sammy Morgan/Sidney Crooks' All Stars (Prod: Sidney Crooks (UK)) 1971 [ALSO ISSUED ON BULLET BU 455]

PH 58 Listen To The Beat/Sounds Only (actually 'African Zulu') – Herman Chin-Loy/The Aquarius All Stars (actually by Lloyd Charmers And The Hippy Boys) (Prod: Herman Chin-Loy/Lloyd Charmers and Herman Chin-Loy) 1971

PH 59 Johnny Too Bad/Johnny Too Bad (Version) – The Slickers (Prod: Sid Bucknor) 1971

PH 60 Strange Things/Want Money (actually 'Want Money – Version') – John Holt/Winston Wright (actually by The GG All Stars) (Prod: Phil Pratt/Alvin Ranglin) 1971

PH 61 Mosquito One/Out The Light – El Passo (actually Dennis Alcapone) (Prod: Byron Smith) 1971

PH 62 Love I Madly/Especially For You – Charley And Lloyd (actually by Tony Binns And Busty Brown)/Charley And Alton (actually by Winston Blake And Alton Ellis) (Prod: Lloyd Charmers/Lloyd Daley) 1971

PH 63 Iron Bird/Cat Hop – Top Cat (actually Sylvan Williams) (Prod: Les Foster (UK)) 1971

PH 64 NYT

PH 65 Cholera/Blackbird – The Justins (actually by The Jesters)/Lloyd's All Stars (actually Lloyd Daley's All Stars) (Prod: Lloyd Daley) 1971

PH 66 Come Ethiopians/Zion Gate – The Robinsons (actually by The Melodians)/The Matadors (Prod: Lloyd Daley) 1971

PH 67 Do Something/Run Babylon – Charley Ace/The Maytones (Prod: Alvin Ranglin) 1971

PH 68 NYT

PH 69 What A Confusion/Small Axe – Dave Barker/Bob Marley (actually with The Wailers) (Prod: Lee Perry) 1971

PH 70 Stop Your Crying/Suffering Through The Nation – Ken Boothe/The Conscious Minds (Prod: BB Seaton and Ken Boothe) 1971

PH 71 Put Your Sweet Lips/Stand By Me – Raphael Stewart And The Hot Tops/The Justins (Prod: Raphael Stewart/Lloyd Daley) 1971

PH 72 You Inspire Me/Inspire Version – Busty Brown/Busty Brown (actually by The Upsetters) (Prod: Lee Perry) 1971

PH 73 Chie Chie Bud/Chie Chie Bud (Version) – Max Romeo/Max Romeo (actually by The Impact All Stars) (Prod: Victor Chin) 1971

PH 73 Chie Chie Bud/Missing You – Max Romeo (Prod: Victor Chin) 1971 [DUPLICATE ISSUE]

PH 74 Goodnight My Love/There Is A Land – Winston And Errol (Prod: Claudius Perara) 1971

PH 75 Hard Fighter (actually titled 'The Hardest Fighter')/Back To Africa Version 2 – Little Roy/Count Ossie (actually with Alton Ellis) (Prod: Lloyd Daley) 1971

PH 76 Don't Say/Version – James Brown (Ja)/Trans Am All Stars (Prod: James Brown (Ja)) 1971

PH 77 Down Presser/Got The Tip – Peter Tosh And The Wailers/Junior Byles (Prod: Lee Perry) 1971

PH 78 NYT

PH 79 Cherrio Baby (actually 'Cherry Oh Baby')/Civilisation – The Classics (UK) (actually Denzil Dennis And Eugene Paul) (Prod: Lee Perry) 1971

PH 80 NYT

PH 81 Fussing And Fighting/The Man I Should Be – The Slickers (Prod: Sid Bucknor) 1971

PH 82 Don't Give Up/Give Up (Version) – Paul Freeman/The Upsetters (Prod: Lee Perry) 1971

PH 83 Where Love Goes/You Can Run – Donald Smythe/The Hurricanes (actually by The Righteous Flames) (Prod: Lee Perry) 1971

PH 84 You'll Be Sorry/Knock Three Times – David Isaacs (Prod: Lee Perry) 1971

PH 85 NYT

PH 86 NYT

PH 87 Sincerely/Hold On I'm Coming – Owen Gray (Prod: Lord Koos (UK)) 1971

PH 88 Soulful Love/One For All (3 In One) – Pat Kelly/John Holt (actually by U Roy And The Paragons) (Prod: Phil Pratt/Lloyd Daley) 1971

PH 89 Lonely World/Put It On Version – Afro/Alton Ellis's All Stars (Prod: Alton Ellis) 1971

PH 90 NYT

PH 91 Rudies' Medley/Rude Boy Version – Third And Fourth Generation (actually by Peter Tosh And The Soulmates)/Joe Gibbs And The Soulmates (Prod: Joe Gibbs) 1971

PH 92 NYT

PH 93 Christmas Message/Cool It Girl – DD (Denzil) Dennis (Prod: Noel Blake (UK)) 1971

PH 94 Winey Winey (actually 'One In Three (Medley)')/There Is A Place (actually Titled 'Where Must I Go') – Phil Pratt All Stars (actually by Jackie Bernard And The Kingstonians)/Phil Pratt All Stars (actually by Barrington Spence) (Prod: Phil Pratt) 1971

PH 95 Royal Chord/Soul Beat (actually titled 'In The Spirit') (1969) – The Jaylads (actually by The Melodians)/The Jaylads (actually by Lloyd Charmers) (Prod: BB Seaton/Lloyd Charmers) 1972

PH 96 Solid As A Rock/Solid As A Rock (Version) – The Ethiopians/Rupie Edwards' All Stars (Prod: Rupie Edwards) 1972

PH 97 Paul, Marcus And Norman/Paul, Marcus And Norman (Version) – The Gaylads (actually by Ken Boothe And BB Seaton)/The Conscious Minds (actually by The Aquarians) (Prod: BB Seaton And Herman Chin-Loy) 1972

PH 98 Nobody Told Me (actually titled 'Nobody Told Her')/Don't Play That Song (Instrumental) – Carl Lewin (actually by Carl Lewis)/Wing (actually The Marvels) (Prod: Ranny Williams (UK)/Dimples Hinds (UK)) 1972

PH 99 1, 2, 3, A, B, C/Zee – The Combinations (Prod: Ranny Williams) 1972

PH 100 Buttercup/I Care – Winston Scotland/Ronald Wilson (Prod: Tony Robinson) 1972

PH 101 Screwface/Face Man (Version) – Bob Marley And The Wailers (Prod: Tuff Gong) 1972

PH 102 Lively Up Yourself/Version (actually titled 'Live') – Bob Marley And The Wailers/Tommy McCook (actually with The Wailers) (Prod: Tuff Gong) 1972

PH 103 Don't Be A Loser/Jamaican Girl – Roy Shirley (Prod: Roy Shirley) 1972

PH 104 Nanny Skank/Skank Version – U Roy/Pittsburg All Stars (Prod: Karl Pitterson) 1972

PH 105 Darling Ooh Wee/Merry Up Version (actually 'Crackers Version') – U Roy And Errol Dunkley/The God Sons (actually by Glen Brown) (Prod: Rupie Edwards/Glen Brown) 1972

PH 106 Dungeon/Kiss Me Honey (actually titled 'Kiss Me Honey Honey, Kiss Me') – Glen Miller/Nora Dean (Prod: Ranny Williams) 1972

PH 107 Forward March/Plenty Of One (Medley) – Derrick Morgan (Prod: Derrick Morgan) 1972

PH 108 A Sugar/Part 2 Sugar – Roy Shirley/Altyman Reid (Prod: Roy Shirley) 1972

PH 109 Pharoah Hiding/Hail To Power – Junior Byles/The Upsetters (Prod: Lee Perry) 1972

PH 110 Have I Seen Her (actually titled 'Have I Sinned')/Have I Seen Her Version (actually 'Have I Sinned Version') – Lloyd (Charmers) And Ken (Boothe) (Prod: Lloyd Charmers) 1972

PH 111 Round And Round/Round Version – The Melodians/The Upsetters (Prod: Lee Perry) 1972

PH 112 People Like People/Softie (actually titled 'Night Fever') – Gerry Meggie (actually by Clancy Eccles)/Max Romeo (actually by Lloydie (Lloyd Charmers) And The Lowbites) (Prod: Clancy Eccles/Lloyd Charmers) 1972

PH 113 Trying To Wreck My Life/Pride And Joy – Leroy Samuel (actually Leroy Smart)/John Holt (Prod: Bunny Lee) 1972

PH 114 You Should've Known Better/Known Better – The Wailing Souls And The Tuff Gong All Stars (Prod: Tuff Gong) 1972

PH 115–PH 120: NOT ISSUED

PH 121 Fattie Bum Bum/Fattie Bum Dub – Laurel Aitken (Prod: Laurel Aitken (UK)) 1975

SUCCESS

RE 901 Look Who A Bust Style/Look Who A Bust Style (Version 2) – The Meditators/Rupie Edwards' All Stars 1969

RE 902 Grandfather's Clock/Promoter's Grouse – Rupie Edwards' All Stars (actually with Winston Wright)/Rupie Edwards' All Stars (actually by Rupie Edwards And Lynford Anderson) 1969

RE 903 Fat Girl, Sexy Girl/Man And Woman – John Holt 1970

RE 904 Don't Let Me Suffer/Red Sun Rise – The Concords/Hugh Roy Henry (actually by The Concords) 1970

RE 905 Handicap/If You Can't Beat Them Join Them – Rupie Edwards' All Stars/Rupie Edwards 1970

RE 906 Crazy/Your New Love (Version) – Dobby Dobson/Rupie Edwards' All Stars (actually by Neville Hinds) 1970

RE 907 Conjunction/Love Is A Wonderful Wicked Thing – Neville Hinds/Rupie Edwards 1970

RE 908 NOT ISSUED

RE 909 Pop Hi/High Tide (Title Incorrect: May Be Called 'Going West') – Rupie Edwards' All Stars (actually with Val Bennett)/The Virtues (actually with Val Bennett) 1970

RE 910 Return Of Herbert Spliffington/Young, Gifted And Black (Instrumental) – Rupie Edwards And Sidy/Rupie Edwards' All Stars 1970

RE 911 Census Taker/Souling Way Out – Rupie Edwards' All Stars/Rupie Edwards' All Stars (actually with Glen Adams) 1970

RE 912 Cry A Little Cry/Revenge Version 3 – Dobby Dobson/Rupie Edwards' All Stars 1970

RE 913 That Wonderful Sound/Don't Make Me Over – Dobby Dobson 1970 [A-SIDE REISSUED ON PAMA SUPREME PS 354]

RE 914 Too Late/You Can't Wine – Gregory Isaacs/The Kingstonians 1970

Note: all issues were produced by Rupie Edwards.

SUPREME

SUP 201 Time To Pray/Young Budd – Mr Foundation (actually by Lloyd Robinson)/Mr Foundation (actually by Leonard Dillon) (Prod: Coxson Dodd) 1969

SUP 202 More Games/Maga Dog – Sound Dimension/Mr Foundation (actually by The Invaders) (Prod: Coxson Dodd) 1969

SUP 203 Work It Up/Chatty Chatty – Jack And The Beanstalk (actually by Jackie Bernard And The Kingstonians) (Prod: Coxson Dodd) 1969

SUP 204 Let It Be/Looking Back – The Mohawks (Prod: Graham Hawk (UK)) 1970

SUP 205 For Our Liberty/Wicked Lady – The Mohawks (Prod: Graham Hawk (UK)) 1970

SUP 206 Surfin'/All The Love (actually titled 'Gonna Give Her All The Love I've Got') – Owen Gray (Prod: Ranny Williams) 1970

SUP 207 Give Me Some/Give Me Some (Part 2) – The Mohawks (Prod: Graham Hawk (UK)) 1970

SUP 208 Funky Funky/Funky Funky (Version) – The Mohawks (Prod: Graham Hawk (UK)) 1970

SUP 209 Hallelujah/Boat Of Joy – The Emotions/Matador All Stars (Prod: Lloyd Daley) 1970

SUP 210 When You Go To A Party/Stop The Party – The Meditators/Rupie Edwards' All Stars (Prod: Rupie Edwards) 1970

SUP 211 Double Attack/Puzzle (actually 'Double Attack Version') – Hugh Roy (actually by U Roy Junior And Ronnie Davis)/Murphy's All Stars (Prod: Albert George Murphy) 1970

SUP 212 Share My Rest/Always – John Holt/Al Brown (Prod: Keith Hudson/?) 1970

SUP 213 Musical Attack/Music Alone (actually 'Music Alone Shall Live (Version)') – Rupie Edwards' All Stars (Prod: Rupie Edwards) 1970

SUP 214 You Must Believe Me/Funk The Funk – Dennis Alcapone And Niney/Rupie Edwards' All Stars (Prod: Rupie Edwards) 1970

SUP 215 Burning Fire/Push And Push (actually 'Burning Fire (Version)') – Joe Higgs/Rupie Edwards' All Stars (Prod: Rupie Edwards) 1971

SUP 216 I Like It Like This (actually titled 'Don't Rock My Boat')/I Am Sorry – Bob Marley/Bunny Gayle (Prod: Lee Perry) 1971

SUP 217 Mount Zion/All Over – The Righteous Souls/Eccle And Neville (Prod: Lee Perry) 1971

SUP 218 Everynight/Ethiopia – Ruddy (Grant) And Sketto (Richards) (Prod: Laurel Aitken (UK)) 1971 [REISSUED ON CAMEL CA 2006]

SUP 219 Stay/You're My Everything – Slim Smith (Prod: Slim Smith) 1971

SUP 220 Just My Imagination/Gotta Get A Message To You – Dave Barker And The Charmers (Prod: Lloyd Charmers) 1971

SUP 221 Love Bug/Sound Of Our Forefathers – The Ethiopians (Prod: Alvin Ranglin) 1971

SUP 222 NYT

SUP 223 Go Back/Go Back Version 2 – Impact (actually by The Vibrators)/Impact (actually by The Impact All Stars) (Prod: Victor Chin) 1971

SUP 224 Don't Get Weary/Don't Get Weary (Version) – Tony Brevitt/Brevitt All Stars (Prod: BB Seaton) 1971

SUP 225 Let It Fall/Can't Change – Eugene And Burst (actually Eugene Paul And Mike Elliott)/Denzil And Burst (actually Denzil Dennis And Mike Elliott) (Prod: Sidney Crooks (UK)) 1971

SUP 226 Starvation/Jordan River – The Ethiopians/Maxie (Max Romeo) And Glen (Brown) (Prod: JJ Johnson/Alvin Ranglin) 1971

SUP 227 My Application/Oh No My Baby – Stranger And Gladdy/Tabby And The Diamonds (Prod: Stranger Cole) 1971

SUP 228 Double Heavy/Johnny Dollar – Dave Barker (Prod: Martin Riley and Ranny Williams) 1971

SUP 229 Not You Baby/Baby (Version) – The Upsetting Brothers (actually by Victor And The Upsetting Brothers)/Dreadlock All Stars (Prod: Dread Lock Label, Ja) 1971

Note: there was a further issue on this label, namely 'What The World Is Coming To'/'Live As One' by King Chubby (actually Junior Byles), which was also put out as the first release on the Pama Supreme imprint. The catalogue number remained the same in both cases (SUP 297) and it is suspected that the release on Supreme came about around the middle of the label's run (ie just prior to the launch of Pama Supreme).

UNITY

UN 500 On Broadway/Unity Is Strength – Slim Smith/Lester Sterling (Prod: Bunny Lee) (1968) [WHITE-LABEL PRE-RELEASE FORMAT ONLY]

UN 501 Last Flight To Reggae City/Watch Dem Go – Stranger Cole And Tommy McCook/Junior Smith (Prod: Bunny Lee/Roy Smith (UK)) 1968

UN 502 Bangarang/If We Should Ever Meet – Stranger Cole And Lester Sterling/Stranger Cole (actually with Gladdy Anderson) (Prod: Bunny Lee/Stranger Cole) 1968

UN 503 Wet Dream/She's But A Little Girl – Max Romeo (Prod: Bunny Lee) 1968 [REISSUED ON OCEAN OC 003]

UN 504 Everybody Needs Love/Come Back Girl – Slim Smith/Junior Smith (Prod: Bunny Lee/Roy Smith (UK)) 1968

UN 505 Reggae On Broadway/Love Can Be Wonderful – Lester Sterling/The Clique (Prod: Bunny Lee/Roy Smith (UK)) 1969

UN 506 The Avengers/Donkey Man – Tommy McCook/Laurel Aitken (Prod: Bunny Lee/Laurel Aitken (UK)) 1969

UN 507 Belly Woman/Please Stay (1968) – Max Romeo (actually by Derrick Morgan)/Paulette (Morgan) And The Lovers (Prod: Derrick Morgan/H Robinson) 1969

UN 508 For Once In My Life/Burning Desire – Slim Smith (Prod: Bunny Lee) 1969 [B-SIDE REISSUE OF UNITY BU 523B]

UN 509 Spoogy/Monkey Fiddle – Lester Sterling/Tommy McCook (Prod: Bunny Lee/Derrick Morgan) 1969

UN 510 Zip-Pa-Di-Do-Dah/On Broadway – Slim Smith (Prod: Bunny Lee) 1969

UN 511 Twelfth Of Never/Solid As A Rock – Max Romeo (actually by Pat Kelly)/The Tartans (Prod: Bunny Lee/Ken Lack) 1969 [A-SIDE REISSUED ON PAMA SUPREME PS 379A]

UN 512 Regina/Bright As A Rose – Lester Sterling (Prod: Bunny Lee) 1969 [B-SIDE REISSUED ON UNITY UN 531B]

UN 513 Let It Be Me/Love Makes Me Do Foolish Things – Slim Smith And Paulette (Morgan) (Prod: Bunny Lee) 1969

UN 514 When I Get My Freedom/Life Can Be Beautiful – Stranger Cole (actually with Roy Richards)/Stranger Cole (Prod: Stranger Cole/Bunny Lee) 1969

UN 515 Somebody To Love/Confusion – Slim Smith (Prod: Bunny Lee) 1969

UN 516 Wine Her Goosie/Fire Ball – Max Romeo/King Cannon [Carl Bryan] (Prod: Derrick Morgan/Bunny Lee) 1969

UN 517 1,000 Tons Of Megaton/Five Card Stud – Lester Sterling/King Cannon [Carl Bryan] (Prod: Bunny Lee) 1969

UN 518 Man About Town/Man At The Door – Lester Sterling (Prod: Bunny Lee) 1969

UN 519 Peyton Place/Red Gal Ring – Don Tony Lee (actually with Roland Alphonso) (Prod: Bunny Lee) 1969

UN 520 Slip Away/Spanish Harlem – Slim Smith (Prod: Bunny Lee) 1969 [REISSUED ON CAMEL CA 81 WITH A- AND B-SIDES REVERSED]

UN 521 NOT USED

UN 522 Thirty Pieces Of Silver (1964)/Everybody Ska (1964) – Prince Buster And The All Stars (Prod: Cat Campbell And AMY Records, USA) 1969

UN 523 NOT USED

UN 524 Sunny Side Of The Sea/Place In The Sun – Slim Smith (Prod: Bunny Lee) 1969 [B-SIDE REISSUED ON PAMA SUPREME PS 373A/BULLET BU 523A]

UN 525 The Return Of Al Capone/The Q Club – Peter Tosh/Lennox Brown (Prod: Bunny Lee) 1969

UN 526 Pepper Seed/Ambitious Beggar – Ranny Williams (actually by Peter Tosh) (Prod: Winston Holness) 1969

UN 527 Blessed Are The Meek (1968)/My Conversation (1968) – Slim Smith And The Uniques (Prod: Bunny Lee) 1969

UN 528 Dreams To Remember/Peace Maker – The Hippy Boys (actually by Gladstone Anderson's All Stars)/The Hippy Boys (Prod: Lloyd Charmers) 1969

UN 529 Sun Valley/Drums Of Fu-Manchu – Peter Tosh/Headley Bennett (Prod: Bunny Lee) 1969

UN 530 What You Gonna Do?/Hot Coffee – The Reggae Boys/Headley Bennett (Prod: Bunny Lee) 1969

UN 531 Lonesome Feeling/Bright As A Rose – Lester Sterling (Prod: Bunny Lee) 1969 [B-SIDE IS REISSUE FROM UN 512B]

UN 532 Mini Skirt Vision/Far Far Away – Max Romeo (actually with The Rudies)/Max Romeo (actually with The Hippy Boys) (Prod: Derrick Morgan (UK)/Ranny Williams (UK)) 1969

UN 533 Hook Up/Full Up – Bunny Lee All Stars (actually with Jackie Mittoo)/Bunny Lee All Stars (actually with Lester Sterling And Tommy McCook) (Prod: Keith Chin) 1969

UN 534 Dream Boat/Tommy's Dream – Tommy McCook (Prod: Bunny Lee) 1969

UN 535 Peanut Vendor/100,000 Tons Of Rock – Tommy McCook (Prod: Bunny Lee) 1969

UN 536 No Matter What/Walk Through This World – Doreen Shaeffer (Prod: Bunny Lee) 1969

UN 537 Keep That Light Shining On Me/Build My World Around You – Slim Smith (Prod: Bunny Lee) 1969

UN 538 How Much Is That Doggy In The Window/As Long As He Needs Me – Doreen Shaeffer (Prod: Bunny Lee) 1969

UN 539 Love Me Tender/This Feeling – Slim Smith (Prod: Slim Smith) 1969 [REISSUED ON ESCORT ERT 852]

UN 540 Derrick Top-The-Pop/Capone's Revenge – Derrick Morgan (actually with Andy Capp)/Glen Adams (Prod: Derrick Morgan/Glen Adams) 1969

UN 541 Day Dream/Joy Ride – Bunny Lee All Stars (Prod: Bunny Lee) 1969

UN 542 Honey/There's A Light – Slim Smith (actually with Sir Harry)/Slim Smith (Prod: Bunny Lee) 1969

UN 543 Ivan Hitler The Conqueror/The Splice – Lloyd Willis And Bunny Lee's All Stars (Prod: Bunny Lee) 1969

UN 544 Melting Pot/Death Rides A Horse (actually titled 'Maxie's Pop A Top') – Max Romeo And The Hippy Boys/The Hippy Boys (Prod: Keith Chin) 1970

UN 545 Clap Clap (aka 'Feel The Spirit')/You've Got Your Troubles – Max Romeo And The Hippy Boys/Max Romeo (actually with The Hippy Boys) (Prod: Keith Chin) 1970

UN 546 Return Of Jack Slade/Fat Man – Derrick Morgan (Prod: Derrick Morgan (UK)) 1970

UN 547 What A Cute Man/Buy You A Rainbow – Max Romeo With The Bunny Lee All Stars (Prod: Bunny Lee) 1970

UN 548 Sometimes/Lash-La-Rue – John Holt/Bunny Lee's All Stars (actually with Niney) (Prod: Bunny Lee/Winston Holness) 1970

UN 549 Sea Cruise/Niney's Hop – John Holt/Bunny Lee's All Stars (actually with Niney) (Prod: Bunny Lee/Winston Holness) 1970

UN 550 NOT USED

UN 551 Why Did My Little Girl Cry/Change Partners – Freddie MacGregor/Peter Austin (Prod: Bunny Lee) 1970

UN 552 Walking Along/Warfare – John Holt/Bunny Lee's All Stars (actually with Count Machuki And Jackie Mittoo) (Prod: Bunny Lee) 1970

UN 553 When You Were Mine (actually titled 'My Girl Has Gone')/The Angles (actually titled 'The Angels Listened In') – Ken Parker/The Clarendonians (Prod: Bunny Lee) 1970

UN 554 My Special Prayer/Never Hurt The One You Love – Errol Dunkley (Prod: Bunny Lee) 1970

UN 555 Ten Cents (actually 'Winey For Ten Cents')/Stay With Me Forever – The Soul Mates/Doreen Shaeffer (Prod: Bunny Lee) 1970

UN 556 Gonna Give Her All The Love I Got/Nobody But You – John Holt/Busty Brown (Prod: Bunny Lee) 1970

UN 557 Do It My Way/Where In This World (Are You Going) – Eric 'Monty' Morris (Prod: Bunny Lee) 1970

UN 558 Goodnight My Love (actually titled 'See You At Sunrise')/Lover Girl – The Corsairs (actually by The Interns) (Prod: Bunny Lee) 1970

UN 559 Drink Wine Everybody/Someone To Call My Own – Delroy Wilson/Joe White (Prod: Bunny Lee) 1970

UN 560 Fish In The Pot/Feel It – Max Romeo (Prod: Derrick Morgan (UK)) 1970

UN 561 No Love/A Little Tear – Little John (actually John Holt) (Prod: Bunny Lee) 1970

UN 562 Slip Up/On Broadway – Lester Sterling/Dave Barker (Prod: Bunny Lee) 1970 [ALSO PRESSED ON BLUE UNITY LABEL]

UN 562 Duppy Conqueror/Justice – Bob Marley And The Wailers/The Upsetters (Prod: Lee Perry) 1970 [DUPLICATE ISSUE – EXISTENCE UNCONFIRMED]

UN 563 Skankee/Skankee (Version 2) – Niney And Bunny Lee's All Stars (Prod: Winston Holness) 1970

UN 564 Love Makes The World Go Round/Love (Version Instrumental) – Ernest Wilson/Ernest Wilson (actually by Bunny Lee's All Stars) (Prod: Ernest Wilson) 1970

UN 565 More Balls/Bum Ball (actually titled 'Musical Hop') – Mark Anthony And The Jets (actually by Earl Lindo)/Mark Anthony And The Jets (actually by Delroy Jones) (Prod: Errol Thompson) 1970

UN 566 Peace And Love/Peace And Love (Version) – The Third Dimension/The Third Dimension (actually by Bunny Lee's All Stars) (Prod: Bunny Lee) 1970

UN 567 Blessed Are The Meek/The People's Voice – Dave Barker And Slim Smith/Jeff Barnes And The Uniques (Prod: Bunny Lee) 1970

UN 568 1,000 Tons Of Version/Wake The Nation – Jeff Barnes And Roland Alphonso/U Roy And Jeff Barnes (Prod: Bunny Lee) 1970

UN 569 Conquering Ruler/Bedweight – Derrick Morgan (Prod: Derrick Morgan) 1970 [REMASTERED VERSIONS OF ORIGINAL 1968 CUTS]

UN 570 Jenny (actually 'Jenny Come Lately')/The Race – Slim Smith (Prod: Slim Smith) 1970

UN 571 Maccabee Version/Music Book – Max Romeo/The Soul Syndicate (Prod: Bunny Lee) 1970

UN 571 Maccabee Version/Music Book – Max Romeo/The Soul Syndicate (Prod: Willie Francis) 1971 [SECOND PRESSING WITH GREEN WRITING CREDITING WILLIE FRANCIS AS PRODUCER)

UN 572 Rent Crisis/Rent Crisis (Version) – Max Romeo (Prod: Winston Holness) 1973

UN 573 Big Hair/Skank In Skank – Dirty Harry (Richard Hall) And Buster's All Stars/Young Doug And Buster's All Stars (Prod: Cat Campbell) 1973

PAMA ALBUMS

SECO/ECO Series (SECO = stereo, ECO = mono)

SECO 1 – *We'll Keep A Welcome/Prince Of Wales' Investiture* – Hammersmith Welsh Male Choir (1969)

Note: the investiture of the Prince of Wales is mentioned on the sleeve together with photographs of him, but this is actually just a marketing ploy aimed at appealing to and attracting the 'royalist' market. The investiture took place around mid-1969 so this would have been a current media topic at the time.

ECO 2 – *Crab Biggest Hits* – Various Artists (1969)

SIDE 1
1. Private Number – Ernest Wilson (Prod: Derrick Morgan)
2. Run Girl Run – GG (George) Grossett (Prod: Harry Mudie)
3. Fire A Muss Muss Tail – The Ethiopians (Prod: H Robinson)
4. Children Get Ready – The Versatiles (Prod: Lee Perry)
5. Seven Letters – Derrick Morgan (Prod: Derrick Morgan)
6. Reggae Hit The Town – The Ethiopians (Prod: H Robinson)

SIDE 2
1. Work It – The Viceroys (Prod: Lloyd Daley)
2. River To The Bank – Derrick Morgan (Prod: Derrick Morgan)
3. Spread Your Bed – The Versatiles (Prod: Lee Perry)
4. What A Big Surprise – The Ethiopians (Prod: H Robinson)
5. Reggae City – Val Bennett (Prod: Bunny Lee)
6. Lonely Heartaches – The Tartans (actually by The Clarendonians) (Prod: Ken Lack)

Note: some copies apparently carry the number 'CRL 4000' in the top right-hand corner of the sleeve.

ECO 3 – *Reggae Hits '69 Volume 1* – Various Artists (1969)

SIDE 1
1. Children Get Ready – The Versatiles (Prod: Lee Perry)
2. Bangarang – Lester Sterling And Stranger Cole (Prod: Bunny Lee)
3. Hey Boy, Hey Girl – Derrick (Morgan) And Patsy (Todd) (Prod: Derrick Morgan)
4. Rhythm Hips – Ronald Russell (Prod: Eric Barnett)
5. River To The Bank – Derrick Morgan (Prod: Derrick Morgan)
6. Reggae Hit The Town – The Ethiopians (Prod: H Robinson)

SIDE 2

1. The Horse – Eric Barnett (actually by Theo Beckford's Group) (Prod: Eric Barnett)
2. I Love You – Derrick Morgan (Prod: Derrick Morgan)
3. Reggae In The Wind – Lester Sterling (Prod: Bunny Lee)
4. Let's Have Some Fun – Devon (Russell) And The Tartans (Prod: H Robinson)
5. Push Push – The Termites (actually by The Hi-Tones) (Prod: Eric Barnett)
6. Last Flight To Reggae City – Tommy McCook And Stranger Cole (Prod: Bunny Lee)

ECO 4 – *Gas Greatest Hits* – Various Artists (1969)

SIDE 1

1. 1,000 Tons Of Megaton – Roland Alphonso (actually with Derrick Morgan) (Prod: Derrick Morgan)
2. How Long Will It Take – Pat Kelly (Prod: Bunny Lee)
3. Reggae In The Wind – Lester Sterling (Prod: Bunny Lee)
4. Walking Proud – Martin Riley (Prod: Winston Lowe)
5. Ain't Too Proud To Beg – The Uniques (Prod: Bunny Lee)
6. The Horse – Eric Barnett (actually by Theo Beckford's Group) (Prod: Eric Barnett)

SIDE 2

1. Soul Call – The Soul Rhythms (Prod: Joe Sinclair)
2. Wanted – Baba Dise (actually Pama Dice) (Prod: Winston Riley)
3. Never Give Up – Pat Kelly (Prod: Bunny Lee)
4. Te Ta Toe – Eric Barnett (actually by Theo Beckford's Group) (Prod: Eric Barnett)
5. Ring Of Gold – The Melodians (Prod: Winston Lowe)
6. Choo Choo Train – The Soul Cats (actually by unidentified male vocal group) (Prod: ? (UK))

SECO 5 – *Butlins' Red Coat Revue* – The Butlins Red Coats (non-reggae) (1969)

ECO 6 – *Nu-Beat's Greatest Hits* – Various Artists (1969)

SIDE 1

1. La La Means I Love You – Alton Ellis (Prod: Alton Ellis)
2. Rescue Me – The Reggae Girls (actually by The Ebony Sisters) (Prod: Harry Mudie)
3. Another Heartache – Gregory Isaacs (Prod: Winston Sinclair And Gregory Isaacs)
4. Rhythm Hips – Ronald Russell (Prod: Eric Barnett)
5. Haile Selassie – Laurel Aitken (Prod: Laurel Aitken (UK))
6. My Testimony – The Maytals (actually by The Ethiopians) (Prod: JJ Johnson)

SIDE 2

1. Train To Vietnam (actually 'Train To South Vietnam') – The Rudies (Prod: Palmer brothers (UK))
2. Hey Girl, Hey Boy – Derrick (Morgan) And Patsy (Todd) (Prod: Derrick Morgan)

3. Blowing In The Wind – Max Romeo (Prod: Bunny Lee)
4. Rhythm And Soul – Bobby Kalphat (actually with The Caltone All Stars) (Prod: Ken Lack)
5. Suffering Still – Laurel Aitken And Girlie (Prod: Laurel Aitken (UK))
6. Give You My Love – Derrick And Paulette (Morgan) (Prod: Derrick Morgan)

ECO 7 – *Unity's Greatest Hits* – Various Artists (1969) (all tracks produced by Bunny Lee except * which was a Stranger Cole production)

SIDE 1
1. Bangarang – Lester Sterling And Stranger Cole
2. Last Flight To Reggae City – Tommy McCook And Stranger Cole
3. Let It Be Me – Slim Smith And Paulette (Morgan)
4. Everybody Needs Love – Slim Smith
5. Reggae On Broadway – Lester Sterling
6. Twelfth Of Never – Pat Kelly

SIDE 2
1. Spoogy – Lester Sterling
2. For Once In My Life – Slim Smith
3. If We Should Ever Meet – Stranger Cole*
4. The Avengers – Tommy McCook
5. On Broadway – Slim Smith
6. Bright As A Rose – Lester Sterling

ECO 8 – *Scandal In A Brixton Market* – Laurel Aitken, Girlie And Rico Rodriguez (all tracks produced by Laurel Aitken (UK)) (1969)

SIDE 1
1. Scandal In A Brixton Market – Laurel Aitken And Girlie
2. Madame Streggae – Laurel Aitken And Girlie
3. Stupid Married Man – Laurel Aitken
4. Tammering – Laurel Aitken
5. Have Mercy – Laurel Aitken
6. Night Cricket – Laurel Aitken

SIDE 2
1. Run Powell Run – Laurel Aitken
2. Teddy Bear – Laurel Aitken
3. Mr Soul – Laurel Aitken
4. Woke Up This Morning – Laurel Aitken
5. Babylon – Rico Rodriguez
6. Stop The War In Vietnam – Laurel Aitken And Rico Rodriguez

ECO 9 – *Everybody Needs Love* – Slim Smith (all tracks produced by Bunny Lee) (1969)

SIDE 1
1. Everybody Needs Love
2. I've Been Terrorised
3. A Place In The Sun
4. Never Let Me Go (With The Uniques)
5. Slip Away
6. Spanish Harlem

SIDE 2
1. Somebody To Love
2. Stranger On The Shore
3. Burning Desire
4. On Broadway
5. Zip-Pa-Di-Doo-Dah
6. Ain't Too Proud To Beg (with The Uniques)

ECO 10 – *In London* – Derrick Morgan (1969) (all tracks produced by Derrick Morgan in Jamaica, despite the album title)

SIDE 1
1. Seven Letters
2. First Taste Of Love
3. How Can I Forget
4. Stand By Me
5. Don't Play That Song
6. Too Bad

SIDE 2
1. One Morning In May
2. Come What May
3. Send Me Some Loving
4. Make It Tan Deh
5. Give Me Back
6. River To The Bank

ECO 11 – *Reggae Hits '69 Volume 2* – Various Artists (1969)

SIDE 1
1. 1,000 Tons Of Megaton – Roland Alphonso (actually with Derrick Morgan) (Prod: Derrick Morgan)
2. Who You Gonna Run To? – The Techniques (Prod: Winston Riley)
3. Down In The Park – The Inspirations (Prod: Lee Perry)
4. Spread Your Bed – The Versatiles (Prod: Lee Perry)
5. Take Your Hand From Me Neck – The Viceroys (Prod: Lloyd Daley)
6. Throw Me Corn – Winston Shand (actually with The Sheiks) (Prod: Ranny Williams)

SIDE 2
1. Soul Call – The Soul Rhythms (Prod: Joe Sinclair)
2. Work It – The Viceroys (Prod: Lloyd Daley)
3. Run Girl Run – GG (George) Grossett (Prod: Harry Mudie)
4. Private Number – Ernest Wilson (Prod: Derrick Morgan)
5. Since You've Been Gone – Eric Fratter (Prod: Harry Johnson)
6. Spoogy – Lester Sterling (Prod: Bunny Lee)

SECO 12 – *Reggae Hits* – Rudy Mills (all tracks produced by Derrick Harriott) (1969)

SIDE 1
1. A Heavy Load
2. Every Beat Of My Heart
3. John Jones
4. I'm Trapped
5. Wholesale Love

SIDE 2
1. Tears On My Pillow
2. Hang Your Heart To Dry
3. Place Called Happiness
4. Time On My Side
5. A Long Story

SECO 13 – *Derrick Harriott Sings Jamaica Reggae* – Derrick Harriott (all tracks produced by Derrick Harriott) (1969)

SIDE 1
1. Sitting On Top
2. Been So Long
3. Close To Me
4. Long Time
5. Standing In

SIDE 2
1. Have Some Mercy
2. The Girl's Alright
3. You Really Got A Hold On Me
4. I'm Not Begging
5. It's Alright

ECO 14 – *Rico In Reggae Land* (a tribute to Don Drummond) (all tracks produced by Bunny Lee And Rico Rodriguez. Ja rhythm tracks overlaid in UK) (1969)

SIDE 1
1. Tribute To Don Drummond (actually with Gene Rondo)
2. Anancy Rumba
3. Rainbow Into The Rio Mino
4. Sweet Chariot
5. Tom Jones
6. Scar Face (actually with Gene Rondo)

SIDE 2
1. Trombone Man
2. Japanese Invasion (actually with Gene Rondo)
3. Top Of The Class
4. Black Milk
5. Stranger On The Shore
6. Place In The Sun

SECO 15 – *Bangarang* – Lester Sterling (all tracks produced by Bunny Lee) (1969)

SIDE 1
1. Bangarang (with Stranger Cole)
2. Reggae In The Wind
3. Spoogy
4. 1,000,000 Tons Of TNT
5. Man At The Door
6. Man About Town

SIDE 2
1. Reggae On Broadway
1. Doctor Satan
2. Danger Man
3. Bright As A Rose
4. Regina
5. Man At Work

SECO 16 – Untraced

SECO 17 – *Boss Reggae* – Various Artists (all tracks produced by CS Dodd) (1970)

SIDE 1
1. Poor Mi Israelites – Winston Jarrett
2. Scare Him – The Flames

3. Give Me True Love – The Meditators
4. Help – The Helpers
5. Night Doctor – Jackie Mittoo
6. Run For Rescue – Lloyd Robinson

SIDE 2
1. Tomorrow – The Meditators
2. Too Many Miles – Winston Wellington
3. Double Crosser – Lloyd Robinson
4. Sweet Talking – The Heptones
5. Just Can't Satisfy – Winston Jarrett
6. Jane – The Gladiators

SECO 18 – *The Best Of Camel – An Oasis Of Sounds* – Various Artists (1970)

SIDE 1
1. Strange Whispering – The West Indians (Prod: Lee Perry)
2. Who You Gonna Run To? – The Techniques (Prod: Winston Riley)
2. Girl What You Doing To Me – Owen Gray (actually with The Rudies) (Prod: Derrick Morgan (UK))
4. Warrior – Johnny (Osbourne) And The Sensations (Prod: Winston Riley)
5. Confidential – Lloyd Charmers (actually with The Hippy Boys) (Prod: Lloyd Charmers)
6. Bongo Nyah – The Little Roys (actually by Little Roy And Don Carlos) (Prod: Lloyd Daley)

SIDE 2
1. Every Beat Of My Heart – Owen Gray (actually with The Rudies) (Prod: Derrick Morgan (UK))
2. In This World – The Federals (Prod: Derrick Harriott)
3. Find Yourself A Fool – The Techniques (Prod: Winston Riley)
4. Danny Boy – King Cannon [Carl Bryan] (Prod: Harry Johnson)
5. Since You've Been Gone – Eric Fratter (Prod: Harry Johnson)
6. Your Sweet Love – The Soul Cats (Prod: Ewan McDermott)

SECO 19 – *Bullet – A World Of Reggae* – Various Artists (1970)

SIDE 1
1. Throw Me Corn – Winston Shand (actually with The Sheiks) (Prod: Ranny Williams)
2. Heart Don't Leap – Dennis Walks (Prod: Harry Mudie)
3. Copy Cats – The Clan (actually Derrick Morgan, Stranger Cole And Owen Gray With The Rudies) (Prod: Derrick Morgan (UK))
4. Each Time – The Ebony Sisters And The Bunny Lee All Stars (Prod: Bunny Lee)
5. Come By Here – Winston And Rupert (Prod: Harry Mudie)
6. What's Your Excuse – The Hippy Boys (actually with Count Sticky) (Prod: Ranny Williams)

SIDE 2
1. Summer Place – Ranny Williams And The Hippy Boys (Prod: Ranny Williams)
2. I'm Just A Minstrel – The Kingstonians (Prod: Albert GeorgeMurphy)
3. Love Of My Life – Dennis Walks (Prod: Harry Mudie)
4. Hog In A Mi Minti – The Hippy Boys (actually with Winston Shand) (Prod: Ranny Williams)
5. That's My Life (wrong title: possibly called 'Because You Lied') – Fitzroy Sterling (actually with The Rudies) (Prod: Fitzroy Sterling (UK))
6. Let Me Tell You Boy – The Ebony Sisters (Prod: Harry Mudie)

SECO 20 – *A Gift From Pama* – Various Artists (1970)

SIDE 1
1. Facts Of Life – The Mellotones (Prod: Lee Perry)
2. If It Don't Work Out (actually titled 'Then You Can Tell Me Goodbye') – Pat Kelly (Prod: Bunny Lee)
3. The Champ – The Mohawks (Prod: Alan Hawkshaw And Harry Palmer (UK))
4. Everybody Needs Love – Slim Smith (Prod: Bunny Lee)
5. Who You Gonna Run To? – The Techniques (Prod: Winston Riley)
6. Sock It To 'Em Soul Brother – Bill Moss (Prod: Bill Moss For Bell Records (USA))

SIDE 2
1. History (actually titled 'Wonderful World') – Harry And Radcliffe (Prod: H Robinson)
2. Everyday Will Be A Holiday – Roy Docker (Prod: Roy Smith (UK))
3. Hold Down – The Kingstonians (Prod: Derrick Harriott)
4. Throw Me Corn – Winston Shand (actually with The Sheiks) (Prod: Ranny Williams)
5. I Know It's Alright – The Crowns (Prod: Harry Palmer (UK))
6. Strange – Dobby Dobson (Prod: Rupie Edwards)

SECO 21 – Untraced

SECO 22 – *Laugh With Bim And Bam* – Bim, Bam And Clover (live recording – continuous dialogue with no individual tracks) (1970)

SECO 23 – Untraced

SECO 24 – *Many Moods Of The Upsetters* – The Upsetters (except where otherwise specified) (Prod: L Perry) (1970)

SIDE 1
1. Ex-Ray Vision
2. Can't Take It Anymore (actually by David Isaacs)
3. Soul Stew

4. Low Lights
5. Cloud Nine (actually by Carl Dawkins)
6. Beware

SIDE 2
1. Serious Joke
2. Goosey (actually by Pat Satchmo)
3. Prove It
4. Boss Society (actually by Pat Satchmo)
5. Mean And Dangerous
6. Games People Play
7. Extra (this track not credited on sleeve or disc)

SECO 25 – *House In Session* – Lloyd Charmers And The Hippy Boys (1970) except where otherwise specified

SIDE 1
1. Soul At Large (Prod: Lloyd Charmers)
2. Soul Of England (actually by The Jokers) (Prod: Lloyd Charmers)
3. African Zulu (Prod: Lloyd Charmers And Herman Chin-Loy)
4. Confidential (Prod: Lloyd Charmers)
5. House In Session (actually by Tommy Cowan And The Hippy Boys) (Prod: Lloyd Charmers)
6. Cooyah (actually titled 'Cat Nip') (Prod: Lloyd Charmers)

SIDE 2
1. Shanghai (Prod: Lloyd Charmers)
2. Everybody Needs Love (Prod: Winston Lowe)
3. Stronger (Prod: Winston Lowe)
4. Sweet Sweet (actually by Lloyd Robinson) (Prod: Winston Lowe)
5. Ling Tong Ting (Prod: Winston Lowe)
6. Yes Sah (Prod: Lloyd Charmers)

SECO 26–29 – Untraced

SECO 30 – *Rising Stars At Evening Time* – Gordon Langford Orchestra, Shake Keane And The Hastings Girl Choir (non-reggae – no track listing available) (1970)

Note: this was the first album in Pama's 'Airborne' series and has the added catalogue number 'NBP 1000' in brackets, NBP standing for Noel Brown Productions. See also PSP 1004.

SECO 31 – *First Lady Of Reggae* – Doreen Shaeffer (1970) (all tracks produced by Bunny Lee)

SIDE 1
1. Walk Through This World
2. Everybody Needs Love
3. No Matter What
4. Try To Remember
5. How Long Will It Take
6. If It Don't Work Out (actually 'Then You Can Tell Me Goodbye')

SIDE 2
1. As Long As He Needs Me
2. How Much Is That Doggie In The Window?
3. I Fall In Love Everyday
4. One Of Us Will Weep
5. June Night
6. Love Me With All Your Heart

SECO 32 – *Birth Control* – Various Artists (1970)

SIDE 1
1. Birth Control – Lloyd Tyrell [Lloyd Charmers] (Prod: Lloyd Charmers)
2. The Pill – Bim, Bam And Clover (Prod: Derrick Morgan (UK))
3. Sock It Onto I – Lloyd Tyrell (actually by Max Romeo) (Prod: Bunny Lee)
4. Feel It – Max Romeo (Prod: Bunny Lee)
5. Ram You Hard – John Lennon (actually by The Bleechers) (Prod: Lee Perry)
6. Benwood Dick – Laurel Aitken (Prod: Laurel Aitken (UK))

SIDE 2
1. Wine Her Goosie – Max Romeo (Prod: Derrick Morgan (UK))
2. Satan Girl – The Ethiopians (Prod: Lloyd Daley)
3. Adults Only (actually titled 'The Big Race') [Mento] – Calypso Joe (actually by Lord Power) (Prod: Harry Johnson)
4. Pussy Price – Laurel Aitken (Prod: Laurel Aitken (UK))
5. Caught You (actually titled 'Musical Bop') – The Upsetters (actually by Count Sticky) (Prod: Ranny Williams)
6. Fire In Your Wire (actually titled 'Madame Streggae') – Laurel Aitken (actually By Girlie) (Prod: Laurel Aitken)

SECO 33 – *Strange* – Dobby Dobson (Prod: Rupie Edwards) (1970)

SIDE 1
1. Strange
2. Crazy
3. Masquerade Is Over

4. That Wonderful Sound
5. Don't Make Me Over

SIDE 2
1. Baby Make It Soon
2. What Love Has Joined Together
3. I Wasn't Born Yesterday
4. Cry A Little Cry
5. Your New Love

Note: this album was also issued by Trojan with the same track listing but a different title and sleeve. Both releases are remarkably thin on the ground, possibly because both companies withdrew their copies after limited pressings due to the obvious duplication of activity.

ECO 34 – *Reggae For Days* – Various Artists (1970)

SIDE 1
1. Souls Of Africa – Tiger (Prod: Laurel Aitken (UK))
2. What A Cute Man – Max Romeo (Prod: Bunny Lee)
3. The Worm (actually 'King Of The Worm') – Lloyd Robinson (Prod: Lloyd Daley)
4. Bumper To Bumper – Eric Barnett (actually by Unidentified Instrumental Outfit) (Prod: Alvin Ranglin)
5. Catch This Sound – Martin Riley (actually with The Uniques) (Prod: Martin Riley)
6. Since You Left – The Maytones (Prod: Alvin Ranglin)

SIDE 2
1. Jumping Dick – Gloria's All Stars (actually The GG All Stars) (Prod: Alvin Ranglin)
2. Shocks Of Mighty – Dave Barker (actually with The Upsetters) (Prod: Lee Perry)
3. Sometimes – John Holt (Prod: Bunny Lee)
4. London Bridge – Neville Hinds (actually with The Matadors) (Prod: Lloyd Daley)
5. Leaving On A Jet Plane – Glen Adams (Prod: Glen Adams)
6. Tammy – Pat Kelly (Prod: Pat Kelly)

ECO 35 – *Young, Gifted And Black* – Various Artists (1970)

SIDE 1
1. And Black – Denzil (Dennis) And Jennifer (Jones) (Prod: Derrick Morgan (UK))
2. Artibella – Ken Boothe (Prod: Phil Pratt)
3. Take Me Back – Laurel Aitken (Prod: Laurel Aitken (UK))
4. Dollars And Bonds – Lloyd Tyrell [Lloyd Charmers] (Prod: Lloyd Charmers)
5. In This World – The Federals (Prod: Derrick Harriott)
6. How Much Is That Doggie In The Window? – Doreen Shaeffer (Prod: Bunny Lee)

SIDE 2
1. Standing At The Corner – Winston Groovy (Prod: Laurel Aitken (UK))

2. Scrooge – Little Roy (Prod: Lloyd Daley)
3. Return Of Jack Slade – Derrick Morgan (Prod: Derrick Morgan (UK))
4. Census Taker – Rupie Edwards' All Stars (Prod: Rupie Edwards)
5. Gold Digger – The Little Roys (actually by The Wailing Souls) (Prod: Lloyd Daley)
6. Need To Belong – Derrick (Morgan) And Jennifer (Jones) (Prod: Derrick Morgan (UK))

FTF Series

FTF 1001 – *The Trouble With Adam* – Exordium

FTF 1002 – *Time To Live* – The Harmonizers

FTF 1003 – *Bound For Glory* – Various Artists

Note: the short-lived FTF ('Face To Face') series consisted of these three gospel-oriented albums for which no track listings, artist credits or years of release are available.

PMLP/PMLP-SP Series

PMLP 1 – *Remember Otis* – Beverley Simmons (all tracks produced by Harry Palmer (UK)) (1968) (first issue with 'altar' sleeve)

SIDE 1
1. Down In The Valley
2. My Boy
3. Old Man Trouble
4. Satisfaction
5. I've Been Loving You Too Long
6. Mr Pitiful

SIDE 2
1. Sad Song
2. These Arms Of Mine
3. Pain In My Heart
4. My Lover's Prayer
5. That's How Strong My Love Is
6. Respect

PMLP-SP 2 – *West Coast Rock And Roll* – The Milwaukee Coasters (Prod: Palmer brothers (UK)) (1968) (first issue in pink sleeve)

SIDE 1
1. Rock Around The Clock

2. Josephine
3. Caldonia
4. Hey Charlie
5. Sick And Tired (Oh Babe)
6. Three Months, Three Weeks, Three Days

SIDE 2
1. When The Saints Go Marching In
2. Whole Lotta Shakin' Going On
3. Don't Look Back
4. Choo Choo Ch'boogie
5. Treat Me Nice
6. Cool Mover
7. Good Golly Miss Molly

PMLP-SP3 – *Ready Steady Go – Rocksteady* – Various Artists (1968)

SIDE 1
1. Soul Food – Lyn Taitt And The Jets (Prod: Lynford Anderson)
2. My Time Is The Right Time – Alton Ellis (Prod: Alton Ellis and Johnny Moore)
3. CN Express, Part 1 – Clancy All Stars (actually Clancy Eccles, Lee Perry And Count Sticky) (Prod: Clancy Eccles)
4. Where In This World – Carlton Alphonso (Prod: Roy Bennett)
5. Eastern Promise – Earl St Joseph (Prod: Harry Palmer (UK))
6. You Were Meant For Me – The Groovers (actually by Lee Perry) (Prod: Clancy Eccles)
7. What Will Your Mama Say – Clancy Eccles (Prod: Clancy Eccles)

SIDE 2
1. Fiddlesticks – Tommy Mckenzie Orchestra (Prod: Harry Palmer (UK))
2. Say What You're Saying – Eric 'Monty' Morris (Prod: Clancy Eccles)
3. The Fight (actually 'The Big Fight') – Clancy Eccles (Prod: Clancy Eccles)
4. Heartbeat – Ernest Ranglin (Prod: Clancy Eccles)
5. The Message – Alton Ellis (Prod: Alton Ellis)
6. They Wash – The Joyce Bond Show (Prod: Carl Palmer (UK))
7. Bang Bang Lulu – Lloyd Tyrell [Lloyd Charmers] (Prod: Lynford Anderson)

PMLP 4 – *Bang Bang Lulu* – Various Artists (1969) (album issued in three different-coloured sleeves – one black, one orange, one red)

SIDE 1
1. Bang Bang Lulu – Lloyd Tyrell [Lloyd Charmers] (Prod: Lynford Anderson)
2. Wet Dream (actually 'Mr Ryha') – Max Romeo (actually Lloyd Tyrell [Lloyd Charmers]) (Prod: Winston Lowe)
3. Making Love – Devon (Russell) And The Tartans (Prod: H Robinson)
4. Push Push – The Termites (actually by The Hi-Tones) (Prod: Eric Barnett)

5. Simple Simon – Eric 'Monty' Morris (Prod: Clancy Eccles)
7. How Come (actually 'I Come') – Lloyd Tyrell (actually by Lee Perry And The Gaylets) (Prod: Lynford Anderson)

SIDE 2
1. Lulu Returns – Lloyd Tyrell [Lloyd Charmers] (Prod: Lynford Anderson)
2. I Love You – Derrick Morgan (Prod: Derrick Morgan)
3. Soul Food – Lyn Taitt And The Jets (Prod: Lynford Anderson)
4. Push It Up – The Termites (Prod: H Robinson)
5. Money Girl – Larry Marshall (Prod: Ken Lack)
6. Rhythm Hips – Ronald Russell (Prod: Eric Barnett)

PMLP 5 – *The Champ* – The Mohawks (Prod: Alan Hawkshaw and Harry Palmer (UK)) (1969)

SIDE 1
1. The Champ
2. Hip Jigger
3. Sweet Soul Music
4. Dr Jekyll And Hyde Park
5. Senior Thump
6. Landscape

SIDE 2
1. Baby Hold On
2. Funky Broadway
3. Rocky Mountain Roundabout
4. Sound Of The Witch Doctors
5. Beat Me Till I'm Blue
6. Can You Hear Me?

PMLP 6 – *Made Of Gold* – The Crowns (Prod: Harry Palmer (UK)) (1969)

SIDE 1
1. Mellow Moonlight
2. I Surrender
3. Let's Go Baby
4. Mr Success
5. My Baby Just Cares For Me
6. Jerking The Dog

SIDE 2
1. She Ain't Gonna Do Right
2. I Know It's Alright
3. I'm So Proud
4. Would I Love You?

345

5. I Need Your Loving
6. Keep Me Going

PMLP-SP7 – *Rocksteady Cool* – Various Artists (1969)

SIDE 1
1. Train To Vietnam (actually 'Train To South Vietnam') – The Rudies (Prod: Palmer bros)
2. Hey Boy, Hey Girl – Derrick (Morgan) And Patsy (Todd) (Prod: Derrick Morgan)
3. Bye Bye Love – Alton Ellis (Prod: Clancy Eccles)
4. Young Love – Horace (Faith) And The Imperials (Prod: H Robinson)
5. On The Town – Bunny And Ruddy (Prod: Ken Lack)
6. Searching – Junior Smith (Prod: Roy Smith (UK))
7. Mini Really Fit Dem – The Soul Flames (actually by Alton Ellis And The Flames) (Prod: Alton Ellis)

SIDE 2
1. La La Means I Love You – Alton Ellis (Prod: Alton Ellis)
2. Blue Socks – Rico Rodriguez (Prod: Harry Palmer (UK))
3. Cover Me – Fitz (Fitzroy Sterling) And The Coozers (Prod: Jeff Palmer (UK))
4. Rhythm And Soul – Bobby Kalphat (actually with The Caltone All Stars) (Prod: Ken Lack)
5. Engine 59 – Dandy And The Rudies (Prod: Jeff Palmer (UK))
6. If Music Be The Food Of Love – Derrick Morgan (actually by unidentified male vocalist) (Prod: Derrick Morgan)
7. Rocksteady Cool – Frederick Bell (Prod: Carl Bradford)

PMLP-SP8 – *Soul Sauce From Pama* – Various Artists (1969)

SIDE 1
1. Jerking The Dog – The Crowns (Prod: Harry Palmer (UK))
2. Feel Good All Over – Betty Lavette (Prod: Don Gardner (UK))
3. The Good Ol'days – Bobby Patterson And The Mustangs (Prod: Jetstar Records, USA)
4. Oh Babe – The Milwaukee Coasters (Prod: Palmer brothers (UK))
5. Tip Toe – Norman T Washington (Prod: Harry Palmer (UK))
6. Baby Hold On – The Mohawks (Prod: Alan Hawkshaw and Harry Palmer (UK))

SIDE 2
1. Dr Goldfoot And His Bikini Machine – The Beas (Prod: Harry Palmer (UK))
2. Same Thing All Over – Norman T Washington (Prod: Carl Palmer (UK))
3. Soul Man – Rico Rodriguez (Prod: Palmer brothers (UK))
4. I'm An Outcast – Roy Docker (Prod: Roy Smith (UK))
5. What A Guy – Beverley Simmons (Prod: Harry Palmer (UK))
6. Broadway Ain't Funky No More – Bobby Patterson And The Mustangs (Prod: Jetstar Records, USA)

PMLP-SP9 – *Remember Otis* – Beverley Simmons (Prod: Harry Palmer (UK))
   (1969) (reissue of PMLP 1 in second (black and white) sleeve)

PMLP-SP10 – *The Best Party Album* – The Milwaukee Coasters (reissue of
   'West Coast Rock And Roll' on PMLP-SP2 in red, yellow and black sleeve) (1969)

PMLP 11 – *A Dream* – Max Romeo. Tracks marked * backed by The Rudies (and
   produced by Derrick Morgan (UK)); tracks marked ** backed by The Hippy Boys (and
   produced by Ranny Williams (UK)) (1969)

   SIDE 1
   1. Wet Dream (re-recorded version)*
   2. A No Fe Me Pickney*
   3. Far Far Away**
   4. The Horn*
   5. Hear My Plea*
   6. Love**

   SIDE 2
   1. I Don't Want To Lose Your Love*
   2. Wood Under Cellar*
   3. Wine Her Goosie*
   4. Club Raid*
   5. You Can't Stop Me*

PMLP-12 – *Pat Kelly Sings* – Pat Kelly (all tracks produced by Bunny Lee except those marked
   *, which were Lee Perry productions) (1969)

   SIDE 1
   1. Since You're Gone *
   2. Troubling Mind
   3. Tracks Of My Tears
   4. How Long Will It Take?
   5. A Thousand Years
   6. Try To Remember

   SIDE 2
   1. Dark End Of The Street *
   2. Festival Time
   3. Workman Song
   4. If It Don't Work Out (actually titled 'Then You Can Tell Me Goodbye')
   5. The Great Pretender
   6. Never Give Up

PMP Series

PMP 2000 – *Revival Time* – The Watford Gospel Singers (gospel – track listing unavailable) (1971)

PMP 2001 – *Reggae Spectacular With Strings* – Various Artists (1971)

SIDE 1
1. Maybe The Next Time – Pat Rhoden (actually with The Mohawks) (Prod: Derrick Morgan (UK))
2. I Wish I Was An Apple – Derrick Morgan (actually with The Mohawks) (Prod: Derrick Morgan (UK))
3. Sugar Dumpling – Owen Gray (Prod: Sidney Crooks (UK))
4. Sweeter Than Honey – Norman T Washington (Prod: Harry Palmer (UK))
5. Here Is My Heart – Winston Groovy (Prod: Laurel Aitken (UK))
6. Don't Let Him Take Your Love From Me – The Marvels (Prod: Derrick Morgan (UK))

SIDE 2
1. Something On My Mind – Errol Dixon (Prod: Errol Dixon (UK))
2. Take Back Your Nicklet – Ferdinand (Dixon) And Dill (Bishop) (Prod: Derrick Morgan (UK))
3. Never Love Another (actually titled 'I'll Never Love Any Girl (The Way I Love You)') – Laurel Aitken (Prod: Laurel Aitken (UK))
4. I'll Do It – Derrick (Morgan) And Paulette (Morgan) (Prod: Derrick Morgan)
5. Fiddlesticks – Tommy Mckenzie Orchestra (Prod: Harry Palmer (UK))
6. For Once In My Life – Slim Smith (Prod: Bunny Lee)

PMP 2002 – *Straighten Up, Volume 1* – Various Artists (1971)

SIDE 1
1. Let It Be – The Mohawks (Prod: Graham Hawk (UK))
2. Last Goodbye – Norman T Washington (Prod: Harry Palmer (UK))
3. Without My Love – Little Roy (actually with Joy Lindsay) (Prod: Lloyd Daley)
4. Got To Get You Off My Mind – Shel Alterman (actually with The Mohawks) (Prod: Harry Palmer (UK))
5. Chariot Coming – The Viceroys (Prod: Sidney Crooks)
6. Straighten Up – The Maytones (Prod: Alvin Ranglin)

SIDE 2
1. Give Her All The Love I've Got – John Holt (Prod: Bunny Lee)
2. Bring Back Your Love – Owen Gray (Prod: Derrick Morgan (UK))
3. Yellow Bird – Winston Groovy (Prod: Laurel Aitken (UK))
4. Someday We'll Be Together – The Marvels (Prod: Derrick Morgan (UK))
5. Too Experienced – Winston Francis (Prod: Coxson Dodd)
6. Pick Your Pocket – The Versatiles (Prod: Laurel Aitken (UK))

PMP 2003 – *Something Sweet The Lady* – Various Artists (1971)

SIDE 1
1. Something Sweet The Lady – Dora (King) And Joe (Marks) (actually with The Pete Weston Orchestra) (Prod: Pete Weston)
2. Nice Grind – The Rebels (Prod: Sidney Crooks (UK))
3. It Don't Sweet Me – Laurel Aitken (Prod: Laurel Aitken (UK))
4. Big Head Walking Stick – Bim And Clover (Prod: Derrick Morgan (UK))
5. My Dickie – Derrick Morgan (Prod: Derrick Morgan (UK))
6. Where It Sore – King Sutch (actually by Count Sticky) (Prod: Ranny Williams)

SIDE 2
1. You Run Come – Little Roy (Prod: Lloyd Daley)
2. Exposure – Lloyd Tyrell [Lloyd Charmers] (Prod: Lloyd Charmers)
3. Fish In The Pot – Max Romeo (Prod: Derrick Morgan (UK))
4. Woman A Love In The Nightime [MENTO/CALYPSO] – Lord Spoon And David (actually by Mix Flour And Sugar) (Prod: Alvin Ranglin)
5. Winey For Ten Cents – The Soul Mates (Prod: Bunny Lee)
6. Blues Dance – Girlie And Laurel Aitken (Prod: Laurel Aitken (UK))

PMP 2004 – *African Melody* – Various Artists (1971)

SIDE 1
1. African Melody – The GG All Stars (Prod: Alvin Ranglin)
2. Man From Carolina – The GG All Stars (Prod: Alvin Ranglin)
3. Stand For Your Right – Lloyd Tyrell [Lloyd Charmers] (Prod: Lloyd Charmers)
4. Warrior – Johnny (Osbourne) And The Sensations (Prod: Winston Riley)
5. Games People Play – Winston Francis (Prod: Coxson Dodd)
6. Oh Me Oh My – Lloyd Tyrell [Lloyd Charmers] (Prod: Lloyd Charmers)

SIDE 2
1. Immigrant's Plight – Bim, Bam And Clover (Prod: Derrick Morgan (UK))
2. Freedom Street – Ernest Wilson (actually by Fitzroy Sterling) (Prod: Fitzroy Sterling (UK))
3. Salaam – Charles Organaire (Prod: Willie Francis)
4. Return Of Herbert Spliffington – Carl Bailey (actually by Rupie Edwards And Sidy) (Prod: Rupie Edwards)
5. Look Who A Bust Style – The Meditators (Prod: Rupie Edwards)
6. Blessed Are The Meek – Slim Smith And The Uniques (Prod: Bunny Lee)

PMP 2005 – *This Is Reggae, Volume 2* – Various Artists (1971)

SIDE 1
1. My Sweet Lord – Fitzroy Sterling (Prod: Sidney Crooks (UK))
2. Denver – Alton Ellis And The Flames (Prod: Alton Ellis)
3. History Of Africa – The Classics (UK) (actually Denzil Dennis And Milton Hamilton) (Prod: Laurel Aitken (UK))

4. Feel It – Sister (actually by Paulette And Gee) (Prod: Alvin Ranglin)
5. Band Of Gold – Joan Ross [TT Ross] (Prod: Derrick Morgan (UK))
6. I'll Never Fall In Love With You Again – Winston Heywood (actually with The Fud Christian All Stars) (Prod: Fud Christian)

SIDE 2
1. Groove Me – Owen Gray (Prod: Sidney Crooks (UK))
2. Keep On Trying – Little Roy (Prod: Lloyd Daley)
3. Back To Africa – Alton Ellis (Prod: Lloyd Daley)
4. Lord Deliver Us – Alton Ellis (Prod: Lloyd Daley)
5. Heaven Help Us All – Winston Groovy (Prod: Sidney Crooks (UK))
6. Maccabee Version – Max Romeo (Prod: Willie Francis)

PMP 2006 – *Hot Numbers, Volume 1* – Various Artists (1971)

SIDE 1
1. Candida – Owen Gray (Prod: Sidney Crooks (UK))
2. Let The Power Fall – Max Romeo (actually with The Hippy Boys) (Prod: Derrick Morgan)
3. Cracklin' Rosie – Lloyd Jackson (Prod: Derrick Morgan (UK))
4. My Love (aka 'Can't Hide The Feeling') – Rupie Edwards All Stars (actually by The Gaylads) (Prod: Rupie Edwards And BB Seaton)
5. All Combine (Part 1) – The Upsetters (Prod: Lee Perry)
6. Knock Three Times – Carl (actually Carl Lewis) (Prod: Sidney Crooks (UK))

SIDE 2
1. I Found A Man In My Bed – Eugene Paul (Prod: Sidney Crooks (UK))
2. Fire Fire – The Youth [I Jah Man Levi] (Prod: Jeff Palmer (UK))
3. Nothing Has Changed – DD (Denzil) Dennis (Prod: Ranny Williams (UK))
4. Do Something – Charley Ace (Prod: Alvin Ranglin)
5. Talk About Love – Pat Kelly (Prod: Phil Pratt)
6. Cholera – The Justins (actually The Jesters) (Prod: Lloyd Daley)

PMP 2007 – *Straighten Up, Volume 2* – Various Artists (1971)

SIDE 1
1. Guilty – Tiger (Prod: Laurel Aitken (UK))
2. Just My Imagination – Dave Barker And The Charmers (Prod: Lloyd Charmers)
3. Farewell My Darling – Eugene Paul (Prod: Sidney Crooks (UK))
4. Don't You Weep – Max Romeo (Prod: Derrick Morgan)
5. John Crow Skank – Derrick Morgan (Prod: Derrick Morgan)
6. Free The People – Winston Groovy (Prod: Winston Tucker and Norton York (UK))
7. My Girl – Slim Smith (Prod: Slim Smith)

SIDE 2
1. Monkey Spanner – Larry And Lloyd (actually by Denzil Dennis And Pete Campbell) (Prod: Laurel Aitken (UK))

2. Love And Emotion – The Righteous Flames (actually with Winston Jarrett) (Prod: Derrick Morgan)
3. Put Your Sweet Lips – Raphael Stewart And The Hot Tops (Prod: Raphael Stewart)
4. I Wanna Be Loved – Winston Groovy (Prod: Winston Tucker (UK))
5. Cheerio Baby (actually 'Cherry Oh Baby') – The Classics (UK) (actually Denzil Dennis And Eugene Paul) (Prod: Lee Perry)
6. Same Thing For Breakfast – Winston (Groovy) And Pat (Rhoden) (Prod: Winston Tucker and Pat Rhoden (UK))
7. Every Night – Ruddy (Grant) And (Sketto) Richards (Prod: Laurel Aitken (UK))

PMP 2008 – *This Is Reggae, Volume 3* – Various Artists (1971)

SIDE 1
1. Piece Of My Heart – Mahalia Saunders (actually Hortense Ellis) (Prod: Lee Perry)
2. What Will Your Mama Say (1967 Cut With Added Strings) – Clancy Eccles (Prod: Clancy Eccles and Norton York)
3. Hold Them 1, 2, 3, 4 (actually titled 'The Great Roy Shirley') – Roy Shirley (Prod: Roy Shirley)
4. Blackman's Pride – Alton Ellis (Prod: Sidney Crooks (UK))
5. African Museum (actually titled 'Jah Picture') – Sounds Combine (actually by Winston Wright) (Prod: Errol Dunkley)
6. Let It Be Me – The Cariboes (Prod: Laurel Aitken (UK))

SIDE 2
1. Seven In One Medley – The Gaylads (Prod: Herman Chin-Loy and BB Seaton)
2. Standing By – Derrick Morgan (Prod: Derrick Morgan)
3. Have You Ever Been Hurt? – Tiger (Prod: Laurel Aitken (UK))
4. I'll Never Let You Down – Laurel Aitken (Prod: Laurel Aitken (UK))
5. One Minute To Zero (1966) – Ken Walker (actually by The Kent Walker Band) (Prod: Kent Walker)
6. Freedom Train – The Gladiators (Prod: Lloyd Daley)

PMP 2009 – *Hot Numbers, Volume 2* – Various Artists (1972)

SIDE 1
1. One Night Of Sin – The Slickers (actually by Jackie Brown And The Gaytones) (Prod: Sonia Pottinger)
2. Rudies' Medley – Third And Fourth Generation (actually by Peter Tosh And The Soulmates) (Prod: Joe Gibbs)
3. Royal Chord – The Gaylads (actually by The Melodians) (Prod: BB Seaton)
4. Maga Dog – Peter Tosh (actually with The Soulmates) (Prod: Joe Gibbs)
5. Sincerely – Owen Gray (Prod: Lord Koos (UK))
6. Rasta Bandwagon – Max Romeo (actually with Lee Perry) (Prod: Winston Holness)
7. Soulful Love – Pat Kelly (Prod: Phil Pratt)

SIDE 2

1. Buttercup – Winston Scotland (Prod: Tony Robinson)
2. You'll Be Sorry – David Isaacs (Prod: Lee Perry)
3. In The Ghetto – Rip 'N Lan (actually by Zip And Len) (Prod: Laurel Aitken (UK))
4. The Coming Of Jah – Max Romeo (actually with Niney) (Prod: Winston Holness and Lee Perry)
5. Dandy Shandy, Version 4 – Impact All Stars (with unidentified DJ) (Prod: Victor Chin)
6. Walk A Little Bit Prouder – Carl Dawkins (Prod: Max Romeo)
7. You Gonna Miss Me – Owen Gray (Prod: Sidney Crooks (UK))

PMP 2010 – *Let The Power Fall* – Max Romeo (1972)

SIDE 1

1. Missing You (Prod: Victor Chin)
2. Puppet On A String (Prod: Derrick Morgan)
3. Crackling Rose (Prod: Derrick Morgan)
4. Chi Chi Bud (Prod: Victor Chin)
5. Black Equality (Prod: Pete Weston)
6. Let The Power Fall (Prod: Derrick Morgan)

SIDE 2

1. Don't You Weep (Prod: Derrick Morgan)
2. Mother Oh Mother (Prod: Rupie Edwards)
3. Chicken Thief (Prod: Derrick Morgan)
4. Ginalship (Prod: Lee Perry)
5. Maccabee Version (Prod: Winston Francis)
6. Batchelor Boy (Prod: Derrick Morgan)

PMP 2011 – *Free The People* – Winston Groovy (all are UK productions) (1972)

SIDE 1

1. I Like The Way (You Hug And Kiss Me) (Prod: Winston Tucker)
2. I've Got To Find A Way To Get Maria Back (Prod: Winston Tucker)
3. Not Now (Prod: Winston Tucker)
4. To The Other Man (Prod: Winston Tucker)
5. Tell Me Why (Prod: Winston Tucker)
6. Yellow Bird (Prod: Laurel Aitken)

SIDE 2

1. I Wanna Be There (Prod: Winston Tucker)
2. Don't Break My Heart (Prod: Sidney Crooks)
3. Free The People (Prod: Winston Tucker)*
4. Standing At The Corner (Prod: Laurel Aitken)
5. The First Time (Prod: Winston Tucker)
6. Groovin' (Prod: Laurel Aitken)

(* this is not the same cut as that on Pama Supreme PS323A)

PMP 2012 – *Reggae To Reggae* – Various Artists (1972)

SIDE 1
1. Lively Up Yourself – Bob Marley And The Wailers (Prod: Tuff Gong)
2. Jamaican Girl – Roy Shirley (Prod: Roy Shirley)
3. Send Me Some Loving – Slim Smith (Prod: Bunny Lee)
4. You Don't Care – Lloyd Parks (Prod: Tony Robinson)
5. I Want To Go Back Home – The Groovers (Prod: F Crossfield)
6. This Tropical Land (aka 'This Beautiful Land') – The Melodians (Prod: Tony Brevett)
7. Beat Down Babylon – Junior Byles (Prod: Lee Perry)

SIDE 2
1. Black Cinderella – Errol Dunkley (Prod: Jimmy Radway)
2. Butter And Bread – Lloyd Young (Prod: Glen Brown)
3. Screw Face – Bob Marley And The Wailers (Prod: Tuff Gong)
4. Solid As A Rock – The Ethiopians (Prod: Rupie Edwards)
7. My Only Love (actually 'My One And Only Lover') – Gregory Isaacs (Prod: Gregory Isaacs)
6. High School Serenade – Lennox Brown (Prod: Tony Robinson)
7. Public Enemy Number One – Max Romeo (Prod: Lee Perry)

PMP 2013 – *Soulful Love* – Pat Kelly (Prod: Phil Pratt) (1972)

SIDE 1
1. Talk About Love
2. Soulful Love
3. I Wish It Would Rain
4. Rain From The Skies
5. Bridge Over Troubled Waters

SIDE 2
1. How Long Will It Take
2. That Special Love
3. Steal Away
4. It Couldn't Be
5. He Ain't Heavy, He's My Brother

Note: while this album appeared in Pama's release sheets, its issue is most certainly unsubstantiated.

PMP 2014 – *Straighten Up, Volume 3* – Various Artists (1972)

SIDE 1
1. Rum Rhythm (actually titled 'Mucking Fuch' – (Roy) Shirley And (Lloyd) Charmers (Prod: Lloyd Charmers)
2. South Of The Border – Denzil Dennis (Prod: Ranny Williams (UK))

3. Nanny Skank – U Roy (Prod: Karl Pitterson)
4. Bend Down Low – The Groovers (Prod: Derrick Morgan (UK))
5. Greatest Hits, Parts 1 And 2 – Owen Gray (Prod: Ranny Williams (UK))
6. Rocksteady – The Marvels (Prod: Lloyd Charmers)
7. A Sugar – Roy Shirley (Prod: Roy Shirley)

SIDE 2
1. Pray For Me – Max Romeo (Prod: Sonia Pottinger)
2. Linger A While – John Holt (Prod: Lloyd Daley)
3. Aily And Ailaloo – Niney And Max Romeo (Prod: Winston Holness)
4. Searching So Long – Derrick Morgan (Prod: Derrick Morgan (UK))
5. Way Down South – U Roy (Prod: Alvin Ranglin)
6. Nothing Can Separate Us – Owen Gray (Prod: Sidney Crooks (UK))
7. Plenty Of One (Medley) – Derrick Morgan (Prod: Derrick Morgan)

PMP 2015 – *Sixteen Dynamic Reggae Hits* – Various Artists (1972)

SIDE 1
1. Sugar Pie (actually titled 'I Can't Help Myself') – The Hammers (Prod: Tom of Brixton (UK))
2. Shocks Of Mighty – Dave Barker (actually with The Upsetters) (Prod: Lee Perry)
3. Girl What You Doing To Me – Owen Gray (actually with The Rudies) (Prod: Derrick Morgan)
4. Guilty – Tiger (Prod: Laurel Aitken (UK))
5. Clint Eastwood – The Upsetters (actually with Lee Perry) (Prod: Lee Perry)
6. Let It Be – The Mohawks (Prod: Graham Hawk (UK))
7. Seven Letters – Derrick Morgan (Prod: Derrick Morgan)
8. How Long Will It Take – Pat Kelly (Prod: Bunny Lee)

SIDE 2
1. Everybody Needs Love – Slim Smith (Prod: Bunny Lee)
2. Let The Power Fall – Max Romeo (actually with The Hippy Boys) (Prod: Derrick Morgan)
3. Mr Popcorn – Laurel Aitken (Prod: Laurel Aitken (UK))
4. Throw Me Corn (actually 'Hold Down') – Winston Shand (actually by The Kingstonians) (Prod: Derrick Harriott)
5. Bumper To Bumper – Eric Barnett (actually by Unidentified Instrumental Outfit) (Prod: Alvin Ranglin)
6. Maybe The Next Time – Pat Rhoden (actually with The Mohawks) (Prod: Derrick Morgan (UK))
7. Who You Gonna Run To? – The Techniques (Prod: Winston Riley)
8. Chariot Coming – The Viceroys (Prod: Sidney Crooks)

PMP 2016 – *This Is Reggae, Volume 4* – Various Artists (1972)

SIDE 1

1. Mr Postman – Cynthia Richards (Prod: Cynthia Richards And Irving (Al) Brown)
2. The Time Has Come – Slim Smith (Prod: Bunny Lee)
3. I Miss My Schooldays – BB Seaton (Prod: Lloyd Charmers)
4. Sad Movies – Barbara Jones (Prod: B Brooks)
5. I'm Feeling Lonely – The Maytones (actually by Vernon Buckley) (Prod: Alvin Ranglin)
6. This Is My Story – The Clarendonians (Prod: Bunny Lee)
7. Are You Sure – Max Romeo (Prod: Rupie Edwards)

SIDE 2

1. Darling Forever – The Clarendonians (Prod: Peter Austin and Ken Wilson)
2. Howdy And Tenky – (Emmanuel) Flowers And Alvin (Ranglin) (Prod: Alvin Ranglin)
3. You've Lost That Loving Feeling – The Heptones (Prod: Rupie Edwards)
4. The King Man Is Back – The Hoffner Brothers (Prod: Glen Brown)
5. Ten Times Sweeter Than You – Tony Gordon (actually by Winston Francis) (Prod: Lynford Anderson)
6. Hail The Man – Owen Gray (Prod: Ranny Williams (UK))
7. Jesamine – Junior English (Prod: Sidney Crooks (UK))

PMP 2017 – *Straighten Up, Volume 4* – Various Artists (1973)

SIDE 1

1. Soul Sister – The Groovers (actually by The Heptones) (Prod: Lee Perry)
2. The Godfather – Jerry Lewis (Prod: Bunny Lee)
3. Lean On Me – BB Seaton (Prod: Lloyd Charmers)
4. Breakfast In Bed – Winston Reedy (Prod: Ranny Williams (UK))
5. My Confession – Cornel Campbell (Prod: Bunny Lee)
6. Here Comes The Heartaches – Delroy Wilson (Prod: Bunny Lee)
7. Life And All Its Dreams – The Avengers (Prod: Kirk Redding (UK))
8. Black Heart – U Roy (Prod: Lloyd Charmers)

SIDE 2

1. Hi-Jack Plane – The Avengers (Prod: Kirk Redding (UK))
2. I Want Justice – BB Seaton (Prod: Rupie Edwards)
3. Our High School Dance – Stranger Cole (actually with Patsy Todd) (Prod: Bunny Lee)
3. The Man In Your Life (aka 'I'm The Nearest Thing To Your Heart') – Les Foster And Ansell Collins (Prod: Derrick Morgan (UK))
5. Fever – Junior Byles (Prod: Lee Perry)
6. Good Hearted Woman – The Clarendonians (Prod: Bunny Lee)
7. I Hear You Knocking – Owen Gray (Prod: Sidney Crooks (UK))
8. I Don't Want To Die – Junior English (Prod: Ellis Breary (UK))

PSP SERIES

PSP 1001 – *The Lovely Dozen* – Various Artists (1969)

SIDE 1
1. Reggae On Broadway – Lester Sterling (Prod: Bunny Lee)
2. Peace On Earth – Premo And Joe (Prod: H Robinson)
3. Reggae City – Val Bennett (Prod: Bunny Lee)
4. Reggae In The Wind – Lester Sterling (Prod: Bunny Lee)
5. Mr Rhya – Lloyd Tyrell [Lloyd Charmers] (Prod: Winston Lowe)
6. Reggae Hit The Town – The Ethiopians (Prod: H Robinson)

SIDE 2
1. Push Push – The Termites (actually by The Hi-Tones) (Prod: Eric Barnett)
2. Lulu Returns – Lloyd Tyrell [Lloyd Charmers] (Prod: Lynford Anderson)
3. The Avengers – Tommy McCook (Prod: Bunny Lee)
4. I Love You – Derrick Morgan (Prod: Derrick Morgan)
5. Spread Your Bed – The Versatiles (Prod: Lee Perry)
6. Diana – Alton Ellis (Prod: Alton Ellis)

PSP 1002 – *Hey Boy, Hey Girl* – Various Artists (1969)

SIDE 1
1. Hey Boy, Hey Girl – Derrick (Morgan) And Patsy (Todd) (Prod: Derrick Morgan)
2. You've Lost Your Date – The Flames (actually by The Righteous Flames) (Prod: Coxson Dodd)
3. Give It To Me – Stranger Cole (Prod: Stranger Cole)
4. Another Heartache – Winston Sinclair (actually by Gregory Isaacs) (Prod: Winston Sinclair and Gregory Isaacs)
5. Give You My Heart – Derrick (Morgan) And Patsy (Todd) (Prod: Derrick Morgan)
6. Blowing In The Wind – Max Romeo (Prod: Bunny Lee)

SIDE 2
1. I'll Do It – Derrick (Morgan) And Patsy (Todd) (Prod: Derrick Morgan)
2. Ring Of Gold – The Melodians (Prod: Winston Lowe)
3. Come On Little Girl – Winston Sinclair (Prod: Winston Sinclair)
4. Simple Simon – Eric 'Monty' Morris (Prod: Clancy Eccles)
8. If Music Be The Food Of Love – Derrick Morgan (actually by unidentified male vocalist) (Prod: Derrick Morgan)
9. Choo Choo Train – The Soul Cats (actually by unidentified male vocal group) (Prod: ? (UK))

PSP 1003 – *This Is Reggae, Volume 1'* – Various Artists (1970)

SIDE 1
1. Moon Hop – Derrick Morgan And The Rudies (Prod: Derrick Morgan (UK))
2. Girl What You Doing To Me – Owen Gray (actually with The Rudies) (Prod: Derrick Morgan (UK))
3. How Long Will It Take – Pat Kelly (Prod: Bunny Lee)
4. Clint Eastwood – The Upsetters (actually with Lee Perry) (Prod: Lee Perry)
5. Wet Dream – Max Romeo (Prod: Bunny Lee)
6. Sentimental Man – Ernest Wilson (Prod: Bunny Lee)

SIDE 2
1. Pretty Cottage – Stranger Cole (actually with Gladdy Anderson) (Prod: Stranger Cole)
2. Sentimental Reason – The Maytones (Prod: Alvin Ranglin)
3. Derrick Top-The-Pop – Derrick Morgan (Prod: Derrick Morgan)
4. Jesse James – Laurel Aitken (Prod: Laurel Aitken (UK))
5. Cat Nip (actually titled 'Yes Sah') – The Hippy Boys (actually with Lloyd Charmers) (Prod: Lloyd Charmers)
6. Honey – Slim Smith (actually with Sir Harry) (Prod: Bunny Lee)

PSP 1004 – *Reggae To UK With Love* – Various Artists (all tracks produced by Noel Brown and Timmy George, with orchestra conducted by Ranny Williams) (1970)

SIDE 1
1. Live Only For Love – The Progressions
2. Summertime Rock – The Progressions
3. So Long, Farewell – Frederick McLain (actually Freddy McKay)
4. Sunny Sunday Morning – Frederick McLain (actually Freddy McKay)
5. All I Need Is Love – Barry Anthony
6. Love You Most Of All – The Emotions

SIDE 2
1. This Old House – The Emotions
2. Fair Deal – The Progressions
3. Are You Ready? – The Progressions
4. Tears Won't Help You – Frederick McLain (actually Freddy McKay)
5. Ain't That Crude – The Progressions
6. The Dum Dum Song (wrong title: possibly called 'Give Me Love') – The Progressions

Note: this was the second album in Pama's 'Airborne' series and has the added catalogue number in brackets 'NBP 1001' (NBP standing for Noel Brown Productions). See also SECO 30.

PSP 1005 – UNTRACED

PSP 1006 – *Moon Hop* – Derrick Morgan (all tracks produced by Derrick Morgan in the UK except track 1, side 2, although track 2, side 1 does use a Ja rhythm) (1970)

SIDE 1
1. Night At The Hop (with The Rudies)
2. Oh Babe
3. Let's Have Some Fun (with Jennifer Jones And The Mohawks)
4. Man Pon Moon (with The Rudies)
5. Just A Little Lovin' (with Jennifer Jones And The Mohawks)
6. Moon Hop (with The Rudies)

SIDE 2
1. Derrick Top-The-Pop (with Andy Capp)
2. Give Me Lovin' (with unidentified male vocalist and The Mohawks)
3. The Story (actually titled 'I Wish I Was An Apple') (with The Mohawks)
4. This Ain't My Life (with unidentified male vocalist and The Mohawks)
6. Wipe The Tears (with Jennifer Jones And The Mohawks)
7. Telephone (with Jennifer Jones And The Rudies)

Note: the unidentified vocalist(s) referred to above were probably either Owen Gray or Denzil Dennis.

PSP 1007 – *Live At The Cumberland* – Mood Reaction (all tracks produced by Theo Loyla for Frant Productions (UK)) (1970)

SIDE 1
1. Roaring Twenties
2. Problems
3. Moon Hop
4. Sweet And Dandy
5. Liquidator
6. Too Much Loving
7. Live Injection

SIDE 2
1. Wet Dream
2. Pop-A-Top
3. Everybody Needs Love
4. Red Red Wine
5. Runaway Man
6. All Change On The Bakerloo Line

PSP 1008–1011 – UNTRACED

PSP 1012 – *The High Priest Of Reggae* – Laurel Aitken (Prod: Laurel Aitken (UK)) (1970)

SIDE 1
1. Jesse James
2. Mr Popcorn
3. I Got To Have Your Love
4. Sloop John B
5. Shoo Be Doo
6. Haile Selassie

SIDE 2
1. Landlords And Tenants
2. Save The Last Dance For Me
3. Walk Right Back
4. Don't Be Cruel
5. Woppi King
6. Suffering Still (actually with Girlie)

PSP 1013 – UNTRACED

PSP 1014 – *Clint Eastwood* – The Upsetters (except where otherwise specified) (all tracks produced by Lee Perry except * which were co-produced by Perry and Glen Adams) (1970)

SIDE 1
1. Return Of The Ugly
2. For A Few Dollars More
3. Prisoner Of Love (actually by Dave Barker And The Upsetters)
4. Dry Acid (actually by Count Sticky And The Upsetters)
5. Rightful Ruler (actually titled 'Earth's Rightful Ruler') (actually by U Roy With Peter Tosh And Count Ossie)
6. Clint Eastwood (actually by Lee Perry And The Upsetters)

SIDE 2
1. Taste Of Killing
2. Selassie (actually by The Reggae Boys)*
3. What Is This? (actually by The Reggae Boys)*
4. Never Found Me A Girl (actually by David Isaacs And The Upsetters)
5. My Mob
6. Caught You (actually by Count Sticky And The Upsetters)

PTP SERIES

PTP 1001 – *Reggae Hit The Town* – Various Artists (1975)

SIDE 1
1. Sinners – Justin Hinds And The Dominoes (Prod: Duke Reid)
2. Darling It's You – Bill Gentles (Prod: Bill Gentles)
3. Sing About Love – Pat Kelly (Prod: Phil Pratt)
4. Car Pound – Bill Gentles (Prod: Bill Gentles)
5. You Can Never Stop Me Loving You – Derrick Morgan (Prod: Derrick Morgan (UK))
6. Education Rock – Junior Byles (Prod: Lee Perry)

SIDE 2
1. Can't You Understand – Larry Marshall (Prod: Carlton Patterson)
2. If It's Love You Need – Justin Hinds And The Dominoes (Prod: Duke Reid)
3. You Lie – Larry Marshall (Prod: Carlton Patterson)
4. Just Like A Woman – Pat Kelly (Prod: Phil Pratt)
5. Beat Them Jah Jah – The Twinkle Brothers (Prod: Norman Grant)
6. Come What May – Fermena (Edwards) (Prod: Ranny Williams (UK))

Note: pressed with both Pama and Star labels, although copies of the latter seem to be more abundant.

Sources

Throughout the book we have referred to *Black Echoes/Echoes* and *Black Music* issues for general information. Any particular usage we have noted within the text and/or in the sources.

We have also regularly checked our facts with the excellent *Reggae – The Rough Guide* by Steve Barrow and Peter Dalton (Rough Guides/Penguin) and *The Guinness Who's Who Of Reggae* (Guinness).

Other sources are as follows (by chapter). A key to interviewers cited is given directly below.

Key
MA – Mike Atherton
MdK – Michael de Koningh
MG – Marc Griffiths
LCH – Laurence Cane-Honeysett

Chapter 1
Public Records Office
Keep On Moving – The Windrush Years – Tony Sewell (Voice Enterprises Ltd 1998)
The Jamaican Gleaner
After The Windrush – Gary MacFarlane
Notting Hill Riots And British National Identity – Tim Helbing
Pete Fontana interview – MdK 2003
Rico Rodriguez interview – MdK 2003
Count Suckle interview – MdK 2003
Post Office directories
Rob Bell interview – MdK 2003
Siggy Jackson interview – LCH 1994

Chapter 2

Rob Bell interview – MdK 2003
DD Dennis interview – LCH 2003
Eddy Grant interview – Roger St Pierre, *Black Echoes* 1976
Winston Groovy interview – MG 2003
Jack Price interview – LCH 2003
Pat Rhoden interview – MdK 2003
Bruce White interview – MdK 2002/2003
Bruce Ruffin interview – LCH 2001
The Guinness Book Of Hit Singles – Paul Gambaccini, Tim Rice, Jonathan Rice
    (Guinness)
The Complete Book Of The British Charts Singles And Albums – Tony Brown, Jon
    Kutner and Neil Warwick (Omnibus Press)
John Kpiaye interview – LCH 2003
Mike Cole interview – MA 2003
Monty Neysmith interview – LCH 2003
Roy Shirley interview – MG 2003
Cimarons – Carl Gayle *Black Music* March 1974/December 1977
Sid Bucknor interview – MdK 2003
Freddie Notes interview – MdK 2003
Glenroy Oakley interview – MdK 2003
Jackie Robinson interview – MdK 2003
Dave Barker interview – MdK 2003
Bob Andy interview – MdK 2003
Rico Rodriguez interview – MdK 2003
Jah Music (Chapter 7 – The British Scene) – Sebastion Clarke (Heinemann Educational
    Books Ltd 1980)

Chapter 3

Public Records Office
Guild Hall
Post Office directories
Monty Neysmith interview – LCH 2003
Alan Hawkshaw email – MA 2003
Rico Rodriguez interview – MdK 2003
DD Dennis interview – LCH 2003
Joe Sinclair interview – MdK 2003
Alan Wallace (Wally – Mood Reaction) interview – MdK 2003
The London Gazette 15 June 1973
The London Gazette 22 February 1974

Chapter 4

Rob Bell interview – MdK 2003
Sid Bucknor interview – MdK 2003
Dennis Harris interview – Steve Barrow *Black Echoes* 30 October 1976
Joe Sinclair interview – MdK 2003

Cymande – uncredited *Black Music* February 1974
UK Reggae Scene – Chris May – *Black Music* July, August, September 1977

Chapter 5
Dennis Bovell interview – *Reggae International* Stephen Davis and Peter Simon
    (Thames & Hudson 1983)
Pat Rhoden interview – MdK 2003

Chapter 6
Rob Bell interview – MdK 2003
Winston Groovy interview – MG 2003
Brian Harris interview – MA 2003
Steve Jukes interview – MA 2003
Ian Smith interview – MG 2001

Chapter 7
Burning Spear – *NME* Ian MacDonald November 1975
Small Reggae Labels Explosion – Carl Gayle *Black Music* October 1975
Delroy Washington – *Black Music* December 1977
Merger original line-up – *The Encyclopaedia Of Popular Music*
Dave Hendley interview – MdK 2003

Chapter 8
Pat Rhoden interview – MdK 2003
Keith Stone – MG – interview 2003 plus previous conversations taking place over
    several years
Noel Hawks interview – MdK 2003
Fatman overview – Dave Hendley
Greensleeves overview – Chris Cracknell/MdK

Index

BBC 214
Beat & Commercial Records
(see *B&C*)
beatniks 21
Beckford, Theo 84
Bed Bugs, The 40
Bees, The 31, 38, 39
Beginner, Lord 22
Bel Cantos, The 29
Bell, Rob 16–18, 53–4, 56,
69–70, 105–6, 158
Bell, Robert 'Kool' 111
Bell, William 83
Bell label 74
Bellott, Errol 195
Beltones, The 149
Bennett, Fay 99
Bennett, Roy 77, 78
Bennett, Scotty (see *Reel, Penny*)
Bennett, Val 80
Bennett, Winston 192
Benton, Brook 60, 151, 156
Benup, Desmond (see *Bryan,
Desmond*)
Berry, Chuck 18
Bert, Carl 186
Betteridge, Dave 42, 69
Beverley Music 103
Big Apple Records, Nottingham
166, 168
Big Dread 142, 204
Big Joe 146
Big R Soul Band, The 172
Big Roy 113, 145, 192
Big Shot label 132, 153, 200
Big Youth 59, 60, 128, 133,
147
Biggs, Barry 38–9, 64, 68, 130,
182
Biggs, Sir 139
Biko, Steve 192
Bilk, Acker 22
Binns, Sonny 42, 45, 47, 48, 52,
86, 119
Birds, Dr 194
Birmingham, reggae scene
158–66, 196–7
Black, Michael 140
Black Ark Studio 120, 127, 159
Black Art label 165
Black Beat label 141
Black Echoes (magazine) 61,
102, 123, 124, 125, 131,
134, 138, 188, 191, 196,
213, 222–3
Black Harmony 139, 140, 205
Black Joy label 224
black music, fragmentation of
174
Black Music label 224

Black Music (magazine) 76, 93,
94, 101, 103, 114, 116, 117,
122, 124, 131, 146, 148,
159, 163, 171, 177, 189,
196–7, 216, 221–3
Black Roots 197
Black Roots label 189, 224
Black Slate 44, 189, 191–2, 207
Black Swan label 150
Black Uhuru 211
Black Wax label 101, 162, 163,
215
Black and White label 121
Blackbeard (see *Bovell, Dennis*)
Blackburn, Tony 35, 51
Blackstones, The 122, 123, 198,
216
Blackwell, Chris 23, 24, 27,
30–1, 55, 74, 161, 175, 210
Blackwood, Lloyd (see *Coxson,
Lloyd*)
Blood Sisters, The 188
Bloom, Bobby 49
Bloxham, Dave 51, 54
Blue Beat label 15, 16, 20, 21,
23–7, 28, 31, 38, 48, 53, 55,
57, 63, 73, 161, 167, 209
Blue Cat 167, 168
Blue Cat label 79, 155
Blue Flames, The 16, 25
Blue Mountain label 52
Blues & Soul (magazine) 218,
220, 223
blues beat 15, 22, 23, 160, 162
Blues Busters, The 68
blues dances 15, 112
Blues Unlimited 18
Bluesville Club 50
Bob and Marcia 52–3, 66, 85,
149, 221
Bob Marley And The Wailers
(see *Marley, Bob*)
Body Music 116
Bohannon, Hamilton 130
Bojangles, Mr 149
Bond, Joyce 21, 54, 74, 75
Bones, Mr T (see *Noel, John*)
Booker T 119
Boom, Barry (see *Robinson,
Paul*)
Boothe, Admiral Ken 50
Boothe, Ken 46, 61, 107, 149
Bop, Jah 216
Boss label 211
Boss Sounds 9, 105, 118
Boucher, Judy 72, 156
Bovell, Dennis 122, 124, 125,
126, 134–6, 138, 187, 195,
198, 199, 202, 203, 207, 208
Bow, Trevor 195

Box Tops, The 74
Boyo, Billy 226
Bradford 173
Bradley, Junior 30, 148, 159, 160
Bradshaw, Tiny 18
Branson, Richard 175, 191
Breary, Ellis 157
Brentford Road All Atars 149
Brevett, Tony 146
Brightly, Anthony 'Tony' 191,
192
Briscoe, Lambert 45, 61, 62
Bristol, reggae scene 174, 197
Brixton 14
Brooks, Cedric 130
Broonzy, Big Bill 21
Brother Dan All Stars 47
Brown, Al 114
Brown, Barry 179
Brown, Bertram 194, 224
Brown, Carol 129
Brown, Castro 102, 137–9, 199,
204
Brown, Dennis 59, 99, 102,
117, 121, 122, 137–9, 147,
150, 177, 178, 191, 204, 216
Brown, Glen 155
Brown, Jackie 137
Brown, James 45, 49, 111, 112,
113
Brown, John 211
Brown, Lloyd 121
Brown, Lovett 19
Brown, Oscar Junior 47–8
Brown, Vic 48
Brown, Wally 146
Brown Sugar 124–5, 187,
201–2, 204
Brownie T (see *Kpiaye, John*)
Bryan, Desmond 56, 70, 126,
128–9, 150, 224
Bryan, Rad 35
Buchanan, Manley (see *Big
Youth*)
Bucknor, Norman (Sid) 35, 46,
47, 108–10, 114, 198, 206
Buggis 115
Bulleit, Jim 85
Bullet label 85, 86, 90, 91, 98,
101, 143
Bullimore, Tony 169
Burke, Sonny 55
Burning Sounds label 140, 146,
195, 198, 203, 208
Burning Spear 26, 46, 56, 149,
175, 176, 189, 196
Burrell, Frank 55
Bush Productions 126, 128
Bushay, Clement 117, 139–40,
143, 198, 205, 206

Bushay's label 140, 206
Bushranger label 140
Bushrangers, The 206
Buster, Prince 9, 16, 24–6, 28, 39, 56, 57, 58, 59–61, 69, 75, 161, 165, 168
Butler, Jerry 144
Byles, Junior 95, 118, 122
Byrne, Jerry 18
Byron Lee And The Dragonaires 23, 28, 65, 68

Cactus label 67, 68, 94, 144
Cadillac Music 59
Cadogan, Susan 111, 122, 128, 157, 197
Caesar, Imruh 222
Caitlin, Carolyn 124
Caltone label 29
calypso 22, 26, 27, 155, 225
Camel label 85, 86, 98, 101
Campbell, Al 119
Campbell, Bill 114, 140–1, 144, 167, 197
Campbell, Cecil (see Buster, Prince)
Campbell, Cornel 59, 115, 117, 127, 128, 216
Campbell, Enid 24, 60
Campbell, Errol 207–8
Campbell, Lloyd 63, 154, 155
Campbell, Michael 'Ruben' 190
Campbell, Mikey (see Dread, Mikey)
Campbell, Nola 75
Campbell, Pete 79, 140–1, 144, 167
Campbell, Wilbert (see Suckle, Count)
Cannon, King 30
Capital Letters 196–7
Capital Radio 157, 214
Captain Sinbad 179
Caretaker 207
Carib Gems 140, 143, 184, 224
Carib-Arawak Publications 222
Carib-Disc-O 77, 81
Caribbean label 128, 198
Caribou Records 23
Carifta label 81, 121
Carlos, Don 180, 211, 225
'Carnival Boycott' 14
Carolyn And Roland 124
Carter, Linval (see Jazzbo, Prince)
Cartridge label 156
Casinos, The 84
Cassandra 124
Castell, Lacksley 179
Castle Hill Music 171

Cats, The 37–8
CBS 190, 193, 199
Cha Cha label 224
Chain Reaction 36
Chalk Farm Studios 33, 34, 46, 47, 51, 52, 61, 66, 108, 109, 110, 144, 198
Champions, The 152
Chanan-Jah label 94, 119, 184
Chandell, Tim 155, 156
Chang, Ken 150, 151
Channel, Bruce 74
Channel One Studio 114, 122, 127, 136, 147, 163
Chantells, The 129
Charm label 104
Charmers, Lloyd 80, 86, 88, 94, 96, 99, 114
Checker, Chubby 34
Chek label 24
Chi-Lites, The 34, 64, 113, 200
Chicken, Funky 173
Childs, Rev AA 27
Chin, Kes 28
Chin, Leonard 'Santic' 102, 188, 212, 225
Chin, Victor 95
Chin, Vincent (Randy) 14
Chin-Loy, Herman, 65, 95, 148, 159
Chisholm, George 27
Chosen Few 113
Christy, John 153
Chuck And Dobby 28
Chuckles, The 30
Chung, Geoffrey 65, 129, 130
Chung, Mikey 130
Churchill, Trevor 74
Churchill, Winston 50
Cimarons, The 9, 33, 44–7, 62, 65, 108, 111, 127, 145
Circle International label 198
Clan, The 90
Clancy Eccles And The Dynamites 45
Clarendonians, The 58, 65, 144
Claridge, Mo 157, 173, 179, 182–3
Clarke, George 'Flea' 193
Clarke, Johnny 114, 117, 121, 127, 175
Clarke, Sebastian 222
Clash, The 180, 181
Classics, The 79–80, 150
Clay, Judy 83
Cliff, Jimmy 31, 33, 93, 108, 153
Cliff, Les (see St Lewis, Cliff)
Clint Eastwood And General Saint 218

Club 31: 72, 75, 169
Clue J And The Blues Blasters 24
Coach House Studio 34, 144
Coke, Russell 43, 94, 99, 119–21, 126
Coke, Winifred 120
Cole, Mike 37–8
Cole, Nat 63
Cole, Nat King 21
Cole, Stranger 80, 82, 85, 89–90, 95, 103
Collins, Ansel 34, 35, 36, 60, 66, 67, 98, 172, 221
Collins, Clancy (aka Sir Collins) 74, 141–2, 148, 149, 204, 207
Collins, Dave (see Barker, Dave)
Collins, Leonie 142
Collins, Steve 142
Collins Down Beat label 74, 141–2
Colour Supplement, The 75
Coloured Raisins, The 48, 50
Columbia Blue Beat label 31, 38, 74, 132
Comic, Sir Lord 149
Commercial Entertainments 65
Commodores, The 212
compilation albums 185–6
Concords, The 91
Concrete Jungle label 123, 125, 135, 162, 196, 198, 202, 208
Conflict label 181
Congo label 199
Conley, Arthur 50
Conscious Sounds 212
Contempo 215
Continentals, The 18
Cooke, Paul (see Paul, Eugene)
Cooke, Sam 135, 200
Copasetic label 224
Copyright Control label 57
Cosmo, Frank 55
Cotton, Joseph 219
Count Shelly label 43, 106, 107, 108, 109, 113–16, 117, 128, 133, 139, 140, 144, 155, 199
Counter Point label 121
Cousins, Roy 122, 225
Cousins, Tony 41, 65–8
Cowan, Tommy 127
Coxson label 74, 78, 148, 166
Coxson, Lloyd 9, 134, 137, 140, 207, 210, 212–13
Crab label 79–80, 83–4, 86, 98
Cracknell, Chris 217
Crane River Band 21
Creation Steppers, The 212